MANAGEMENT:
PRINCIPLES AND POLICY

Third edition July 1990

ISBN 0 86277 812 3 (previous edition 0 86277 219 2)

A CIP catalogue record for this book is available
from the British Library

Published by

BPP Publishing
Aldine House, Aldine Place
142-144 Uxbridge Road
London W12 8AW

We are grateful to the Institute of Chartered Secretaries and Administrators,
the Chartered Institute of Bankers and the Chartered Institute of Management
Accountants for permission to reproduce past examination questions in this
text. Suggested solutions, where provided, have been prepared by BPP Publishing
Ltd. We also express our gratitude to United Biscuits plc for permission to
make references to their corporate Ethics and Operating Principles.

BPP Publishing Limited

1990

CONTENTS

CONTENTS

SYLLABUS

Objective

> To develop a knowledge and understanding of the concepts, problems and practices of management. To introduce students to the skills of analysing changes in market, technological, legal, social and political factors in the environment.
>
> The paper will adopt a practical focus throughout and will be concerned with improvement of management and organisation. It will include a compulsory case study to provide students with the opportunity of outlining how they would use the concepts and ideas from the course to solve a management problem. In dealing with the case study and with other questions, students should be encouraged to draw upon material from other relevant subjects from the course.

Syllabus

The manager. The role of management in public and private sector organisations. Direction and motivation, including the management of managers; training and development; management succession. The transition from functional to general management. The development of new managerial work practices, including working at home and sub-contracting.

Managerial accountability and authority. Managerial accountabilities and authority. The constraints and choices facing managers. The exercise of delegation; authority and responsibility; objective setting and management by objectives.

Organisation. Organisation structures and design: the application of contingency theory; matrix or project structures. The impact of technology and the environment on organisations in the private and public sectors. The organisation and co-ordination of the main organisational functions of production or operations, marketing, research and development. The development of corporate plans including an introduction to business and technological forecasting. The problems of large organisations; centralisation and decentralisation: autonomy and control; problems of diversification and mergers. Management and small business.

The management of change. The conditions for effective change. The management of change and creativity. The management of growth, stability and contraction. Implementation and the politics of change. Organisational effectiveness. The role of general and functional management in organisation change and the contribution of a Management Services Division. The role and value of internal and external consultants. New venture strategies.

Social responsibilities of management. The relationship between the Government and Management in both the public and private sectors. The social regulation of business. The responsibilities of managers to consumers, suppliers, employees and the environment. Managers as a profession.

Note. The **compulsory case study** will either comprise one question which is more or less equally valid for public and private sector candidates or two questions (one to be answered), one of which will be for candidates in the Company Secretarial or General and Financial Administration streams and the other orientated towards the Local Government and Public Service Administration Stream.

From June 1990, the compulsory case study comprises one question which is equally valid for public and private sector candidates.

FOREWORD

Format of the examination paper

The examination paper is divided into two sections.

(a) *Section A* consists of a single, *compulsory* question, and takes the form of a case study.

One third of the total marks in the examination may be gained from this question.

(b) *Section B* consists of seven 'essay-type' questions, and candidates must answer *any three* of these questions.

Two thirds of the total marks in the examination may be gained from Section B.

The Section A question, being a case study, takes some time to read and digest. It is usually divided into three or four parts, with equal marks being awarded for the answers to each part. In answering such questions, you should try to give equal time to each part of the question. A comment of the examiner on the performance of candidates in a past examination is quite telling:

> 'The main problem here was a tendency for responses to tail off. Two pages devoted to part (i), two paragraphs to part (ii) and sometimes as little as two lines to part (iii). Yet each part carried equal marks, a fact clearly stated in the question. It followed, therefore, that some candidates were awarded marks out of little more than half the marks the question would have attracted. This is an important matter of examination technique.'

Section B questions are more straightforward 'essay-type' questions, some examples of which are shown in this text.

Time allowed for the examination – 3 hours.

With effect from the June 1990 examinations, the examination scheme structure has changed. *Management: Principles and Policy* is now set for the Professional Programme Part A (Common Professional Modules) instead of 'Part 4'. The syllabus and paper format, however, are unchanged.

Review of past papers

You may find it helpful to have an idea of the topics examined in recent papers.

December 1989

Section A

1. Case study in which a departmental manager has failed to meet his profit targets for the first quarter of a year. These targets were set using an MBO approach, which proceeded well until the manager was pressurised into revising them upwards. He has three drastic remedies which can be used to meet return on assets targets but he also has profits and sales targets to meet. You are required:

   (a) to analyse the root causes of the problem; and
   (b) to advise the manager on what to do.

FOREWORD

Section B

2. Definition of management.
3. Executive and non-executive directors.
4. Classical school - division of labour.
5. Effect of computerisation on job satisfaction.
6. Management of change.
7. Government regulation of business.
8. Effects of inadequate co-ordination.

June 1989

Section A

1. Case study in which a company selling advertising space is experiencing a variety of short and long term problems. As a consultant called in to advise on future policy, you are required to give:

   (a) your initial views on the situation;
   (b) an explanation of how you would structure your approach to this task; and
   (c) your recommendations, on the basis of the information provided, to the managing director.

Section B

2. The dynamics of a managerial career; coping with barriers to advancement.
3. Explanation of Management by Objectives; an examination of its usefulness as a basis for performance measurement and evaluation.
4. Effects of microelectronics on organisational design.
5. Analysis of responsibilities and interface relationships of:
   (a) marketing
   (b) production
   (c) finance
   (d) personnel.
6. Motivation of a long-serving supervisor who is underperforming.
7. Justification of financial expenditure on enhancement of a company's public image.
8. Processes to achieve organisational change; reasons why change is resisted.
9. Ways in which a Chief Executive Officer or General Manager differs from other managers.

December 1988

Section A

1. Case study in which an organisation is involved in a number of joint ventures, one of which is experiencing delays. In a meeting, those responsible revealed themselves to be mutually suspicious. The question requires ideas for:

   (a) managing a meeting to ensure teamwork;
   (b) improving the workings of the main department responsible for the delays;
   (c) avoiding similar problems in future.

Section B

2. Human aspects of budgeting.
3. Management skills for large division.
4. Organisation's 'image'.
5. Encouraging innovation in large organisations.
6. Customer relations.
7. Matrix organisation structures.
8. Time management.

June 1988

Section A

1. Case study involving a General Manager of a poorly-performing division of a large organisation. The General Manager's style is old-fashioned and autocratic. He cannot delegate; he does not trust his staff; he refuses to train his junior managers. In short, he is having difficulties coping with change and he seems incapable of resolving the 'human relations' issues within his division. The question required:

   (a) an action plan to improve the division's performance and management effectiveness;

   (b) a discussion as to how the Chief Executive would approach these issues with the General Manager;

   (c) an outline management development program for the division to improve cooperation, communication and managerial performance.

Section B

2. Management development.
3. Managerial responsibility for employment security.
4. Performance appraisal and performance accountability.
5. Long range plans.
6. Making decisions.
7. Motivation, in particular the use of rewards.
8. Assessing organisational effectiveness.

December 1987

Section A

1. Case study in which a consultant is hired to analyse the problems that supervisors are having in achieving a high work performance from staff. The consultant makes certain recommendations, and the question asked:

   (a) for your views on how effective you would expect the proposals to be;
   (b) what questions you, as general divisional manager, would want to ask the consultant and your departmental managers;
   (c) how the general manager can overcome cynicism amongst staff about the value of the consultant's survey.

Section B

2. Conflict between line and staff management.

3. Outline a management development programme, in an organisation which wants to show concern for clients and markets, and to be flexible.

4. Motivation of individuals to carry out senior management jobs effectively.

5. Performance appraisal in *one* of the following:
   (i)   retail store
   (ii)   manufacturing company
   (iii)   financial services company
   (iv)   local government organisation
   (v)   hospital
   (vi)   professional body

6. Decision-making: its rationality, the effect of inadequate information and management style.

7. Careful planning of major organisational change.

8. Responsibility of managers to their employees. Helping the career development of subordinates.

June 1987

Section A

1. Case study involving proposals to decentralise the management accounting function, by appointing a management accountant for each operating unit (division). Head office would have a Finance Director responsible for certain matters, and so each management accountant would report to two bosses, the operating unit's general manager and the Finance Director. The Finance Director also wishes to change the role of the head office finance division, by encouraging a more constructive and co-operative problem-solving approach in dealings with divisional managers. The question asked:

   (a) what will be the likely problems and advantages of decentralised management accounting?

   (b) what measures should be adopted to support the changed role of the head office finance division?

   (c) what actions should the top management team take to prepare for the changes?

FOREWORD

Section B

2. How should senior managers deal with ineffective performance by functional managers?

3. The issues to consider in developing a corporate strategy for *one* of the following:
    (i)   a bank
    (ii)   a building society
    (iii) a college
    (iv)   a national charity
    (v)   a retail store
    (vi)   a local authority.

4. The role of performance appraisal in a programme of management development.

5. The contribution of a Management Services Division to the introduction of a computerised management information system into an organisation.

6. The transition from functional to general management: training and development issues.

7. Differences in the role of general managers in large compared with small organisations

8. The extent to which managers should take account of wider responsibilities other than economic and performance objectives.

December 1986

Section A

1. Case study about a company with seven decentralised operating divisions, with a chief executive at head office who uses a participative style of leadership. One unit is performing badly, and is under several external and internal pressures, which are listed in the question. The problems of the division are explained. The question asks for an outline strategy on:

    (a) how to prepare the division's employees for the organisational changes that will be necessary to improve performance;
    (b) how to plan and monitor a programme of change;
    (c) how to help employees at all levels in the division to cope with change;
    (d) how to achieve improvement in the division's performance.

Section B

2. The leadership role of general management in major organisational change.

3. Achieving collaboration between staff of a Management Services Division and staff in functional departments.

4. Modifying objectives as circumstances change: effect on the motivation of functional managers.

5. The managerial skills needed for dealing with people in other organisations in a collaborative venture.

6. Impact of changing technology on an organisation and its employees.

7. Achieving effective control over a functional department in *one* of the following functions:
   (i)   production
   (ii) marketing
   (iii) research and development
   (iv) sales
   (v)   a service department.

8. Challenges for managers of small organisations in *one* of the following:
   (i)   finance
   (ii) product/service development
   (iii) training and development.

What do you need to know to pass the examination?

The examination syllabus tests your knowledge of management principles and policy, and so you need to be aware of the general principles of effective management and organisation.

The examination also takes things further, and tests your ability to relate the principles to practical 'real-world' problems.

(a) This is evident in the case study approach in Section A.

(b) Section B questions also try to present problems in such a way that you cannot provide a 'stock' or 'standard' answer. Instead, you must *adapt* your knowledge to a particular situation or problem given to you in the question, and show practicality, realism and common sense. Often, it will help to bring your own personal work experience into a solution, to explain the points you are making.

This study text presents the principles that you need to know, and tries to present ideas in such a way that the practical and 'real world' aspects of management problems are clearly seen. Where appropriate, some simple case studies are used for illustration, and you might like to compare what you would do in the situations described with the 'recommended' approach that we give in the text. You would also do well to read the management pages in the *Administrator* and the *Financial Times* in order to see how management principles affect real life decisions.

What you should always try to do, however, is to see the syllabus as a test of your own potential as a general manager. Studying for *Management: Principles and Policy* should be a step in your personal career training and development programme. Use it well!

BPP Publishing Ltd
July 1990

SECTION A

THE MANAGER

Chapter 1

THE ROLE AND FUNCTIONS OF MANAGEMENT

This chapter covers the following topics

1. The role of managers: private and public sector organisations
2. The functions of management
3. Managerial dilemmas
4. The use of managerial time
5. Theories of management
6. Managerial roles: Henry Mintzburg
7. New managerial work practices

Purpose of this chapter

To look in broad terms at what the role and functions of managers are, using the ideas of theorists such as Fayol, Taylor and Mayo on which to base the analysis.

Some of the practical difficulties in performing the role and functions of managers will be discussed, using simple case studies.

1. THE ROLE OF MANAGERS: PRIVATE AND PUBLIC SECTOR ORGANISATIONS

1.1 In broad terms, the collective role of the managers in an organisation is to:

(a) act on behalf of the owners of the organisation. In a company, these are the shareholders, to whom the senior management should ultimately be accountable;

(b) to set objectives for the organisation;

(c) to achieve those objectives through the process of managing;

(d) to sustain corporate values in their dealings with other organisations, customers, employees and the general public.

1: THE ROLE AND FUNCTIONS OF MANAGEMENT

1.2 In a public sector organisation, management acts on behalf of the government and its 'political masters'. Politicians in a democracy are in turn accountable to the general public. A possible difference of some importance between public and private sector organisations is that some of the objectives of a public sector organisation might be set by the 'owners' - ie the government - rather than by the management. The government might also tell senior management to carry out certain policies or plans, thereby restricting management's discretion.

1.3 As just one example, when the UK government in 1988 announced its plans to privatise the electricity industry:

(a) not all managers in the industry agreed with the government's objective/policy of de-nationalising the industry; and

(b) the chief executive of the industry was reported to disagree strongly with major points of detail in the plan for privatisation, which the government was imposing on the industry's senior management.

1.4 Given some such differences, though, the role and functions management in both the private and public sectors are similar.

1.5 It is worth emphasising the role of managers - and all employees - *to sustain corporate values*. This is an aspect of management which can easily be overlooked. United Biscuits (1987) issued a handbook for its staff on the company's ethics and operating principles, and in this, it is stated that:

> 'A company is more than a legal entity engaged in the production and sale of goods and services for profit. It is also the embodiment of the principles and beliefs of the men and women who give it substance; it is characterised by guiding principles which define its view of itself and describe the values it embraces. Such values have, for our company, existed implicitly for very many years - United Biscuits is what it is and as good as it is because a great many individuals over a long period of time have contributed their own best efforts to preserving and enhancing the values that cause it to endure'.

2. THE FUNCTIONS OF MANAGEMENT

2.1 The process of management and the functions of management have been analysed many times in various ways by different writers, who have taken the view that:

(a) management is an operational process, which can be understood by a close study of management functions;

(b) the study of management should then lead to the development of certain principles of good management, which will be of value when put into practice.

Henri Fayol: functions of management

2.2 Henri Fayol, a French management theorist working in the early decades of this century, listed the functions of management as follows:

4

(a) *Planning*. This involves selecting objectives, and the strategies, policies, programmes and procedures for achieving the objectives either for the organisation as a whole or for a part of it. Planning might be done exclusively by managers who will later be responsible for performance: however, *advice* on planning decisions might also be provided by 'staff management' who do not have 'line' authority for putting the plans into practice. Expert advice is nevertheless a part of the management planning function.

(b) *Organising*. This involves the establishment of a structure of tasks which need to be performed to achieve the goals of the organisation, grouping these tasks into jobs for an individual, creating groups of jobs within sections and departments, delegating authority to carry out the jobs, and providing systems of information and communication, and for the co-ordination of activities within the organisation.

(c) *Commanding*. This involves giving instructions to subordinates to carry out tasks over which the manager has authority for decisions and responsibility for performance.

(d) *Co-ordinating*. This is the task of harmonising the activities of individuals and groups within the organisation, which will inevitably have different ideas about what their own goals should be. Management must reconcile differences in approach, effort, interest and timing of these separate individuals and groups. This is best achieved by making the individuals and groups aware of how their work is contributing to the goals of the overall organisation.

(e) *Controlling*. This is the task of measuring and correcting the activities of individuals and groups, to ensure that their performance is in accordance with plans. Plans must be made, but they will not be achieved unless activities are monitored, and deviations from plan identified and corrected as soon as they become apparent.

2.3 Fayol's analysis of management functions is only one of several similar types of analysis. Other functions which might be identified, for example, are *staffing* (ie filling positions in the organisation with people), *leading* (unlike commanding, 'leading' is concerned with the impersonal nature of management) and *acting as the organisation's representative* in dealing with other organisations (ie an ambassadorial or public relations role).

2.4 Some theorists reject Fayol's argument that managers are commanders, and argue instead that they are persuaders and motivators.

Peter Drucker: the management process

2.5 Peter Drucker worked in the 1940s and 1950s as a business adviser to a number of US corporations. He was also a prolific writer on management. Drucker grouped the operations of management into five categories:

(a) *Setting objectives for the organisation*. Managers decide what the objectives of the organisation should be and quantify the targets of achievement for each objective. They must then communicate these targets to other people in the organisation.

(b) *Organising the work*. The work to be done in the organisation must be divided into manageable activities and manageable jobs. The jobs must be integrated into a formal organisation structure, and people must be selected to do the jobs.

(c) *Motivating* employees and communicating information to them to enable them to do their work.

(d) *The job of measurement.* **Management** must:
  (i) establish objectives or **yardsticks** of performance for every person in the organisation;
  (ii) analyse actual performance, appraise it against the objectives or yardsticks which have been set, and analyse the comparison;
  (iii) communicate the findings and explain their significance both to subordinate employees and also to superiors.

(e) *Developing people.* The manager 'brings out what is in them or he stifles them. He strengthens their integrity or he corrupts them'.

2.6 Every manager performs all five functions listed above, no matter how good or bad a manager he is. However a bad manager performs these functions badly, whereas a good manager performs them well. Drucker emphasised the importance of *communication* in the functions of management, which should be evident in items (a), (c) and (d) above.

2.7 Drucker has also argued that the manager of a business has a basic function of management - economic performance. In this respect, the business manager is different from the manager of any other type of organisation. Management of a business can only justify its existence and its authority by the economic results it produces, even though as a consequence of their actions, significant non-economic results occur as well.

2.8 He then described the jobs of management within this basic function of economic performance as follows. (It is worth noting in particular the inclusion of *innovation* in this list. Innovation and change are a major feature of the syllabus.)

(a) *Managing a business.* The purposes of the business are:
  (i) to create a customer; and
  (ii) innovation;

(b) *Managing managers.* The requirements here are:
  (i) management by objectives;
  (ii) proper structure of managers' jobs;
  (iii) creating the right spirit in the organisation;
  (iv) making a provision for the managers of tomorrow;
  (v) arriving at sound principles of organisation structure;

(c) *Managing worker and work.*

2.9 A manager can improve his performance in all areas of management, including management of the business, by a study of the principles of management, the acquisition of 'organised knowledge' (eg management techniques) and the systematic appraisal of his own performance in all aspects of his work, at whatever level of management this happens to be.

2.10 The three jobs in paragraph 2.8 are carried out within a time dimension.

(a) Management must always consider both the short-term and longer-term consequences of their actions. A business must be kept profitable into the long-term future, but at the same time short-term profitability must be maintained to avoid the danger that the long term will never be reached, and the business liquidated or taken over.

(b) Decisions taken by management are for the future, and some have a very long 'planning horizon' - ie the time between making the decision and seeing the consequences of that decision can be very long. For example, if a decision is made to build a factory, it might be years before the building is erected, equipped and in operation, and years more before it earns sufficient profits to pay back the investment.

Charles Handy: being a manager

2.11 Charles Handy suggested that a definition of a manager or a manager's role is likely to be so broad as to be fairly meaningless. His own analysis of being a manager was divided into three aspects:

(a) the manager as a general practitioner;
(b) the managerial dilemmas;
(c) the manager as a person.

2.12 *The manager as a general practitioner.* A manager is the first recipient of an organisation's problem and he must:

(a) identify the symptoms in the situation (eg low productivity, high labour turnover, severe industrial relations problems etc);
(b) diagnose the disease or cause of the trouble;
(c) decide how it might be dealt with - ie develop a strategy for better health;
(d) start the treatment.

2.13 Typical strategies for health were listed as:

(a) *People:* ie changing people, either literally or figuratively;
  (i)   hiring and firing;
  (ii) re-assignment;
  (iii) training and education;
  (iv) selective pay increases;
  (v)   counselling or admonition;

(b) *The work and the structure:*
  (i)   re-organisation of reporting relationships;
  (ii   re-definition of the work task;
  (iii) job enrichment;
  (iv) re-definition of roles;

(c) *The systems and procedures:* to amend or introduce:
  (i)   communication systems;
  (ii) rewards systems (payment methods, salary guides);
  (iii) information and reporting systems;
  (iv) budgets or other decision-making systems (eg stock control, debtor control).

1: THE ROLE AND FUNCTIONS OF MANAGEMENT

3. MANAGERIAL DILEMMAS

3.1 Managers are paid more than workers because they must face some constant dilemmas which have to be resolved, and it is management's job to resolve them. These dilemmas are as follows.

    (a) *The dilemma of the cultures.* The cultures of organisations are described in a later chapter of this text. It is management's task to decide which culture of organisation and management is required for his particular task. As a manager rises in seniority, he will find it necessary to behave in a culturally diverse manner to satisfy the requirements of his job and the expectations of his employees. In other words, managers must be prepared to show flexibility and good judgement in their choice of organisation culture. The manager 'must be flexible but consistent, culturally diverse but recognisably an individual with his own identity. Therein lies the dilemma. Those . . . who relapse into a culturally predominant style will find themselves rightly restricted to that part of the organisation where their culture prevails. Middle layers of organisations are often overcrowded with culturally rigid managers who have failed to deal with this cultural dilemma'.

    (b) *The dilemma of time horizons.* This is the problem of responsibility for both the present and the future at the same time, described above in paragraph 2.10(a).

    (c) *The trust-control dilemma.* This is the problem of balance between management's wish to control the work for which they are responsible, and the necessity to delegate work to subordinates, thereby trusting them to do the work properly. The greater trust a manager places in subordinates, the less control he retains himself. Retaining control implies a lack of trust in subordinates. 'The managerial dilemma is always how to balance trust and control'.

    (d) *The commando leader's dilemma.* In many organisations, junior managers show a strong preference for working in project teams, with a clear task or objective, and working outside the normal bureaucratic structure of a large formal organisation. Unfortunately, there can be too many project groups (or 'commando groups') for the good of the total organisation, and a manager's dilemma is to decide how many project groups he should create to satisfy the needs of his subordinates, and how much bureaucratic organisation structure should be retained for the benefit of the total organisation despite the wishes of his subordinates.

3.2 *The manager as a person.*
Management is developing into a 'semi-profession' and managers expect to be rewarded for their professional skills. The implications for individual managers are that 'increasingly it will come to be seen as the individual's responsibility to maintain, alter or boost his skills, to find the right market for his skills and to sell them to the appropriate buyer'. In other words, management must continue to develop their own professional skills and sell them to the best bidder.

3.3 The dilemmas of management help to explain why the process of managing might often seem easy in theory, but is more complex in 'real life'.

3.4 When a manager faces problems or dilemmas, his or her subordinates are bound to suffer too.

3.5 In an article in the *'Administrator'* (Jan 1987), Sarah Rookledge describes the findings of an American report entitled: 'Working Well: Management for Health and High Performance'.

The report pointed out particular management traits that were held responsible by workshop interviewees for causing stress and health problems (eg high blood pressure - hyper-tension - insomnia, coronary heart disease and alcoholism). These included:

(a) unpredictability - staff work under constant threat of an outburst;
(b) destruction of workers' self esteem - making them feel helpless and insecure;
(c) setting up win/lose situations - turning work relationships into a battle for control;
(d) providing too much - or too little - stimulation.

3.6 In British research, according to the same article, managers are criticised for:

(a) not giving credit where it is due;
(b) failing to communicate policy or involve staff in decisions;
(c) supervising too closely; and
(d) not defining duties clearly enough.

The most 'harmful' style is said to be 'leave alone and zap' - where the employee (frequently young and inexperienced) is given a task, left without guidance, and then 'zapped' with a reprimand or punishment when mistakes are discovered. This simply creates a vicious circle of anxiety and guilt.

4.   THE USE OF MANAGERIAL TIME

4.1 A manager's use of his time is affected by a number of factors, such as:
(a)   the nature of his job;
(b)   his own personality;
(c)   the influence of colleagues; and
(d)   his work environment.

4.2 *The nature of the job.*
A manager's job involves regular contact with other people in the organisation. It is important to ensure that the inevitable interruptions which this causes are not allowed to encroach too much upon the supervisor's time. Keeping a detailed time diary is a common method of highlighting the amount of time taken up by interruptions and may suggest ways of reducing them.

Typical causes of wasted time in a manager's job might be prolonged or unnecessary meetings with colleagues or the preparation of unnecessary paperwork (which could be replaced with a brief oral communication). Managers should be on their guard against this and should consider whether such meetings and paperwork can be dispensed with.

4.3 *The personality of the manager.*
In one respect this is linked with the previous heading; a manager whose personality is confident and assertive will be better able to resist interruptions than one who is diffident. Other suggestions under this heading include the following.

(a) Do work which is different and requires concentration at times when interruptions are least likely, perhaps very early in the morning or late in the afternoon. Some people find that they work better in the morning than in the evening, or vice versa, and this should also be taken into account.

    (b)   Cultivate an organised and methodical approach, finishing one task before beginning on the next.

    (c)   Set appropriate personal targets which will contribute to the goals of the organisation.

4.4   *The influence of colleagues.*
Colleagues are defined as including superiors and subordinates as well as fellow managers.

    (a)   Although communication skills are important in a manager's job, the need to avoid unnecessary and time-wasting communication (eg. in prolonged meetings) has already been mentioned.

    (b)   A superior who interferes too much in the manager's job can be very disrupting. Tact in warding off such attention can be a valuable attribute.

4.5   *The work environment.*

    (a)   The physical surroundings in which a person works may affect his use of time. Even if a manager does not have an office of his own, he should try to appropriate a reasonably quiet area where concentrated work can be carried out without interruptions.

    (b)   Trips to the photocopier or to computer terminals should be minimised, particularly if they are housed in distant parts of the building.

    (c)   Fixed procedures and red tape can be time-consuming. Managers should try to minimise the time they spend on merely complying with laid-down procedures, without cutting corners that might lead to lower quality of output.

5.   THEORIES OF MANAGEMENT

5.1   The principles of management might suggest to you that there are some 'correct' ways of being a good manager or supervisor. Various writers have indeed put forward their ideas about how to be an effective and an efficient manager. Two of the early 'schools' of thinking about this were:
    (a)   the scientific management school; and
    (b)   the human relations or behavioural school.

Scientific management and F W Taylor

5.2   Frederick W Taylor (1856-1971) was the 'father' of the 'scientific management' movement. He argued that management should be based on 'well-recognised, clearly defined and fixed principles, instead of depending on more or less hazy ideas'.

> His purpose was to maximise efficiency and he suggested that by offering workers more money for being efficient, both the workers and the employees would benefit. Instead of arguing about how profits should be divided between them, workers and employers together should work for greater efficiency and productivity, so that there are more profits to share out.

5.3 Taylor felt that productivity would not be improved by the offer of more money alone, and he argued that a radical change of attitudes, on the part of both management and workers, was essential if his system were to be successful.

"The great mental revolution that takes place in the mental attitude of the two parties under scientific management is that both parties take their eyes off the division of the surplus as the all-important matter, and together turn their attention toward increasing the size of the surplus until this surplus becomes so large that it is unnecessary to quarrel about how it should be divided. They come to see that when they stop pulling against one another and instead, both turn and push shoulder to shoulder in the same direction, the size of the surplus created by their joint efforts is truly astounding. They both realise that when they substitute friendly co-operation and mutual helpfulness for antagonism and strife, they are together able to make this surplus so enormously greater than it was in the past that there is ample room for a large increase in wages for the workmen and an equally great increase in profits for the manufacturer." (Testimony to the House of Representatives Committee, 1912).

5.4 His famous four principles of scientific management were:

(a) *the development of a true science of work:* all knowledge which has hitherto been kept in the heads of workmen should be gathered and recorded by management. 'Every single subject, large and small, becomes the question for scientific investigation, for reduction to law'. Very simply, he argued that management should apply techniques to the solution of problems and should not rely on experience and 'seat-of-the-pants' judgements;

(b) *the scientific selection and progressive development of workmen:* workmen should be carefully trained, and given jobs to which they are best suited. Although 'training' is an important element in his principles of management, 'nurturing' might be a more apt description of his ideas of worker development;

(c) *the bringing together of the science and the scientifically selected and trained men:* the application of the techniques to decide what should be done, using workmen who are both properly trained and willing to maximise output, should result in maximum productivity;

(d) *the constant and intimate co-operation between management and workers:* 'the relations between employers and men form without question the most important part of this art.' (Taylor, *'Shop Management'* 1903)

5.5 The four principles should be applied together; unfortunately, it is possible to apply 'scientific management' techniques in order to improve productivity, without training the workforce or paying them for the improvement in output. This resulted in great hostility from trade union leaders, who condemned scientific management as a means of overworking the labour force and reducing the number of jobs. Taylor was eventually obliged to defend his ideas before a committee of the House of Representatives (Congress) in 1912.

5.6 It is useful to consider an application of Taylor's principles. In testimony to the House of Representatives Committee, Taylor used as an example the application of scientific management methods to shoveling work at the Bethlehem Steel Works:

(a) facts were first gathered by management as to the number of shovel loads handled by each man each day, with particular attention paid to the relationship between weight of the average shovel load and the total load shifted per day. From these facts, management was

11

able to decide on the ideal shovel size for each type of material handled in order to optimise the speed of shoveling work done. (Thus, scientific technique was applied to deciding how work should be organised);

(b)   by organising work a day in advance, it was possible to minimise idle time and the moving of men from one place in the shoveling yard to another. (Once again, scientific method replaces 'seat-of-the-pants' decisions by supervisors);

(c)   workers were paid for accepting the new methods and 'norms' and received 60% higher wages than those given to similar workers in other companies in the area. Workers were carefully selected and trained in the art of shoveling properly; anyone falling below the required norms consistently was given special teaching to improve his performance;

(d)   'the new way is to teach and help your men as you would a brother; to try to teach him the best way and show him the easiest way to do his work. This is the new mental attitude of the management towards the men . . .';

(e)   at the Bethlehem Steel Works, Taylor said, the costs of implementing this method were more than repaid by the benefits. The labour force required fell from 400 - 600 men to 140 men for the same work.

5.7   A summary of scientific management, in Taylor's own words, might be:

> (a)   'the man who is fit to work at any particular trade is unable to understand the science of that trade without the kindly help and co-operation of men of a totally different type of education';
>
> (b)   'it is one of the principles of scientific management to ask men to do things in the right way, to learn something new, to change their ways in accordance with the science and in return to receive an increase of from 30-100% in pay. . . .'.

5.8   Early supporters of the principles of scientific management included the following writers:

(a)   Frank and Lillian Gilbreth. A husband and wife team, they did much work in advancing the techniques of time and motion study (work study). As an example Frank Gilbreth made a study of 'wasted motions' ie physical movements which are unnecessary to get a job done - and he was able in one case the reduce the number of motions in bricklaying from 18 to 5, thereby doubling productivity without the need for an increase in effort. Lillian Gilbreth was an industrial psychologist, and her interest in human attitudes at work was blended with her husband's concern for efficiency;

(b)   Harrington Emerson was a leading advocate of standards and standardisation;

(c)   Henry Gantt, an associate of Taylor, did much work on the scientific selection of workmen, their training and development, and the formulation of incentive bonus schemes. Gantt is best-known for his development of the bar chart (Gantt chart) in which the time-relationship of activities in an overall project are depicted and time-critical activities can be identified.

(This was a fore-runner of network and critical path analysis and PERT techniques).

5.9 Hicks wrote 'by the end of the scientific management period, the worker had been reduced to the role of an impersonal cog in the machine of production. His work became more and more narrowly specialised until he had little appreciation for his contribution to the total product ... Although very significant technological advances were made . . . the serious weakness of the scientific approach to management was that it de-humanised the organisational member, who became a person without emotion and capable of being scientifically manipulated, just like machines'.

5.10 The worker's skills became devalued. Previously, the worker was felt to have some sort of expertise in the task he was performing, and, as a consequence, a degree of responsibility for it. In scientific management, the worker's knowledge of his craft was recorded and examined scientifically, so that eventually the *responsibility* for planning work processes was taken over by management.

5.11 The scientific management approach may be summarised as follows:

(a) an organisation should be an alliance of management and workers, to increase efficiency and productivity, so as to improve profitability;

(b) management should contribute towards this greater efficiency by the application of scientific techniques, and certain principles of management;

(c) the attitude of workers should not be ignored, and attention must be given to industrial psychology. Human attitudes began to attract increasing attention from management theorists so that a sociological approach to management and the 'behavioural' school of thought began to emerge as an alternative to scientific management.

The human relations or behaviouralist school: Elton Mayo

5.12 In the period from about 1930 a school of management thought developed which emphasised the importance of human relationships in organisations. In many ways, it was a reaction against the de-humanising aspects of the scientific management school of thought. (Note: 'de-humanising' refers not so much to the thinking of Taylor himself, but to the tendency of (scientific) management techniques to be introduced without the co-operation and approval of the workforce).

5.13 Elton Mayo was perhaps the most important contributor to this school of thought, as a result of his experiments at the Hawthorne plant of the Western Electric Company (known as the 'Hawthorne experiments').

5.14 Like Taylor and most of the other members of the scientific management movement, Mayo was primarily interested in management as it affected those at the rank and file level. But his viewpoint was entirely different. He not only agreed with the critics of the movement who felt that it paid insufficient attention to the human factor in productivity, he went even further. He believed that the economic motive, on which Taylor laid such stress, was unimportant compared to emotional and non-logical attitudes and sentiments in improving the efficiency and productivity of the employees at work.

5.15 The experiments arose from an attempt by Western Electric to find out the effects of lighting standards on worker productivity, ie the investigation began as 'scientific management' research. As a test, it moved a group of girls into a special room with variable lighting, and moved another group of girls into a room where the lighting was kept at normal standards. To the astonishment of the company management, productivity shot up in both rooms.

When the lighting was then reduced in the first room, as a continuation of the test, not only did productivity continue to rise in the first room, but it also rose still further in the second room. Mayo was called in to investigate further.

5.16 Mayo's Hawthorne experiments took place in Chicago during the thirties. The researchers were trying to find a relationship between fatigue and output. Five girls were the 'guinea pigs' of the experiment. At every point in the programme, the workers were consulted. Checks were kept in quarterly periods, with records not only of their work conditions, lighting, heating, rest periods, etc but also of their private lives. Nothing of any value came out of the experiments until they returned to the conditions of work that they had started with. This was a 48 hour week, with no rest breaks and not very good lighting, but output in the experiment still kept rising!

The improvements in productivity could not be explained by lighting, rest periods, hours of work or any other physical work conditions, but Mayo suspected that the attitudes of the girls in the experiment might explain the results.

5.17 Following a series of interviews with the guinea pigs in the experiments, the Hawthorne researchers concluded that it was the interest and attention that was the previously unrecognised motivation. This, they decided, was of far greater importance than all the improved conditions and other variables that they had been introducing. They said: 'Attitudes to people, as people, may be more important than such factors as rest periods, benefits, money etc. People are not merely instruments.'

5.18 Mayo wrote 'Management, by consultation with the girl workers, by clear explanation of the proposed experiments and the reasons for them, by accepting the workers' verdict in several instances, unwittingly scored a success in two most important human matters - the girls became a self-governing team, and a team that co-operated wholeheartedly with management'.

5.19 A hypothesis was developed that motivation to work, productivity and the quality of output were all related to:

(a) the 'psychology of the work group' - ie social relations among the workers; and
(b) the relationship between the workers and their supervisor/boss.

5.20 The hypothesis was tested further by Roethlisberger and Dickson, who selected a new group of 14 men, wirers and solderers, who were put under observation. Results of the experiment revealed that:

(a) the group developed a keen sense of its own identity; however, it divided into two separate cliques, one of which felt that it did more difficult, 'higher status' work than the other;

(b) the group as a whole developed certain 'norms' with regard to both output and supervision;

      (i)   with regard to output:

           (1)   the group appeared to establish a standard amount of production which was 'fair' for the pay they received;

           (2)   members of the group who produced above this normal level of output, or who shirked work and did less than the norm, were put under 'social pressure' by work-mates to get back into line;

      (ii)   with regard to supervision, the group view was that supervisors should not be officious and take unpleasant advantage of their position of authority. One officious supervisor was put under 'social pressure' by the group, so that he asked for a transfer out of the group;

(c)   the group did not follow company policy on some issues, with regard to work practices. In addition, daily reports of output were 'fiddled'; sometimes workers recorded more output than they actually produced, and on other days, they recorded less than they produced. The effect was to report constant volumes of daily production, whereas actual daily volume, according to tiredness or morale on the day, fluctuated considerably;

(d)   individual production rates varied significantly, but not according to individual ability or intelligence. Members of the 'high status' clique produced more than members of the other clique; but both the highest-producing employees and lowest-producing employees were the 'social outcasts' from either group. The men were paid a productivity incentive, and the high-status group felt that the other group were shirking; this resulted in considerable ill-feeling, and an eventual decline in the productivity of the group as a whole.

5.21   The experiments appeared to confirm that human attitudes (both of individuals and work groups) and the relationship between management and work groups or individual subordinates, were of key importance in establishing motivation to work and production efficiency.

Taylor and Mayo – who was right?

5.22   The scientific management school and the human relations school were both interested in increasing productivity on the shop floor, but their opinions on the proper way to motivate workers were diametrically opposite. It might seem, therefore, that one must be right and the other wrong. However, this is not necessarily true, since they were looking at the work situation from two entirely different angles.

5.23   Moreover, study shows that there were some important similarities in their goals and attitudes. Both were keen to advance the cause of science in management, and both were concerned with the working man and with social justice.

5.24   However, Mayo insisted: 'We have failed to train students in the study of social situations; we have thought that first class technical training was sufficient in a modern and mechanical age. As a consequence we are technically competent as no other age in history has been; and we combine this with utter social incompetence. This defect of education and of administration has of recent years become a menace to the whole future of civilisation. The administrator of the future must be able to understand the human-social facts for what they actually are, unfettered by his own emotion or prejudice. He cannot achieve this ability except by careful training – a training that must include knowledge of relevant technical skills, of the systematic ordering of operations, and of the organisation of co-operation.'

5.25 Drucker ('*The Practice of Management*' 1955) made some very interesting and useful comments on both the scientific management and human relations schools of thought. Remember, however, that since he wrote his comments further work has been carried out, and new ideas have emerged.

5.26 His comments about scientific management are as follows.

(a) Scientific management has contributed a philosophy of worker and work. 'As long as industrial society endures, we shall never lose again the insight that human work can be studied systematically, can be analysed, can be improved by work on its elementary parts. Like all great insights, it was simplicity itself'.

(b) However, it is capable of providing solutions to management problems only up to a certain point, and it seems incapable of providing further developments in future. 'Scientific Management . . . has been stagnant for a long time . . . During the last thirty years, it has given us little but pedestrian and wearisome tomes on the techniques, if not on the gadgets, of narrower and narrower specialities . . . The reason for this is that Scientific Management, despite all its worldy success, has not succeeded in solving the problem of managing worker and work. As so often happens in the history of ideas, its insight is only half an insight'.

(c) One major weakness of scientific management is that breaking work down into its elementary parts, and analysing a job as a series of consecutive 'motions', the solution to management problems the analysis often provides is that each separate 'motion' within the entire job could be done by a separate worker.

This is a mistake. It is correct to analyse work into its constituent parts, but it is wrong to create jobs for each different part. 'It is possible that Taylor himself saw the need to integrate . . . But practically all other writers – and all practitioners – see in the individual motion the essence of good work organisation'.

The boring nature of assembly-line work is the most obvious example of Drucker's criticism – and one which you are no doubt familiar with. It is much more satisfying to assemble a whole motor car than to be given a single part of the overall job, eg paint spraying. Scientific management therefore assumes that the human being, organised in a specific way to do specific tasks, is a (poorly designed) 'machine tool'.

Drucker concluded that in doing a work task 'every one of the operations should be analysed by means of scientific management to the point where they can be done by unskilled people. But the operations must be integrated again into a job';

(d) A further criticism of scientific management is that it divorces planning work from doing the work. The divorce of planning from doing reflects 'a dubious and dangerous philosophical concept of an elite which has a monopoly on esoteric knowledge entitling it to manipulate the unwashed peasantry'.

It is perfectly correct to realise that a job will be done better if it properly planned beforehand. This is a significant contribution of scientific management.

Drucker's objection was that the people who do the planning beforehand should be the people who later do the job itself. 'Planning and doing are separate parts of the same job; they are not separate jobs'.

5.27 Drucker concluded that his criticisms of scientific management explain the resistance to change in work practice which is often found amongst workers. 'Because the worker is supposed to do rather than to know – let alone plan – every change represents the challenge of the incomprehensible and therefore threatens his psychological security'.

5.28 In contrast, the human relations theory of management starts out with the right basic concepts – that people want to work; management's task is therefore to get the best out of them; and to do so, work must not be organised as a series of unrelated activities. However, at the time of writing (1955) Drucker argued that:

(a) 'Human Relations is, at least in the form in which it exists thus far, primarily a negative contribution. It freed management from the domination of viciously wrong ideas, but it did not succeed in substituting new concepts'.
(*Note:* the work of theorists such as Herzberg and Likert came later).

(b) Human relations thinking, whilst recognising the importance of work groups (Roethlisberger and Dickson of the 'Chicago school' pioneered this work) did not properly recognise that some work groups might have their own separate interests and objectives. The most significant reason for Drucker's criticism was the failure to recognise the 'political' and 'visionary' interests of trade unions.

(c) Human relations thinking might be used to 'manipulate' employees, and Drucker believed that there was a possibility that it would be used as 'a mere tool for justifying management's actions, a device to 'sell' whatever management is doing. It is no accident that there is so much talk in Human Relations about 'giving workers a sense of responsibility' and so little about their responsibility, so much emphasis on their 'feeling of importance' and so little making them and their work important'. This criticism was later echoed by McGregor in his analysis of Theory X and Theory Y management (described in a later chapter).

The problems of applying human relations ideas in practice remain an insuperable practical problem for many managements, which are simply reluctant to do anything more than pay lip service to the principles.

5.29 It might also be added that the principles of human relations thinking have not yet been successfully introduced in the management 'hierarchy' of many organisations, and yet they are intended to apply to workers as well as to junior managers. Clearly, there is still a long way to go, even today.

6. MANAGERIAL ROLES: HENRY MINTZBURG

6.1 Henry Mintzburg's book *The Nature of Managerial Work* was published in 1973, and was the result of empirical research into how managers in fact do their work. His main contention is:

"The classical view says that the manager organises, coordinates, plans and controls; the facts suggest otherwise."

6.2 Mintzburg instead identifies three types of role which a manager must play.

(a) *Interpersonal* roles which arise from the manager's formal authority include:

    (i)   the *figurehead* or ceremonial role, which according to Mintzburg's studies took up 12% of Chief Executive's time spent in contact with other people;

    (ii)   the *leader* role involves hiring, firing and training staff, motivating employees, reconciling individual needs with the requirements of the organisation;

    (iii)   the *liaison* role, rarely mentioned in many management texts, is what managers perform when making contacts outside the vertical chain of command. Some managers spend up to half their meeting time with their peers rather than with their subordinates and as such are the ambassadors of the departments they control. They need to know what is happening in other departments to act accordingly. Senior managers may spend a great deal of time with people outside their organisation. Mintzburg says that the purpose of these contacts is to build up an informal information system, but at the same time they are a means of extending influence both within organisations and outside.

(b) Managers also perform *informational* roles. As a leader, a manager has access to every member of staff, and is likely to have more external contacts than any of them. A manager's liaison contacts means that he or she is a channel of information from inside the department to outside and vice versa. Mintzburg, in an article published in the *Harvard Business Review* in 1975, states:

"The manager does not leave meetings or hang up the telephone in order to get back to work. In a large part communication *is* his work."

Mintzburg identifies three types of informational role.

    (i)   The manager *monitors* the environment, and receives information from subordinates or peers in other departments. Note that much of this information is of an informal nature, derived from his or her network of contacts and might be gossip or speculation.

    (ii)   The manager *disseminates* information, which he or she has acquired both formally through the vertical chain of command and informally through the network of contacts, to subordinates in the department.

    (iii)   As a *spokesman* the manager provides information to interested parties, either within or external to the organisation.

(c) Finally the manager has a number of *decisional* roles. The manager's formal authority and access to information means that no one else is in a position to take decisions relating to the work of the department.

    (i)   A manager acts as a sort of *entrepreneur* by initiating projects quite possibly of a small scale, a number of which may be on the go at any one time, to improve the department or to help it react to a changed environment.

    (ii)   A manager has to respond to pressures over which the department has no control. A manager is therefore a *disturbance handler* taking decisions in unusual situations which are impossible to predict.

(iii) A manager takes decisions relating to the *allocation of scarce resources*. The manager determines the department's direction, and authorises decisions taken by subordinates.

(iv) *Negotiation* both with inside and outside the organisation takes up a great deal of management time, but is a vital component of managerial work.

6.3 Mintzburg was led to draw a number of conclusions about certain assumptions relating to managerial work.

(a) Mintzburg's researches revealed that the belief that a manager is a reflective and systematic planner is a myth. Managerial work is disjointed and discontinuous; planning is conducted on a day to day basis, in between more urgent tasks.

(b) Another myth is that a manager has no regular or routine duties to perform, as these have been delegated to juniors. Mintzburg discovered that managers perform a number of routine duties, particularly of a ceremonial nature (eg receiving important guests).

(c) Thirdly, it has often been assumed that managers need aggregated information which they can best obtain from a formal management information system. Mintzburg's research indicated that managers prefer *verbal* communication. Information conveyed by word of mouth in an informal way is likely to be more 'current' and also more concrete thus easier to grasp.

(d) Finally, Mintzburg says that management cannot be a science or even a profession, as "A science involves the enaction of systematic analytically determined procedures or programs. If we do not even know what procedures managers use, how can we describe them by scientific analysis? And how can we call management a profession when we cannot specify what managers are to learn?"

Mintzburg states that general management is, in practice, a matter of judgement and intuition, gained from experience in particular situations rather than from abstract principles.

"The manager is . . . forced to do many tasks superficially. Brevity, fragmentation and verbal communication characterise his work."

His criticism of management science is that it has only concentrated on ideas that are easily susceptible to scientific analysis.

Exercise

Summarise for yourself the ways in which the functions of management can be analysed. At the same time, try to come up with your own description of what managerial work actually involves. Can you see any discrepancies between theory and practice?

6.4 Some theorists have suggested that managers can be efficient if they apply certain techniques or philosophies, and the scientific management school and the behavioural school of thinking were early contrasting approaches towards being an efficient and effective manager. However, managing isn't so easy in practice, and at the end of this chapter some case studies will illustrate aspects of the problem.

7. NEW MANAGERIAL WORK PRACTICES

7.1 New technology, especially production technology and information technology (robots, computers, communication systems etc) is changing the way that managers do their work.

    (a) *Technical skills*. Managers are becoming increasingly involved in using information technology (IT). Many have a microcomputer at their desk (or 'workstation'), which they might use for:

        (i) design work (computer-aided design, or CAD);
        (ii) planning and budgeting (eg using financial models or spreadsheet models);
        (iii) creating and using a central 'database' of information;
        (iv) carrying out complex calculations (eg mathematical models and techniques, preparing financial accounts);
        (v) carrying out repetitive standard calculations; or
        (vi) communicating via electronic mail.

    (b) *General management skills*. The functions of management haven't changed - they are still to plan, control, organise, command, motivate, co-ordinate, communicate and so on. But the proportion of time spent by a manager or supervisor on each function is likely to change. For example, if robotics or computers reduce the number of shopworkers and office clerks, the number of junior managers might remain the same, but with less time spent on directing and motivating others and more time spent, perhaps, on planning and co-ordinating.

7.2 Examples of technological change aren't hard to come by. The table on the next page illustrates some fairly recent changes in the field of microelectronics

New developments in microelectronics

A Products	A1 New products	*Examples* Compact disks Personal (home) computers Portable phones
	A2 Radically improved products	Digital watches
	A3 Improvements to existing products	Many domestic products, such as TVs, videos, washing machines, microwave ovens.
B Manufacturing	B1 Robots B2 Computer aided design (CAD) linked to computer aided manufacture (CAM) B3 Computerised stock control and production control.	
C Services	C1 Finance	Home banking Cash dispenser machines Electronic funds transfer at point of sale
	C2 Retailing	Point of sale systems Stock control - bar coding
	C3 Information services	External databases.
D Office work	D1 Office computers D2 Communications	Word processing Facsimile, electronic mail, networking.

7.3 The *strategic purpose* of new technology might be:

(a) to reduce operating costs
   (i) robotics save labour and labour costs, and also often save accommodation space;
   (ii) stock control and production control systems reduce stock levels and wastage;

(b) to increase flexibility. For example, computer-aided design helps a firm to experiment with more product designs before finally selecting an optimal design;

(c) to improve the quality of a product or service (eg to provide faster and more accurate service);

(d) to provide better control and integration by means of:
   (i) better information,
   (ii) better error detection processes.

7.4 The consequences of technological changes for the practice of management might be as follows.

---

1. Semi-skilled jobs will be taken over by robots and computers. There will be fewer jobs or more part-time jobs, and so less need for supervision.

2. There may be a degrading of old skills, or an ending to the need for old skills. New skills will be needed, and:

   2.1 there will be more pressure on managers to provide training or re-training for staff;

   2.2 management development will be more important, to keep managers up-to-date, and to motivate them as advancement gets harder.

3. As equipment becomes simpler to use, there could be opportunities for greater flexibility in manning, with one worker able to carry out more varied tasks. In manufacturing, there may be more continuous shift working (24 hours a day), to keep expensive assets in constant use.

5. Since more jobs will be part-time, there will be less need for full-time employees. More work will be sub-contracted, and full-time jobs axed. Managers will have to deal with external contractors instead of issuing directions to their own staff.

6. Better communications systems, portable computers etc reduce the need for people to work together in an office. There will be *more working at home*. Several managers can then share the same small office, and go into work only occasionally.

7. Working at home is likely to speed up the progression towards 'sub-contracting', and some managers might become self-employed consultants with a 'main client' (their erstwhile employer) and a number of smaller clients who are picked up as the individual gradually markets his services more widely.

8. Improved information systems should help managers to plan and control work more effectively (eg using databases and models for planning, and obtaining fast feedback for better control).

9. Better information systems open up opportunities for:

   9.1 more *centralisation* of decision-making by top management and

   9.2 a reduced need for middle managers. The size of the middle management workforce might be reduced.

7.5 *In The Age of The Smart Machine* by Shoshana Zuboff, published in 1989, reviews the far reaching effects that information technology and computerisation will have on work and future management practice. She begins by examining what computerisation actually does. For example, assume that a complicated production process has now been computerised. What effects does this have on the way that the process is controlled?

   (i)   The process has been *automated*. Effectively, this means that tasks are performed with the minimum of human judgement and intervention and according to set routines. Arguably, automation is the triumph of Taylorism as described earlier.

   (ii) The process has been *informated*. As the process is controlled by computer, human beings can only monitor it *indirectly* by observing the data that the computer displays on, say, a VDU screen.

7.6 So what? How does this affect management?

   (a)   Firstly, effective production control in a computerised environment depends on the ability of the workforce to interpret and manipulate abstract data, and to do this they need an overall theoretical knowledge of the system.

   (b)   Secondly, dealing with problems thrown up by data on a screen requires an ability to discuss them in a cooperative way, and so decisions may be arrived at by consensus. A critical questioning attitude towards data presented on the screen is needed. Traditional management practice requires that managers control information, and managers alone take decisions. However, if the workforce needs to manipulate information in order to function at all, it is obvious that information and information-handling skills can no longer be exclusive to management. The days when managers were a priestly caste with a privileged control over knowledge are numbered: *shared access to information threatens the distinction between managers and the managed*, returns responsibility for the work process back to the workers and thus would appear to undermine the logic of Taylor's analysis completely.

   (c)   Thirdly, information technology itself is becoming more user friendly. Fourth generation languages are relatively easy to use, which may lead to employees gaining more control over their own work. With the growth of database technology, routine transactions can be taken over by the machines, so that human beings can be freed to make use of the wealth of information easily available.

   (d)   Fourthly, computerisation has largely been seen as a means of *cutting costs*. Cost savings are easily identified. However, it is Zuboff's contention that few organisations consider that information, intelligently used, can be a means of *adding value*.

7.7 Zuboff cites a real life example where middle managers, by insisting on implementing old forms of control, measurably impeded growth in productivity after a computerised system had been installed.

7.8 Zuboff believes the problem to be cultural. Managers have looked on themselves as an elite, and their authority has always been felt to rest on a commonly held set of values: in short managerial authority has to be seen to be *legitimate*. Zuboff cites a number of ideas about management used over the past two centuries to justify management's 'right to manage'.

(a) If the manager is also an owner, the manager has rights over the business as the business is personal property.

(b) Managers are harder working, and so deserve to be in authority.

(c) Managers and workers have inherent psychological differences and managers get where they are by natural selection ('Survival of the fittest' or Social Darwinism).

(d) Management is a science, and managers are dispassionate scientists free from normal human motivations (power, political rivalry etc).

(e) Managers are better educated than the workers, and only the educated are fit to manage.

7.9 The 'informating' power of the new technology requires the workforce to be educated as well. Managers can no longer pretend that they are in some way different from the people they are managing. In the long run, information technology may be a threat to the status of management as a group, and may even require the redefinition of 'management' itself.

7.10 The extent to which these changes in management practice occur over time will depend on certain conditions or contingencies; including:

(a) the speed of technological change;
(b) the amount of judgement needed in management decisions;
(c) the extent of personal service in work;
(d) the unpredictability of work;
(e) the risks involved should an electronic system break down.

When (b), (c), (d) and (e) are high, the progress of change will probably be relatively slow.

7.11 Changes are happening all the time. You might know of some that have affected your own work. If so, be ready to describe them in your examination. Make a distinction, though, between:

(a) changes that affect the skills you use as a manager (eg using micros);
(b) changes that affect the way you do your work (eg working at home); and
(c) changes that alter your functions as a manager. These shouldn't change at all, except that you might perform some functions more and some functions less than before.

CASE STUDY 1

Let's finish this chapter on the functions of management with two simple case studies.

The following exchanges were overheard in an office of a public company:

Manager: I asked for this report on Friday - what delayed you?

Supervisor: I was trying to clear up the end-of-quarter returns.

Manager: But it's already the fourth of the month.

Supervisor: Yes, but I had two of my staff away on holiday at the same time.

Manager: How did that happen?

Supervisor: Well they asked me separately - a few weeks apart - and I hadn't realised what the consequences would be.

Manager: I'm afraid it's not good enough. I am constantly having to complain about work which is produced at the last moment - or later. It is often badly prepared and faulty. What are you going to do about it?

Supervisor: I don't know. I never have the time to think ahead.

How would you help this supervisor?

Discussion

Let's start by analysing the features of the case.

(a) The supervisor is late with his reports and they are often badly prepared.
(b) He has failed to anticipate and plan for the effects of two staff being on holiday.
(c) These situations are not rare occurrences since the manager is 'constantly' complaining.
(d) The supervisor appears to be hard-working, but is this enough for effective management?

This appears to be a problem of a failure to *plan*. The problem might be aggravated by:

(a) inability of the supervisor to *delegate;*
(b) the failure of his manager to provide help.

The problem directs us to show *how* we would help this particular supervisor. To do this rationally we must diagnose the causes of the problem. Possible causes could include:

(a) inability of the supervisor;
(b) overwork of the supervisor;
(c) poor help and advice from his manager.

Either (a) or (b) would mean that the supervisor is not carrying out his functions properly, and (c) would mean that the manager is not doing his job of developing his staff properly.

In more detail, the possible factors causing the problem would include:

(a)   the supervisor does not know how to plan, or does not see the need for planning;

(b)   the supervisor is overworked, or fails to delegate and therefore has not got the time to plan and organise;

(c)   the supervisor may have been badly selected and does not possess the qualities to be an effective manager;

(d)   the manager has given no coaching or guidance to help him overcome his difficulties;

(e)   the manager does not give enough information or time to allow his subordinates to plan.

The appropriate help would depend on a complete diagnosis of the facts related to this problem which could only be made after interviewing both the manager and the supervisor, checking the records for evidence of the kinds of mistakes and their effects on the performance of the supervisor's section, with careful distinctions between facts and opinions.

The nature of the help needed to solve this problem would depend on its causes but could be any of the following measures.

The *manager* might need the help, not the supervisor! The manager should be counselled to:

(a)   ensure that his subordinates understand their jobs and their wider significance on performance;

(b)   provide the resources and information necessary for effective planning;

(c)   provide feedback on their performance and be prepared to coach, train or counsel to ensure they plan effectively;

(d)   provide an example by his own approach to planning and reward those who follow his example.

The *subordinate* should be counselled:

(a)   so that he sees the need for planning and delegation within the wider framework of effective management of his section;

(b)   so that he accepts the need for further training if this is considered necessary;

(c)   to accept the help of his manager and to follow his example and discuss with his own subordinates the appropriate approaches to delegation.

The best course of action might be a combination of these alternatives. The actions must be combined into a plan of action which is adequately discussed and communicated to both individuals to ensure that they know their part in the plan.

Allow a suitable amount of time for the plan to take effect, and then follow it up, to check whether the problem has been solved. It might be necessary to consider:

(a)   further training and counselling;
(b)   transfer of the subordinate to other duties;
(c)   dismissal in the unlikely case of wilful dereliction of duties.

CASE STUDY 2

> Bill Brown, your friend and fellow section leader, possesses many admirable qualities and skills. He is clear-headed and logical, a good organiser and planner, and has a good understanding of the technical aspects of his work. Despite all this, his staff often seem to be puzzled because he does not always make himself clear to them, and, as a result, mistakes are made and the staff become annoyed and frustrated.
>
> How would you advise Bill Brown to communicate more effectively?

Discussion

This is a problem involving poor personal communications between Bill and his staff which result in mistakes at work and frustration for his subordinates. Communication is an important function of management.

Communication is the exchange of ideas and values between two or more people. It consists of:

(a) *Technical process*
Selecting the correct symbols (eg words, numbers, illustrations), selecting the correct media to transmit the message (eg verbal, written), repeating the message, allowing feedback of the message from the receiver.

(b) *Social process*
Involves social relationships of trust and friendliness, perception and values which influence the meaning of a message to both parties.

To help Bill, it would be necessary to find out the exact causes of the problem. Since Bill is a friend and fellow section leader, this would involve talking to both Bill himself, to explore his own views, and (with Bill's permission) to his staff.

Find out:

(a) the exact nature of the failures in communication, eg are they caused by misunderstandings?

(b) what annoys and frustrates his staff?
   - does he talk above their heads and fail to explain things in terms that they can understand?
   - does he not communicate at all?
   - does he communicate too late or only when they ask?

   Only by identifying the real causes will it be possible to help Bill, but advice would possibly include the points below.

Advice and help for Bill
It is often difficult for a person who is as bright and intelligent as Bill to appreciate the limitations and inabilities of other people. Good leadership requires such an understanding.

(a) Bill must be clear in his own mind as to the content of any message he wants to give his staff and why he needs to communicate it.

(b) Bill should organise his ideas before speaking.

(c) He should ensure that:

   (i) the timing is right for his message (eg a relatively unimportant piece of information should not be given to a person working hard to meet a deadline);

   (ii) the setting is right (eg a personal comment should not be delivered in front of the whole office;

   (iii) communication has taken place within the context of the organisation's customs and normal practices.

(d) Use simple and direct language and avoid technical terms and jargon whenever possible.

(e) Try to anticipate their technical limitations and explain using illustrations and examples whenever possible.

(f) Select the appropriate media for the message (eg verbal for simple or 'personal' messages; written if the message is complex).

(g) Bill must ensure that he communicates the importance of the message to the receiver so that full attention is given.

(h) Always obtain feedback of the message/instruction. Ensure that what the message means to his staff is what Bill intended it to mean.

(i) Recognise that the perception and values of each individual will be different. The sense in which we see things and the importance we attach to them will depend on our education, family background and social status. Bill must develop a sensitivity to the world of his staff and understand how this influences their attitudes towards messages.

(j) Encourage Bill to use more face-to-face communications so that the person's reaction can be seen and understood. (Non-verbal signals can be important.)

(k) Try to encourage a more open superior/subordinate relationship, so that his staff can ask questions and do not feel they might be criticised for needing to ask.

(l) Try to be a good listener, and show an interest in their ideas. When they are wrong, explain and discuss their point of view in a sympathetic way and avoid using:
   (i) his superior position to rule out their arguments;
   (ii) superior intelligence ('I know all the answers') to reinforce his position.

(m) Bill's words must be supported by his actions.

TEST YOUR KNOWLEDGE

(The numbers in brackets refer to paragraphs in this chapter)

1. What is the broad role of managers, and how does this role differ between public and private sector organisations? (1.1-1.4)

2. Describe the skills of a manager responsible for the effective running of a functional department within an organisation (discussion point below).

3. Criticise the ideas of

    (a)   scientific management, and
    (b)   the human relations approach to management. (5.26-5.28)

4. List ways in which the *practice* of management might change or develop due to technological advances. (7.1-7.2)

Discussion point

Question 2.   Some technical skills appropriate to the department are needed. Also skills of management - ie skills at planning, controlling, problem-solving, making decisions, motivating or commanding, dealing with other people, co-ordinating, counselling, encouraging creativity and innovation.

Chapter 2

DIRECTION: LEADERSHIP STYLE AND EFFECTIVE MANAGEMENT

This chapter covers the following topics

1. The manager as leader
2. Trait theories of leadership
3. Leadership styles
4. Task management
5. The management hierarchy
6. A systems approach to leadership
7. A contingency approach to leadership
8. The importance of leadership style

Purpose of this chapter

To consider the various styles of leadership, which managers use either to direct or to motivate others.

Motivation will be studied in further detail in the next chapter.

1. THE MANAGER AS LEADER

1.1 Leadership is the process of influencing others to work willingly towards an organisation's goals, and to the best of their capabilities. ' The essence of leadership is followership. In other words it is the willingness of people to follow that makes a person a leader' (Koontz, O'Donnell, Weihrich). Leadership would also be listed as *one* of the functions of management.

1.2 Leadership comes about in a number of different ways:

(a) a manager is appointed to a position of authority within the organisation. Leadership of his subordinates is a function of the position he holds;

(b) some leaders (eg in politics or in trade unions) might be elected;

(c) other leaders might emerge by popular choice and through their personal drive and qualities. Unofficial spokesmen for groups of people are leaders of this style.

1.3 Our main concern, of course, is with managers who are appointed as leaders by virtue of their position in the organisation.

1.4 If a manager had indifferent or poor leadership qualities his subordinates would still do their job, but they would do it ineffectually or perhaps in a confused manner. By providing leadership, a manager should be able to use the capabilities of subordinates to better effect, ie leadership is the 'influential increment over and above mechanical compliance with the routine directives of the organisation' (Katz and Kahn *The Social Psychology of Organisations*).

1.5 Since leadership is concerned with influencing others, it is necessary to have some understanding about what motivates people to work. Motivation is the subject of the next chapter of this text, but it may be summarised briefly as the effort, energy and excitement which a person is prepared to expend in his work. Koontz, O'Donnell and Weihrich formulate the principle that 'since people tend' to follow those whom they see as a means of satisfying their own personal goals, the more managers understand what motivates their subordinates and how these motivations operate, and the more they reflect this understanding in carrying out their managerial actions, the more effective leaders they are likely to be.'

2. TRAIT THEORIES OF LEADERSHIP

2.1 Early theories suggested that there are certain qualities, personality characteristics or 'traits' which make a good leader. These might be aggressiveness, self-assurance, intelligence, initiative, a drive for achievement or power, appearance, interpersonal skills, administrative ability, imagination, a certain upbringing and education, the 'helicopter factor' (ie the ability to rise above a situation and analyse it objectively) etc.

2.2 This list is not exhaustive, and various writers attempted to show that their selected list of traits were the ones that provided the key to leadership. The full list of traits is so long that it appears to call for a man or woman of extraordinary, even superhuman, gifts to be a leader.

2.3 Jennings (1961) wrote that 'Research has produced such a variegated list of traits presumably to describe leadership, that for all practical purposes it describes nothing. Fifty years of study have failed to produce one personality trait or set of qualities that can be used to distinguish between leaders and non-leaders.' Trait theory, although superficially attractive, is now largely discredited.

Alternative approaches to leadership theory have been developed over the years, and some of these will be described under the headings of:

(a) style theories, mainly of the 'behaviouralist' school of thought;
(b) systems theory and leadership;
(c) contingency theories of leadership.

3. LEADERSHIP STYLES

3.1 A leader cannot try to forget that he is the 'boss' by being friendly and informal with subordinates, or by consulting them before making any decision. Douglas McGregor (*Leadership and Motivation*) wrote about his own experiences as a college president that : 'It took a couple of years, but I finally began to realise that a leader cannot avoid the exercise of authority any more than he can avoid responsibility for what happens in the organisation.' A leader can try to avoid acting dictatorially, and he can try to act like 'one of the boys', but he must accept all the consequences of being a leader. McGregor wrote that 'since no important decision ever pleases everyone in the organisation, he must also absorb the displeasures, and sometimes severe hostility, of those who would have taken a different course'.

3.2 However, although a leader must exercise his authority, he can do it in a number of different ways. In other words, his *style* of leadership might vary. It is generally accepted that a leader's style of leading can affect the motivation, efficiency and effectiveness of his subordinates.

3.3 Four different types of leadership were identified by Huneryager and Heckman (1967).

(a) *Dictatorial style:* the manager forces subordinates to work by threatening punishment and penalties. The psychological contract between the subordinates and their organisation would be coercive. Dictatorial leadership might be rare in commerce and industry, but it is not uncommon in the style of government in some countries of the world, nor in the style of parenthood in many families.

(b) *Autocratic style:* decision-making is centralised in the hands of the leader himself, who does not encourage participation by subordinates; indeed, subordinates' ideas might be actively discouraged and obedience to orders would be expected from them. The autocratic style is common in many organisations, and you will perhaps be able to identify examples from your own experience. Doctors, matrons and sisters in hospitals tend to practise an autocratic style; managers/directors who own their company also tend to expect things to be done their way.

(c) *Democratic style:* decision-making is decentralised, and shared by subordinates in participative group action. To be truly democratic, the subordinate must be willing to participate. The democratic style is described more fully later.

(d) *Laissez-faire style:* subordinates are given little or no direction at all, and are allowed to establish their own objectives and make all their own decisions. The leader of a research establishment might adopt a laissez-faire style, giving individual research workers freedom of choice to organise and conduct their research as they themselves want (within certain limits, such as budget spending limits).

3.4 These four divisions or 'compartments' of management style are really a simplification of a 'continuum' or range of styles, from the most dictatorial to the most laissez-faire.

2: DIRECTION: LEADERSHIP STYLE AND EFFECTIVE MANAGEMENT

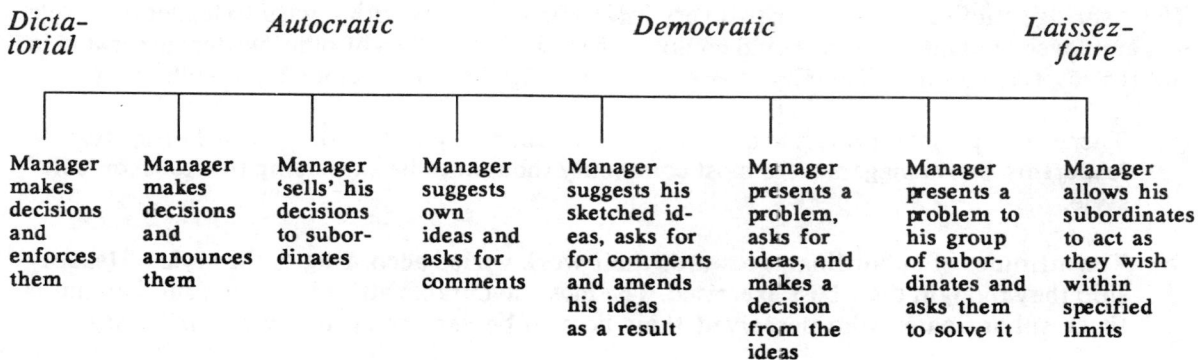

Dicta-torial	*Autocratic*			*Democratic*			*Laissez-faire*
Manager makes decisions and enforces them	Manager makes decisions and announces them	Manager 'sells' his decisions to subordinates	Manager suggests own ideas and asks for comments	Manager suggests his sketched ideas, asks for comments and amends his ideas as a result	Manager presents a problem, asks for ideas, and makes a decision from the ideas	Manager presents a problem to his group of subordinates and asks them to solve it	Manager allows his subordinates to act as they wish within specified limits

This 'continuum' of leadership styles was first suggested by Tannenbaum and Schmidt (1958).

3.5 There are differing views as to which of these leadership styles (especially (a), (b) or (c)) is likely to be most effective. The probable truth is that the degree of effectiveness of a particular leadership style will depend on the work environment, the leader himself, and his subordinates.

The Ashridge studies

3.6 A slightly different analysis of leadership styles, based on this continuum, was made by the Research Unit at Ashridge Management College, based on research in several industries in the UK (reported 1966). This research distinguished four different management styles.

(a) The autocratic or *'tells'* style. This is characterised by one-way communication between the manager and the subordinate, with the manager telling the subordinate what to do. The leader makes all the decisions and issues instructions, expecting them to be obeyed without question.

(b) The persuasive or *'sells'* style. The manager still makes all the decisions, but believes that subordinates need to be motivated to accept them before they will do what he wants them to. He therefore tries to explain his decisions in order to persuade them round to his point of view.

(c) The *consultative* style. This involves discussion between the manager and the subordinates involved in carrying out a decision, but the manager retains the right to make the decision himself. By conferring with his subordinates before making any decision, the manager will take account of their advice and feelings. Consultation is a form of limited participation in decision-making for subordinates, but there might be a tendency for a manager to appear to consult his subordinates when really he has made up his mind beforehand. Consultation will then be false and a facade for a sells style of leadership whereby the manager hopes to win the acceptance of his decisions by subordinates by pretending to listen to their advice.

(d) The democratic or *'joins'* style. This is an approach whereby the leader joins his group of subordinates to make a decision on the basis of consensus or agreement. It is the most democratic style of leadership identified by the research study. Subordinates with the greatest knowledge of a problem will have greater influence over the decision. The joins style is therefore most effective where all subordinates in the group have equal knowledge and can therefore contribute in equal measure to decisions.

3.7 The Ashridge studies made one or two very interesting findings with regard to leadership style and employee motivation. You should compare these with the views of other writers described in the rest of this chapter. The findings of the Ashridge studies included the following.

(a) There was a clear preference amongst the subordinates for the *consultative* style of leadership but managers were most commonly thought to be exercising the 'tells' or 'sells' style.

(b) The attitudes of subordinates towards their work varied according to the style of leadership they thought their boss exercised. The most favourable attitudes were found amongst those subordinates who perceived their boss to be exercising the *consultative style*.

(c) The least favourable attitudes were found amongst subordinates who were unable to perceive a consistent style of leadership in their boss. In other words, subordinates are unsettled by a boss who chops and changes between autocracy, persuasion, consultation and democracy. The conclusion from this finding of the study is that *consistency* in leadership style is important.

3.8 Below are listed some of the strengths and weaknesses of each type of style.

		Strengths	*Weaknesses*
(a) *Tells style*	(1)	Quick decisions can be made when speed is required	(1) It does not encourage the subordinate to give his opinions when these might be useful.
	(2)	It is the most efficient type of leadership for highly-programmed not routine work.	(2) Communications between the manager and subordinate will be one-way and the manager will know until afterwards whether his orders have been properly understood.
			(3) It does not encourage initiative and commitment from subordinates.
(b) *Sells style*	(1)	Employees are made aware of the reasons for decisions.	(1) Communications are still largely one-way. Subordinates might not buy his decisions.
	(2)	Selling decisions to staff might make them more willing to co-operate.	(2) It does not encourage initiative and commitment from subordinates.
	(3)	Staff will have a better idea of what to do when unforeseen events arise in their work because the manager will have explained his intentions.	

(c) *Consultative style*

(1) Employees are involved in decisions before they are made. This encourages motivation through greater interest and involvement.

(1) It might take much longer to reach decisions.

(2) An agreed consensus of opinion can be reached and for some decisions consensus can be an advantage rather than a weak compromise.

(2) Subordinates might be too inexperienced to formulate mature opinions and give practical advice.

(3) Employees can contribute their knowledge and experience to help in solving more complex problems.

(d) *Joins style*

(1) It can provide high motiva-tion and commitment from employees.

(1) The authority of the manager might be undermined.

(2) It shares the other advantages of the consultative style.

(2) Decision-making might become a very long process, and clear decisions might be difficult to reach.

(3) Subordinates might lack enough experience.

3.9 The views of 'classical' theorists were that a leader should be task-orientated. By applying the scientific method to work problems, managers would maximise efficiency. Taylor advocated a benevolent paternalism or autocratic style of leadership. Another 'classical' view was that dictatorial leadership is more effective.

3.10 There was a general agreement that a person is born with leadership qualities or traits, ie he 'has what it takes' to be leader; this is known as 'the great man' theory and has already been discussed.

3.11 The 'great men' theory was challenged by subsequent writers of the human relations and behaviouralist schools. Stodgill wrote (1948) 'A person does not become a leader by virtue of the possession of some combination of traits, but the pattern of personal characteristics of the leader must bear some relevant relationship to the characteristics, activities and goals of the followers'. The conclusion was that if leadership is not an innate gift, a style of leadership appropriate to a given work situation can be learned and adopted.

3.12 *Human relations*' views on leadership styles will be discussed by considering the contributions of:

(a) Lewin, Lippitt and White;
(b) McGregor (Theory X and Theory Y); and
(c) Likert.

2: DIRECTION: LEADERSHIP STYLE
AND EFFECTIVE MANAGEMENT

Lewin, Lippitt and White (1939)

3.13 Although Elton Mayo is considered to be the pioneer of the human relations movement, Lewin was another important theorist who did much research on group dynamics and leadership styles. With his colleagues Lippitt and White he reported the results of well-known experiments which were carried out in boys' clubs established for the purposes of their studies.

3.14 Club leaders were trained to act as autocratic, democratic or laissez-faire leaders, and the purpose of the experiments was to learn how the children reacted to different styles of leadership. The leaders were moved from one club to another every six weeks and by means of rotation each club (consisting of 10-year-old boys) experienced three different styles of leadership, under three different leaders.

    (a) The *autocratic* leader tended to give orders, and to interrupt the activities of the boys by giving commands to do something else. Criticism and praise were given out non-objectively, ie at the whim of the leader.

    (b) The *democratic* leader suggested what the boys should do, showed concern for each boy's individual welfare, participated in the activities of the group, but left the decisions about what to do to the boys themselves.

    (c) The *laissez-faire* leader also made suggestions, but was more 'stand-offish' and did not involve himself with the boy's welfare, nor did he join in the group activities, so that the boys were effectively left to do what they wanted by themselves.

3.15 Lewin, Lippitt and White were particularly interested in aggressive social behaviour, either within the group or shown to outsiders. Their findings may be summarised as follows:

    (a) in one experiment, aggressive behaviour was very much more common among the autocratic group than the democratic group, but none of the aggression or hostility was directed at the leader himself:

    (b) in a subsequent experiment, boys in four out of five autocratic groups showed 'apathetic' behaviour and lack of aggression. This apathy was attributed by the experimenters to the repressive style of the club leader;

    (c) 95 per cent of boys preferred a democratic to an autocratic leader, and 70 per cent preferred a laissez-faire leader to an autocratic one;

    (d) aggression is only partly caused by leadership style. Other factors arousing hostile behaviour are tension, restriction of physical space and the cultural background of the boys in the group. Nevertheless, leadership style contributes towards such behaviour.

3.16 In a subsequent publication many years later (1960) Lippitt and White investigated the effect of leadership on productivity in different groups. They concluded that:

    (a) work-orientated conversation was greatest in a democratic group, less in an autocratic group and, interestingly, least in a laissez-faire group;

    (b) the amount of work actually done was greatest in an autocratic group and least in a laissez-faire group. Motivation was strongest in a democratic group where boys often carried on working even when a leader left the room. Interestingly, however, motivation was not sufficient to increase output above the level of the autocratic group;

(c) as mentioned above, hostility and discontent were greatest in an autocratic group. Four dropped out of the experiment, and all belonged to an autocratic group at the time. Boys in an autocratic group were more dependent on their leader, and submissive; their hostility was towards each other. In contrast, originality, group-mindedness and friendly playfulness were greatest in a democratic group.

Douglas McGregor: Theory X and Theory Y

3.17 Douglas McGregor in his book *The Human Side of Enterprise* claims that a manager's choice of leadership style will stem from his theories about how his subordinates behave. He offers two theories held by managers, which he calls Theory X and Theory Y.

3.18 *Theory X.*
This is the theory that the average human being has an inherent dislike of work and will avoid it if he can. Because of this human characteristic of dislike of work, most people must be coerced, controlled, directed, threatened with punishment to get them to put forth adequate effort towards the achievement of organisation objectives. The human being prefers to be directed, wishing to avoid responsibility. He has relatively little ambition and wants security above all.

3.19 *Theory Y.*
The expenditure of physical and mental effort in work is as natural as play or rest. The ordinary person does not inherently dislike work: according to the conditions it may be a source of satisfaction or punishment. Extensive control is not the only means of obtaining effort. Man will exercise self-direction and self-control in the service of objectives to which he is committed.

3.20 The most significant reward that can be offered in order to obtain commitment is the satisfaction of the individual's self-actualising needs. The average human being learns, under proper conditions, not only to accept but to seek responsibility. Many more people are able to contribute creatively to the solution of organisational problems than do so. At present the potentialities of the average person are not being fully used.

3.21 You will have your own viewpoints on the validity of Theory X compared with Theory Y. In fact McGregor intentionally polarised his theories, and recognises that people are too complex to be categorised in this way. Inevitably a manager's choice of leadership strategy will arise from his theories on the causes of behaviour of his subordinates.

3.22 Theory X is often misunderstood, and confused with a 'hard' or a 'soft' style of direction. 'Theory X is not a straw man for purposes of demolition, but is in fact a theory which materially influences managerial strategy in a wide sector of American industry today.' What was true in 1960 remains true even now. 'Theory X explains the *consequences* of a particular managerial strategy, it neither explains nor describes human nature although it purports to...What sometimes appear to be new strategies - decentralisation, management by objectives, consultative supervision, "democratic" leadership - are usually but old wine in new bottles, because the procedures derived to implement them are derived from the same inadequate assumptions about human nature...These new approaches are no more than different tactics - programmes, procedures, gadgets - within an unchanged strategy based on Theory X.'

In more general words, lip service is paid to Theory Y but Theory X is practised.

3.23 Theory X implies the optimum *integration* of organisational requirements with individual goals.

'Authority is an inappropriate means for obtaining commitment to objectives. Other forms of influence - help in achieving integration for example - are required for this purpose'. Management should adopt policies that promote satisfaction of needs in the job, and individual development and self-expression.

3.24 Theory X stresses domination and dependence in work relationships; Theory Y emphasises independence. But the seeming 'either/or' conflict suggested by these opposing views does not exist; leadership styles can vary in degrees, ranging from extreme Theory X to extreme Theory Y. McGregor was unable to prove that one extreme was objectively better than another (ie more productive) nor could he disprove that a middle of the road leadership style might not be better:

(a) Theory X supervision, when the 'rules' are properly applied, should be successful in achieving stated objectives. It is unlikely, however, that the stated objectives will be surpassed, ie the minimum objectives become the maximum objectives as well. Much potential might be unrealised.

(b) Theory Y supervision has been implemented on occasions. For example, the Lincoln Electric Company in the USA made each employee responsible for his own supplies (both purchasing and control) and for setting the quality and quantity of his own output. Theory Y, however, depends on mature individuals; maturity, given the influence of group psychology etc, does not exist sufficiently on the shop floor to be practicable in its extreme form. *Progress* along the road to Theory Y is all that is realistically possible.

McGregor concluded that 'Theory Y is an invitation to innovation'.

3.25 A manager who operates on a Theory X basis will closely direct and control workers and will operate through specific instructions and detailed control. On the other hand, the Theory Y based manager will naturally delegate and develop his staff and encourage them to take greater responsibility and tackle more challenging work. It is important to link McGregor's Theory Y with Likert's participative style manager, who is proved by research to be the most effective manager.

Rensis Likert

3.26 Rensis Likert distinguished four systems of management:

(a) exploitive authoritative;
(b) benevolent authoritative;
(c) consultative authoritative;
(d) participative group management.

Managers, to be effective and to communicate, must adjust to the people they are managing.

3.27 Likert attempted to show that the effective manager is one who uses the participative style of management, although the ideal manager must be able to use the right leadership style for the right situation. Everyone in an organisation is interdependent with other people (as a manager is dependent upon his subordinates). Authority alone is insufficient to obtain good performance. It can only be effective in certain situations and with certain people. The complete manager is one who uses (normally) a supportive, participative approach but who can use any style effectively in the right situation.

3.28 In his books *New Patterns of Management* and *The Human Organisation* he attempted through research to answer the question 'what do effective managers have in common?' His research showed that four main elements are normally present in any effective manager:

(a) they expect high levels of performance. Their standards and targets are high and apply overall, not only to their subordinates' performance, but also to other departments and their personal performance;

(b) they are employee-centred. They spend time getting to know their workers and develop a situation of trust whereby their employees feel able to bring their problems to them. When necessary, their actions can be hard but fair, akin to the actions of a fond and responsible parent. Such managers are typified by their ability to face unpleasant facts in a constructive manner and help their staff to grow and develop a similar constructive attitude;

(c) they do not practise close supervision. The truly effective manager is aware of the performance levels that can be expected from each individual and he has helped them to define their own targets. Once this has been achieved, the manager judges results and does not closely supervise the actions of his staff. In this way he not only develops his people, he also frees himself to spend more time on other aspects of his work (for example, planning decisions, communications with other areas and personnel problems);

(d) they operate the participative style of management as a natural style. This means that if a job problem arises they do not impose a favoured solution. Instead, they pose the problem and ask the staff member involved to find the best solution. Having then agreed their solution the participative manager would assist his staff in implementing it.

3.29 Likert emphasises that all four features must be present for a manager to be truly effective. For example, if a manager is employee-centred, if he delegates and is participative, then he will have a happy working environment but he will not produce a high performance unless he also establishes standards of performance. A manager's concern for people must be matched by his concern for achieving results. This linking of the human relations approach with scientific management targets will provide the recipe for real effective performance. It is important to remember that management techniques such as time and motion study, financial controls etc are used by high producing managers 'at least as completely as by the low producing managers, but in quite different ways.' The different application is caused by a better understanding of the motivations of human behaviour.

3.30 In *New Patterns of Management* Likert examined the results achieved by managers and supervisors who were practising the participative style of management. He analysed these results in terms of output, wastage rates, labour turnover and absenteeism. In summary, his research showed that on the whole, supervisors with the best performance were those who concentrated their main efforts on the human aspects of their staff's problems and attempted to build work groups with high performance standards. On the other hand, supervisors with poor performance are described as spending more time in ensuring that their staff were busily employed in fulfilling specified stages of work.

3.31 His research further showed that the participative, supportive supervisor who was transferred to a low-production unit was able to raise the performance at a fast rate.

3.32 It is necessary to understand how the principle of supportive relationships would affect an organisation structure.

(a) Each individual must believe that the organisation has desirable, significant objectives, and that he makes an indispensable contribution to the objectives of the organisation. Jobs which do not fulfil this purpose must be re-organised so that they do. 'Experiences, relationships etc are considered to be supportive when the individual involved sees the experience (in terms of his values, goals, expectations, and aspirations) as contributing to or maintaining his sense of personal worth and importance.'

(b) An organisation must recognise the importance of the well-motivated work group in setting his high-performance goals. 'Management should deliberately endeavour to build these effective groups, linking them into an overall organisation by means of people who hold overlapping group membership.'

(c) 'Linking pins' perform a key function in the 'overlapping group form of organisation'. A leader of one group is also a subordinate member of a group higher in the hierarchical structure, so that he acts as a link between his subordinates and a higher authority. Diagrammatically this would be shown as follows:

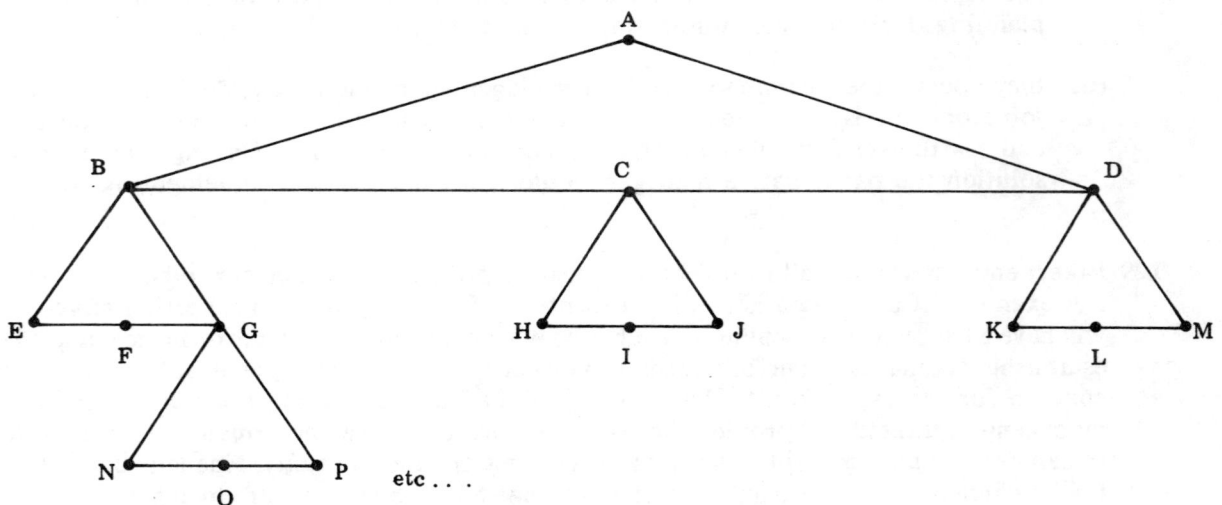

3.33 In this example, G is a linking pin between the group of B and his own group of N, O and P. Similarly, B is a linking pin to decisions at the top level - ie A's group of A, B, C and D.

Committee organisation could be employed effectively in addition to the overlapping group structure of the formal hierarchy.

The group leader retains responsibility for what occurs, even though the group practises collective decision-making.

2: DIRECTION: LEADERSHIP STYLE
AND EFFECTIVE MANAGEMENT

The integration of organisational goals and objectives with those of every individual in the organisation is essential.

Every employee must receive rewards (pay etc) which give them equitable compensation for their efforts.

3.34 Likert's conclusion was that the style of supervision is more important in achieving better results than any more general factors such as job interest, loyalty towards the company etc.

3.35 These conclusions can be correlated with the results of an RAF attitude survey amongst air crews, published in the late 1940s. This survey showed that the loyalty and 'identifying with' attitude of an individual was greater towards the smaller unit than to the larger unit to which he belonged. Thus an air crew member has a closer identification with his air crew than with his squadron, a closer identification with his squadron than with the RAF, and a closer identification with the RAF than with his King and country. The conclusion is that motivation will be more effectively raised by the local manager than by higher management.

3.36 There are clearly difficulties involved in the practical application of Likert's ideas:

(a) for the overlapping group structure to be applied, the entire organisation must adopt the new management style. This 'new style' however, tends to be 'localised' in individual managers and their own work groups;

(b) in a large organisation, a worker at the bottom of the hierarchy will have difficulty in relating his own contributions to the setting of the organisation objectives at the top of the hierarchy;

(c) the ever-present problems of conflict between the self-interest of rival sub-units (eg production, sales, marketing and accountancy departments) will tend to blur a proper appreciation of what company objectives really are.

3.37 The Financial Times of 25 June 1986 reported the ideas of Rosabeth Moss Kanter on leadership styles. Moss Kanter is a business consultant whose services are much in demand. She criticises excessively authoritarian and non-participative management on the ground that it stifles innovation and entrepreneurship.

3.38 Her list of 'Rules for stifling innovation' is a critique of 'management by terror'.

1. Regard any new idea from below with suspicion.
2. Insist that people who need your approval first go through several other levels of management.
3. Get departments/individuals to challenge each other's proposals.
4. Express criticism freely, withhold praise, instil job insecurity.
5. Treat identification of problems as signs of failure.
6. Control everything carefully. Count everything in sight - frequently.
7. Make decisions in secret, and spring them on people.
8. Do not hand out information to managers freely.
9. Get lower-level managers to implement your threatening decisions.
10. Above all, never forget that you, the higher-ups, already know everything important about the business.

2: DIRECTION: LEADERSHIP STYLE AND EFFECTIVE MANAGEMENT

4. TASK MANAGEMENT: A RETURN TO TRADITIONAL VIEWS

4.1 The writings of the human relations school (McGregor etc) tended to obscure the 'task' element of a manager's responsibilities. By emphasising style of leadership and the importance of human relations, it is all too easy to forget that a manager is primarily responsible for ensuring that tasks are done efficiently and effectively.

4.2 Robert R Blake and Jane S Mouton designed the management grid (1964). It is based on two fundamental ingredients of managerial behaviour, namely:

(a) concern for production, ie the 'task'; and
(b) concern for people.

4.3 The results of their work were published under the heading of 'Ohio State Leadership Studies', but are now commonly referred to as Blake's grid.

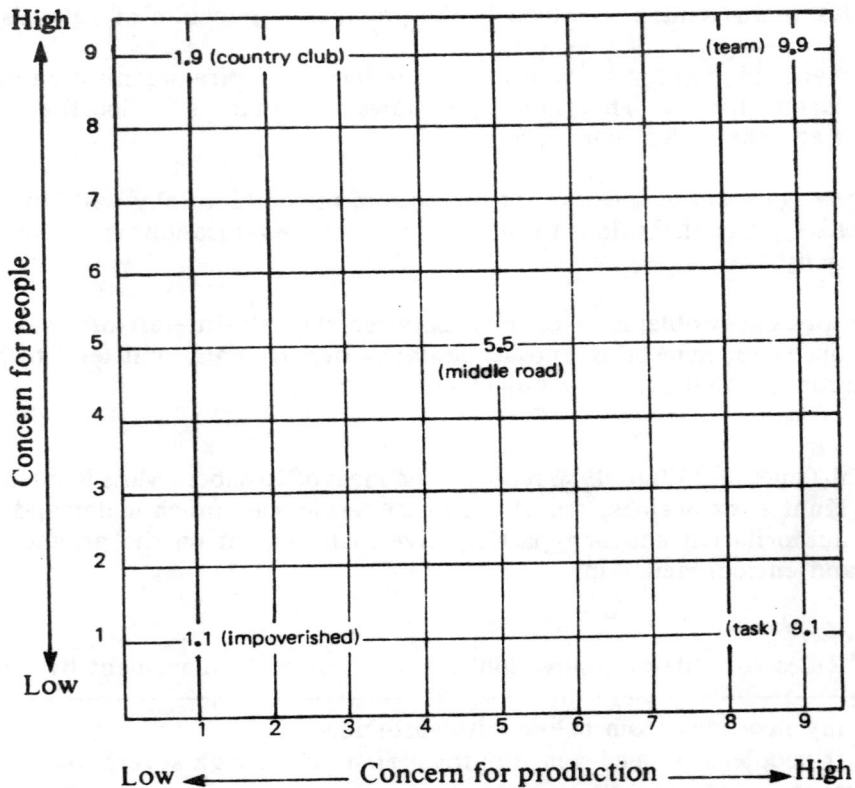

4.4 The extreme cases shown on the grid are defined by Blake as being:

    (a) 1.1 *impoverished*: manager is lazy, showing little effort or concern for staff or work targets;

    (b) 1.9 *country club*: manager is attentive to staff needs and has developed satisfying relationships. However, there is little attention paid to achieving results;

    (c) 9.1 *task management*: almost total concentration on achieving results. People's needs are virtually ignored and conditions of work are so arranged that people cannot interfere to any significant extent;

    (d) 5.5 *middle of the road or the dampened pendulum*: adequate performance through balancing the necessity to get out work while maintaining morale of people at a satisfactory level;

    (e) 9.9 *team*: high performance manager who achieves high work accomplishment through 'leading' committed people who identify themselves with the organisational aims.

4.5 The conclusion is that the most efficient managers combine concern for the task with concern for people.

4.6 It is worth being clear in your own mind about the possible usefulness of Blake's grid. Its primary value is obtained from the appraisal of a manager's performance, either by the manager himself or by his superiors. The ideal manager is a 9.9 man (or woman) with high concern for both production and people. An individual manager can be placed on the grid, and his position on the grid should help him to see how his performance as a leader and a manager can be improved. For example, a manager rated 3.8 has further to go in showing concern for the task itself than for developing the work of his subordinates.

4.7 You should also be aware that Blake's grid is based on the assumption that concern for production and concern for people are not incompatible with each other. In this respect, Blake and Mouton accept the Theory Y view of leadership style.

5. THE MANAGEMENT HIERARCHY

5.1 A further consideration is whether the style of leadership should vary with the level in the hierarchy. It could be argued, for instance, that shop-floor workers are likely to be less mature as individuals and therefore in need of Theory X supervision, whereas higher managers are more mature and worthy of a different leadership style from their superiors.

5.2 With reservations, the answer could possibly be that democratic leadership is preferable at all levels:

    (a) *first line supervisors*: these do much technical work themselves, and are faced with more immediate, day-to-day problems of leadership. These managers must recognise the importance of co-operation, perhaps because they work in an area where it is most ignored.

Many managers vastly underrate the honesty, helpfulness and common sense of their fellow man without realising that it is the social surrounding of the factory which largely makes them as they are. There is no behaviour on the part of the workers which is not copied exactly by management, eg questions of status, indulgence in restrictive practices, stealing and so on.

It is generally forgotten that in modern industry compulsion has to be replaced by co-operation, because the unco-operative worker is a danger in modern industry where sabotage may be catastrophic. Co-operation cannot be produced by force, and the factory manager is liable to forget that whilst, as the representative of formal authority in the factory, he may exert some control by reason of his power to hire or fire, the workers, because of their informal authority, have the much greater power of accepting or rejecting co-operation with the formal hierarchy.

No agitator can organise a mass of well adjusted people into an aggressive movement but unrest caused by underlying frustrations which are already there can be utilised by a potential leader. Similarly, no leader can increase productivity, raise morale, or impose social conditions in the factory without the co-operation of others;

(b) *middle managers*: 'Middle management is in a state of acute competition.' (Hunter). Managers on their way up the promotion ladder may feel under pressure from people they can see as rivals. This can make it difficult for them to take a cool, objective view of long-term results.

Because of this, they may become depressed, insecure and impetuous and some companies are trying to find a remedy for this by appraisal or development schemes which ensure a fair chance to all worthy of it.

Communication from below upwards is a major problem adding stresses to the 'man in between'. Perhaps it is in the area of the middle managers where the problems of leadership style are most acute.

Exercise

Try to summarise for yourself the different descriptions of leadership style put forward by the style theorists. Can you think of any situation where you or your boss displays more than one type of style? Why is this so?

---

6. A SYSTEMS APPROACH TO LEADERSHIP

6.1 Systems theory is concerned with the complex inter-relationships between the many different parts of a system (organisation), and the effect of the environment on the system (and vice versa). Katz and Kahn have developed ideas on how leadership can contribute to the better functioning of a system.

6.2 Early research by Katz and Kahn (reported in 1951) into the effect of leadership style on productivity suggested that there were three aspects of leader behaviour which affected productivity:
(a) assumption of the leadership role;
(b) closeness of supervision;
(c) degree of employee-orientation.

6.3 Comparisons were made between high-production and low-production groups and it was found that:

(a) in the most efficient groups the supervisor assumed the leadership role and used his supervisory talents to get the best out of his group. The leader has special functions and cannot therefore behave as an ordinary group member (ie be 'one of the boys'). In large organisations the assumption of the supervisory role is often made easier by transferring staff on promotion so that they can make a fresh start among strangers;

(b) supervision was closer in low-production than in high-production groups. Workers expect to have some control over the means by which they perform a set task, and they resent having means specified in too much detail. Supervisory behaviour was found to reflect management leadership styles, ie the organisational context affects leadership;

(c) studies of the attitudes held by supervisors towards their subordinates revealed that the men in charge of high-production groups were more employee-oriented (ie intent on promoting their welfare). In the research experiment, the attitudes of a manager were gauged by asking subordinates to rate bosses; results showed that the efficient bosses were seen by their subordinates to be more *considerate*.

6.4 Katz and Kahn have since developed their ideas and have suggested that the reason why the most effective managers show consideration and understanding towards their subordinates is because they supplement their formal position in the organisation and appreciate that their employees:

(a) have interests and roles outside their job;
(b) are subject to pressures and influences from their external environment;
(c) need information to do their job with greater understanding;
(d) need to be guided in the dynamic, changing organisation, and to understand the significance of change.

6.5 Good leaders show a true awareness that organisations are 'open' systems, reacting to and changing with their environment, of which their subordinates are also a part. Leaders influence those aspects of their subordinates' interests, energies and drive which cannot be harnessed by simple organisation structure, job definitions, or more formal management techniques.

7. A CONTINGENCY APPROACH TO LEADERSHIP

7.1 A contingency approach to leadership is one which argues that the ability of a manager to be a leader, and to influence his subordinate work group, depends on the particular situation, and will vary from case to case. Factors which vary in different situations are the personality of the leader, his leadership style, the nature of the group's tasks, the nature and personality of the work group and its individual members, conditions of work and 'external environmental' factors.

7.2 Perhaps the leading advocate of contingency theory is F E Fiedler. In an earlier work (1960) he studied the relationship between style of leadership and the effectiveness of the work group. Two styles of leadership were identified:

(a) *psychologically distant managers* (PDMs) who maintain distance from their subordinates by:

    (i) formalising the roles and relationships between themselves and their superiors and subordinates;

    (ii) being withdrawn and reserved in their inter-personal relationships within the organisation;

    (iii) preferring formal consultation methods rather than seeking opinions of their staff informally;

(b) *psychologically close managers* (PCMs) who:

    (i) do not seek to formalise roles and relationships with superiors and subordinates;

    (ii) are more concerned to maintain good human relationships at work than to ensure that tasks are carried out efficiently;

    (iii) prefer informal contacts to regular formal staff meetings.

7.3 In this study, Fiedler identified certain other significant qualities of the psychologically distant manager:

(a) He judges subordinates on the basis of their performance, he expects them to make mistakes and plans accordingly.

(b) He prefers ambitious subordinates.

(c) He attempts to obtain considerable freedom of action from his superiors.

(d) Though reserved in his interpersonal relationships he nevertheless displays good interpersonal skills.

(e) He is primarily task-orientated, and gains satisfaction from seeing a task performed.

7.4 Given these qualities of the PDMs, it is perhaps not surprising that in his 1960 study Fiedler concluded that the most effective work groups were led by psychologically distant managers and not by psychologically close managers. The explanation for this appeared to be that a manager cannot properly control and discipline subordinates if he is too close to them emotionally.

7.5 Fiedler went on to develop his contingency theory in *A Theory of Leadership Effectiveness*. He suggested that the effectiveness of a work group depended basically on two factors: .

(a) the relationship between the leader and his group;
(b) the nature of the work or tasks done by the group.

2: DIRECTION: LEADERSHIP STYLE AND EFFECTIVE MANAGEMENT

7.6 He concluded that:

(a) a structured (or psychologically distant) style works best when the *situation* is either very favourable, or very unfavourable to the leader;

(b) a supportive (or psychologically close) style works best when the *situation* is moderately favourable to the leader.

7.7 A situation is 'favourable' to the leader when:

(a) the leader is liked and trusted by the group;
(b) the tasks of the group are clearly defined;
(c) the power of the leader to reward and punish with organisation backing is high.

'Group performance will be contingent upon the appropriate matching of leadership styles and the degree of favourableness of the group situation for the leader, that is, the degree to which the situation provides the leader with influence over his group members.' (Fiedler)

7.8 Fiedler's analysis can be described by a 3-dimensional cube in which one dimension represents the level of respect and trust for the leader amongst subordinates, a second dimension is the degree to which the tasks of the group are clearly defined, and a third dimension is the degree to which the leader has power and authority to reward or punish subordinates.

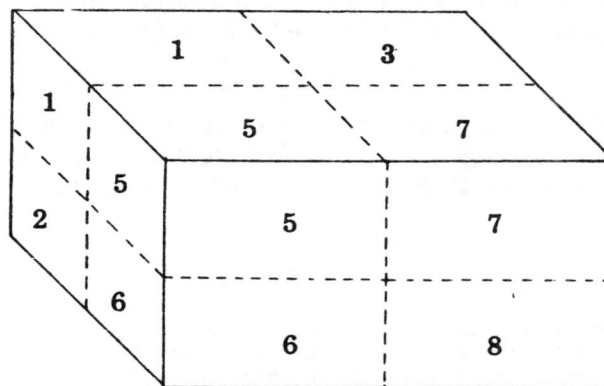

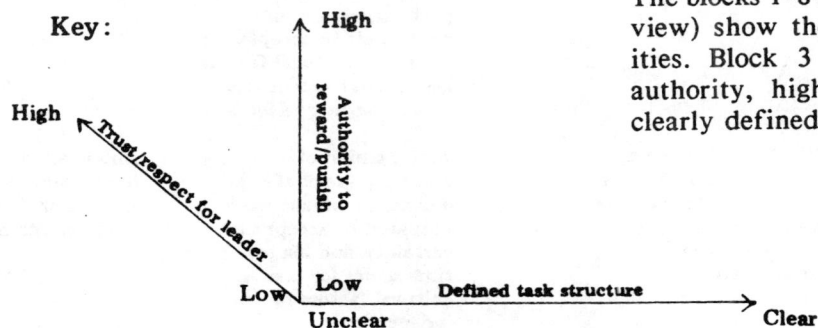

The blocks 1–8 (4 is hidden from view) show the eight possibilities. Block 3 illustrates high authority, high respect and a clearly defined task.

(a)   When the situation is very favourable for the leader, he can afford to concentrate on the task, and be a task-orientated, psychologically distant manager. The leader of a research group might be in this position.

(b)   When the situation is only moderately favourable for the leader, he will need to show more concern for people - ie be a psychologically close manager.

(c)   When the situation is unfavourable for the leader, he will need to be task-orientated, and a psychologically distant autocrat.

(d)   Concern for task and concern for people should be balanced according to the needs of the situation, and the degree to which it favours the leader.

7.9   The *situation* is the key to deciding how effective a leadership style can be. 'If we wish to increase organisational and group effectiveness we must learn not only how to train leaders more effectively, but also how to build an organisational environment in which the leader can perform well.'

7.10 Handy has also suggested a contingency approach to leadership. The factors in any situation which contribute to a leader's effectiveness are:
(a)   the leader himself - his personality, character and preferred style of operating;
(b)   the subordinates - their individual and collective personalities, and their preference for a style of leadership;
(c)   the task - the objectives of the job, the technology of the job, methods of working etc;
(d)   the environment - which is discussed separately.

7.11 Essentially, Handy argues that the most effective style of leadership in any particular situation is one which brings the first three factors - a leader, subordinates and task - into a 'best fit'. For each of the three factors, a spectrum can be drawn ranging from 'tight' to 'flexible'.

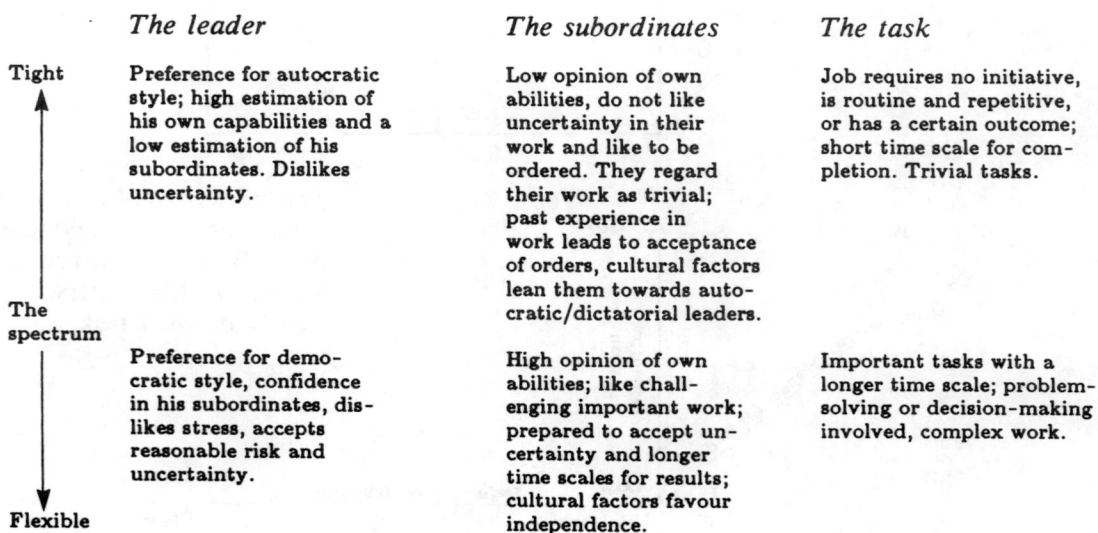

	The leader	*The subordinates*	*The task*
Tight ↑	Preference for autocratic style; high estimation of his own capabilities and a low estimation of his subordinates. Dislikes uncertainty.	Low opinion of own abilities, do not like uncertainty in their work and like to be ordered. They regard their work as trivial; past experience in work leads to acceptance of orders, cultural factors lean them towards auto-cratic/dictatorial leaders.	Job requires no initiative, is routine and repetitive, or has a certain outcome; short time scale for com-pletion. Trivial tasks.
The spectrum ↓ Flexible	Preference for demo-cratic style, confidence in his subordinates, dis-likes stress, accepts reasonable risk and uncertainty.	High opinion of own abilities; like chall-enging important work; prepared to accept un-certainty and longer time scales for results; cultural factors favour independence.	Important tasks with a longer time scale; problem-solving or decision-making involved, complex work.

7.12 A best fit occurs when all three factors are on the same level in the spectrum. In practice, there is likely to be a misfit. Confronted with a lack of fit, the leader must decide which factor(s) should be changed to bring all three into line. The factor over which a leader has most influence is himself and his style; hence, Handy argues, the great emphasis on 'leaderships' in management literature. 'However, although the leader's style is theoretically the easiest to alter in the short term, there are often long-term benefits to be achieved from re-defining the task (eg job enlargement) or from developing the work group.'

7.13 The fourth factor identified by Handy in the situational jig-saw is the environment, ie:

(a) *the position of 'power' held by the leader in the organisation and the relationship of the leader and his group.* Power might be a position of authority but it might also be the expertise or the charisma of the leader. A person with great power has a bigger capacity to set his own style of leadership, select his own subordinates and re-define the task of his work group;

(b) *organisational 'norms' and the structure and technology of the organisation.* No manager can flout convention and act in a manner which is contrary to the customs and standards of the organisation. If the organisation has a history of autocratic leadership, it will be difficult to introduce a new style. If the formal organisation is highly centralised, there will be limits to how far a task can be re-structured by an individual manager. In mass-production industries, where routine, repetitive work is in-built into the production technology, challenging tasks will be difficult to create, and leadership will tend, perforce, to be autocratic;

(c) *the variety of tasks and the variety of subordinates.* If the tasks of a work group are simple, few in number and repetitive, the best style of leadership will be different from a situation in which tasks are varied and difficult. In many groups, however, tasks vary from routine and simple, to complex 'one-off' problem-solving. Managing such work is complicated by this variety.

7.14 Similarly, the individuals in a work group might be widely different. One member of the group might seek participation and greater responsibility, whereas another might want to be told what to do. Furthermore, labour turnover may be frequent, and the individual persons who act as leaders or subordinates are constantly changing; such change is unsettling because the leadership style will have to be altered to suit the new situation, each time a personnel change occurs.

7.15 The 'environment' can be improved for leaders within an organisation if top management act to ensure that:

(a) leaders are given a clear role and 'power';
(b) organisational 'norms' can be broken;
(c) the organisational structure is not rigid and inflexible;
(d) subordinates in a work group are all of the same quality or type;
(e) labour turnover is reduced, especially by keeping managers in their job for a reasonably lengthy period of time.

8. THE IMPORTANCE OF LEADERSHIP STYLE

8.1 The relevance of leadership style to the practice of management may be summarised as follows.

2: DIRECTION: LEADERSHIP STYLE AND EFFECTIVE MANAGEMENT

(a) Leadership involves a concern for the task itself and also a concern for people.

(b) Concern for people requires an understanding of what will motivate individuals to work harder and more effectively, and also an understanding of what can make a work group as a whole improve its motivation and norms of working.

(c) Leadership style is a factor influencing the motivation of individual subordinates and the attitudes of work groups.

(d) Training and management development programmes might help a manager to improve his leadership style.

(e) The most appropriate style of management for raising the level of employee efficiency and effectiveness will vary according to circumstances. This means that either:

   (i) a manager might have to change his leadership style as the circumstances of his job change (eg when he is moved to a new job). However, since it is difficult to turn an autocrat into a democrat, or vice versa - ie since a leopard cannot change its spots...

   (ii) ...it might be necessary instead to appoint managers who have a particular style of leadership to jobs where that style will be the most productive in the circumstances. However, at senior levels, a consultative or democratic style of leadership will almost certainly be the most productive.

CASE STUDY 1

Now let's see how an understanding of leadership styles might apply in practical situations.

> George Gillespie is a section leader. Sometimes he makes decisions unilaterally. At other times he will not decide unless he has the consensus of his entire team. It is never clear on which basis he decides to act. As a result, the members of his team are often confused and demoralised. How would you help him?

Discussion

First of all, we must diagnose the problem and its causes. The problem concerns George Gillespie's approach to decision making. It also suggests that his leadership style should also be investigated since the warning signs of confusion and demoralisation of his team indicate that they don't know what to expect from him, and he lacks consistency.

The factors causing the problems may include the following.

(a) George might never have had any formal training as regards decision making or participation. As a result he is continually changing from one management style to another in order to find the one which feels best, ignoring the fact that no one style can be correct for all the various types of decisions he had to make.

(b) He might not have a clear idea of the relative improtance of the decisions he has to make. Some will be his sole preserve, others could be given to subordinates, others might involve consulting the whole section for a consensus opinion.

(c)   George may be having difficulty in reconciling the need to be seen to be in charge of his section and a desire to involve his group in the decision making process.

(d)   George may not be suited to leadership.

To find out which factor (or factors) is the main cause of the problem, we would need to obtain the following information:

(a)   the nature of the work allocated to the section;
(b)   the importance of the decisions that have to be make by George and his department;
(c)   the quality of his staff.

George should be given a couselling interview and asked to discuss his approach to dexision making. It should be explained to him that he must learn to distinguish between decisions that he must take unilaterally and decisions which should be made by the group or by subordinates. The factors relevant to this distinction are:

(a)   the importance of the decision. The cost of making a mistake should be considered and evaluated. Important decisions should be taken by George himself;

(b)   the subject matter of the decision. Sometimes delegation or sharing is not possible because of either company policy in relation to confidentiality or the technical and complex nature of the decision;

(c)   the amount of time available and the ability of his team to deal with such situations;

(d)   the importance of his subordinates' acceptance of the decision. With some decisions such acceptance is vital to successful implementation, and so the decisions should either involve or be taken by the subordinates;

(e)   the quality of the members of the department and supervisor's confidence in them;

(f)   George's own preference for leadership style. He might prefer to be autocratic or democratic, a Theory X, Y or Z manager and so on, but he should be *consistent* whatever style he chooses to adopt.

George may well benefit from a training course in the art of decision making. He would be told that the choice is not a simple one between unilateral decision or group consensus. The department can be involved in the process by:

(a)   obtaining information for George so that he will be better equipped ot make the right decision;

(b)   offering opinions either as individuals or as a group for George to consider although he would not be bound to follow any suggested course of action;

(c)   making decisions George feels can be safely delegated. This should improve morale as employees feel more regularly involved;

(d)   reaching a decision by consensus which George then endorses.

The situation should be reviewed after a period to see if a more consistent pattern of decision making had evolved and staff morale improved while an acceptable standard of work had been maintained. If the problem persisted, further training may be necessary.

CASE STUDY 2

> John Frost is having problems in managing his group, the members of which all express a variety of dissatisfactions. Basically, they say that he does not given them any leadership. John himself is very confident and takes many initiatives. He likes to get on with things and cannot understand why others are so slow and reactionary.
>
> One of John's subordinates, Ken Marshall, is in his fifties. He has always worked in the same department, and is very disturbed at John's apparently arbitrary and risky decisions. Ian Prince, on the other hand, is very frustated. He has a lot of ideas for change but John never has time to listen to them. The result is that Ian feels resentful and frustrated. A third subordinate, Frank Cadell, is frightened of John who is always in a hurry, does not appear to care whether Frank is there or not, never asks how he is getting on, and does not help to overcome his anxieties about whether he is doing his job properly.
>
> How would you advise John to change his behaviour?

Discussion

John Frost's problem is one of leadership style. We do not know what the performance standards of his work group are, and so we do not know whether his group is achieving or exceeding its targets. However, in view of the dissatisfaction of his group members, it is likely that the group's performance is not good, in spite of the work done by John Frost personally.

We are told that John Frost is very confident and takes many initiatives, but does not understand why others resist his decisions. His style of leadership might be described as the 'tells' kind of leadership, or autocratic style, because he appears to take decisions himself without consulting his subordinates and then tells them what his decision is. His style of leadership might also be described in some ways as 'laissez-faire' because having taken decisions, he appears to leave his staff to get on with their work and shows no obvious interest in what they are doing.

The problems with his leadership style are evident in the dissatisfactions of the subordinates.

(a)   Ken Marshall has been inthe department a long time, and might be nearing retirement. He is upset by the radical approach of John Frost to the decisions he takes. Ken is obviously well used to established ways and resistant to change. John Frost is failing to explain his reasons and persuade Ken of the need for change.

(b)   Ian Prince is frustrated because he is not allowed to participate int he decision-making processes. His opinions are not asked for, and his ideas are ignored, even though, unlike Ken Marshall, he does not object to change.

(c)   Frank Cadell wants to do his job well and wants to be a well-liked subordinate, but he gets no personal interest or attention from John Frost, and he is intimidated by John Frost's distant and 'busy' manner.

The consequence of John Frost's poor supervision in each case is low morale, and probably poor performance, from his staff.

John Frost should be given advice on each individual subordinate's problem.

(a) *Ken Marshall*. Ken Marshall is quite probably too much stuck in his ways and resistant to changes for the better. On the other hand, he has had a lot of experience in the department, and some of his words of caution might not be inappropriate.

The problem in his case is probably a need for respect for his experience and security in the face of change. John Frost should explain the reasons for changes. Knowing why change is needed helps to reduce resistance to change. He should also explain hwo Ken will be affected personally by any changes, and how he can adapt to them. His specific responsibilities and targets as a result of any change should be spelled out clearly, and John Frost should try to convince Ken that hs is capable of carrying out his new tasks well. If there are any risks that Ken can see in change, John Frost should be willing to discuss them. Ken Marshall's experience should be used constructively, whereas it is currently expressing itself negatively, in frustration and resistance to change.

(b) *Ian Prince*. In his case, John Frost should be much more prepared to listen to his subordiante's ideas for change. These ideas might not always be good one, but a task of supervision is to develop staff. This can be done by encouraging ideas and initaiative, discussing them, and then explaining why they might or might not be good ones. A more consultative or participative style of leadership will almost certainly reduce Ian Prince's frustrations, and also help to develop his own skills and experience.

When Ian's ideas are accepted, he should be informed about the progress of implementing them, and their success or failure. He might be responsible for implementing the ideas himself, in which case feedback about his performance should be given to him, and John Frost should regularly counsel him about it.

(c) *Frank Cadell*. Frank Cadell needs closer supervision, in the sense that John Frost should spend more time him. He should show an interest in him and his work. Frank needs more social contact, and to be reassured by praise for doing his job well. John Frost must be prepared to give these.

Conclusion

It is not easy for a manager to change his leadership style overnight, and the advice to John Frost should include suggestions for setting about making changes. Regular staff meetings would be one suggestion. It might also help him to make a record of the time he spends each day with each of his subordinates.

John Frost should be counselled regularly by his boss as he tries to change. A formal review of his success in changing his style, and the effects of his new approach on group performance and attitudes, should be made after some months.

TEST YOUR KNOWLEDGE

(The numbers in brackets refer to paragraphs in this chapter)

1. Are there born leaders? (2.1-2.3)

2. Styles of leadership can be described in various ways. Name some of them. (3.3, 3.6, 3.17, 3.26)

3. How do leaders stifle innovation in their work groups or departments? (3.38)

4. Explain Blake's grid. (4.1-4.3, 4.5)

5. How does a manager's position in the management hierarchy affect his management style? (5.2)

6. Describe the systems approach to leadership. (6.1-6.5)

7. What is a contingency approach to leadership? (7.1) Explain one such approach. (7.8, 7.11)

Chapter 3

PRINCIPLES OF MOTIVATION

This chapter covers the following topics:

1. Motivation
2. Motivation theories
   - Maslow: hierarchy
   - Herzberg
   - Expectancy theory
3. Systems and contingency approaches to motivation
4. Carrot or stick?
5. Work groups and motivation
6. Creating an effective work group
7. The characteristics of effective and ineffective work groups

---

Purpose of this chapter

To consider what motivation is, why it matters and how it occurs. Both individual motivation and group attitudes will be discussed.

1. MOTIVATION

1.1 An organisation has goals, which can only be achieved by the efforts of the people who work in the organisation. Individual people also have their own 'goals' in life, and these are likely to be different from those of the organisation. A major consideration for supervisors and management is the problem of getting the employees to work in such a way that the organisation achieves its goals; in other words, employees must be motivated.

1.2 You may be wondering why motivation is important. It could be argued that if a person is employed to do a job, he will do that job and no question of motivation arises. If the person doesn't want to do the work, he can resign.

1.3 The point at issue, however, is the *efficiency* with which the job is done. It is suggested that if individuals can be motivated, by one means or another, they will work more efficiently (ie productivity will rise) or they will produce a better quality of work. There is some debate as to what the actual effects of improved motivation are, efficiency or quality, but it has become widely accepted that motivation is beneficial to the organisation.

3: PRINCIPLES OF MOTIVATION

> "If we could understand, and could then predict , the ways in which individuals were motivated we could influence them by changing the components of that motivation process. Is that manipulation - or management?"
>
> *Charles Handy - Understanding Organisations*

1.4 It has been argued that some individuals need the 'big stick' treatment to be forced into doing their work well, but that mature, self-disciplined individuals do not need this treatment and will be motivated by a more 'enlightened' approach to supervisor-subordinate relationships. The best approach to motivating individuals in an organisation will vary with the particular circumstances, or situation, of each organisation.

1.5 In the most basic terms, an individual has needs which he wishes to satisfy. The means of satisfying his needs are 'wants'. For example, an individual might feel the need for power, and to fulfil this need, he might want money and a position of authority. Depending on the strength of hits needs and wants, he may take action to achieve them. If he is successful in achieving them, he will be satisfied. This can be shown in a simple diagram.

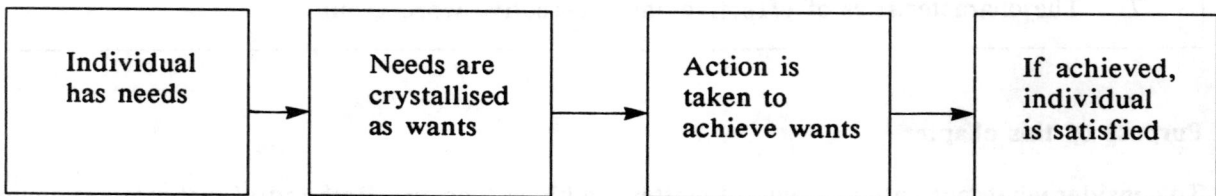

| Individual has needs | → | Needs are crystallised as wants | → | Action is taken to achieve wants | → | If achieved, individual is satisfied |

1.6 *Motivators* can be established which act as the 'wants' of the individual. For example, the position of sales director might serve as a 'want' to satisfy an individual's need for power, or access to the senior executive's dining room might serve as a 'want' to satisfy a need for status; a chartered secretarial qualification might serve as means of satisfying the need for prestige.

Motivators may exist which are not directly controllable by management; for example, an individual might want to be accepted by his work-mates, to satisfy his need for friendship and affiliation with others, and he might therefore choose to conform to the norms and adopt the attitudes of the work group - which are not necessarily shared by the 'organisation' as a whole.

1.7 'Motivation' is then the urge or drive to take action to achieve wants. For example, an individuals might want to be promoted, but he might not be sufficiently motivated to work harder or more efficiently in order to win the promotion: he might also want leisure, or he may not believe that the company really will promote him if he does work harder etc. Management has the problem of creating or 'manipulating' motivators which will actually motivate employees to perform in a desired way.

1.8 The kind of theory that we subscribe to, about what motivation is and what can be 'done' with it, will influence all our attitudes to management and individuals in organisations. There are various ways of looking at motivation. Handy groups early motivation theories under three headings:

(a) *satisfaction theories*. These theories are based on the assumption that a 'satisfied' worker will work harder, although there is little evidence to support the assumption. Satisfaction may reduce labour turnover and absenteeism, but will not necessarily increase individual productivity. Some theories hold that people work best within a compatible work group, or under a well-liked leader;

(b) *incentive theories*. These theories are based on the assumption that individuals will work harder in order to obtain a desired reward - ie. positive reinforcement, although most studies are concentrated on money as a motivator. Handy notes that incentive theories *can* work, if:

(i) the individual perceives the increased reward to be worth the extra effort;
(ii) the performance can be measured and clearly attributed to that individual;
(iii) the individual wants that particular kind of reward; and
(iv) the increased performance will not become the new minimum standard;

(c) *intrinsic theories*. These theories are based on the belief that higher-order needs are more prevalent in modern man than we give him credit for. People will work hard in response to factors in the work itself - participation, responsibility etc.: effective performance is its own reward.

2. MOTIVATION THEORIES

Maslow's hierarchy of needs

2.1 Apart from 'biogenic needs' or 'drives', that is biological determinants of behaviour, activated by deprivation, there are *'psychogenic needs'* - emotional or psychological needs. The American psychologist Abraham Maslow argued that man has seven innate needs - of which only the first two include primary needs such as we have described. Maslow's categories are:

- physiological needs   - the need for food, shelter etc.

- safety needs   - freedom from threat, but also security, order, predictability

- love needs   - for relationships, affection, sense of belonging

- esteem needs   - for competence, achievement, independence, confidence and their reflection in the perception of others, ie. recognition, appreciation, status, respect

- self-actualisation needs   - for the fulfilment of personal potential: 'the desire to become more and more what one is, to become everything that one is capable of becoming'

- freedom of inquiry and expression needs   - for social conditions permitting free speech and encouraging justice, fairness and honesty

- knowledge and understanding needs   - to gain and order knowledge of the environment, to explore, learn, experiment etc.

According to Maslow, the last two needs are the channels through which we find ways of satisfying all the other needs, ie. they are the basis of satisfaction. The first two needs are essential to human survival. Satisfaction of the next two is essential for a sense of adequacy and psychological health. Maslow regarded self actualisation as the ultimate human goal, although few people ever reach it. We will discuss the 'hierarchy' into which Maslow put his needs when we come to work-related theories of motivation, later in this chapter.

2.2 Roethlisberger and Dickson add on to physiological and safety needs:

- Friendship and Belonging Needs
- Needs for Justice and Fair Treatment
- Dependence-Independence
- Needs for Achievement

2.3 Maslow put forward certain propositions about the motivating power of man's innate needs.

(a) Man's needs can be arranged in a 'hierarchy of relative pre-potency'.

(b) Each 'level' of need is dominant until satisfied; only then does the next level of need become a motivating factor.

(c) A need which has been satisfied no longer motivates an individual's behaviour. The need for self-actualisation can never be satisfied.

2.4 There is a certain intuitive appeal to Maslow's theory. After all, you are unlikely to be concerned with status or recognition while you are hungry or thirsty - primary survival needs will take precedence. Likewise, once your hunger is assuaged, the need for food is unlikely to be a motivating factor.

2.5 Needs can be satisfied by aspects of a person's life outside work. However, since work provides a livelihood and takes up such a large part of a person's life, it is obviously going to play an important role in the satisfaction of his needs/wants.

2.6 Maslow said that the various levels of the need hierarchy overlap to some extent, and an individual may still be motivated by needs at a lower level when he acquires needs at a higher level.

For example, a manager might want something which fulfils his need for esteem, but he might also be concerned about reducing the threat of redundancy, which would take away the satisfaction afforded by his job with regard to social needs and safety needs. At any time, therefore, a person might have needs at differing levels in the hierarchy. Even so, there is a general progression upwards as some needs are at least partially satisfied, and others gain importance.

2.7 Subsequent researchers have shed doubt on Maslow's assumptions that needs can be put into a hierarchy. Why, for instance, can an individual realise himself fully only when his safety, social and esteem needs have been satisfied? In Maslow's terms, an individual experiences several needs at different levels of the hierarchy at the same time.

2.8 Maslow's theories may be of general interest, but have no clear practical application. It has not been proved that stimulating an individual's needs (providing motivators) will in its turn spark off a certain behaviour reaction (from that individual motivation).

The same need may cause different behaviour in different individuals. One person might seek to satisfy his need for esteem by winning promotion whereas another individual might seek esteem by leading a challenge against authority.

It is occasionally difficult to reconcile the willingness of individuals to forego the immediate satisfaction of needs and to accept current 'suffering' to fulfil a long-term goal (eg the long studentship of the medical profession or accounting profession).

Herzberg's 'Work and the Nature of Man' (1966)

2.9 Frederick Herzberg in his book *Work and the Nature of Man* identified the elements which cause job dissatisfaction, and those which can cause job satisfaction. He distinguished between 'hygiene factors' and 'motivator factors'.

2.10 Factors which cause dissatisfaction at work are:

(a) company policy and administration;
(b) salary;
(c) the quality of supervision;
(d) interpersonal relations;
(e) working conditions;
(f) job security.

2.11 'When people are dissatisfied with their work it is usually because of discontent with the environmental factors' (Herzberg).

He calls such factors *'hygiene'* factors; hygiene because they are essentially preventative. They prevent or minimise dissatisfaction but do not give satisfaction, in the same way that sanitation minimises threats to health, but does not give 'good' health.

2.12 Hygiene factors are also called *maintenance factors*, because they have to be continually reviewed. Satisfaction with environmental factors is not lasting. In time dissatisfactions will occur. For example:

(a) an individual might want a pay rise which protects his income against inflation. If he is successful in obtaining the rise he wants, he will be satisfied for the time being, but only until next year's salary review;

(b) an individual who is newly recruited into a job might want to establish good personal relations with his colleagues. If he is successful, he will be satisfied at first, but in time he will get used to working with them, and may start to get fed up with seeing the same familiar faces day after day.

2.13 The important concept is that motivation through the above-mentioned factors is a necessary but thankless task. It is never-ending. Even if effective it will still not motivate the employee to work well (at a higher than usual level of performance) except for a short period of time.

On the other hand, if the environment is deficient in some way then the subordinates are likely to become annoyed and show their displeasure by industrial conflict, decreased productivity, grumbling etc. Yet, if the deficiency is corrected the best that can be expected is that output/effort will return to 'normal'.

2.14 *Motivator factors* create job satisfaction and are effective in motivating an individual to superior performance and effort. These factors consist of:

(a) status (although this may be a hygiene factor as well as a motivator factor);
(b) advancement;
(c) gaining recognition;
(d) being given responsibility;
(e) challenging work;
(f) achievement;
(g) growth in the job.

2.15 Herzberg saw two separate 'need systems' of individuals.

(a) There is a need to avoid unpleasantness. This need is satisfied at work by hygiene factors. Hygiene satisfactions are short-lived; individuals come back for more, in the nature of drug addicts.

(b) There is a need for personal growth, which is satisfied by motivator factors, and not by hygiene factors.

(c) A lack of motivators at work will encourage employees to concentrate on bad hygiene (real or imagined) eg to demand more pay.

(d) Some individuals are not mature enough to want personal growth; these are 'hygiene seekers' because they can only ever be satisfied by hygiene factors.

(e) 'The superior who is a hygiene seeker cannot but have an adverse effect on management development, which is aimed at the personal growth and actualisation of subordinates.' Managers must therefore be motivator seekers.

2.16 The job itself can be interesting and 'exciting'. It can satisfy the desire for a feeling of 'accomplishing something', for responsibility, for professional recognition, for advancement and so on, and the need for self-esteem.

2.17 'Dissatisfaction arises from environmental factors - satisfaction can only arise from the job.' (Herzberg).

If there is sufficient challenge, scope and interest in the job, there will be a lasting increase in satisfaction and the employee will work well; productivity will be above 'normal' levels.

2.18 Hygiene needs, when satisfied, eliminate potential dissatisfaction but do little or nothing to create direct motivation. However, satisfaction of the motivating factors will raise output and stimulate performance.

2.19 The extent to which a job must be challenging or creative to a motivator seeker will depend on each individual's ability and tolerance for delayed success.

2.20 Herzberg suggested means by which motivator satisfactions could be supplied. Stemming from his fundamental division of motivator and hygiene factors, he encourages managers to study the job itself (ie the type of work done, the nature of tasks, levels of responsibility) rather than conditions of work. Only this way will motivation improve. (Concentrating on environmental factors will merely stave off job dissatisfaction.) He specified three typical means whereby work can be revised to improve motivation.

(a) *Job enrichment:* this is the main method of improving job satisfaction and can be defined as 'the planned process of up-grading the responsibility, challenge and content of the work'. Typically, this would involve increasing delegation to provide more interesting work and problem-solving at lower levels within an organisation.

(b) *Job enlargement:* although often linked with job enrichment, it is a separate technique and is rather limited in its ability to improve staff motivation. Job enlargement is the process of increasing the number of operations in which a worker is engaged and so moving away from narrow specialisation of work. Herzberg tells us that this is more limited in value, since a man who is required to complete several tedious tasks is unlikely to be much more highly motivated than a man performing one continuous tedious task.

(c) *Job rotation:* this is the planned operation of a system whereby staff members exchange positions with the intention of breaking monotony in the work and providing fresh job challenge.

Job enrichment, job enlargement and job rotation are described in more detail later on.

2.21 One of the implications of Herzberg's theories is that there are two separate problems for supervisors about the motivation of employees.

(a) They should learn to recognise the symptoms of poor motivation. These symptoms are likely to be caused by 'hygiene' factors, and include:

(i) a high or increasing rate of labour turnover;

(ii)   high absenteeism;

(iii)   numerous incidences of industrial disputes and stoppages;

(iv)   declining quality of output, and higher spoilage rates;

(v)   more customer complaints about bad service;

(vi)   a large number of accidents at work;

(vii)   excessive lateness for work;

(viii)   poor productivity.

The remedy for many of these symptoms can be provided by paying more attention to hygiene factors (eg improving conditions at work, redundancy protection, better rates of pay etc).

However, these remedies might eliminate poor motivation, but they will not create commitment or positive motivation.

(b)   They should also concentrate on other methods of improving motivation and employee commitment. These include job enrichment, participation and delegation.

Expectancy theory

2.22   Expectancy theory states that the strength of an individual's motivation to do something will depend on the extent to which he *expects* the results of his efforts to contribute towards his personal needs or goals, to reward him or to punish him.

2.23   Put another way, expectancy theory states that people will decide how much they are going to put into their work, according to what they perceive they are going to get out of it, and also according to the value that they place on this outcome (whether the positive value of a reward, or the negative value of a punishment).

2.24   Charles Handy (*Understanding Organisations*) puts forward an 'admittedly theoretical' form of expectancy model.

2.25   Handy suggests that for any individual decision, there is a conscious or unconscious 'motivation calculus' which is an assessment of three factors:

(a)   the individual's own set of needs (these may be defined in any of the ways suggested by Maslow, Herzberg, McClelland and others);

(b)   the desired results – what the individual is expected to do in his job;

(c)   'E' factors. Handy suggests that motivational theories have been too preoccupied with 'effort'. He notes that there seems to be a set of words, coincidentally beginning with 'e', that might be more helpful. As well as effort, there is energy, excitement in achieving desired results, enthusiasm, emotion, and expenditure (of time, money etc.).

3: PRINCIPLES OF MOTIVATION

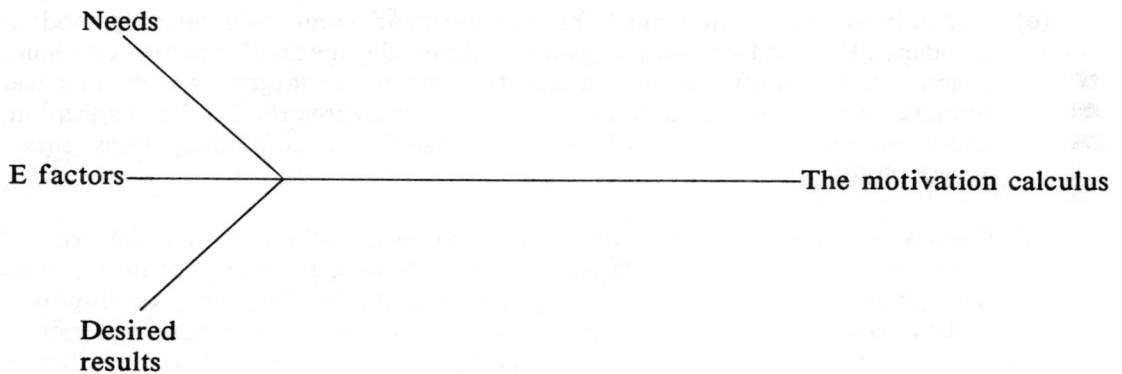

```
        Needs
            \
             \
E factors ————————————>————————————————————————————The motivation calculus
             /
            /
        Desired
        results
```

2.26 The 'motivation decision' - how strong the motivation to achieve the desired results will be - will depend on the individual person's judgement about:

(a) the strength of his needs;
(b) the *expectancy* that expending 'E' will lead to a desired result; and
(c) how far the result will be 'instrumental' in satisfying his needs.

For instance, a person may have a high need for power. To the degree that he believes that a particular result, eg. a completed task, will gain him promotion (expectancy) *and* that promotion will in fact satisfy his need for power ('instrumentality') he will expend 'E' on the task.

2.27 In terms of organisation practice, Handy suggests that several factors are necessary for the individual to complete the calculus, and to be motivated.

(a) *Intended results* should be made clear, so that the individual can complete his 'calculation', and know what is expected of him, what will be rewarded and how much 'E' it will take.

(b) Without knowledge of *actual results*, there is no check that the 'E' expenditure was justified (and will be justified in future). *Feedback* on performance - good or bad - is essential, not only for performance but for confidence, prevention of hostility etc.

2.28 Child has added that expectancy theory emphasises the need for *managers* to decide what they want, and reward employees for achieving it. They shouldn't want to achieve A and reward employees for achieving B. This might seem obvious enough, but it isn't so easy in practice!

2.29 Handy's calculus helps to explain various phenomena of individual behaviour at work.

(a) Individuals are more committed to specific goals - particularly those which they have helped to set themselves. Kay, French and Myer found that, in job appraisal, 62.5% of *specific* goals for self-improvement were achieved by their interviewees, as opposed of 27.3% where no specific goals were set.

(b) If an individual is *rewarded* according to performance tied to standards (ie. 'management by objectives'), however, he may well set *lower* standards: the 'instrumentality' part of the calculus (ie. likelihood of success and reward) is greater if the standard is lower, so less expense of 'E' is indicated.

(c) Individuals with a high need for 'achievement' frequently set only moderately high standards. Row and Russell set up an experimental game and found that continual *failure* to reach targets eventually made individuals set lower targets, which they were able to achieve. At the same time, continual *success* increases the level of aspiration, and also increases the desirability of the goal itself: the individual feels that it is 'all worthwhile'.

(d) Inertia, withdrawal or even breakdown can occur where the possible variables in the calculus (amount of 'E', obtainable results, time-span etc.) become too many for the individual to cope with (usually in emotionally insecure, or highly analytical individuals). Reducing the available alternatives, or the time-span under consideration, may enable the calculus to function again: a holiday, for instance, is often beneficial.

3. SYSTEMS AND CONTINGENCY APPROACHES TO MOTIVATION

3.1 Stemming from the early research work of Mayo, a systems and contingency approach to motivation has been developed by a number of writers, notably Kurt Lewin. A systems and contingency approach means that:

(a) the motivation of an individual cannot be seen in isolation but depends on the system within which he operates, his work group and his environment;

(b) the motivation of the individual will also depend on circumstances. Different people react to the same environment in different ways, and a person's motivation is likely to vary from day to day, according to his mood, events at work, his fatigue as well as 'hygiene' and 'motivator' factors in his work.

3.2 Writing in 1938, Lewin developed his 'field theory' in which he compared an individual's environment to a magnetic field, with various forces in that field pulling him in different directions and affecting his attitudes from day to day. His formula for human behaviour was:

$B = (P,E)$ where

B is a person's behaviour, which depends on

P the person himself/herself and

E his or her environment.

3.3 This means that an individual's motivation, varying over time, could be illustrated on a graph as follows:

**Amount or
degree of
motivation
of individual**

Poor
supervision

Work-group
norms restrain
his efforts

Fatigue

Good
supervision

Given an
interesting task

Pay
incentive

Time

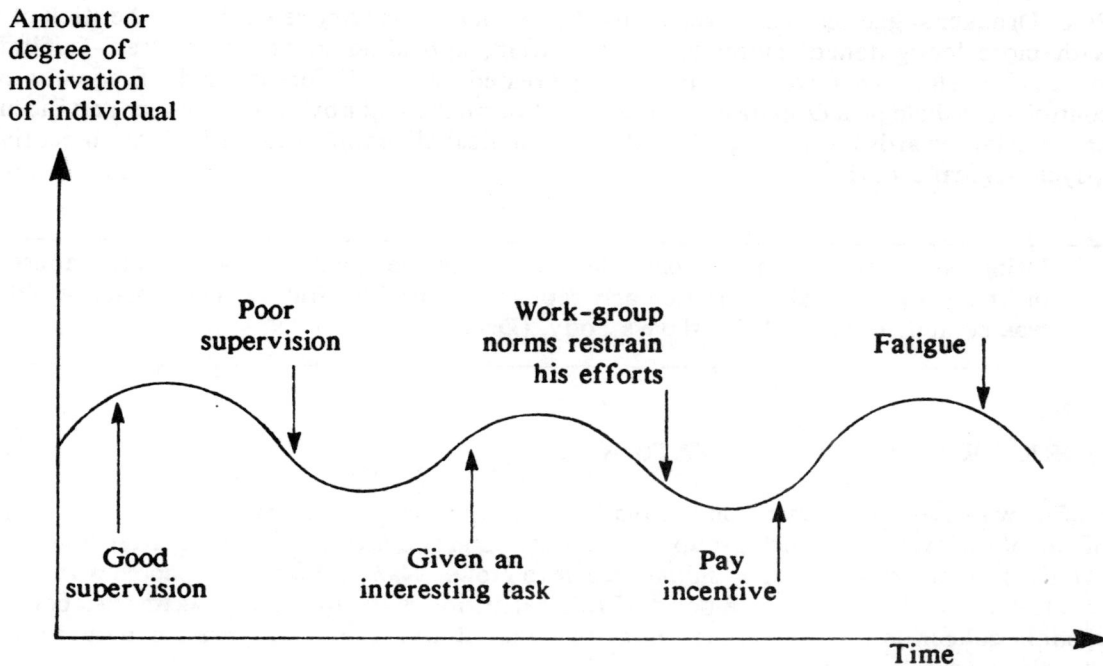

3.4 The systems and contingency school of thought is that if a manager wishes to improve the motivation of subordinates, he must take all the circumstances of the particular situation into account, differences between individuals, the external environment, individuals' expectations, work groups, variations in circumstances from day to day or month to month etc.

3.5 One conclusion from this approach might be that motivation depends on so many interrelated factors that a manager wishing to improve motivation is faced with a complex problem for which there may be no obvious ready-made solution.

4. CARROT OR STICK?

4.1 You might have noted that 'motivation' can be a negative process (ie. appealing to an individual's need to *avoid* unpleasantness, pain, fear etc.) as well as a positive one (ie. appealing to the individual's need to attain certain goals).

(a) Negative motivation is 'wielding the big stick' - threatening dismissal or demotion, reprimand etc. - ie. negative reinforcement.

(b) Positive motivation is 'dangling the carrot', and may be achieved by:

(i) the offer of 'extrinsic' rewards, such as pay incentives, promotion, working conditions etc.
(ii) 'internal' or psychological satisfaction for the individual, ie. 'virtue is its own reward', a sense of achievement, a sense of responsibility and value etc.

"Have managers outsmarted motivational theory, and become cynical about carrots, world-weary about sticks?" (Ray Proctor: Finance for the perplexed executive)

4.2 Peter Drucker suggested that in replacing the carrot of monetary rewards and the stick of fear with more 'enlightened' methods of motivation, appealing to needs for 'self-fulfilment, 'creativity' etc., what was actually being created was a different kind of equally strict control - psychological despotism. Workers are "controlled - not by fear of hunger and incentive of material rewards but through fear of psychological alienation and through the incentive of 'psychological security'."

> Using psychology to control, dominate, and manipulate others is self-destructive abuse of knowledge. It is also a particularly repugnant form of tyranny. The master of old was content to control the slave's body. (Drucker)

5. WORK GROUPS AND MOTIVATION

5.1 So far, we have concentrated on motivation of individuals. In reality, it is often the attitudes of people within their work group - ie. collective group attitudes - that matter much more. Handy in *Understanding Organisations* defines a group as 'any collection of people who perceive themselves to be a group'. The point of this definition is the distinction it implies between a random collection of individuals and a 'group' of individuals who share a common sense of identity and belonging.

5.2 Groups may be quite large, but are more likely to be small. This is because the sense of identity is likely to be fostered by interactions of individuals and this is less likely to occur when the number of individuals is large.

5.3 A group may be a unit within the formal organisation of an enterprise such as an office section, a work team, a committee or a board of directors. Alternatively, informal groups might form including individuals from different departments or sections.

5.4 The *function* of groups may be looked at from two different standpoints: that of the organisation and that of the individuals who comprise the group.

5.5 From the individual's standpoint groups perform some important functions.

   (a) They satisfy social needs for friendship and belonging.

   (b) They help individuals in developing images of themselves (eg a person may need to see himself as a member of the corporate planning department or of the works snooker team).

   (c) They enable individuals to help each other in matters which are not necessarily connected with the organisation's purpose (eg people at work may organise a baby-sitting circle).

   (d) They enable individuals to share the burdens of any responsibility they may have in their work.

3: PRINCIPLES OF MOTIVATION

Group norms

5.6 A work group establishes 'norms' or acceptable levels and methods of behaviour, to which all members of the group are expected to conform. This group attitude will have a negative effect on an organisation if it sets unreasonably low production norms (anyone producing more is made the social outcast of the group). Groups often apply unfair treatment or discrimination against others who break their 'rules'.

5.7 In a classic experiment by Sherif, participants were asked to look at a fixed point of light in a black box in a darkroom. Although the point of light is fixed, it so happens that in the darkness, it *appears* to move. Each participant was asked to say how far the light moved, and their individual estimates were recorded.

5.8 They were next put into a small group where each member of the group gave their own estimates to the others. From this interchange of opinions, individuals began to change their minds about how far the light had moved, and a group 'norm' estimate emerged.

5.9 When the groups were broken up, each individual was again asked to re-state his estimate; significantly, they retained the group norm estimate and rejected their previous individual estimate.

5.10 The experiment showed the effect of group psychology on establishing norms for the individual himself; even when, as in the case of the experiment, there is no factual basis for the group norm.

5.11 From these findings, that an individual's opinions can be changed or swayed by group consensus, it may be argued that it would be more effective, and probably also easier in practice, to change group norms than to change individual norms. Motivation should therefore involve the work group as a whole, because changes agreed by a group are likely to be more effective and longer-lasting.

5.12 In addition to specialist terms and processes, an established group will have its own values and ways of looking at things. These last may be termed 'attitudes'. In many cases they are implicitly accepted rather than expressed in definite terms, having grown up unnoticed and irrationally; nevertheless, there is a strong group pressure towards conformity.

5.13 Until a newcomer is seen to be versed in the group attitudes, and until he gives evidence of sharing and accepting them, he will not be fully assimilated into the group. Groups where the attitudes are very rigid and irrational will have great difficulty in assimilating newcomers. Individuals, on the other hand, who are set in their own attitudes and insensitive to those of others will have difficulty in being accepted by new groups.

3: PRINCIPLES OF MOTIVATION

5.14 Implications for management include the following.

(a)   The work group can put pressure on unpopular supervisors by displaying negative and hostile attitudes to them personally. In the Hawthorne experiments, Roethlisberger and Dickson described how such hostility might force a supervisor into asking for a transfer. Supervisors as leaders need to win the active support of the group as a whole, while at the same time attempting to improve group efficiency.

(b)   A group's attitude to management may depend on the size of the organisation, and the remoteness of the group from top management; the greater the distance between management and workers, the less probable will be the group motivation to achieve the organisation's goals. This has significance in terms of the design of formal organisations.

(c)   Inter-group hostility is easily aroused, and once aroused, difficult to subdue. The management of inter-group relations is therefore of some importance in achieving organisational effectiveness.

5.15 Owing to the fact that attitudes are implicitly accepted rather than openly expressed, and that they are often irrational rather than based upon adequate information, not a great deal can be done to change them in the short term. Induction training and propaganda have some effect, but to build up a real sense of identification with a company there is no substitute for *good communications* and *good relationships* in the small face-to-face groups of which it is composed.

Competition and co-operation within groups and between groups

5.16 In an experiment reported by Deutsch (1949), psychology students were given puzzles and human relation problems to work at in discussion groups. Some groups (the 'co-operative' ones) were told that the grade each individual got at the end of the course would depend on the performance of his group. Other groups (the 'competitive' ones) were told that each student would receive a grade according to his own contributions.

5.17 No significant differences were found between the two kinds of group in the amount of interest and involvement in the tasks, or in the amount of learning. But the co-operative groups, compared with the competitive ones, had greater productivity per unit time, better quality of product and discussion, greater co-ordination of effort and sub-division of activity, more diversity in amount of contribution per member, more attentiveness to fellow members and more friendliness during discussion.

5.18 Another experiment, conducted in 1949 by Sherif and Sherif, set out to investigate how groups are formed, and how relationships between groups are created. The 'guinea pigs' of the experiment were 24 boys of about 12 years old who were taken to a summer camp, and after a few days divided into two 'formal' groups, the Bulldogs and the Red Devils.

5.19 It was found that when the groups were formed there was a noticeable switch of friendships. Boys whose previous 'best friends' were moved into the other group began to switch 'best friendships' to someone else who belonged to their group. The group identity thus had a significant effect on the attitudes of individual members.

5.20 The experimenters also tried to create friction between the groups; these efforts were so successful that by the end of the experiment such intense inter-group rivalry existed that subsequent attempts to re-unite the entire camp were insufficient to restore common goodwill. From this, and other research, it is argued that new members of a group quickly learn the norms and attitudes of the others, no matter whether these are 'positive' or 'negative', friendly or hostile.

5.21 All members of a group will act in unison if the group's existence or patterns of behaviour are threatened from outside.

6. CREATING AN EFFECTIVE WORK GROUP

6.1 One common management problem is how to create an effective, efficient work group. If managers can motivate groups (and individuals) to work harder and better to achieve organisational goals, the sense of pride in their own competence (*competence motivation*) might create job satisfaction through belonging to the group and performing the group's tasks. Competitive motivation is often strong in successful football teams and highly trained army units.

6.2 Handy takes a contingency approach to the problem of group effectiveness, which, he argues, depends on:

(a)	the group	}
(b)	the group's task	} The 'givens'
(c)	the group's environment	}
(d)	motivation of the group	}
(e)	leadership style	} The 'intervening factors'
(f)	processes and procedures	}
(g)	productivity of the group	} The 'outcomes'
(h)	satisfaction of the group members	}

Handy's approach to groups

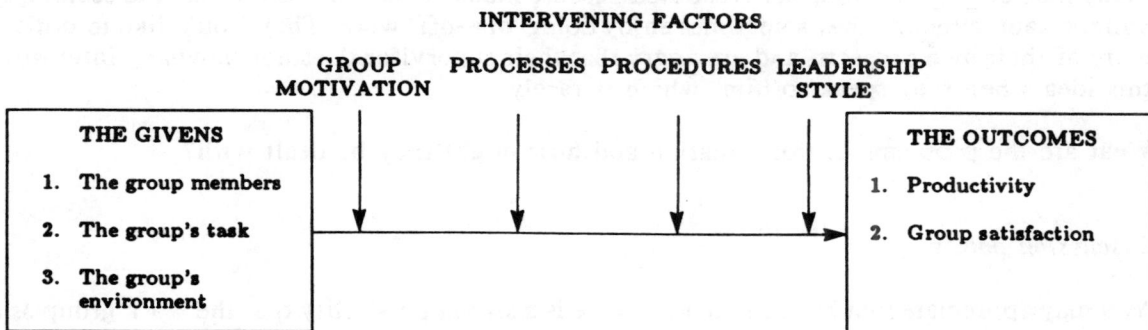

INTERVENING FACTORS

GROUP   PROCESSES   PROCEDURES   LEADERSHIP
MOTIVATION   STYLE

THE GIVENS	THE OUTCOMES
1. The group members	1. Productivity
2. The group's task	2. Group satisfaction
3. The group's environment	

6.3 The personalities and characteristics of the individual members of the group, and the personal goals of these members, will help to determine the group's personality and goals. An individual is likely to be influenced more strongly by a small group than by a large group in which he may feel like a small fish in a large pond, and therefore unable to participate effectively in group decisions.

6.4 The nature of the task must have some bearing on how a group should be managed. If a job must be done urgently, it is often necessary to dictate how things should be done, rather than to encourage a participatory style of working. Jobs which are routine, unimportant and undemanding will be insufficient to motivate either individuals or the group as a whole. If individuals in the group want authoritarian leadership, they are also likely to want clearly defined group targets.

6.5 The group's environment relates to factors such as the physical surroundings at work and to inter-group relations. An open-plan office, in which the members of the group are closely situated, is more conducive to group cohesion than a situation in which individuals are partitioned into separate offices, or geographically distant from each other. Group attitudes will also be affected, as described previously, by its relationship with other groups, which may be friendly, neutral or hostile.

Exercise

As an example, suppose that a work group consists of five people, who work closely together in an open-plan office. Their supervisor has his office two floors above in the same building. All the group members are well-educated, but most of them are new to the company.

The task of the group is to prepare market forecasts, which are submitted to marketing managers whose offices are in a different building. The forecasts are mostly routine, although occasionally 'one-off' requests for special information are received. The volume of work is not really sufficient to keep all five group members busy.

The group's leader is more concerned with the special responsibilities which keep him fully occupied, and he is inclined to leave the group alone, ie he displays a 'laissez-faire' approach to leadership.

Many members of the group are frustrated because much of the work is boring, and seemingly unimportant, although they sometimes enjoy doing 'one-off' work. They would like to initiate more of their own projects, and are angry that their supervisor does not show any interest in this idea when they speak to him, which is rarely.

What are the problems in this situation and how might they be dealt with?

Discussion points

You may appreciate that in this situation there is a strong possibility that the work group as a whole will tend to develop negative feelings towards their work and the organisation, to become slack and uncaring about their work, to develop strong interests outside work and to display a hostile attitude to other departments in the organisation. This would be because of:

(a) *the nature of the group:* its size is small therefore individuals will more readily identify with it. Individual members may be too well qualified for the work they do, especially the routine report preparation;

(b) *the task:* routine work is unsuited to individuals who seek more challenging work. A shortage of work is likely to lead to boredom;

(c) *the environment:* the group is 'physically intact' but remote from its supervisor and the marketing managers it serves;

(d) *the 'laissez-faire' style of leadership* is unlikely to encourage group motivation. Motivation will also be discouraged by the lack of a clear purpose for the group's task, the absence of the right to show initiative and the apparent absence of any kind of reward for doing the job efficiently;

(e) left to its own devices, and without an organised sense of purpose, the procedures of the group are likely to be 'muddled'.

A management approach to dealing with this particular situation might be as follows:

(a) to reduce the size of the work group;

(b) to upgrade the work of the group, or to employ less skilled individuals, so that the group is more suited to the task;

(c) to change the supervisor, and to introduce a leader whose style is more suited to the reorganised group;

(d) to re-arrange office space so that the supervisor works close to his group, and maintains effective communication links with the marketing department;

(e) to consider various methods of motivating the group which would be more efficient;

(f) to provide the group with an identifiable task, and to organise their work procedures and processes.

As a result the group might be motivated so as to achieve a more clearly thought-out purpose more efficiently.

---

7. THE CHARACTERISTICS OF EFFECTIVE AND INEFFECTIVE WORK TEAMS

7.1 If a manager is to try to improve the effectiveness of his work team he must be able to identify the different characteristics of an effective group and an ineffective group. Some pointers to group efficiency are quantifiable measures; others are more qualitative factors and are difficult to measure. These are shown on the next page.

EFFECTIVE WORKGROUP	INEFFECTIVE WORKGROUP
Quantifiable factors	
(1) Low rate of labour turnover	(1) High rate of labour turnover
(2) Low accident rate	(2) High accident rate
(3) Low absenteeism	(3) High absenteeism
(4) High output and productivity	(4) Low output and productivity
(5) Good quality of output	(5) Poor quality of output
(6) Individual targets are achieved	(6) Individual targets are not achieved
(7) There are few stoppages and interruptions to work	(7) Much time is wasted owing to disruption of work flow
	(8) Time is lost owing to disagreements between superior and subordinates
Qualitative factors	
(1) There is high commitment to the achievement of targets and organisational goals	(1) There is no understanding of organisational goals or the role of the group
(2) There is a clear understanding of the group's work	(2) There is a low commitment to targets
(3) There is a clear understanding of the role of each person within the group	(3) There is confusion and uncertainty about people's roles within the group
(4) There is a free and open communication between members of the group and trust between members	(4) There is mistrust between group members and suspicion of group's leader
(5) There is idea sharing	(5) There is little idea sharing
(6) The group is good at generating new ideas	(6) The group does not generate any good new ideas
(7) Group members try to help each other out by offering constructive criticisms and suggestions	(7) Group members make negative and hostile criticisms about each other's work
(8) There is group problem solving which gets to the root causes ofthe work problem	(8) Work problems are deaslt with superficially, with attention paid to the symptoms but not the cause
(9) There is an active interest in work decisions	(9) Decisions about work are accepted passively
(10) Group members seek a united consensus of opinion	(10) Group members hold strongly opposing views
(11) The members of the group want to develop their abilities intheir work	(11) Group members find work boring and do it reluctantly
(12) The group is sufficiently motivated to be able to carry on working in the absence of its leader	(12) The group needs its leader there to get work done

7.2 The importance of a group for social contacts by its individual members is worth a bit more thought. You might think that the social nature of groups is obvious to recognise. However, some formal groups do not provide strong social links, when its individual members do not work closely together and do not meet often. One example is a committee. Committee members in a large business organisation often do not have strong social links.

7.3 It will be helpful if you try to make a distinction in your mind between:

(a) what work groups can be organised to do (perform a task, control work, make decisions, ratify decisions, create ideas, exchange ideas and co-ordinate work etc); and

(b) the implication for management that since some groups develop certain characteristics and norms, it would be advisable to give some attention to the leadership of groups and to making group norms and attitudes work in the organisation's favour (perhaps through participation in decision-making etc).

TEST YOUR KNOWLEDGE

(The numbers in brackets refer to paragraphs in this chapter)

1. What is motivation in terms of an individual's needs and wants? (1.1-1.7)

2. Distinguish between hygiene and motivator factors in a job, as described by Herzberg. (2.12, 2.14)

3. What is the expectancy theory of motivation? (2.22)

4. Describe Lewin's systems and contingency approach to motivation. (3.2, 3.3)

5. What is a group norm? (5.6) What implications does the existence of group norms have for motivation and management? (5.11, 5.14)

6. What are the characteristics of:
   (a) effective, and
   (b) ineffective work groups? (7.1)

7. It has been suggested that managerial effectiveness is a function of the individual manager's motivation, the abilities the manager brings to any managerial job, and the opportunities available to that manager. Do you agree?

   (No solution given. Consider each of the 3 factors in turn and how each might be a contributory element to a manager's performance)

Chapter 4

MOTIVATION IN PRACTICE

This chapter covers the following topics

1. Motivation and acceptance of responsibility
2. Job design
3. Pay systems
4. Participation as a means of motivation
5. Conclusions on motivation of individuals
6. Discipline

Purpose of this chapter

First, to consider how motivation might be achieved in practice. This will take us into related areas of the syllabus, such as job design and pay (organisation) and participation in decision-making (delegation).

Also to make the point that even with a well-motivated work force, there will still be a need for a disciplinary code for staff who step out of line.

1. MOTIVATION AND ACCEPTANCE OF RESPONSIBILITY

1.1 Drucker (writing before Herzberg) suggested that motivation through 'employee satisfaction' is not a useful concept because employee satisfaction is such a wishy-washy idea. It doesn't mean anything in particular, and if it is to have some meaning, it must be defined more constructively. His suggestion was that employee satisfaction comes about through encouraging – if need be, by 'pushing' – employees to accept *responsibility*. There are four ingredients to this:

(a) *careful placement of people in jobs*. The selection or recruitment process is an important one, because the person selected should see the job as one which provides a challenge to his abilities. There will be no motivation for a university graduate in the job of shop assistant, whereas the same job can provide a worthwhile challenge to someone of lesser academic training and intelligence;

(b) *high standards of performance in the job*. Targets for achievement should be challenging. However, they should not be imposed in an authoritarian way by the employee's bosses. The employee should be encouraged to expect high standards of performance from himself;

(c) *providing the worker with the information he needs to control his own performance.* The employee should receive routine information about how well or badly he is doing without having to be told by his boss. (The design of a reporting system is important in this respect). Being told by a boss comes as a praise or reprimand, and the fear of reprimand will inhibit performance. Access to information as a routine matter overcomes this problem of inhibition;

(d) *opportunities for participation in decisions that will give the employee managerial vision.* Participation means having some say and influence in the way the employee's work is organised and the targets for his work are set. Participation does not mean that his boss relinquishes the job of managing the business! However, bosses should manage people to make them efficient; and managing people to manage themselves is a potentially valuable way of achieving such efficiency.

Methods of improving motivation

1.2 There are various ways in which management can attempt to increase the motivation of their subordinates:

> (a) Herzberg and others recommended better *job design* - that is job enrichment, job enlargement and job rotation;
>
> (b) *pay* and incentive schemes are frequently regarded as powerful motivators;
>
> (c) various writers have suggested that *participation* by subordinates in decision-making will improve motivation through self-realisation.

2. JOB DESIGN

Job enrichment

2.1 Job design is the process of deciding:

- on the content of a job in terms of its duties and responsibilities;

- on the methods to be used in carrying out the job, in terms of techniques, systems and procedures; and

- on the relationships that should exist between the job holder and his/her superiors, colleagues and subordinates.

2.2 As its objectives, the job design process seeks to improve productivity, efficiency and quality and to satisfy the individual's needs for interest, challenge and accomplishment.

2.3 The process has two main steps:

(a) job analysis - analysing and establishing what work has to be done; and
(b) job enrichment - allowing the individual greater opportunity for personal achievement.

> In this chapter we shall concentrate on job enrichment, the size of the job and job rotation.

2.4 Job enrichment is planned, deliberate action to build greater responsibility, breadth and challenge of work into a job. A job may be enriched by:

(a) giving it greater variety (although this could perhaps also be described as job enlargement);

(b) allowing the employee in the job greater freedom to decide for himself how the job should be done;

(c) encouraging employees to participate in the planning decisions of their superiors; and

(d) ensuring that the employee receives regular feedback on his performance, comparing his actual results against his targets.

2.5 Job enrichment attempts to add further responsibilities to a job by giving the job holder decision-making capabilities of a 'higher' order.

2.6 For instance, an administrator's responsibilities for producing quarterly management reports ended at the stage of producing the figures. These duties were then extended so that he prepared the actual reports and submitted them, under his own name, to the senior management. This alteration in responsibilities not only enriched his job but also increased his work-load. This in turn led him to delegate certain responsibilities to clerks within the department. These duties were in themselves job enrichment to the clerks and so a cascading effect was obtained.

> This highlights one of the basic elements of job enrichment - that what is tedious, mundane detail at a high level can represent significant job interest and challenge at a lower level in the organisation where a person's experience and scope is much less.

2.7 Some experiments have been made whereby *work groups* were given collective job enrichment. Child (in *'Organisation: A Guide to Problems and Practice'*) cited the example in the UK of Phillips. A work group responsible for manufacturing black and white television sets carried out the entire assembly operation and also had authority to deal directly with purchasing, stores and quality control, without a supervisor acting as intermediary. The change in work organisation meant, however, that the company had to incur additional costs in re-equipment and training.

2.8 Perhaps a more well-known example is the case of Volvo in Sweden, where a new factory was built so as to facilitate greater flexibility for work groups with considerable responsibilities for major stages of manufacture, to organise their jobs as they considered best. Once again, job enrichment necessitated large capital expenditure.

2.9 Job enrichment has not been widely developed, and only a few reported cases exist in both the USA and Europe, although there may be other schemes 'masquerading' as job enrichments whch are not thorough-going applications of the principle. The reasons for its slow progress may be:

(a)   the technology of working conditions. It would be difficult to introduce a scheme of job enrichment into mass production and assembly line working, without spending considerable amounts of money on re-organisation of working conditions and equipment. Child suggested that 'in some cases, the conditions for job enrichment via autonomous group working involve capital investment which is more expensive than in traditional technologies; examples are Volvo's Kalmar automobile plant and Renault's Le Mans axle factory.'

(b)   jobs with a low level of skill may be difficult to enrich (but it should be easier to enrich jobs of subordinate managers);

(c)   job enrichment should be wanted by subordinates. An attempt by senior managers to impose job enrichment schemes according to their own particular views as to what job enrichment actually means, is unlikely to be long lasting or productive.

2.10 It would be wrong, however, to suppose that job enrichment alone will automatically make employees more productive. 'Even those who want their jobs enriched will expect to be rewarded with more than job satisfaction. Job enrichment is not a cheaper way to greater productivity. Its pay-off will come in the less visible costs of morale, climate and working relationships'. (Handy).

2.11 If jobs are enriched, employees will expect to be paid fairly for what they are doing. It might be more correct therefore to say that job enrichment might improve productivity through greater motivation, but only if it is rewarded fairly.

Job enlargement versus micro-division of labour

2.12 *Job enlargement* is frequently confused with job enrichment though it should be clearly defined as a separate technique. Job enlargement, as the name suggests, is the attempt to widen jobs by increasing the number of operations in which a job holder is involved.

This has the effect of lengthening the 'time cycle' of repeated operations, and by reducing the number of repetitions of the same work, the dullness of the job should also be reduced. Job enlargement is therefore a 'horizontal' extension of an individual's work, whereas job enrichment is a 'vertical' extension.

2.13 Job enlargement has often been described as an approach to a job design which is at the opposite end of a spectrum to the *'micro-division'* of labour. The micro-division of labour is based on a production line approach to the organisation of work:

(a)   a job is divided up into the smallest number of sequential tasks possible. Each task is so simple and straightforward that it can be learned with very little training;

(b)   if labour turnover is high, this does not matter because unskilled replacements can be found and trained to do the work in a very short time;

(c)   since the skill required is low, workers can be shifted from one task to another very easily. The production flow will therefore be unaffected by absenteeism;

(d)   if tasks are closely defined and standard times set for their completion, production is easier to predict and control;

(e)   standardisation of work into simple tasks means that quality is easier to predict. There is less scope for doing a task badly.

2.14 The arguments against the micro-division of labour are:

(a)   the work is monotonous and makes employees tired, bored and dissatisfied. The consequences will be high labour turnover, absenteeism and spoilage;

(b)   the boredom of employees in their work will provide a breeding ground for industrial unrest and strikes;

(c)   men, unlike machines, work more efficiently when their work is variable;

(d)   an individual doing a simple task feels like a small cog in a large machine. This prevents him from having any sense of his contribution to the organisation's end product;

(e)   excessive specialisation isolates the individual in his work and inhibits social contacts with 'work mates'.

2.15 A well-designed job should therefore:

(a)   give the individual scope for setting his own work standards and targets;
(b)   give the individual control over the pace and methods of working;
(c)   provide variety by allowing for inter-locking tasks to be done by the same person;
(d)   give the individual a chance to add his comments about the design of the product, or his job;
(e)   provide feedback of information to the individual about his performance.

2.16 Arguably, job enlargement is limited in its ability to improve motivation since, as Herzberg points out, to ask a worker to complete three separate tedious, unchallenging tasks is unlikely to motivate him more than asking him to fulfil one singe tedious, unchallenging task;

> 'To paraphrase Herzberg, adding one Mickey Mouse job to another does not make any more than two Mickey Mouse jobs' (Child).

(The same criticism would be applied to job rotation, which has a similar purpose to job enlargement - giving subordinates more varied work to do, but of a similar nature or degree of difficulty.)

2.17 Job enlargement might succeed in providing job enrichment as well, provided that the nature of the extra tasks to be done in the bigger job give the employee a greater challenge and incentive.

(a)   When work is organised as a production line, with each employee responsible for just a small part of the total work, the dullness and monotony of the employee's work will be exceptionally high. Just by giving an employee a task which spans a larger part of the total production work - ie by enlarging the job - the dullness and monotony are likely to be reduced.

(b) Enlarged jobs can provide a challenge and incentive. For example, a trusted employee might be given added responsibilities for:

(i) checking the quality of output. (There is a view that concern for quality of manufactured goods is a major reason for the success of Japanese industry. An employee who is allowed to monitor his own work quality, as well as the work of others, might easily see a challenging responsibility in such a job);

(ii) training new recruits.

2.18 Enlarged jobs might also be regarded as 'status' jobs within the department, and as stepping stones towards promotion.

2.19 *Participation* in decision-making by employees (which will be discussed more fully later) is a form of both job enlargement and job enrichment. Drucker (in 'The Practice of Management' (1955)) quoted the example of IBM where the final details of the design of the first electronic computers by the company were worked out on the factory floor in consultation with the work-force. Workers were able to offer suggestions based on their experience and practical know-how for the improvement of the computer design. The effects of this innovation in job design were found by IBM management to be:

(a) better product design;
(b) lower production costs;
(c) greater speed of production;
(d) greater worker satisfaction.

2.20 Delegation is another factor in the design of jobs. Job enlargement and enrichment cannot be taken too far unless more authority is delegated to subordinates. Handy suggests that although delegation is one of those 'good' words which managers pay lip service to, they are often reluctant to delegate in practice. This is because by delegating, a manager loses to his subordinates control over decisions, and he does not necessarily trust his subordinates to do the job as well as he could himself.

2.21 This is what Handy calls a *'trust control' dilemma:* the manager wants to have control over decisions, but would like to delegate and so show his trust in the subordinates' abilities. He cannot show more trust (delegate) without losing more control.

'Trust . . . is cheap. Trust leaves the superior free to do other things; trust, if given and accepted, breeds responsibility and obviates the need for controls, as the controls become, in a sense, self-administered (the secretary refers the letters she is worried about to her boss, the salesman consults his manager in doubtful cases). But trust is risky, for the superior is held accountable for things that others did, even if they did them in ways he would not himself have chosen.

Trust can be misplaced, trust can be abused. And since trust means the absence of superior-administered controls, trust can leave the superior feeling naked and a little lonely, (what are they all up to, I wonder?), like an anxious mother when the children are mysteriously quiet.'

Job rotation

2.22 *Job rotation* might take two forms:

(a) an employee might be transferred to another job after a period of, say, 2-4 years in an existing job, in order to give him or her a new interest and challenge, and to bring a fresh person to the job being vacated;

(b) job rotation might be regarded as a form of training. Trainees might be expected to learn a bit about a number of different jobs, by spending six months or one year in each job before being moved on. The employee is regarded as a 'trainee' rather than as an experienced person holding down a demanding job.

2.23 No doubt you will have your own views about the value of job rotation as a method of training or career development. It is interesting to note Drucker's view: 'The whole idea of training jobs is contrary to all rules and experience. A man should never be given a job that is not a real job, that does not require performance from him'.

It is generally accepted, however, that the value of job rotation as a motivator is limited.

3. PAY SYSTEMS

3.1 A view held by many employers is that employees can be motivated to do their work more quickly and efficiently if they are given the incentive of higher pay for better effort. The pay system should usually offer the incentive of a wage or salary in excess of a basic, minimum level. Incentive schemes may take a variety of different forms, for example:

(a) *Piece-work:* by this method, employees are paid a stated amount for each unit or 'piece' of work they do. In many cases, employees receive a basic wage, plus a bonus calculated on piece-work principles. This method of payment is often applied to salesmen, who receive a basic salary plus a commission based on the sales they obtain.

The disadvantages of piece-work are that:
(i) employees may worry about losing pay due to illness or holidays;
(ii) the quality of output may be reduced in an effort to increase quantities;
(iii) employees might decide how much they wish to earn each week and produce enough output to earn this amount (no less, but no more either);
(iv) as with many productivity schemes, there may be the fear amongst employees that if they work harder, the new level of efficiency will become the 'norm' or standard, and employers may then reduce the value of the pay incentive whilst at the same time expecting the same level of efficiency to continue.

(b) *A measured day rate:* a number of progressive firms have been abandoning piece-work systems as no longer appropriate to their circumstances and have introduced a system of measured day work, under which an employee is paid a time rate, plus a bonus which is conditional on his maintaining a pre-determined level of output. The standard required is high and if the level of performance is not maintained a lower payment is made.

(c) *An individual bonus scheme:* employees may be paid a basic wage ('day rate') but be rewarded with a bonus at the end of each week, month or year, on the strength of their performances during that period. The difficulty with such schemes in many organisations is that individuals do not work alone and in isolation, but depend on colleagues for assistance.

An individual bonus scheme may therefore be seen as unfair by other individuals, who feel that they are unrewarded for their share of the effort. There are not many jobs where *individual* output can be properly measured.

(d) *Merit rating.* This is a system in which an individual is rewarded (eg. given a bonus) according to how well his boss thinks he has done in the period - ie. according to his merit. Merit rating is subjective and might be used where quantitative measurement of a person's achievements is not possible, such as with managerial work, where achievements are often intangible.

(e) *A team bonus or group bonus scheme:* the idea behind a group bonus is to promote co-operation between members of a work-team and thereby improve efficiency and output collectively, perhaps by accepting a *productivity agreement* or *flexible working practices.* Such schemes are usually *negotiated* between management and unions, but they have the usual disadvantages of most incentive schemes, ie

(i) quality may be sacrificed for the sake of output quantity;
(ii) more materials may be wasted because jobs are rushed;
(iii) productivity achievements might not be 'real'.

Additional problems would be:

(i) establishing a scheme that is fair to all members of the group. Some may work harder than others, and will resent a share of the bonus going to those who have done no real work to earn it. It is possible, for example, that the size of a 'group' may be so large that some bonus for productivity by members working in, say, Newcastle, might be shared by other members of the 'group' at head office in, say, London;

(ii) there may be inter-group rivalry, with one work group trying to secure a higher bonus for itself at the expense of the performance (and bonus) of another group.

(f) *A high day-rate system:* some employees are paid a high hourly rate of pay, with the intention that top-quality individuals will apply for the jobs, and high rates of pay will stimulate them to work well. The drawback of such a 'bonus' scheme is that high rates of pay are likely to encourage regular attendance at work, but will not necessarily stimulate high productivity.

(g) *A profit-sharing plan:* whereby all employees receive an end-of-year bonus (possibly in the form of shares in the company) based on the profits of the company. The aim of such schemes is to motivate employees to show an interest in the profitability of their company. In practice, however, problems may arise due to labour turnover; for example, if an employee thinks he might leave the company during the year, and therefore receive no profit-share, he will have no interest in the incentive scheme. New staff joining during the year will not work long enough to earn a full share of the profits, and might also be uninterested in the scheme.

The timescale of rewards - ie annual payments - is perhaps too long to be of effective interest to a work-force, unless the work-force is settled and labour turnover is low. Nevertheless, many companies have introduced profit-sharing schemes and have been pleased with their 'success'.

3.2 Incentive schemes are devised for indirect workers as well as direct workers, eg for office workers, supervisors and managers. The incentive may be:

(a) a bonus based on profits of the company, eg if a 12 per cent dividend is paid on shares then the bonus is 12 per cent on salaries;

(b) the issue of shares in the company or an option to subscribe for shares at favourable rates in the future (ie a share option scheme);

(c) a bonus related to the output of the department for which the supervisor or manager is responsible;

(d) a 'value added' bonus, based on the proportion of labour cost to 'value added'. (Value added is the difference between sales revenues and material costs).

3.3 We must remember that an employee needs income to live. The size of his income will affect his standard of living, and although he would obviously like to earn more, he is probably more concerned:

(a) that he should earn *enough* pay; and

(b) that his pay should be fair in comparison with the pay of others both inside and outside the organisation.

3.4 There is a possible conflict between the organisation's view of pay and its employee's view of pay:

(a) organisations regard pay as a cost. Profits are earned only when revenues have first of all covered costs. When revenues are low, an organisation should seek low wages too. When revenues are high, it should be able to afford more in wages;

(b) employees regard pay as income. No matter how low profits are, they will want both job stability and a stable income. It is all right for wages to go up, but it is not so good for wages to come down. Organisations look for high profits before paying high wages. Employees look for good wages first and foremost, and if anything, tend to be hostile towards the profit motive.

3.5 This conflict might explain the frequent failure of some types of pay incentive schemes to motivate employees to work harder to earn more profits:

(a) profit sharing is welcomed when profits are high. However, it is difficult to convince workers to put more into their work now to earn profits in future in order to earn more bonuses in future. The link between current efforts and future bonuses is not necessarily clear or convincing;

(b) share-ownership schemes in theory should interest employees in profits, because dividends will be paid out of profits to shareholders. It would appear, however, that an employee's resistance to profits and concern for good wages goes deeper, and a small shareholding will not persuade him to put profits before wages.

3.6 This conflict might also help to explain why a work force might demand higher wages and salaries for accepting technological innovations into work practices. New technology provides greater productivity (lower costs, higher output) but replaces people with machines or robots. People using the machines do not themselves bring about the cost savings. However, new technology threatens jobs, security and therefore income. The loss of security and the threat to income should therefore be paid for by an increase in income to the employees who are still employed.

3.7 It should be apparent that pay as a motivator is commonly associated with payment by results, whereby a worker's pay is directly dependent upon his output.

3.8 All such schemes are based on the principle that people are willing to work harder to obtain more money. However, the work of Elton Mayo and Tom Lupton has shown that there are several constraints which can nullify this basic principle. For example:

(a) the average worker is generally capable of influencing the timings and control systems used by management, and so can 'fiddle the figures';

(b) workers remain suspicious that if they achieved high levels of output and earnings then management would alter the basis of the incentive rates to reduce future earnings;

(c) generally, workers conform to a group output norm and the need to have the approval of their fellow workers by conforming to that norm is more important than the money urge.

3.9 Further drawbacks to the use of money as a form of motivation are:

(a) rates of pay are perhaps more useful as a means of keeping an organisation adequately staffed by competent, qualified people, rather than as a means of getting them to work harder;

(b) in most large companies, salary levels and pay levels are usually structured carefully so as to be 'equitable' or fair. Managers and workers will *compare* the pay of each other, or with people working in other organisations in the same area, and will be dissatisfied if the comparison is unfavourable. Pay is therefore more likely to be a 'hygiene' factor at work than a motivator;

(c) when employees expect a regular annual review of salary, increases in pay will not motivate them to work harder. Indeed, if the increase is not high enough, it may be a source of dissatisfaction.

Management criteria for pay systems

3.10 A major problem with using pay systems as a form of motivator for employees is that management should want to achieve other objectives with the pay structure they set up. Motivation isn't the only factor to consider when we think about pay.

3.11 Child has suggested that there are six management criteria for a reward system.

(a) It should encourage people to fill job vacancies and to stay in their job (ie. not leave).

(b) It should increase the predictability of employees' behaviour, so that employees can be depended on to carry out their duties consistently and to a reasonable standard.

(c) It should motivate (increase commitment and effort).

(d) It should increase willingness to accept change and flexibility. (Changes in work practices are often 'bought' from trade unions with higher pay).

(e) It should foster and encourage *innovative behaviour*.

(f) Pay differentials should reflect the nature of jobs in the organisation and the skills or experience required. The reward system should therefore be consistent with seniority of position in the organisation structure, and should be thought *fair* by all employees.

3.12 On the other hand, money *can* be a motivator, depending on the individual's need for money. Thus a young married man with a family to support may want money very badly, so that he can afford enough to achieve a desired standard of living. Money is not usually an end in itself, but it provides the means of buying the things an individual wants in order to satisfy his physiological, safety, social, esteem and self actualisation needs.

It is generally agreed that if there is a clear, short-term and direct link between extra effort, results and higher pay, then an individual can be considerably motivated by money. Salesmen paid on a commission basis could be a clear example of this principle in practice.

3.13 Drucker suggested that pay is an incentive to produce better output only where a willingness to perform better already exists.

3.14 We return, therefore, to the view that if higher pay must be directly related to extra effort to be a real motivator, then incentive schemes can be effective motivators.

3.15 To avoid some of these difficulties, some companies have moved from individual to group incentive schemes. Where this has been linked to a job enrichment programme then effective working groups with healthy rivalry can be formed, thus gaining some advantages from both worlds. On the other hand, an individual will not work harder unless the group as a whole raises its norms, and there will be some resentment against group members who are seen to be 'shirking'.

3.16 It has become clear from the experiences of many companies that profit sharing schemes, incentive schemes (productivity bonuses) and joint consultation machinery do not in themselves improve productivity or ease the way for work to get done. Company-wide profit sharing schemes cannot be related directly to extra effort by individuals and are probably a 'hygiene' factor rather than a motivator.

Better organisation, better technology and motivation of employees are also needed to improve productivity; a major problem is to put all these into practice.

4. PARTICIPATION AS A MEANS OF MOTIVATION

4.1 There is a theory that if a superior invites his subordinates to participate in planning decisions which affect their work, if the subordinates voluntarily accept the invitation, and results about actual performance are fed back regularly to the subordinates so that they can make their own control decisions, then the subordinate will be motivated:

(a) to be more efficient;
(b) to be more conscious of the organisation's goals;
(c) to raise his planning targets to reasonably challenging levels;
(d) to be ready to take appropriate control actions when necessary.

4.2 It is obvious that participation will only be feasible if the superior is willing to apply it.

4.3 What exactly does participation involve and why might it be a good thing? Handy commented that: 'Participation is sometimes regarded as a form of job enlargement. At other times it is a way of gaining commitment by workers to some proposal on the grounds that if you have been involved in discussing it, you will be more interested in its success. In part, it is the outcome of almost cultural belief in the norms of democratic leadership. It is one of those 'good' words with which it is hard to disagree'.

4.4 The advantages of participation should perhaps be considered from the opposite end - ie what would be the disadvantages of not having participation? The answer to this is that employees would be told what to do, and would presumably comply with orders. However, their compliance would not be enthusiastic, and they would not be psychologically committed to their work.

4.5 Participation can involve employees and make them committed to their task, but only if:

(a) participation is *genuine*. It is very easy for a boss to pretend to invite participation from his subordinates but end up issuing orders. If subordinates feel the decision has already been taken, they might resent the falsehood of management efforts to discuss the decision with them. A good example would be the offer by management to discuss redundancies with its employees when employees believe that the decisions about redundancies have already been taken, and management's offer of genuine discussions is false;

(b) the efforts to establish participation by employees are *continual* and pushed over a long period of time and with a lot of energy. However, 'if the issue or the task is trivial...and everyone realises it, participitative methods will boomerang. Issues that do not affect the individuals concerned will not, on the whole, engage their interest'. (Handy);

(c) the *purpose* of the participation of employees in a decision is made quite clear from the outset. 'If employees are consulted to make a decision, their views should carry the decision. If, however, they are consulted for advice, their views need not necessarily be accepted;

(d) the individuals really have the *abilities* and the *information* to join in decision-making effectively;

(e) the supervisor or manager *wishes* for participation from his subordinates, and does not suggest it because he thinks it is the 'done thing'.

Motivation through participation in practice

4.6 Present social and educational trends show that people's expectations have risen above the basic requirement for money. The current demand for more interesting work and to have a say in decision-making. These expectations are a basic part of the movement towards greater participation at work. Participation should involve the work group.

This movement towards greater participation is not limited to the UK. In most industrially developed countries (eg USA, West Germany, Sweden, Australia, France) there is the desire for increased involvement in decisions on the part of those people who will be affected by them.

4.7 The methods of achieving increased involvement have largely crystallised into two main streams. These can be described as:

(a) industrial action towards greater day-to-day involvement and participation in the process of management;

(b) political action towards industrial democracy.

4.8 These two streams have been described by Strauss and Rosenstein as immediate and distant participation.

(a) *Immediate participation* is used to refer to the involvement of employees in the day-to-day decisions of their work group. Typical examples of this type of participation in the past have come from Scandinavia, eg Volvo, Saab, etc.

(b) *Distant participation* refers to the process of including company employees at the top levels of the organisation which deal with long-term policy issues (eg investment, employment et al). Typical examples of this type of participation would be found in any major West German company with the two tier board structure. (In 1951, a German law was passed which requires labour representatives on the supervisory board and executive committee of certain large companies. The executive committee should include one labour representative as a director. Despite EEC attempts at European harmonisation, the UK is still some way off having such 'worker-directors'.)

4.9 Because the word 'participation' is so emotive, it has tended to become a catch phrase, being used by individuals in different contexts without definition, thereby causing much misunderstanding. In business, participation can cover a range of views, depending on the point of view from which one looks.

5. CONCLUSIONS ON MOTIVATION OF INDIVIDUALS

5.1 The following conclusions might be drawn about motivation of individuals and its consequences for management.

(a) Individuals vary in the kind of needs they have and the satisfactions they want. Supervisors and managers should study these needs and try to satisfy the needs of their employees by providing satisfaction in their work.

(b) When staff is recruited, the capacity of an individual to be motivated might be just as important as the individual's basic abilities and paper qualifications.

(c) Supervisors and managers should continually seek ways of trying to generate motivation through job design the job should:

(i) have a clear meaning and purpose in relation to the objectives of the organisation;

(ii) be as self-contained as possible, so that the employee will be doing a 'complete' job;

(iii) provide opportunities for making decisions or participating in decisions which affect his work and targets (eg in deciding the methods for doing work). In this respect, a decentralisation of authority throughout the organisation is likely to encourage employee motivation;

(iv) provide a regular feedback of information to the employee about his performance;

(v) avoid monotony and repetitiveness.

(d) There are numerous problems to using pay incentives and salary schemes as a means of motivation, due to the complex ways in which people respond to matters affecting the pay of themselves and others. However, pay remains a potential motivator, in spite of Herzberg's doubts on this subject.

6. DISCIPLINE

6.1 Managers can try to motivate their staff. But they must also organise and control their work and behaviour, and there must usually be a sense of discipline too.

6.2 Discipline can be considered as:

> 'a condition in an enterprise in which there is orderliness in which the members of the enterprise behave sensibly and conduct themselves according to the standards of acceptable behaviour as related to the goals of the organisation. Discipline therefore can be considered as positive (or good) when employees willingly follow the rules of the enterprise. Discipline is negative (or bad) when subordinates either follow the rules reluctantly or actually disobey regulations and violate the standards of acceptable behaviour.'

6.3 The best discipline is self discipline. It is based upon the normal human tendency to do what needs to be done, to do one's share, to do the right thing, and to follow reasonable standards of acceptable behaviour set for the enterprise. Positive self-discipline is based upon the premise that most employees want to do the right thing. Even before they start to work, most mature persons accept the idea that following instructions and fair rules of conduct are normal responsibilities that are part of any job. Most employees can be counted on to exercise self discipline. They believe in performing their work properly, in coming to work on time, in following the supervisor's instructions, and in refraining from fighting, drinking at work, or stealing etc. Self-imposed discipline involves conformity with legitimate rules, regulations, and orders which are necessary for the proper conduct of the enterprise. It is a normal human tendency to subordinate one's personal interests and personal idiosyncracies to the needs of the organisation.

6.4 Once employees know what is expected of them and feel that the rules are reasonable, self-disciplined behaviour becomes a part of 'group norms' ie the way in which employees behave as a work group, and their collective attitudes. When new rules are introduced, the supervisor must try to convince employees of their purpose and reasonableness. If the work group as a whole accepts change, a strong sense of group cohesiveness on the employees' part will usually exert group pressure on possible dissenters, thus reducing the need for corrective action.

6.5 Unhappily, there are always some employees in every organisation who, for various reasons, will fail to observe the established rules and standards even after having been informed of them. These employees simply do not accept the responsibility of self discipline. Since the job must be accomplished, the supervisor cannot afford to let the few 'get away' with violations. Firm action is required to correct those situations which interfere with the acccepted norms of responsible employee behaviour. The test of a good line manager/supervisor is how he deals with disciplinary situations, however caused.

6.6 There are many types of disciplinary situations which require attention by the supervisor. Internally the ones most frequently occurring are:

(a) excessive absenteeism;

(b) excessive lateness in arriving at work;

(c) defective and/or inadequate work performance;

(d) poor attitudes which influence the work of others or which reflect on the public image of the firm;

(e) breaking rules regarding rest periods and other time schedules such as leaving work to go home early;

(f) improper personal appearance;

(g) breaking safety rules;

(h) other violations of rules, regulations and procedures;

(i) open insubordination, such as the refusal of an employee to carry out a legitimate work assignment.

6.7 In addition to these types of job situations supervisors might be confronted with disciplinary problems stemming from employee behaviour off the job. These may be an excessive drinking problem, the use of drugs or involvement in some form of law breaking activity. In such circumstances, whenever an employee's off-the-job conduct has an impact upon performance on the job, the supervisor must be prepared to deal with such a problem within the scope of the disciplinary process.

6.8 Situations involving disciplinary action are usually not pleasant ones, but the supervisor must learn to deal with disciplinary situations rather than trying to avoid issues by pretending to ignore them. Disciplinary action requires that the supervisor should utilise some of the authority inherent in his supervisory position, even though the supervisor might prefer to 'pass the buck' to someone in higher management. It is vital that supervisors take appropriate action when it is required, because if they don't some employees who are on the borderline may be encouraged to follow the poor examples, and lack of discipline will become more extensive. When defects in employee self-discipline become apparent, it is the supervisor's responsibility to take action firmly and appropriately, however, unpleasant it might be.

Taking disciplinary action

6.9 Any disciplinary action must be undertaken with sensitivity and sound judgement on the supervisor's part. The purpose of discipline is not punishment or retribution. Disciplinary action must have as its goal the improvement of the future behaviour of the employee and other members of the organisation. The purpose obviously is the avoidance of similar occurrences in the future.

6.10 Normally, a good supervisor will not have too many occasions to take disciplinary action. But whenever it becomes necessary, it is the supervisor's job to take whatever action is necessary, even though it is an unpleasant task, and unless absolutely necessary, the supervisor should not call on someone else to handle the problem. Taking disciplinary action will involve an interview with the 'offender' and the supervisor should try to prepare himself properly for it.

(a) *Investigate first*
The supervisor must guard against undue haste or unwarranted actions.

The ACAS *code of practice requires that before doing anything, a supervisor must investigate what happened and why. Consideration should be given to the employee's past record and all other pertinent information about the situation before any disciplinary action is taken.
(* ACAS is the Advisory Conciliation and Arbitration Service).

(b) *Discipline in private*
As a general rule, the supervisor should take disciplinary action with the employee involved, in private. Only under extreme circumstances should disciplinary action be taken in public. A public reprimand builds up resentment in the employee being censured and other factors enter the situation.

About the only exception to this would be in those circumstances where a supervisor's authority is challenged directly and publicly. For example, if the employee openly refuses to carry out a reasonable work request, or if an employee is drunk or fighting on the job, it may be necessary for the supervisor to reach a disciplinary decision quickly and in front of others in order to regain control of the situation. By failing to act decisively in such stress situations, the supervisor may lose the respect of the other subordinates.

Progressive discipline

6.11 Following ACAS guidelines for disciplinary action which emphasise no dismissal on first offence except for gross misconduct, many enterprises have accepted the idea of progressive discipline, which provides for an increase of the severity of the penalty with each offence. The following is a list of suggested steps of progressive disciplinary action and many companies have found these steps to be workable.

(a) *The informal talk*
If the infraction is of a relatively minor nature and if the employee is one whose record has no previous marks of disciplinary action, an informal, friendly talk will clear up the situation in many cases. Here the supervisor discusses with the employee his or her behaviour in relation to standards which prevail within the enterprise. But if a friendly talk is not sufficient to bring about desired results, then it will become necessary for the supervisor to take the next step, the oral warning.

(b) *Oral warning or reprimand*
In this type of interview between employee and supervisor, the supervisor emphasises the undesirability of the subordinate's repeated violation, and that ultimately it could lead to serious disciplinary action.

(c) *Written or official warning*
A written warning is of a formal nature insofar as it becomes a permanent part of the employee's record. Written warnings, not surprisingly, are particularly necessary in unionised situations, so that the document can serve as evidence in case of grievance procedures.

The employee should receive a duplicate copy of the written warning, which should contain a statement of the violation and the potential consequences of future violations. Another copy of this warning is sent to the personnel department, so that it can be inserted in the employee's permanent record.

(d) *Disciplinary layoffs, or suspension*
This course of action would be next in order if the employee has committed repeated offences and previous steps were of no avail. Disciplinary lay-offs usually extend over several days or weeks.

(e) *Demotion*
Another disciplinary measure, the value of which has been seriously questioned, is demoting an employee to a lower-paying job. This course of action is likely to bring about dissatisfaction and discouragement, since losing pay and status over an extended period of time is a form of constant punishment. This dissatisfaction of the demoted employee may easily spread to co-workers, therefore most enterprises avoid downgrading as a disciplinary measure.

(f) *Discharge*
Discharge is the most drastic form of disciplinary action. It should be reserved only for the most serious offences. Due to the serious implications of discharge, supervisors should resort to it infrequently.

6.12 In any disciplinary system the time element is significant. For example, there is the question of how long the breaking of a rule should be held against an employee. Generally, it is desirable to disregard minor offences which have been committed more than a year or two years previously. Therefore, an employee with a poor record on account of tardiness would be given a type of 'clean bill of health' for maintaining a good record for one year, in some enterprises six months or even less.

6.13 In some situations the time element is of no importance. For example, if an employee is caught brandishing a loaded gun in a heated argument during work there is no need to worry about any time element or previous offences. This violation is serious enough to warrant immediate discharge.

The task of the supervisor: administering discipline without being resented

6.14 A supervisor is placed in a difficult position when taking disciplinary action. In spite of the supervisor's use of sensitivity and judgement, imposing disciplinary action tends to generate resentment because it is an unpleasant experience. The challenge to the supervisor is to apply the necessary disciplinary action so that it will be least resented.

6.15 Following these four basic rules will help the supervisor reduce the resentment inherent in all disciplinary actions.

(a) *Immediacy*
Immediacy means that after noticing the offence, the supervisor proceeds to take disciplinary action as speedily as possible, while at the same time avoiding haste which might lead to unwarranted actions.

(b) *Advance warning*
In order to maintain proper discipline and to have employees accept disciplinary action as fair, it is essential that all employees know in advance what is expected of them and what the rules and regulations are.

Many companies find it useful to have a disciplinary section in an employee handbook, which every new employee receives. However, each new employee should also be informed orally about what is expected by explaining the information in the employee handbook.

(c) *Consistency*
A further requirement of good disciplinary technique is that supervisors be consistent in application and enforcement. Consistency of discipline means that each time an infraction occurs appropriate disciplinary action is taken. Inconsistency in application of discipline lowers the morale of employees and diminishes their respect for the supervisor. Inconsistency also leads to employee insecurity and anxiety, and creates doubts in their minds as to what they can and cannot do.

(d) *Impersonality*
It is only natural for an employee to feel some resentment towards a supervisor who has taken disciplinary action against him. Yet the supervisor can reduce the amount of resentment by making disciplinary action as impersonal as possible. Penalties should be connected with the act and not based upon the personality involved.

CASE STUDY 1

This has been quite a long chapter, but an important one. Let's now see how some of the principles might be applied in a practical situation.

> You are concerned about the attitude and performance of Ian Dalgleish, a member of your section. Since your appointment as supervisor of the section a few months ago, you have been able to come to terms with the rest of the team. Performance was mediocre when you arrived but you have obtained improvements by discussing and agreeing new ideas, by establishing clear short-term goals for all your staff, and by giving them frequent feed-back. It has not worked with Ian.
>
> His work is sloppy and untidy. He misses deadlines. He sometimes comes in late and goes early. He seems to resent you and to take perverse pleasure in thwarting your intentions. You know he has considerable potential. He is honorary treasurer of two local societies both of which are full of praise for him. He runs a football team very successfully and is popular with his colleagues.
>
> What will you do now? If your proposed actions fail, what will be your next step?

Discussion

The problem is Ian Dalgleish's failure to use his obvious talents in making a real contribution to the departmental goals and objectives of the organisation. The problem is complicated by an attempt to challenge your leadership of the section: many of his failures (timekeeping) are public failures which can be observed by other members of the department.

Possible reasons for his behaviour

(a) He wanted promotion, or it was widely assumed (by the section) that he would be promoted to supervisor. Therefore he is personally frustrated and publicly embarrassed by your appointment and his behaviour is an attempt to compensate for his frustration.

(b) His outside activities give him more challenge and responsibility and therefore provide more satisfaction of his 'need to achieve' therefore his work does not command a high priority on his enthusiasm and efforts.

(c) He does not respond to your chosen leadership style. Possibly he prefers an authoritarian to a participative approach.

(d) He has personal problems which are affecting his attitude to work.

The fact-finding procedures would include:

(a) a discussion with the previous supervisor as to Ian's work before you came, his ambitions and objectives, and attitude towards your predecessor's leadership;

(b) an examination of Ian's personal file to discover his background, appraisal ratings and any factors which may be influencing his behaviour, eg problems at home, family bereavement;

(c) perhaps informal discussions with other members of the group, although care must be taken to ensure that this does not appear as gossiping behind Ian's back.

Any course of action can only be selected after a full counselling interview with Ian to establish the cause rather than the symptom.

NB. This would be a difficult interview since Ian is unlikely to volunteer easily that his frustration at not being appointed is behind his behaviour, if this is the case. You should examine if you have the necessary social skills and consider obtaining specialist advice from the personnel manager.

The following courses of action could be undertaken, depending on the cause identified for Ian's behaviour:

(a) Consider the areas of your authority you can delegate to Ian. This will depend on the extent to which you can win back his trust and build a cooperative relationship.

(b) Attempt to provide more challenging work (see (a) above) and also try to accommodate his pressures by providing facilities to help his work: calculators, paper, photocopier etc. Demonstrate your admiration for his work in front of his colleagues.

(c) Explain the benefits to Ian of a participative style of management, and point out that managers of the future would be expected to display their skills with people just as much as their ability to complete tasks.

(d) Give him advice and sympathy, and possibly time off to let him sort out his personal problems.

The success or failure of the course of action must be followed up. If the actions fail then transfer to another section might be the answer, particularly if it has promotion prospects. Organisations depend on the talent of their human resources and attempts to keep Ian and channel his abilities are a necessary aspect of organisational adaptation.

CASE STUDY 2

> You have recently been appointed to supervise a group of 10 people who have to cooperate to achieve the goals of their section. You have found disquieting evidence that all is not well. The output of the section is not high as you feel it should be. Although overtime is regularly worked, there are substantial backlogs and targets are missed. Absenteeism in this section is higher than that of any other section. The same people seem to be absent regularly and often produce poor excuses or none at all. People fall out over trivial issues and the lack of cooperation impairs efficiency. You feel a general air of lethargy, if not hostility. What do you propose to do about it? How will you know when you are succeeding?

Discussion

This case study deals with the subject of *work groups*. The information given in the question strongly suggests that there has been poor leadership in the past, and that the group is inefficient, badly-motivated and that some individuals are poorly-disciplined. Do not forget, however, that the problem might not simply lie with bad management of staff. There might be a genuine grievance that the group is overloaded with work, and does not have the resources it needs, hence its poor attitudes.

The group appears to have been badly led in the past. Its output is low, in spite of overtime working, its level of efficiency is low, there is a backlog of work and targets are missed. There is conflict over trivial issues and a lack of co-operation between members of the group, and there is a general air of lethargy or even hostility. Absenteeism is high, especially among particular individuals who are able to get away with poor excuses or no excuses at all.

The possible causes of this serious situation are various. The failure to achieve targets might be due to inadequate planning, failure of the supervisor to tell individuals what their targets are, and a lack of feedback and control system to ensure that action is taken when results fail to meet targets. To some extent the workload of the group might be excessive, so that the group is understaffed, and the heavy workload has demoralised the group members who no longer try to achieve targets and efficiency standards. However, an improvement in efficiency would increase output and ease the backlog and the group is clearly not performing well enough in this respect.

The problem of absenteeism might be caused to some extent by low morale, but the absence of disciplinary action against persistent offenders can only create a sense of unfairness amongst the others. This could help to explain the hostility and conflicts over trivial matters between group members.

The lack of co-operation might be caused by poor planning and supervision, or by poor motivation of staff and inter-personal dislikes. Staff have clearly been reluctant to refer matters to their supervisor, since conflicts have arisen over trivial matters. Good supervision should prevent minor disagreements from escalating into conflict in the first place.

Some individual group members might be unsuited to their jobs and this might help to explain poor efficiency. To some extent or inadequate working conditions and poor organisation of the group's work routines might also be at fault.

What should be done?

(a) The effectiveness of the group should be assessed initially in terms of the group itself, the group's task and the group's working environment.

   (i)   The personalities, characteristics, skills and experience of each individual group member should be assessed. It will take time to make this assessment, but the supervisor should make an immediate start. If possible, inter-personal hostility between particular individuals should be identified. Habitual absentees should be identified from the beginning.

   (ii) The tasks of the group should be assessed. Are the tasks of the group too difficult for the group members? Is the workload too heavy for a group of ten?

   (iii) The environment of the group should be examined. Do they work closely together in an open-plan office, or are they partitioned off into small offices, or even geographically distant from each other? Do the individuals who have to co-operate closely with each other actually sit close together? Is the equipment used by the group adequate for their job?

(b) After an initial assessment of these matters, the supervisor should call a group meeting as soon as possible. At the meeting, he or she should express disquiet at the state of affairs, and explain the reasons for disquiet. The group members should be encouraged to state their own views, after which the supervisor should state his or her intention to do something about the problem. An outline of the proposed steps (suggested below) should be given at the meeting.

(c) The group as a whole must know what its planning targets are, and each individual member of the group should be given standards or targets to work towards.

(d) The work load of the group should be measured within the plan, and if there is a need for overtime, the quantity of overtime that ought to be required should be built into the plan. The supervisor should ask any individuals whether they are unable or unwilling to work these amounts of overtime. If there is a need for more staff, the supervisor could pursue the matter through his or her superiors, and let the staff know what is happening about it.

(e) There should be a regular feedback to individual group members on their actual performance, and how this compares against their targets. If their performance is below standard or target, the supervisor should ask for reasons and discuss what control action or remedies might be necessary.

(f) Persistent absenteeism must be stopped. It should be made clear to all group members that disciplinary measures will be taken against offenders. The supervisor should than apply discipline consistently and keep to his word.

(g) The need for co-operation between group members should be made clear. Co-operation within the group can be improved by good planning, and by regular group meetings to review progress and iron out difficulties. Progress meetings will also have the advantage of providing a forum in which problems can be identified at an early stage, and in which the supervisor can indicate whether the group as a whole is achieving its targets or not.

(h) Any disagreements that cannot be settled amicably should be referred up to the supervisor.

(i) The supervisor should give time and attention to individual members of the group. Training needs should be identified, and group members given appropriate training where required. The supervisor should get to know each individual, identifying their needs and interests, and trying to encourage them in such a way as to improve their attitude, motivation and performance.

(j) If some individuals continue to show personal animosity, or to perform badly, the supervisor should express concern, and indicate that their next formal appraisal will not be favourable.

(k) The techniques and equipment used by the group should be improved where necessary (and if resources are available). The supervisor should make whatever alterations to the office layout and environment seem beneficial and practicable.

(l) The supervisor should set a timescale for improvements and use regular group progress meetings to announce to the group how matters are developing.

How to know when measures are succeeding. The supervisor will know when measures are succeeding because:

(a) the productivity of the group should improve and targets will be achieved;
(b) there should be an apparent improvement in the attitudes of group members.

More specifically:

1   Absenteeism should be much less frequent.

2   There should be higher output and productivity.

3   Individual targets as well as group targets should be achieved.

4   Individuals should display a greater commitment to their work and the achievement of targets. Individuals should also show a clear awareness of what their targets are.

5   Communication between group members should be more free and open.

6   Conflicts over minor matters should no longer occur.

7   Group members should show signs of trying to help each other by offering constructive suggestions and ideas.

8   Group members will begin to show signs of wanting to develop their abilities further.

Some signs of success will be quantifiable (1 to 3 above), other signs will be qualitative and unquantifiable (items 4 to 8 above).

CASE STUDY 3

Because of the unexpected resignation due to illness of the previous manager, George Smith has taken charge of a department of his father's business. The department employs 50 people, and is divided into six sections headed by junior managers. Although the department is efficient and running well, there are half a dozen employees whose time-keeping is irregular, and who periodically leave early or take time off. What steps should George take to eliminate this problem?

Discussion

The problem concerns the irregular time-keeping of half a dozen specific employees in a department which is otherwise efficient and running well. It is a problem which may become worse if it is ignored; for example, the motivation of other employees may suffer if they see that irregular time-keeping is apparently considered acceptable by management.

Some possible causes of irregular time-keeping and absenteeism are listed below:

(a)   The department is quite a large one. Large organisational structures sometimes appear cold and impersonal, which may have a damaging effect on morale.

(b)   The employees concerned may resent the style of leadership displayed by the junior managers, or by the previous manager. The question does not specify whether the previous manager's illness was in any way connected with his work.

(c)   Physical working conditions may be poor.

(d)   The work being done may not be very interesting, either generally, or specifically to the poor time-keepers.

(e)   The employees may be dissatisfied with their career prospects.

More information is needed on the causes of the problem before a solution can be proposed.

(a) The junior managers should be consulted, either individually or in a group. Individual meetings would certainly be preferable if it appears that the problem is confined to a particular department and that one junior manager in particular may therefore be the cause of the problem. These interviews should be conducted with tact. George Smith has been appointed to a position which one or all of the junior managers may have aspired to. The fact that George is the proprietor's son may lead to resentment and lack of respect from his subordinates.

(b) The personnel records of the problem employees should be inspected for any clues to their behaviour.

Solutions to the problem will depend very much on the causes identified. Possibilities are:

(a) Counselling and advice for any junior manager whose actions are diagnosed as contributing to the problem.

(b) Counselling and advice for individual employees. This would be appropriate if the problem is one of lack of motivation caused by dull work or unsatisfactory career prospects.

(c) Improvement in any organisational factors which may be found to be deficient (eg. improvement in physical working conditions).

(d) In the extreme case, disciplinary action might be needed. It would then be important to follow the organisation's recognised disciplinary procedures, possibly involving communication with employee representatives.

Once a solution has been chosen and implemented it should be followed up. In the worst case, if employees have been dismissed recruitment of new staff may be necessary. If less extreme measures have been taken, it will be necessary to review the position after a reasonable interval to ensure that action has had its intended effect.

TEST YOUR KNOWLEDGE

(The numbers in brackets refer to paragraphs in this chapter)

1. In what ways might motivation be improved? (1.2)

2. Distinguish between job enrichment, job enlargement and job rotation. (2.4, 2.12, 2.22)

3. What pay systems are there, and how might they motivate employees? (3.1)

4. What criteria should management wish to apply to the pay system in their organisation? (3.11)

5. In what circumstances will participation in decision-making be a successful means of motivation? (4.5)

6. When might disciplinary action be needed? (6.6)

Chapter 5

MANAGEMENT TRAINING AND DEVELOPMENT: SUCCESSION

This chapter covers the following topics

1. The management of managers
2. Management education, training and development
3. Management education and training (E&T)
4. Management development
5. Transition from functional to general management
6. Management succession

Purpose of this chapter

To look at management education, training and development, as a process of grooming individuals for management jobs. Two particular problems of development are given special attention: the transition from functional to general management and the problems of succession into the very top management positions.

1. THE MANAGEMENT OF MANAGERS

1.1 In the previous chapters, we looked at the function of managers to provide leadership, direction and motivation to employees and subordinates. The subordinates of middle-ranking and senior managers are managers themselves, and so the principles and policies described apply to the management of other managers, as well as to the management of rank-and-file 'workers'.

The broad features of the management of managers might be summarised as follows:

Function	How it might be done
1. Plan and control the activities of other managers.	(a) Corporate planning (b) Budgeting, budgetary control (c) Performance measurement (d) Accountability.
2. Direct and motivate other managers. *Note.* Motivating subordinate managers is necessary if their own subordinates in turn are to stand much chance of being motivated. Managers set an example for their staff.	(a) Delegation of authority or centralisation of decision-making authority. (b) Allowing subordinate managers decision-making discretion.
3. Organise the work of other managers. Co-ordinate their work.	(a) Suitable organisation structure (b) Good communication.
4. Fill managerial vacancies. Staff, recruit, guide and develop managers.	(a) Selection procedures (b) Management development and appraisal programmes (c) Training and education.

1.2 In this chapter, we shall concentrate on item (4). An organisation should have:
   (a) a capable management team, with a suitable blend of abilities and experience;
   (b) a system for filling management positions when vacancies arise, either through:
      (i)   promotion from within; or
      (ii)   appointments of managers from 'outside'; or
      (iii) a mixture of (i) and (ii).

2. MANAGEMENT EDUCATION, TRAINING AND DEVELOPMENT

2.1 You might subscribe to the trait theory of leadership, that some individuals are 'born' with the personal qualities to be a good manager, and others aren't. There might be some bits of truth in this view, but very few individuals, if any, can walk into a management job and do it well without some guidance, experience or training.

2.2 In every organisation, there should be some arrangements or system whereby:

   (a) managers gain *experience*, which will enable them to do another more senior job in due course of time;

   (b) subordinate managers are given *guidance* and *counselling* by their bosses;

   (c) managers are given suitable *training* and *education* to develop their skills and knowledge.

If there is a planned programme for developing managers, it is called a *management development programme*.

5: MANAGEMENT TRAINING AND DEVELOPMENT: SUCCESSION

2.3 A useful distinction between management education, training and development was given in the report *'The Making of British Managers'*, prepared for the BIM and CBI in 1987 by Constable and McCormick. The report gave the following definitions.

(a) '*Education* is that process which results in formal qualifications up to and including post-graduate degrees.'

(b) *Training* is 'the formal learning activities which may not lead to qualifications, and which may be received at any time in a working career.'

(c) '*Development* is broader again: job experience and learning from other managers, particularly one's immediate superior, are integral parts of the development process.'

Development will include features such as:
(i) career planning for individual managers;
(ii) job rotation;
(iii) standing in for the boss while he is away on holiday;
(iv) on-the-job training;
(v) counselling, perhaps by means of regular appraisal reports;
(vi) guidance from superiors or colleagues;
(vii) education and training.

2.4 Education is therefore an element of training, which is an aspect of development.

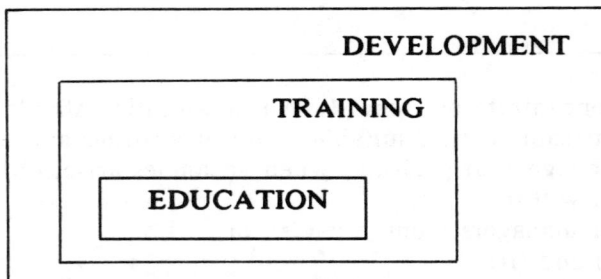

```
┌─────────────────────────────────────────────┐
│                DEVELOPMENT                    │
│   ┌───────────────────────────────────────┐  │
│   │              TRAINING                 │  │
│   │   ┌───────────────────┐               │  │
│   │   │    EDUCATION      │               │  │
│   │   └───────────────────┘               │  │
│   └───────────────────────────────────────┘  │
└─────────────────────────────────────────────┘
```

2.5 It is worth getting clear in your mind at the beginning why management training and development are needed.

(a) Without training and development, managers are unlikely to be ready for promotion when the time comes, and they will not do their new job well until they have learnt by mistakes.

(b) The selection of individuals for promotion is unlikely to be reliable, and the 'wrong people' might be selected for senior jobs. Individuals will rise to their level of incompetence!

(c) Vacancies will often have to be filled by recruitment from outside the organisation, because not enough 'in-house' managers will be good enough or sufficiently ready for promotion.

(d) An organisation should show an interest in the career development of its staff, so as to motivate them and encourage them to stay with the firm. Management development is an important feature of being a good employer.

3. MANAGEMENT EDUCATION AND TRAINING (E & T)

3.1 *Education*, for successful students, leads on to a formal qualification. For managers in the UK, these qualifications include:

(a) undergraduate business and management degrees;
(b) undergraduate degrees in related subjects such and Economics and Accountancy;
(c) postgraduate business and management degrees (MBA course);
(d) the Diploma in Management Studies (DMS);
(e) qualifications from professional institutes, such as the ICSA. Accountancy qualifications (ACA, ACCA, ACMA, AAT) are the most common professional qualifications in the UK.

3.2 *Formal training* which does *not* lead on to a qualification consists mainly of:

(a) post-experience management courses, provided by training companies or colleges and polytechnics;
(b) in-company management training, using the company's own training staff and/or consultants brought in from outside.

3.3 *In-company management training* ranges from:

(a) basic training for those without any formal education and training, such as induction courses for new recruits into junior management posts;

(b) continuing internal development programmes, for managers as they progress through their careers and up the seniority scale;

(c) senior general management programmes. Fairly senior managers need training too, to help their development into even more senior positions!

3.4 The report by Constable and McCormick found from a survey of UK employers that:

(a) most employers regard innate ability and experience as the two key ingredients of an effective manager. But education and training help, *especially in broadening the outlook of managers with only functional experience previously, and without experience of general management;*

(b) there was agreement that it would be both inappropriate and impossible to make management a controlled profession similar to accountancy and law. However, making a managerial career more similar to the professions and *having managers require specific competences appropriate to each stage of their career,* were seen as beneficial.

Skills training

3.5 Skills training is concerned with teaching a person how to do a particular job, or how to do it better. Functional managers, especially supervisors and junior managers, should be given skills training to help them to do their job better.

3.6 A systematic approach to skills training involves identification of technical work which will lend itself to training, the design of a training scheme (including a cost/benefit analysis of the scheme), implementation of the scheme and subsequent review to decide whether or not it has succeeded in achieving its purpose. The stages in a systematic approach of this kind may be listed as follows:

(a) Identify areas where training will be beneficial.
(b) Set training objectives.
(c) Decide on the training method.
(d) Compare the costs and benefits of the proposed course.
(e) Introduce a pilot or test scheme.
(f) Implement the scheme in full.
(g) Monitor the results to check that:
    (i)   training works; and
    (ii) benefits exceed costs.

3.7 Functional department heads should suggest to the training department an area of work where they think that training would be beneficial. Alternatively, the training department itself looks for areas of work where training might be provided.

3.8 In addition to skills training, an organisation should provide training to potential managers or existing managers in management techniques and skills. It has already been suggested that employees might want promotion, but cannot be offered it yet, either because there are not enough vacancies yet and they must wait their turn, or because they are not good enough yet, or even because they might never be good enough for further advancement. Large organisations have a problem of:

(a) motivating their existing staff and keeping them where they might be expected to wait for further promotion;

(b) providing training to ensure that sufficient staff are available to fill management positions capably when vacancies do arise. (In this respect, management training and development should be planned within the framework of the manpower plan).

3.9 Training follows on from recruitment and selection, and also appraisal of performance.

(a) Potential managers can be given training in management skills, either on internal courses or on courses with external organisations such as business schools.

(b) Existing managers can be given training in new skills required for their existing job (eg the technological changes in organisations and the development of computer usage suggest the need for training in computer applications and software for management work).

(c) Existing managers can be given training in the skills required for higher, general management (eg with discussions of organisation policy, and lectures given by directors).

5: MANAGEMENT TRAINING AND DEVELOPMENT: SUCCESSION

3.10 A successful programme for management education and training should involve both senior management and the individual managers who should expect to receive training.

Recommendations

Senior management	*Individual managers*
1. Create an atmosphere within the organisation where continuing management training and development is the norm.	1. Actively want and seek training and development. 'Own' their own career.
2. Utilise appraisal procedures which encourage management training and development.	2. Recognise what new skills they require, and seek them out positively.
3. Encourage individual managers, especially by *making time available* for training.	3. Where appropriate, join a professional institute and seek to qualify as a professional member.
4. Provide support to local educational institutes (eg. colleges) to provide management education and training (E & T).	
5. Integrate in-house training courses into a wider system of management E & T. *Make the subject matter of in-house courses relevant to managers' needs.* Work closely with academic institutions and professional institutions (eg. the ICSA) to ensure that the 'right' programmes are provided.	

3.11 Designing appropriate in-house courses and encouraging some managers to obtain a professional qualification should be two key features of an E & T programme for managers.

3.12 The time given to managers for education could be provided by:

(a) a full year off, to study for an MBA qualification, say;
(b) block release to attend study courses or revision courses;
(c) day release, perhaps to attend courses at a local college;
(d) reducing the workload on individuals, so that they don't have to work long hours and overtime, to give them time to attend evening classes or study at home.

Time off for studying should be paid for by the employer, who might also contribute towards the cost of text books and courses for professional examinations.

4. MANAGEMENT DEVELOPMENT

4.1 Management development is the process of improving the effectiveness of an individual manager by training him/her in the necessary skills and understanding of organisational goals. Although management development is in some respects a natural process, the term is generally used to refer to a conscious policy within an organisation to provide a programme of individual development. The techniques of management development include:

    (a)   formal education and training;
    (b)   on-the-job training;
    (c)   group learning sessions;
    (d)   conferences;
    (e)   counselling.

4.2 The principle behind management development is that by giving an individual time to study the techniques of being a good manager, and by counselling him about his achievements in these respects, the individual will realise his full potential. The time required to bring a manager to this potential is *possibly* fairly short.

4.3 It is important to emphasise the planned nature of management development programmes. As an illustration:

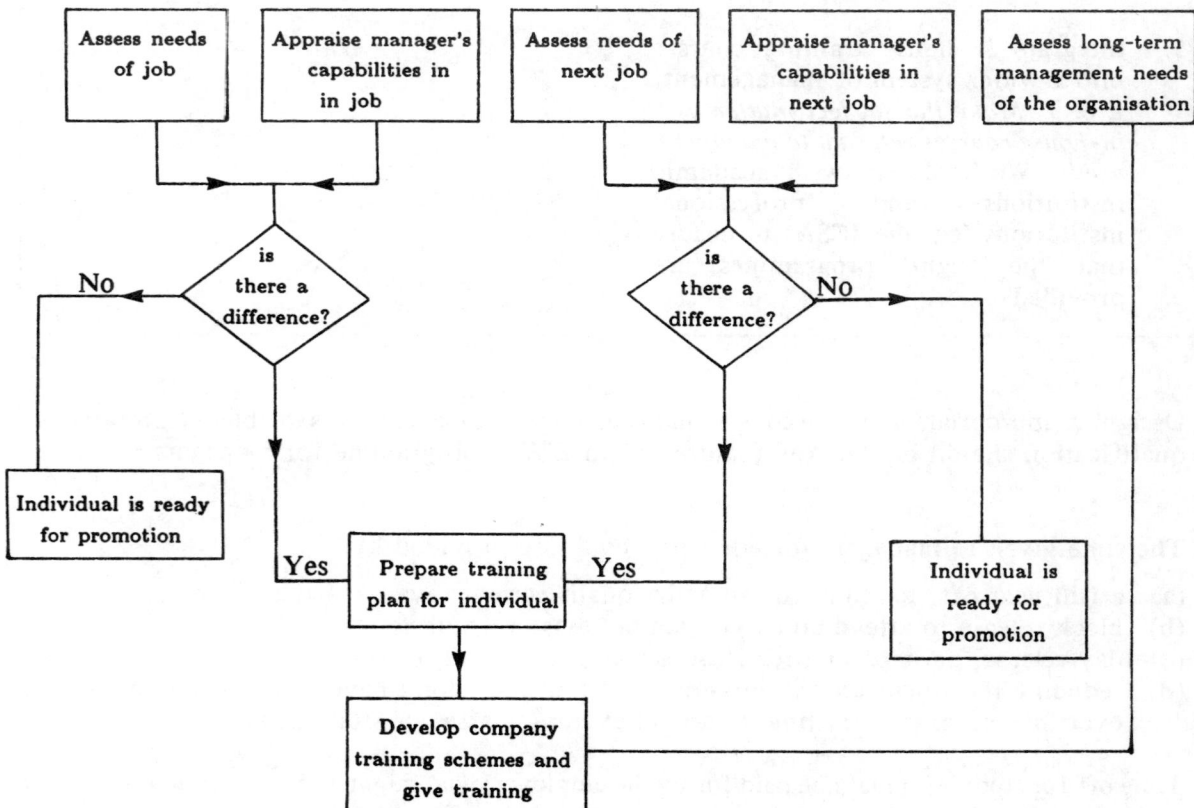

5: MANAGEMENT TRAINING AND DEVELOPMENT: SUCCESSION

4.4 This diagram brings out the importance of *appraisal* in a system of development. Although we have been discussing the development of managers, staff appraisal is important for all grades of employees.

Appraisal schemes

4.5 Management appraisal is the process of:

(a) looking at the past performance of a subordinate manager, and assessing its strengths and weaknesses;

(b) considering the suitability of the manager for promotion (ideally by considering his potential to do a more senior job well);

(c) considering how the performance of the manager can be improved (or developed), by training, moving to another job to obtain more experience, or by counselling the manager about his faults and how to overcome them.

4.6 In many organisations, a formal appraisal is carried out once each year, and an annual report on the manager prepared for personnel records.

4.7 The purpose of formal appraisal schemes is to:

(a) gather information about the skills and potential of existing managers;

(b) assess the performance of managers, so as to reward them (eg with the promise of promotion);

(c) let the manager know how well he or she has performed, and the assessment of his/her strengths and weaknesses;

(d) allow the person being appraised and his/her superior to discuss how they should plan to achieve the objectives of both the person and his/her job.

4.8 Appraisal schemes are therefore means of rewarding, criticising, encouraging, counselling and so developing individual managers. The superior of the person appraised is meant to be both critic and counsellor, but in practice these twin roles tend to be incompatible.

4.9 The 'traditional' method of individual appraisal in bureaucracies is *trait appraisal*. The individual's superior (and perhaps the superior's boss) will be asked to complete an appraisal report on the individual, grading him/her with regard to certain characteristics or traits, such as intelligence, initiative, enthusiasm, skill, punctuality, appearance etc. A typical form of appraisal report is shown on the next page. Each quality of the employee (intelligence etc) is graded from A (excellent) to E (very weak). The completed report may then be discussed in an interview between the individual and his superior.

APPRAISAL REPORT						
Name Position Age	Years in position					
	A	B	C	D	E	Comments
Intelligence Skills in the job Enthusiasm Initiative ....etc....						

4.10 In theory, such appraisal schemes may seem very fair to the individual, but in practice the system often goes wrong because:

(a) appraisal interviews are often defensive on the part of the subordinate, who believes that any criticism will lessen the rewards for his performance - (eg promotion will be missed);

(b) interviews are also often defensive on the part of the superior, who cannot reconcile the role of judge and critic with the 'human relations' aspect of the interview. The superior may therefore misrepresent the extent of the criticism of the subordinate which is contained in the report;

(c) the superior might show bias etc in his report (in the same way that an interviewer might show incorrect judgement in the interview process);

(d) reports from one area might be more favourable or lenient than reports from another area. However, when a standard appraisal report is used throughout the organisation, there is a reasonable prospect that reporting will be fairly consistent in all areas and in all departments.

4.11 Criticism can only be beneficial if it is constructive, and if the threat of withholding rewards is not present (or at least does not dominate the counselling interview). A mutual trust and respect must exist between the superior and the subordinate; and in practice, this is all too rare. In other words, it is easy to write appraisal reports, but it is not so easy to use them in counselling interviews. Criticism is easily taken the wrong way by subordinates, and sometimes given harshly by superiors.

4.12 Various ideas have been put forward to suggest how appraisal can be made more effective:

(a) Its purpose should be constructive, which means that the superior and subordinate in a counselling interview should agree on goals for the subordinate to achieve. The interview should preferably take place at the instigation of the subordinate, who is ready to be given more goal-direction by the superior.

(b)   Instead of trait appraisal, the individual might be judged on his/her success in achieving stated objectives. The drawback to this idea, however, is that the individual may expect to be in a job for only two or three years, so that he/she will not be concerned with longer-term objectives. There will also be a tendency to suppress any trouble until promotion is secured - ie keep the lid on a problem and leave it to blow up in the face of the individual's successor in the job.

(c)   The link between past performance and future reward should be broken unless the organisation clearly intends a connection to exist, perhaps using a system of merit rating. In many formal organisations:

   (i)   promotion tends to depend on seniority, not performance; and

   (ii)   there is a rigid pay structure. Employees and their trade unions believe in *equity of pay* so that there is a clearly defined pay structure for managers in different grades. The pay of an individual is not related to his performance.

Unless the connection between performance and reward is a very real one, it is damaging to the system of appraisal for employees to believe that the connection exists.

(d)   When a manager is promoted, he or she will move into a job which calls for a different mixture of skills. It is widely agreed that as managers move up an organisation's hierarchy, they do less technical work and more general management work. Senior managers spend most of their time on strategic planning - ie design work.

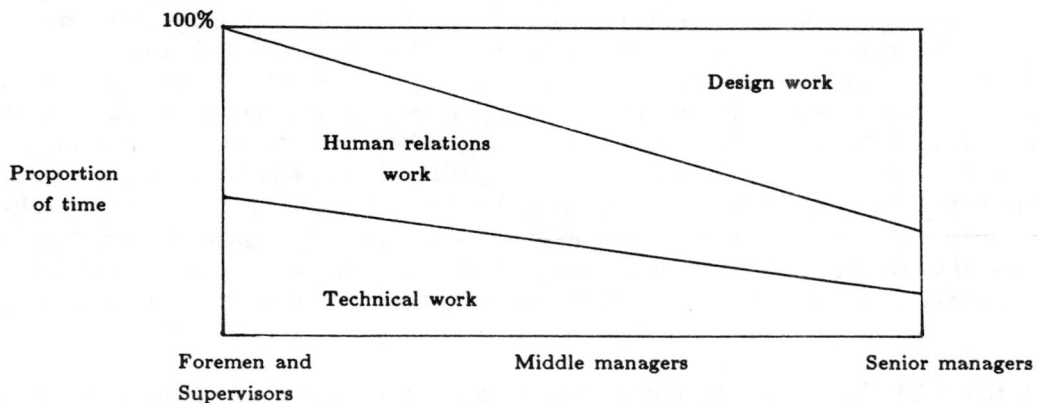

4.13   The argument can be made that if an individual is assessed on the basis of past performance, the assessment will not properly show whether the individual will be capable of handling a more senior job with a demand on different abilities. (Indeed, by using past performance as a guide to promotion prospects, the organisation is likely to promote managers to their level of incompetence).

4.14   Appraisal for promotion might therefore be based on an assessment, not of an individual's traits or past performance, but in terms of his/her *potential skills* as a more senior manager, ie the individual can be graded on his known ability to plan, be a controller and make decisions, skills in human relations and leadership, ability to organise, gather, analyse and communicate information, innovate etc.

5: MANAGEMENT TRAINING AND DEVELOPMENT: SUCCESSION

4.15 You might have gained the impression from the previous paragraphs that job appraisal can be used to identify why a person might not yet be ready for promotion, and to arrange for more training or job experience which will give that person what he needs to gain promotion at some time in the future.

4.16 However, in a large organisation not everyone can be promoted, because:

(a) there are not enough management jobs to go round; and
(b) some people are not management material, or have already risen as high in the organisation as they are likely to get.

4.17 This creates a bit of a problem for the manager making an appraisal for his subordinate. Should he tell the subordinate that he is unlikely ever to be promoted? or that he will not progress far up the hierarchy of management? Or should he pull the wool over the subordinate's eyes, and give him false hopes so as not to discourage him from trying? As long as promotion (and with it, higher pay) remain a valuable reward which motivates individuals to work, it must always be questioned whether honest appraisals might not backfire when employees are disillusioned about their prospects. It would seem to be essential that employees should not be discouraged by their appraisal. The solution is to encourage all employees to improve themselves and develop in their work. In particular, employees must be encouraged to do their existing work better, and in this respect the counselling and help towards their further development seems essential.

4.18 Drucker has suggested that management development should be provided for all managers, not just the ones who are considered promotable material. 'The promotable man concept focuses on one man out of ten - at best one man out of five. It assigns the other nine to limbo. But the men who need management development the most are not the balls of fire who are the ...promotable people. They are those managers who are not good enough to be promoted but not poor enough to be fired. These constitute the great majority; and they do the bulk of the actual managing of the business. Most of them will, ten years hence, still be in their present jobs. Unless they have grown up to the demands of tomorrow's jobs, the whole management group will be inadequate, no matter how good....the promotable people. And whatever can be gained by developing the chosen few will be offset by the stunting....the resentment of those passed over... The first principle of manager development must therefore be the development of the entire management group'.

4.19 On the other hand, Handy noted that '....it remains true that career planning in many organisations is not a development process so much as a weeding-out process'.

4.20 Even so, it is interesting to ask what makes a person a potential manager, and others not. For example, if an organisation recruits 100 school leavers into clerical jobs, what characteristics would separate those who will become managers from those who will not? The possible factors are:

(a) some employees are more motivated than others, and get greater satisfaction from their job. They are more likely to be high-achievers who set themselves high standards;

(b) ambition, and a desire to be more powerful in the organisation;

(c) an ability in management skills, such as:
 (i) an ability to persuade or influence other people;
 (ii) an ability in administration (planning, co-ordinating, providing information, organising);

(iii) an ability to see opportunities in a situation rather than be weighed down by problems.

(d) successful achievement of targets in his job;

(e) a drive or determination to develop himself without having to wait for other people to give encouragement or push;

(f) the desire to earn more money;

(g) good interpersonal relations, in particular an ability to understand the views of other people and not ride rough-shod over them;

(h) a willingness to accept change and new ways of getting things done;

(i) an ability to take a helicopter view rather than a worm's eye view of a situation - in other words, the ability to take a broad view of a problem and be realistic;

(j) a willingness to be moved around in his job to where the opportunities are, even if this means moving geographically to take up a position in a different part of the country, or even abroad.

The factors listed above might therefore be items for inclusion in an appraisal report which considers promotion potential.

On-the-job training

4.21 On-the-job training is very common, especially when the work involved is not complex. Trainee managers require more coaching, and may be given assignments or projects as part of a planned programme to develop their experience. Unfortunately, this type of training will be unsuccessful if:

(a) the assignments do not have a specific purpose from which the trainee can learn and gain experience; or

(b) the organisation is intolerant of any mistakes which the trainee makes. Mistakes are an inevitable part of on-the-job learning.

4.22 Experienced managers, either promoted from within the organisation or recruited from outside, will need a period of *orientation* in their new job. It takes time to settle down, and learn the way the 'system' operates. There must be tolerance of mistakes during this orientation period, because it is a form of on-the-job training.

4.23 Different methods of on-the-job training include:

(a) *coaching*: ie the trainee is put under the guidance of an experienced employee who shows the trainee how to do the job. The length of the coaching period will depend on the complexity of the job and the previous experience of the trainee;

(b) *job rotation*: ie the trainee is given several jobs in succession, to gain experience of a wide range of activities. (Even experienced managers may rotate their jobs, to gain wider experience; this philosophy of job education is commonly applied in the Civil Service, where an employee may expect to move on to another job after a few years);

(c) *temporary promotion*: ie an individual is promoted into his/her superior's position whilst the superior is absent owing to illness. This gives the individual a chance to experience the demands of a more senior position;

(d) *'assistant to' positions*: ie a junior manager with good potential may be appointed as assistant to the managing director or another executive director. In this way, the individual gains experience of how the organisation is managed at the top;

(e) *committees*: ie trainees might be included in the membership of committees, in order to gain an understanding of inter-departmental relationships.

4.24 One particular problem of staff development has recently been discussed in the Harvard Business Review by Jay W Lorsch and Haruo Takagi.

4.25 Lorsch and Takagi looked at the problem of the *plateaued manager*. Long-serving managers may reach a plateau in an organisation, beyond which they recognise that they are unlikely to make progress. They may be faced with a further ten or fifteen years before retirement during which they will feel uncommitted and frustrated.

4.26 Lorsch and Takagi argue that this common problem can be converted into a benefit both for the organisation and for the manager concerned. Experienced executives who have spent a number of challenging 'mainstream' years in an organisation will identify with it and will care about the development of its next generation of professionals and managers. If they participate in the training of newer management staff they will benefit from a renewed sense of importance; meanwhile, the new generation will benefit from their experience and advice.

Recommendations for management development

4.27 The recommendations for a management development programme which were made in the Constable and McCormick report (1987) are similar to their recommendations for management education and training.

> 'This research ... indicates that the total scale of management training is currently at a very low level. The general situation will only improve when many more companies conscientiously embrace a positive plan for management development. This needs to be accompanied by strong demand on the part of individual managers for continuing training and development throughout their careers.'

> *Recommendations in the report*
>
> 'Chief executives should see continuing **management** development as a major area of their responsibility. It should be a regular item for boardroom discussion and an important aspect of long-term corporate plans.'
>
> 'The implementation of strategic initiatives should be accompanied by well-designed management development activities.'
>
> 'Employers should seek to create personal development programmes for all **managers.**'
>
> 'Individual managers should be encouraged to 'own' their development programme.'
>
> 'Employers should establish strong links with external providers of management training with a view to both influencing the design of programmes and obtaining maximum use of expertise.'

4.28 It should also be added that a senior **manager** in the organisation – perhaps the personnel director – should be given the responsibility for implementing a planned management development programme, and the issue of management development within the organisation should be regularly discussed at board level.

4.29 There are two more aspects of management development and training that we need to look at closely. These are:

    (a) *the transition from functional to general management.* At some stage in his or her career, a manager will be promoted from a job which is concentrated mainly on functional expertise (eg. knowledge of production **techniques,** personnel techniques, accountancy skills, marketing skills) into a job where the requirement is for broader and more general management skills – eg. organising, staffing, controlling, dealing with other departments or organisations, long-term planning and so on; and

    (b) *management succession:* in particular, planning for the replacement of the top executive (MD or Chairman) on his or her retirement or resignation.

5.   TRANSITION FROM FUNCTIONAL TO GENERAL MANAGEMENT

5.1 Functional managers are managers whose job is to plan and control functional activities, such as production, research and development, technical engineering, personnel, accountancy, selling and marketing, distribution and so on.

5.2 The change in a manager's work caused by moving from a functional to a general management position can be seen by highlighting some of the important differences in the two types of role.

	Functional manager	General manager
Orientation	● task orientated – focus on the functional tasks in hand	● goal orientated – focus on achievement of organisational (and divisional) goals and objectives
Role	● organiser	● facilitator – eg. co-ordinating interdepartmental activities; obtaining and allocating resources
Information	● defined sources ● usually through formal channels	● poorly defined sources ● often acquired by informal contacts
Goals	● short term	● long term

5.3 The transition from functional to general manager is usually accompanied by promotion to a more senior position in the management hierarchy and therefore the contrast in roles between functional and general management is also found between junior and senior management. But this comparison must not be overstated; much depends on the structure of the organisation concerned. The traditional, functional structure tends to keep managers in functional roles until they reach very senior levels and sometimes for their entire careers.

5.4 A *divisional structure*, however, gives relatively junior managers experience of general management roles, usually as the chief executive of small business units. Organisational structure can therefore have a significant impact on the age and seniority of managers making the transition from functional to general management and therefore the extent of the difficulties it may create. More will be said about divisionalisation in a later chapter.

5.5 Recent research has brought to light the difficulties which managers face in changing from one role to another and these are often particularly acute when the change involves moving from a functional to a general management position. In addition to the normal problems of switching jobs, the manager taking up a general management post has to deal with an abrupt change in the skills needed to perform his role effectively.

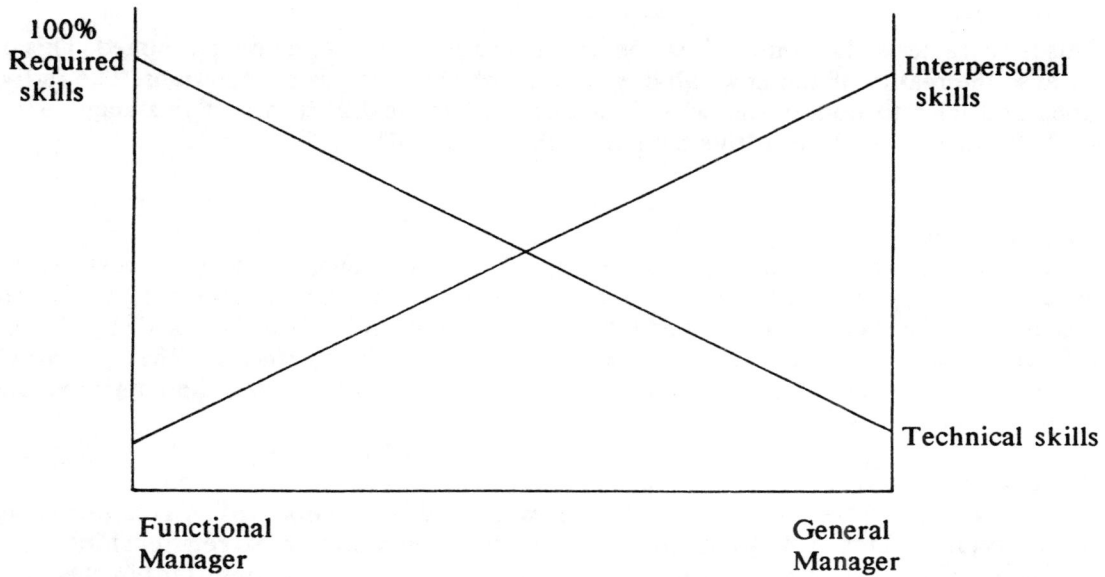

5.6 Technical skills are concerned with an ability to cope with large quantities of data and information and to select the appropriate key points to form the basis for decision-taking. Interpersonal skills involve inspiring, motivating, leading and controlling people to achieve goals which are often poorly defined. For the general manager, the latter are more important.

The transition curve

5.7 The transition from functional to general manager is a complex process and the time taken to complete the 'learning curve' varies depending on the degree of perceived change. Since a move from functional to general management is often, and correctly, viewed as a major change, transitions of this sort take longer than average to complete. The diagram below shows a typical transition curve.

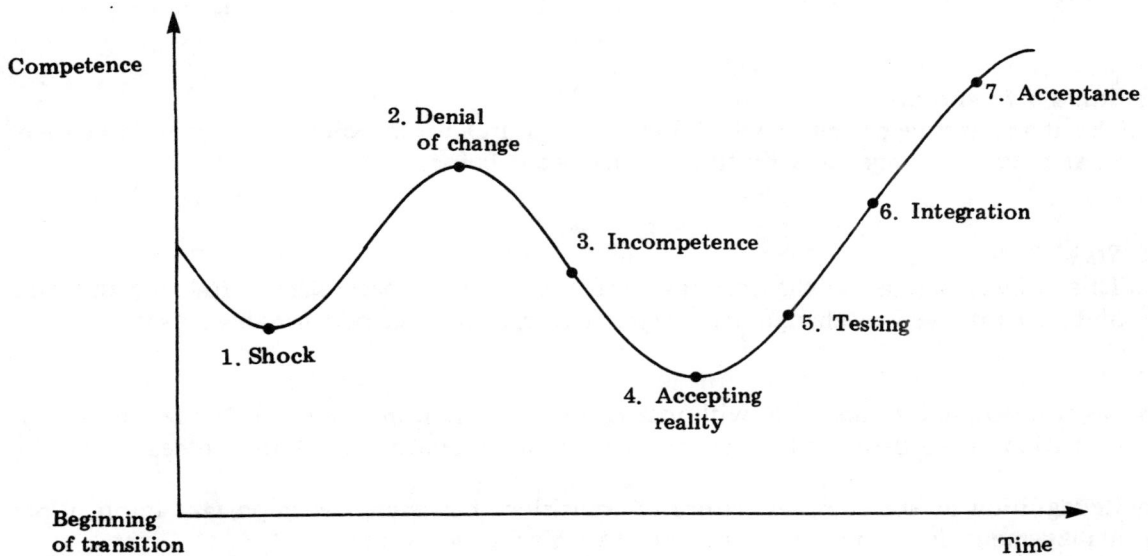

113

5.8 *Stage 1 Shock.*

This is characterised by immobilisation or shock; a sense of feeling overwhelmed. This occurs because the reality of the new job does not match the person's expectations. The individual stops and tries to understand what is happening. Typical attitudes at this stage are "did I really want this job?" and "this isn't the job I expected".

5.9 *Stage 2 Denial.*

This is characterised by a denial of change. There is a reversion to previously successful behaviour. This can be useful if it is temporary, but becomes a handicap if it goes on too long and inappropriate behaviour becomes dominant. Sometimes individuals do remain at this point on the curve indefinitely and this is what is described in the *Peter Principle*. They perform badly because their behaviour is based on their past activities rather than their current ones.

5.10 *Stage 3 Incompetence.*

This involves an awareness that change is necessary and is accompanied by frustration because the individual finds it difficult to cope with the new situation or relationships. A fall in performance level is common but, despite this, the phase is very important in the transition process since, without the realisation of change, people can never develop new attitudes and patterns of behaviour. Organisations which adopt a "sink or swim" approach to transition actually hinder the process in that this phase is commonly regarded as the start of "sinking". Consequently, individuals are reluctant to share their current experience with others.

5.11 *Stage 4 Realism*

This is the time when the reality of the new situation is accepted for the first time. Up to this point managers have been concerned with hanging on to past values, attitudes and behaviours. There is now a preparedness and willingness to experiment with change.

5.12 *Stage 5 Testing*

This is concerned with testing new behaviour and approaches. There is a lot of activity and energy as the testing progresses and mistakes are liable to be made. But the experimentation needs to be encouraged since only by doing this can effective approaches be found.

5.13 *Stage 6 Integration*

This is a reflective period, in which individuals search for meaning in an attempt to understand all the activity, anger and frustration that went before.

5.14 *Stage 7 Accepting*

This is the final phase of the transition. Effective new approaches are introduced and the sense of being involved in change disappears. Self-esteem, and performance, rises.

5.15 No two people face and deal with managerial transition in exactly the same way and so the transition curve described above can only be a general model of the process.

5.16 Recognition of the complex nature of transition, however, has important implications for management development in general and training in particular.

(a) Transition takes time; research indicates that, on average, people feel in control only after a period of 24-30 months.

(b)   Changes which involve considerable adaptation, such as moving from a functional to a general management position, take longer than the average.

(c)   Because transition is often a lengthy process, managements should avoid moving people from position to position too frequently.

(d)   For succession planning and training to be successful, it needs to go beyond the point of entry to the new job.

(e)   People in transition often have more severe entry problems than newcomers, since they are frequently not given a "breathing space" before being expected to perform adequately. This increase the pressures on them and may ultimately reduce their performance and that of the organisation as a whole.

5.17   To help with the transition from technical to general management, an organisation should have a planned management development programme.

(a)   Individuals should be encouraged to acquire suitable educational qualifications for senior management. 'High-fliers' for example might be encouraged to study for an MBA degree early on in their career. Top finance managers (eg. the finance director) ought to have an accountancy or similar qualification.

(b)   Provide in-house training programmes for senior managers and individuals who are being groomed for senior management. Formal training in general management skills can be very helpful.

(c)   Careful promotion procedures. Only managers with the potential to be a good senior manager should be promoted into a senior management position.

(d)   A system of regular performance appraisal, in which individuals are interviewed by their boss (or their boss's boss) and counselled about:

(i)   what they have done well;
(ii)   what they have not done so well;
(iii)   how to improve their performance in their current job;
(iv)   how to develop their skills for a more senior job.

(e)   Provide suitable experience to managers for more senior positions. This can be done, as mentioned earlier, by means of:

(i)   allowing subordinates to stand in for their boss whenever the boss is away;
(ii)   using 'staff officer' positions to groom future 'high fliers'. More is said about these jobs later;
(iii)   job rotation;
(iv)   using a divisionalised organisation structure, to delegate general management responsibilities further down the management hierarchy. Divisional organisation can give managers experience of general management at a fairly early stage in their careers.

5.18   The same problems of transition from functional to general management occur in public sector organisations. In an article in *The Administrator* (January 1988) Jeffrey Greenwell, chief executive of Northamptonshire County Council, wrote about the management of local government that:

5: MANAGEMENT TRAINING AND DEVELOPMENT: SUCCESSION

(a) many junior managers are trained as professionals, such as engineers and social workers. Professionalism helps them to do their functional tasks better;

(b) however, local government's most senior managers are appointed from the ranks of these professionals, who have had no previous experience of general management and have often worked throughout their career to date in just a single functional department.

5.19 As a step towards dealing with this problem, Northamptonshire County Council began a system (from 1983) of giving promising young functional managers some experience of general management early on in their careers - ie. teaching them general management by means of 'hands on' experience. This has been done by creating the job of 'assistant to' or 'staff officer' to the chief executive. A manager from one of the functional departments is appointed for a *temporary period* (perhaps 1-2 years) to act as staff officer to the chief executive of the County Council, and this experience of the general management at a fairly early stage in their career helps to groom them for a full general management job later on.

5.20 Some large companies use a similar system themselves by giving general management experience to young 'high fliers', as staff officer or assistant to either the company chief executive or the chairman.

6. MANAGEMENT SUCCESSION

6.1 Appointing a person as managing director or chief executive, to succeed someone who is retiring or has resigned, is similar in many respects to appointments for *any* management vacancy. But there are some important differences too.

1. The managing director, along with the chairman, is one of the leaders of the organisation. It is crucially important that an able person is appointed to the job.

2. New men often bring innovation, especially if they are appointed from outside (ie. external recruitment rather than internal promotion).

   A new managing director or chairman might bring:
   (a) new ideas and changes in products, services, organisation etc;
   (b) a new style of leadership.

3. The MD and chairman are seen as the embodiment of an organisation's corporate values. A new man at the top can change these. The period just before and after the succession of the new man can be a period of great *anxiety* and *tension* within the organisation.

4. The top man can be especially important for either of two reasons.

   (a) In a small entrepreneurial company, he might be the man who set up the company in the first place. He might still be autocratic, having refused to delegate much authority. He might be reluctant to retire, and need persuading. He might have failed to 'groom' a successor. And he might have run out of ideas, so that the organisation is stagnating under his control and needs a new top man to breathe fresh life into it.

   (b) In a large public company or public sector organisation, the top man often attracts widespread publicity. The new top man must be capable of attracting good PR for the organisation, and must have the 'personal' status to operate at the top level - eg. in dealings with senior politicians and other top industrialists.

5: MANAGEMENT TRAINING AND DEVELOPMENT: SUCCESSION

6.2 The successor to a retiring MD or chairman might be appointed from within the organisation, or externally.

(a) Internal promotion will usually be favoured *unless:*
  (i) there is no one in the organisation who is suitable for the job;
  (ii) the top man needs powerful and influential contacts with outside organisations (eg. the government), and so an external appointment might be preferable.

(b) To provide a suitable successor from within the organisation, there should be a well-planned management development programme. The successor should have been 'groomed' for the succession, eg. by senior management training, and regular introduction to major external contacts, clients, suppliers etc.

6.3 Internal promotion is likely to be preferred by employees in the organisation itself, rather than an external appointment, because the new boss would be 'known', and less likely to change existing corporate values significantly.

6.4 If an external appointment might be appropriate, the organisation will probably appoint a firm of *consultants* (or 'head hunters') to find a person for the job.

6.5 If no ideal successor can be found straightaway, an organisation might decide on a temporary appointment. For example, if a managing director retires, a successor cannot be found externally and no one inside the company is yet 'ready' or suitable for the job, the company's board of directors might ask the chairman or a non-executive director to stand in as temporary MD.

6.6 Whoever is appointed to succeed the outgoing man, someone with ambitions is likely to be disappointed because he or she didn't get the job. Such a person might decide to resign, and so there could be another senior management vacancy to fill too. Succession to the top job can be the start of a major change in personnel, as well as in ideas and outlook!

CASE STUDY 1

Let's look now at a simple case study on management training and development.

You have recently been made responsible for training in your company's head office. This morning, six young graduates, all of whom are on a two-year management programme, have complained about the quality of the training they have been receiving. Departmental heads seem to be unclear as to what sort of training they are supposed to provide for the graduates. The graduates are given dull routine work which they could master in five days, but they are kept at it for a month at a time. They are not told whether they are doing well or badly. They are bored and dispirited.

Required:

(a) What is wrong with the management training programme?
(b) What action should you take to improve the training of the graduates?

5: MANAGEMENT TRAINING AND DEVELOPMENT: SUCCESSION

Discussion

The graduates' complaint relates to the dull work they are given to do. It is assumed therefore that the problem relates entirely to on-the-job training and not to formal tutorial training.

Deficiencies in the management training programme

(a) Highly-qualified management trainees should be capable of mastering new techniques and work procedures very quickly. Department heads seem to be under-estimating the graduates' ability to do so. Graduates are being assigned for a whole month to routine work which they can master in a week. Department heads may have failed to realise the difference in learning speeds between recruits of school-leaving age and graduates specially selected for accelerated management training programmes.

(b) The graduates are poorly motivated because they are bored and do not experience any challenge in their work. Department heads are said to be 'unclear as to what sort of training they are supposed to provide'. They apparently do not realise that the purpose of a management training programme should be to introduce graduates as quickly as possible to *managerial* work, rather than the routine work they are doing now.

(c) There seems to be no system of appraisal and feedback. The trainees are not told whether they are doing well or badly. As well as being poor for morale, this is inefficient in that the graduates will not be able to improve their performance if they are not told where improvements are needed.

Suggestions for improvement

(a) Job rotation. The purpose of this is to broaden the knowledge and experience of the trainees. They can be shifted to a variety of posts, not all of them necessarily including supervisory duties. But the results may be unsatisfactory if insufficient time is allowed in each position.

(b) Use of 'assistant to' positions. Acting managers, preferably those with talent and experience as teachers, are assisted in their jobs by trainees. The trainees are able to observe the managers in the exercise of their normal duties, as well as carrying out useful work themselves.

(c) Temporary promotions. If managers are ill or on holiday trainees can be appointed as 'acting managers' in their absence. This can be a convenience for the organisation as well as an element in staff development. Obviously the trainees may need assistance in carrying out their duties and they should be encouraged to discuss any difficulties with their superiors.

(d) Committees. Trainees might be included in the membership of committees in order to gain an understanding of inter-departmental relationships.

(e) Establishing objectives. The graduates are likely to find their work more satisfying if targets are set for them. As it is, they appear not to know what is expected of them and cannot understand why they spend long periods on work which they have already mastered.

(f) Appraisal reports. A formal system of feedback should achieve improvements in staff performance as well as being a good motivator.

5: MANAGEMENT TRAINING AND DEVELOPMENT: SUCCESSION

Formal education and training should back up on-the-job training. Each graduate should be encouraged to take an *active* interest in his or her own education, training and development.

TEST YOUR KNOWLEDGE

Here are some examination-style problems. Jot down some ideas that you think are relevant to answering them.

1. Describe the main elements of a management development programme in *either* a public *or* a private sector organisation.

2. Outline a development programme for managers taking account of the need to be adaptive and flexible with a particular concern for clients or markets.

3. What would you define as the main management development needs of a functional manager identified for promotion to general management?

4. Discuss the role of performance appraisal as part of a programme of management development aimed at improving managerial effectiveness.

5. What are the advantages and problems of a policy of "promotion from within an organisation"?

6. Discuss the problems of management succession in ONE of the following:
   (i)   a small business run by the founder-entrepreneur;
   (ii) a medium sized manufacturing company;
   (iii) a large public sector organisation.
   What approaches may be adopted to deal with the problems identified?

Discussion points

Question 1
This problem could be answered within the framework of paragraph 2.1. A development programme would be broadly the same for either a public or a private sector organisation, although there will be differences of detail, eg. in skills training and, possibly, succession.

Question 2
Points to cover would include:
(i)   a *planned* programme;
(ii)   putting a senior manager (eg. personnel director) in charge of the programme;
(iii) education;
(iv)   careful recruitment;
(v)   skills training;
(vi)   continuous in-house training;
(vii) general management training;
(viii) on-the-job training with job rotation, delegation, 'assistant to' positions etc;
(ix)   formal and regular appraisal and counselling;
(x)   guidance from superiors for subordinates;
(xi)   planned transition from functional to general management;
(xii) planning for succession into senior management positions.

5: MANAGEMENT TRAINING AND DEVELOPMENT: SUCCESSION

The question emphasises the need to be adaptive and flexible, with particular concern for clients and markets. Flexibility and change are likely to be encourage by involving as many managers as possible in the process of adapting and innovation. Delegation of authority would be advisable. In particular, a divisionalised organisation structure based on products or markets would seem particularly suitable.

Question 3
Here, the need is for a gradual introduction to the skills of general management. The differences between functional and general management should be pinpointed (paragraph 50) and recommendations for helping transition described (paragraph 5.16).

Question 4
The role of performance appraisal is described in paragraphs 4.2-4.8, 4.12-4.14, 4.15-4.20.

Question 5

Advantages	*Disadvantages*
1. Career opportunities for employers.	1. Appointees from outside likely to be more innovative, bringing fresh ideas.
2. Appointees understand the corporate values.	2. Possibly better people available outside.
3. Individuals can be *trained* and *developed* for promotion.	3. Organisation might lack a good management development programme.
4. Makes a career with the organisation more attractive, and reduces staff turnover.	4. Outside appointees should have broader experience.
5. Likely to be greater continuity.	
6. Appointees likely to have a better technical understanding of the business.	

Question 6
The problems of succession are much the same in any organisation: see paragraphs 68-73. Succession in small organisations is often characterised by the retirement of the company's founder, with perhaps a son ready to take over (who may not be a good manager). Succession in a large public sector organisation is quite likely to be a political appointment, perhaps of a person with a high profile in the news media and whose views are in sympathy with those of the government of the day. Appointments to the top post in public sector organisations are often for a fixed term (say 5 years) which might be renewed subsequently - eg. governorship of the Bank of England.

SECTION B

MANAGERIAL ACCOUNTABILITY

AND AUTHORITY

Chapter 6

DECISION MAKING: AUTHORITY, RESPONSIBILITY AND DELEGATION

This chapter covers the following topics:

1. Decision making
2. Authority, responsibility and delegation
3. Delegation of authority
4. Pooled authority
5. Committees
6. Centralisation or decentralisation

Purpose of this chapter

To consider the nature of management decision making and discretion. This leads on to a broad study of authority, responsibility, the delegation of authority and the relative merits of centralising and decentralising authority. More will be said about delegation and centralisation versus decentralisation in the next chapter.

1. DECISION MAKING

1.1 Managers are employed to make decisions. There are different ways of categorising decisions. One useful analysis of decisions is into five categories.

(a) *Routine planning decisions;* typically, budgeting and scheduling.

(b) *Short-run problem decisions;* typically, decisions of a non-recurring nature. For example, a manager might have to deal with a staff problem, or give instructions to a subordinate about what to do next.

(c) *Investment or disinvestment decisions.* For example, should an item of equipment be purchased? Should a department be shut down? Decisions of this nature often have long-term consequences.

(d) *Longer-range decisions;* decisions made once and reviewed infrequently, but which are intended to provide a continuing solution to a continuing or recurring problem. Shillinglaw (1963) calls these 'quantitative policy decisions', and they include decisions about selling and distribution policies (eg. Should goods be sold through middlemen or direct to customers? What type of customer should the sales force attempt to attract? What should the company's discount policies be? Should a company employ its own delivery fleet, or should it hire contractors for distribution? Should a new product or service be launched? Should an additional shift be established in order to raise production levels to meet growing sales demand?).

(e)   *Control decisions;* ie. decisions about what to do when performance is disappointing and below expectation.

1.2   Decisions are needed to resolve problems, when there is a choice about what to do. Problems vary, not just according to what they are about, but also according to:

(a)   how easy or complex they are to resolve;

(b)   how frequently they arise;

(c)   whether the problem can be quantified, or whether there are qualitative matters of judgement involved;

(d)   how much information is available to help the manager to make the decision;

(e)   how serious the consequences would be if a bad decision were made;

(f)   whose job it is to make the decision about how to deal with it.

1.3   *Complexity*
Some problems are difficult to resolve, and call for:

(a)   careful judgement; or
(b)   a lot of thought; or
(c)   technical skill or experience on the part of the manager.

1.4   The manager who has the job of making any decision should have the technical skills to make a sensible decision and avoid unnecessary mistakes.

Due to the technical complexity of some decisions, management jobs are often *specialised by function,* with managers being trained and developed to acquire the technical skills - in engineering knowledge, accountancy, personnel administration, marketing, and so on - to run a functional department and make good management decisions for that department.

1.5   *Frequency*
Some problems are recurring, and have to be resolved fairly regularly. Other problems are occasional, perhaps unique, and difficult to foresee.

(a)   Problems which recur regularly can be dealt with in a routine or standardised way, with the help of *rules and procedures.* For example:

(i)   if a member of staff is continually late for work, a disciplinary code of practice should be available to give guidance to the employee's supervisor about what steps to take;

(ii) if a supplier is late with a delivery, there should be procedures in the purchasing department for chasing up the delivery.

(b) Problems of a non-recurring and non-foreseeable nature cannot be provided for in a book of rules and procedures.

1.6 A higher decision making ability is usually needed from managers to deal with problems in (b) compared with problems in (a).

1.7 *Quantifiable or qualitative*
Quantifiable problems are problems where the likely outcome of each decision option can be measured, or quantified, and the option which offers the 'best numbers' will be selected.

1.8 The outcome of a decision might be measured in:

(a) money terms - eg. revenue, costs, profits;
(b) units of output or work - eg. number of items produced or sold, quantities of stock, hours of work, number of employees or items of equipment;
(c) productivity or efficiency - ie. units of work produced per unit of input resource employed, such as units produced per manhour or units processed per machine per week.

1.9 Quantifiable problems can be resolved by mathematical techniques, to produce a quantifiable decision.

1.10 However, not all problems can be dealt with mathematically. Even with quantifiable problems, there will often be matters of doubt and uncertainty, where 'qualitative' factors will affect the outcome too. Qualitative factors include:

(a) risk; and
(b) human behaviour and attitudes.

1.11 Some simple examples might help to illustrate qualitative influences.

(a) A sales manager estimates that to launch a new product on to the market will cost £200,000 in development and marketing costs. Each product that is sold will earn a gross profit margin of £20, and so the company would need to sell 10,000 units to break even. He *thinks* that the company will be able to sell 12,000 units. A decision has to be made whether or not to launch the new product.

In quantitative terms the product is expected to make a net profit of (12,000 x £20) - £200,000 = £40,000, but only if the forecast of sales is correct. It could be wrong, and the product might make a loss, if sales fail to reach 10,000 units. Some *judgement* is needed about the risk element, in deciding whether or not to launch the product.

(b) An office manager has to decide whether to change the procedures in his office for handling routine transactions. His ideas for change would involve some re-grouping of staff, and some need for training with new computer software. He thinks the changes would improve the productivity of the office and enable it to handle more work each week. However, he suspects that his work force will resist the change, and will insist on alterations to his proposals, and create a hostile atmosphere in the office. Quantifiably, the decision should be in favour of change, but a qualitative factor that could change the decision is what the reaction of staff might be. Again, *judgement* is needed by the manager in his or her decision.

> The key point being made with these examples is that decisions *involving qualitative factors* call for the use of *judgement* by the manager.

1.12 *Information*
Decision makers need information to help them to reach a decision.

The decision is made easier if information is:	*The decision becomes more a matter of guesswork and judgement if information is:*
1. Accurate	1. Inaccurate
2. Complete	2. Incomplete
3. Available in time	3. Too late to help
4. Clear	4. Unclear
5. Concise and to the point	5. Rambling
6. Quantified	6. Qualitative
7. Is given to the person who makes the decision	7. Is given to someone other that the person making the decision - eg. the decision maker's boss - and is passed on in an altered, 'second hand' form.

1.13 The greater the preponderance of qualitative issues over quantitative issues, the more judgement will be needed in making decisions.

1.14 The writer on management theory, Herbert Simon, made a distinction between:

(a) programmed decisions; and
(b) non-programmed decisions.

1.15 *Programmed* decisions, as the name implies, are decisions of a *routine* nature or *quantitative* nature for which decision rules can be predetermined. Many operational decisions can be programmed and a computer used to make them, instead of a manager. Alternatively, programmed decisions can be entrusted to a fairly junior level of management.

1.16 *Non-programmed decisions* are required when a manager must use his judgement, and these exist:

    (a)   where decisions *could* be computerised, but are currently taken by managers or staff;

    (b)   where qualitative factors affect the decision.

Exercise

Can decision-making be an entirely rational process? In what ways is decision-making limited by inadequate information and by the style of management in an organisation?

Discussion points

With inadequate information, decision-making becomes a matter of guesswork and judgement. Inadequate information is caused by any one of the problems listed in paragraph 1.12.

The style of management will determine the way in which decisions are taken. A rational decision is a reasoned, logical decision. An autocratic, dictatorial leader is less likely to make entirely rational decisions about everything, because of his inability to digest enough facts and keep his eye on everything.

Subordinates of an autocratic manager, when required to make decisions, might find themselves unable to make rational decisions due to inadequate information, where the boss has 'sat on' the necessary information, and not made it available to his subordinates.

1.17 *Consequences*
Sometimes, the difference between making a good decision, an 'ordinary' middle-of-the road decision and a bad decision might not be important, in terms of its outcome or consequences. At other times, the beneficial consequences of a good decision, or the harmful consequences of a bad decision, can be enormous.

1.18 As you will imagine, decisions where the consequences could be significant should call for greater management skills

1.19 *Decision makers*
Decisions can be made either by one manager alone or by two or more people jointly, eg in committee.

1.20 Just who makes the decisions depends on organisation structure, and the extent to which authority is delegated within the organisation. We shall look at these issues more fully later on.

1.21 Discretion is the 'liberty of deciding as one thinks fit, absolutely or within limits.' (Concise Oxford Dictionary).

    1.   There is little or no room for discretion with programmed decisions.

    2.   The exercise of discretion in decision making can be associated with the use of judgement.

3. Discretion means freedom to make decisions as one thinks fit. Such freedom can only be exercised if the manager has the full authority to make decisions, without the need to ask a boss for approval, and without the chance that a boss might step in and alter or reverse the subordinate's decisions.

4. A significant motivating factor for managers is the right to exercise discretion - ie. to have authority - over a particular area of work.

Exercise

How important is intuition and judgement in management decision-making? Give reasons for your answer.

Discussion points

The importance of intuition and judgement is apparent in non-programmed decisions, but not in programmed decisions. This point is well covered in the early part of this chapter.

Intuition and judgement might also be needed where the decision *could* be programmed, but is not, due to inadequate information.

---

2. AUTHORITY, RESPONSIBILITY AND DELEGATION

2.1 *Organisational authority* refers to the scope and amount of discretion given to a person to make decisions, by virtue of the position he or she holds in the organisation.

The authority and power structure of an organisation defines:

(a) the part which each member of the organisation is expected to perform; and
(b) the relationship between the members;

so that their concerted efforts should be effective in achieving the purpose of the organisation.

2.2 Authority can be delegated. *Delegation of authority* occurs in an organisation where a superior gives to a subordinate the discretion to make decisions within a certain sphere of influence. This can only occur if the superior initially possesses the authority to delegate; a subordinate cannot be given organisational authority to make decisions unless it would otherwise be the superior's right to make those decisions.

2.3 Delegation of authority thus refers to the process by which a superior gives a subordinate the authority to carry out an aspect of the superior's job. Without delegation, a formal organisation could not exist.

2.4 *Responsibility* refers to the liability of a person to be called to account for his/her actions and results. A subordinate may have a responsibility for which he will be called to account by his superior; a board of directors may have a responsibility to its shareholders; and a government in a democracy will have a responsibility to the electorate.

6: DECISION MAKING: AUTHORITY, RESPONSIBILITY AND DELEGATION

Responsibility is therefore the obligation to do something; in an organisation, it is the duty of an official to carry out his assigned tasks.

2.5 *Unlike authority, responsibility cannot be delegated.* Where a supervisor delegates authority to his subordinate, he remains responsible for ensuring that the work gets done, albeit by the subordinate rather than by himself personally. The superior will exact responsibility from the subordinate for the authority delegated but he will remain responsible himself too.

2.6 With responsibility, we must associate *accountability*. A manager is accountable to his superiors in the organisation for his actions and he is obliged to report to his superior how well he has exercised his responsibility and the use of the authority delegated to him.

2.7 The command structure of authority may be shown by an organisation chart, or may be documented in schedules or manuals. It may be easily appreciated that authority, responsibility and delegation are critical aspects of an organisation structure, and are significant factors in determining the efficiency with which an organisation operates. It has been suggested that the main causes of dissension and stress in day-to-day operations of an organisation are weaknesses in the organisation structure.

2.8 L F Urwick developed a number of the principles of good organisation. These included:

   (a) the principle of *specialisation:* as far as possible, each individual should perform one function only, in which he can be a specialist;

   (b) the principle of *authority:* there should be clear lines of authority (or chains or command) from the top of an organisation down to every individual working in it;

   (c) the principle of *definition:* the duties, authority and responsibility of each position and its relationships with other positions, should be defined in writing and made known to everyone concerned;

   (d) the principle of *correspondence:* authority should match responsibility;

   (e) the principle of *span of control:* managers should not control more than 5 or 6 subordinates if they have interlocking responsibilities.

2.9 If an organisation is to function as a co-operative system of individuals, some people must have authority or power over others. Authority and power flow downward through the formal organisation.

   (a) Authority is the right to do something, ie in an organisation it is the right of a manager to require a subordinate to do something in order to achieve the goals of the organisation. Managerial authority thus consists of:

      (i)   making decisions within the scope of one's own managerial authority;
      (ii)   assigning tasks to subordinates;
      (iii) expecting and requiring satisfactory performance of these tasks from subordinates.

   (b) Power is distinct from authority, but is often associated with it. Whereas authority is the right to do something, power is the ability to do it.

2.10 Three aspects of authority developed by Hicks and Gullet (*'Management'*) are as follows.

(a) *Responsibility and accountability* are coupled with managerial authority. When a manager is given the authority to do something, it is automatically presupposed that he has the ability to do it, the facilities that he needs and that the desired results will be achieved.

The manager is responsible for the actual results achieved, and he is held *accountable* because information about his achievements will be fed back to his superiors, and they can then call him to account to explain his performance.

(b) *Authority is subjective.* Amitai Etzioni made a study of authority and motivation in differing environments. He found that the way in which authority and power are exercised will differ according to the environment, relationships and type of subordinates. Thus the way a prison warder, or even a shopfloor supervisor, exercises authority to get subordinates to do what he wants will be different from the way in which the director of a public company or the managing director of an audit firm will exercise theirs. It will differ again in the case of the captain of the rugby team, or a parish priest. In general, at the bottom end of the management hierarchy, authority must be exercised with more coercion whilst at the top end of the hierarchy, authority is more discreet and immediate subordinates more self-motivated.

(c) *Sources of authority.* The authority of a manager might come from one or more sources.

   (i) *Top down authority* refers to the authority conferred on a *manager* because of the position he holds in the organisation's hierarchy and the extent to which authority has been delegated. It is the official authority 'traditionally' associated with management, which goes down the scalar chain. In most organisations, top down authority goes hand-in-hand with departmentalisation and the division of work, so that a senior manager in department A cannot tell a junior manager in department B what to do, because his authority does not cross department or sectional boundaries.

   (ii) *Bottom up authority* refers to the authority conferred on a *leader* from the people at lower levels in the organisation. Elected leaders, such as politicians and many trade union officials, have such authority, which they will be expected to exercise in the interests of the electors/union members.

   (iii) *Rank.* In some organisations such as the armed forces, rank is a clear expression of authority, and orders gain credibility because they come from someone of higher rank.

   (iv) *Personal authority or charisma.* Some managers acquire authority through their personal charisma, and as a consequence are capable of influencing the behaviour of others.

   (v) *Tradition.* Some individuals acquire authority by tradition. In old established family firms, the elder members of the family might continue to be obeyed and held in respect, even after they have officially retired.

3.   DELEGATION OF AUTHORITY

3.1   It is generally recognised that in any large complex organisation, management must delegate some authority because:

(a)   there are physical and mental limitations to the work load of any individual or group in authority;

(b)   routine or less important decisions are therefore passed 'down the line' to subordinates, and the superior is free to concentrate on the more important aspects of the work (eg planning);

(c)   the increasing size and complexity of organisations calls for *specialisation*, both managerial and technical. This is the *principle of division of work*.

3.2   However, by delegating authority to subordinates, the superior takes on the extra tasks of calling the subordinates to account for their decisions and performance, and also of co-ordinating the efforts of different subordinates.

3.3   To be truly effective, the process of delegation should consist of four stages:

(a)   the expected performance levels (the expected results) of the subordinate should be clearly specified (ie determine the required results). These should be fully understood and accepted by the subordinate;

(b)   tasks should be assigned to the subordinate who should agree to do them;

(c)   resources should be allocated to the subordinate to enable him to carry out his tasks at the expected level of performance, and authority should be delegated to enable the subordinate to do this job;

(d)   responsibility should be exacted from the subordinate by the superior for results obtained (because ultimate responsibility remains with the superior).

3.4   In addition:

(a)   the subordinate's ability and experience must be borne in mind when allocating tasks and responsibilities, since it is highly damaging to allocate tasks beyond a subordinate's capabilities;

(b)   frequent contact must be maintained between the boss and subordinate to review the progress made and to discuss constructive criticism.

3.5   A subordinate may have written or unwritten authority to do his job. Written authority is preferable because it removes the room for doubt and argument. Authority may also be general or specific.

(a)   It is general if the subordinate is given authority to make any decisions with regard to a certain (specified) area of the operations - ie he is put in charge.

(b) It is specific if the subordinate has authority to make certain limited and identified decisions within that area of operations. General authority gives the subordinate greater discretion and flexibility.

Principles of delegation

3.6 There are certain principles of delegation, recommended by classical theorists, and many of them are still relevant in the context of formal organisation structure. These are discussed in the following paragraphs.

3.7 Authority (and power) and responsibility (and accountability) must be properly balanced within an organisation; there must be parity between authority and responsibility:

(a) A manager who is not held accountable for any of his authority or power may well exercise his authority in a capricious way. It is a common human trait to wish to maximise power and minimise accountability.

(b) A manager who is held accountable for aspects of performance which he has no power or authority to control is in an impossible position.

3.8 As stated previously, responsibility cannot be delegated. A subordinate should be responsible to his superior for achievements with delegated authority, but the superior in his turn remains responsible to his own boss for the achievements of his subordinates.

3.9 There should be delegation of authority according to the results required, ie a subordinate must be given sufficient authority to do all that is expected of him.

3.10 Once authority has been delegated, a superior should not expect his subordinate to refer decisions up the chain of command to him for confirmation (or ratification) provided that the decision is within the subordinate's scope of delegated authority.

3.11 There must be no doubts about the boundaries of authority because where doubts exist, decision-making will be weak, confused and possibly contradictory (if boundaries of authority overlap). Classical theorists such as Fayol therefore argued that the scalar chain of command must be clearly specified in terms of who holds what authority and who is accountable to whom and for what. Information flow does not have to be restricted to passing up and down the scalar chain, but authority should. 'The line of authority is the route followed - via every link in the chain - by all communications which start from or go to the ultimate authority. This path is dictated both by the need for some transmission and by the principle of unity of command, but it is not always the swiftest. It is even at times disastrously lengthy in large concerns, notably in governmental ones.' (Fayol *General and Industrial Administration*).

3.12 When authority is delegated, the relationship between subordinate and superior is critically important. Drucker has argued that although authority is passed down to subordinates, the relationship between subordinates and superiors, and their responsibilities, have three dimensions:

(a)   Every manager has the task of contributing towards what his superior's section must do to achieve its objectives.

(b)   Every manager has a responsibility towards the organisation as a whole, and must define the activities of his own unit so as to contribute towards achieving the organisation's objectives.

(c)   Every manager has a responsibility towards his subordinates (ie to make sure they know what is expected of them, to help them set their own objectives, to help them attain their objectives, to offer counsel and advice etc).

'The vision of a manager should always be upward - towards the enterprise as a whole. But his responsibility runs downwards as well, to the managers on his team'. (Drucker)

3.13 It is an interesting question to ask why, in a formal organisation built up in the 'classical' hierarchical manner, there should be so many levels of management. After all, the purpose of management is to see that the work of the organisation gets done, and the only managers who supervise 'actual work' directly are the 'front-line' or 'first-line' supervisors (eg 'foremen' in manufacturing industries).

3.14 If a first-line supervisor has a superior, the work of the superior must derive from the supervisor. Drucker noted that 'the managers on the firing line have the basic management jobs - the ones on whose performance everything else ultimately rests. Seen this way, the jobs of higher management are derivative, are, in the last analysis, aimed at helping the firing line manager do his job. Viewed structurally and organically, it is the firing line manager in whom all authority and responsibility centre; only what he cannot do himself passes up to higher management'.

3.15 Yet authority is passed down or delegated through the formal organisation; it is not passed up from supervisors to senior managers. Although the front-line supervisor manages the real work, the authority to do so comes from higher up.

(a)   A front-line supervisor only has authority over his part of the work of the organisation and cannot issue instructions to another part. For example, the manager of the Oldham branch of a clearing bank cannot issue instructions to employees in the Huddersfield branch. Senior managers are required to co-ordinate the work of subordinates by having authority over a wider area of work, right up to the chief executive and board of directors.

(b)   Front-line supervisors make short-term day-to-day decisions and have no time for longer-term plans and decisions. Longer-term decisions are kept within the authority of more senior managers.

'Authority and responsibility should always be task-focused. This applies all the way up the management hierarchy to the chief executive job itself'. (Drucker)

6: DECISION MAKING: AUTHORITY, RESPONSIBILITY AND DELEGATION

The relationship between organisation structure and delegation

3.16 To decide how authority and responsibility should be delegated, it is necessary:

(a) first of all, to decide what kind of structure of jobs (and departments) the organisation needs;

(b) and only then to decide how authority should be delegated within this structure.

In other words, the way in which authority should be delegated depends very much on how the organisation's tasks are analysed.

3.17 To decide what structure of jobs is needed, Drucker has suggested the need for three analyses to be made.

(a) An *activities analysis*. This is an analysis of what the major activities carried out by the organisation should be. A typical manufacturing company will have functional activities such as 'manufacturing' 'engineering' and 'sales', but not every manufacturing company may need these functional divisions, and some may need to emphasise other functions as well. As an example, Drucker quoted the case of Crown-Zellerbach, a big West-Coast pulp and paper manufacturer, which found that long-range forest management was such an important activity that it had to be established as a separate department, because otherwise it would not be given the attention its importance warranted.

(b) A *decision analysis*. This analyses the kind of decisions to be made in an organisation, and the activities they affect. The analysis will help the management organiser to determine which managers should make the decisions, and who else should be informed.

Drucker itemised four characteristics of the nature of decisions.

(i) *The degree of futurity in the decision.* For how long in the future does the decision affect the business, and how quickly can the decision be reversed if it is later found to be a bad one? Decisions which can be reversed quickly should be taken by relatively junior management.

(ii) *The impact of the decision on other departments or functions, or on the business as a whole.* If a decision affects only one function (eg one section in manufacturing) it can be taken by fairly junior management. If it affects more than one function, the decision must be taken by a manager senior enough to provide consultation with and co-operation with the other functions affected by the business. For example, if the warehousing department is considering a reduction in finished goods stocks, this will affect production (less output needed) and sales (there may be inadequate stock levels to meet customer demand without a waiting list). The decision would need to be made at a very senior level of management (possibly Chief Executive level).

(iii) *The number of qualitative factors in the decision.* Qualitative factors call for the exercise of managerial judgement, and decisions involving value considerations should be taken, or at least reviewed, at a higher management level.

(iv) Whether the decision is regular and periodic, or rare. For recurrent decisions, a general rule is required. This might be decided by higher management. Then, when the rule is subsequently applied in specific cases, more junior management should be given the authority for its application.

Drucker concluded about decision analysis that: 'A decision should always be made at lowest level and as close to the scene of action as possible....Analysing the foreseeable decisions...shows both what structure of top management the enterprise needs and what authority and responsibility different levels of operating management should have'.

(c) A *relations analysis*. This considers the relationships between a manager in charge of an activity and other managers with whom he will have to work. These relationships are not only downwards (with subordinates) but also upwards (with superiors) and sideways (with managers of different activities). 'Analysing relations is not only indispensable to the decision of what kind of a structure is needed. It is also necessary to make the vital decision how the structure should be manned. Indeed, only an analysis of the relations in a job makes possible intelligent and successful staffing'.

Problems of delegation

3.18 In practice many managers are reluctant to delegate and attempt to do many routine matters themselves in addition to their more important duties. Some common reasons for this are listed below.

(a) A manager may feel that his subordinate will carry out the work badly, and that he himself will ultimately be held responsible for his subordinate's errors.

(b) Some managers believe that they would lose touch with their department (both work-load and staff) unless they retain some routine tasks.

(c) Seniors are often unwilling to admit that subordinates have developed to the extent that they could perform some of the manager's duties.

3.19 Handy writes of a 'trust-control dilemma' in a superior-subordinate relationship, in which the sum of trust + control is a constant amount; ie

$$T + C = Y$$

where T = the trust the superior has in the subordinate, and the trust which the subordinate feels the superior has in him;

C = the degree of control exercised by the superior over the subordinate;

Y = a constant, unchanging value;

Any increase in C leads to an equal decrease in T, ie if the superior retains more 'control' or authority, the subordinate will immediately recognise that he is being trusted less. If the superior wishes to show more trust in the subordinate, he can only do so by reducing C, ie by delegating more authority.

3.20 To overcome the reluctance of managers to delegate, it is necessary to:

(a) provide a system of selecting subordinates who will be capable of handling delegated authority in a responsible way. If subordinates are of the right 'quality', superiors will be prepared to trust them more;

(b) have a system of open communications, in which the superior and subordinates freely interchange ideas and information. If the subordinate is given all the information he needs to do his job, and if the superior is aware of what the subordinate is doing:

(i) the subordinate will make better-informed decisions;
(ii) the superior will not 'panic' because he does not know what is going on.

Although open lines of communication are important, they should not be used by the superior to command the subordinate in a matter where authority has been delegated to the subordinate; in other words, communication links must not be used by superiors as a means of reclaiming authority;

(c) ensure that a system of control is established. Superiors are reluctant to delegate authority because they retain absolute responsibility for the performance of their subordinates. If an efficient control system is in operation, responsibility and accountability will be monitored at all levels of the management hierarchy, and the 'dangers' of relinquishing authority and control to subordinates are significantly lessened;

(d) reward effective delegation by superiors and the efficient assumption of authority by subordinates. Rewards may be given in terms of pay, promotion, status, official approval etc.

4. POOLED AUTHORITY

4.1 Further problems with delegation occur when:

(a) subordinates who must co-ordinate their activities cannot agree about how things should be done; or
(b) the collective authority of subordinates may be required to make a decision.

4.2 Disagreements will inevitably occur within any formal organisation. The general rule is that problems which cannot be solved at lower levels are referred upward through the organisation structure until the problem reaches an official with enough authority and power to solve the problem. The channel for appeals would be described by an organisation chart:

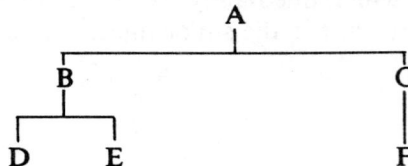

A disagreement between D and E could be referred to B; whereas a disagreement between D and F would need to be settled either by B and C together (using their pooled authority) or by appealing up the scalar chain to A.

4.3 Some organisations may have a special appeals procedure, with problems or grievances referred to an independent arbitrator.

4.4 Pooled authority (or 'splintered' authority) refers to a situation in which two subordinates join together and use their collective authority to make a decision, instead of referring the matter up the chain of command to a superior. In the preceding 'organisation chain' B and C might pool their authority to make a decision affecting their common area of work, or affecting subordinates D, E and F, instead of referring their problem to A. Management conferences are an example of attempts to exchange ideas and reach collective decisions on the basis of pooled authority.

5. COMMITTEES

5.1 Committees might be used within an organisation as a means of either delegating authority or pooling authority. The disadvantages and advantages of committees extend beyond considerations of authority and responsibility and they are described here in full.

Within an organisation, committees can consist entirely of executives (eg. board meetings, budget approvals, project teams, feasibility studies). Alternatively, committees can be an instrument of joint consultation between employers and employees (eg. works councils, joint productivity groups, staff advisory councils).

5.2 Committees may be classified according to the power they exercise, distinguishing between those having the power to bind the parent body and those without such power.

It is also important to consider the function and duration of committees so that the following categories may be defined:

(a) executive committees which have the power to govern or administer. It can be argued that the board of directors of a limited company is itself a 'committee' appointed by the shareholders, to the extent that it governs or administers;

(b) standing committees which are formed for a particular purpose on a permanent basis. Their role is to deal with routine business delegated to them at weekly or monthly meetings;

(c) ad hoc committees are formed to complete a particular task. It can be described as a fact-finding or special committee which is short lived and having achieved its purpose, reports back to the parent body and then ceases to exist;

(d) sub-committees may be appointed by committees to relieve the parent committee of some of its routine work;

(e) joint committees may be formed to co-ordinate the activities of two or more committees, eg. representatives from employers and employees may meet in a Joint Consultative committee. this kind of committee can either be permanent or appointed for a special purpose.

5.3 A psychologist, Janis, has recognised that a group develops a strong feeling of 'we-ness' and it becomes vulnerable to a pattern of behaviour known as 'group think'. This happens as the outcome of group pressure and impedes the official exertion of one's mental processes.

5.4   In order to overcome these difficulties, it has been suggested that members of committees should be encouraged to evaluate decisions critically. The leader should always conduct the meeting impartially and avoid stating his preferences and objections. When the time comes to take a decision, one member should take the part of 'devil's advocate' challenging the majority viewpoint.

5.5   The potential advantages of committees are as follows:

(a)   consolidation of power and authority: whereas an individual may not have sufficient authority to make a decision himself, the pooled authority of a committee may be sufficient to enable the decision to be made. A committee may be referred to in this type of instance as a plural executive. Examples of a plural executive include a board of directors or the Cabinet of the government, which are policy-making and policy-execution committees;

(b)   blurring responsibility: when a committee makes a decision, no individual will be held responsible for the consequences of the decision. This is both an advantage and a disadvantage of committee decisions;

(c)   creating new ideas: group creativity may be achieved by a 'brainstorming committee' or 'think tank';

(d)   they are an excellent means of communication: for example:

    (i)   to exchange ideas of a wide number of interests before a decision affecting the organisation is taken;
    (ii)   to inform managers about policies, plans, actual results etc;

(e)   they are democratic, because they allow for greater participation in the decision-making process;

(f)   combining abilities: committees enable the differing skills of its various members to be brought together to deal with a problem. In theory, the quality of committee decisions should be of a high standard;

(g)   co-ordination: they should enable the maximum co-ordination of all parties involved in a decision to be achieved;

(h)   advisory capacity: a committee is frequently used to offer advice to a decision-maker;

(i)   representative: they enable all relevant interests to be involved int he decision-making process and they bring together the specialised knowledge of working people into a working combination;

(j)   through participation, they may improve the motivation of committee members (and even of their subordinates), and provide managers with wider experience to help with their development;

(k)   a committee may be set up by a board of directors to do 'spade work' and avoid detailed discussions at board meetings.

5.6 The disadvantages of committees may be summarised as follows:

(a) they are apt to be too large for constructive action, since the time taken by a committee · to resolve a problem tends to be in direct proportion to its size.

(b) committees are time consuming and expensive;

(c) delays may occur in the work cycle if matters of a routine nature are entrusted to committees; committees must not be given responsibilities which they would carry out inefficiently;

(d) operations of the enterprise may be jeopardised by the frequent attendance of executives at meetings, and by distracting them from their real duties;

(e) incorrect or ineffective decisions may be made, due to the fact that members of a committee are unfamiliar with the deeper aspects of issues under discussion. Occasionally, there may be a total failure to reach any decision at all;

(f) certain members may be apathetic, due to pressure of work or disinterest, resulting in superficial action;

(g) since there is no individual responsibility for decisions, this might invite compromise instead of clear-cut decisions, besides weakening individual responsibility throughout the organisation. Moreover, members may thereby be enabled to avoid direct responsibility for poor results arising from decisions taken in committee. Weak management an hide behind committee decisions;

(h) committees lack conscience;

(i) proceedings may be dominated by outspoken or aggressive members, thus unduly influencing decisions and subsequent action, perhaps adversely, ie. there may be ; 'tyranny' by a minority.

6. CENTRALISATION OR DECENTRALISATION

6.1 Committees are not used as the main method of delegating authority, and authority is more typically delegated down a formal management hierarchy or chain of command. *Centralisation* and *decentralisation* refer to the degree to which authority is delegated in an organisation. The terms are thereby used to describe the level at which decisions are taken in the management hierarchy.

6.2 Complete centralisation would mean that no authority at all was exercised by subordinates; complete decentralisation would mean that *all* authority was exercised by subordinates (ie there would be no co-ordination of subordinates). It is doubtful whether any organisation approaches to either of these extremes.

In the following paragraphs, we shall use the term 'centralisation' to mean a greater degree of central control, and 'decentralisation' to mean a greater degree of delegated authority.

6: DECISION MAKING: AUTHORITY, RESPONSIBILITY AND DELEGATION

The advantages of centralisation

6.3 The advantages of centralisation are as follows.

(a) Senior management can exercise greater control over the activities of the organisation and co-ordinate their subordinates or sub-units more easily.

(b) With central control, procedures can be standardised throughout the organisation.

(c) Senior managers can make decisions from the point of view of the organisation as a whole, whereas subordinates would tend to make decisions from the point of view of their own department or section. Sub-optimality occurs when one department makes a decision which appears to be a good one, from the departmental point of view, but which is actually damaging to the organisation as a whole. With centralisation, sub-optimality should not occur, but with decentralisation it would be a serious threat to the efficiency of the organisation.

(d) Centralised control enables an organisation to maintain a balance between different functions or departments. For example, if a company has only a limited amount of funds available to spend over the next few years, centralised management would be able to take a balanced view of how the funds should be shared out between production, marketing, research and development, motor vehicles, other fixed asset purchases in different departments etc.

(e) Senior managers ought to be more experienced and skilful in making decisions. In theory at least, centralised decisions by senior men should be better in 'quality' than decentralised decisions by less experienced subordinates. (Note: this raises the issues of trust and the capabilities of subordinates, which have already been discussed in this chapter.)

(f) Centralised management will often be cheaper, in terms of managerial overheads. When authority is delegated, there is often a duplication of management effort (and a corresponding increase in staff numbers) at lower levels of hierarchy. To avoid such costs of duplication some specialised departments (eg data processing, the legal department) may remain centralised.

(g) In times of crisis, the organisation may need strong leadership by a central group of senior managers.

The advantages of decentralisation (delegation)

6.4 Some delegation is necessary in all large organisations because of the limitations to the physical and mental capacity of senior managers. A greater degree of decentralisation, ie over and above the 'minimum' which is essential, has the following advantages.

(a) It reduces the stress and burdens of senior management.

(b) It provides subordinates with greater job satisfaction by giving them more say in decision-making which affects their work. Such participation in decisions, leading to job satisfaction, might motivate the subordinates to work harder and more efficiently and effectively, to achieve the goals of the organisation.

(c) Subordinates may have a better knowledge of 'local' conditions affecting their area of work. With the benefits of such knowledge, they should be capable of more informed, well-judged management. Unfortunately, local managers often think in the short term, whereas senior managers think in the longer term. A subordinate might therefore make a well-informed decision to win a short-term advantage when a different decision would have been preferable in the longer-term view.

(d) Delegation should allow greater flexibility, a quicker response to changing conditions, and speedier decision-making. If problems do not have to be referred up a scalar chain of command to senior managers for a decision, decision-making will be quicker. Since decisions are quicker, they are also more adaptable, and easier to change in the light of unforeseen circumstances which may arise.

(e) By allowing delegated authority to subordinates, management at middle and junior levels are 'groomed' for eventual senior management positions, because they are given the necessary experience of decision-making. Delegation is therefore important for management development.

(f) By establishing appropriate sub-units or profit centres to which authority is delegated, the system of control within the organisation might actually be improved. Targets for performance by each profit centre can be established, actual results monitored against targets and control action taken by appropriate subordinates with the necessary authority; the subordinates would then be held accountable and responsible for their results, and areas of efficiency or inefficiency within the organisation would be more easily identified and remedied.

Summary
*Arguments in favour of centralisation
and decentralisation*

Pro centralisation

1. Decisions are made at one point, and so easier to co-ordinate.

2. Senior managers in an organisation can take a wider view of problems and consequences.

3. Senior management can keep a proper balance between different departments or functions - eg. by deciding on the resources to allocate to each.

4. Possibly cheaper, by reducing number of managers needed and so lower cost of overheads.

5. Crisis decisions are best taken at the centre.

Pro decentralisation

1. Avoids overburdening top managers.

2. Improvers motivation of more junior managers.

3. Helps junior managers to develop and the process of transition from functional to general management.

4. Greater speed of decision making, and response to changing events.

5. Greater awareness of local problems by decision makers Geographically dispersed organisations should often be decentralised on a regional/area basis.

6. Separate spheres of responsibility can be identified, and control systems set up for junior management, and so controls, performance measurement and accountability are better.

CASE STUDY

Your fellow manager, John Birch, finds that he seems to work day and night and the strain is beginning to tell. You have concluded that John does not delegate and is doing everyone's job as well as his own.

What guidance would you offer to John about when he should and should not delegate?

Discussion

John should be taught to appreciate that delegation:

(a)   saves any given individual or group in authority from the stress and strain that he is experiencing. There are physical and mental limitations to the workload that people are capable of shouldering;

(b)   passes routine or less important decisions down the line to subordinates, leaving the superior free to concentrate on the more important aspects of his work (eg. planning), which only he may be competent to undertake. The superior's time is, after all, more costly to the organisation;

(c)   recognises that some specialisation, both managerial and technical, will be required as the organisation grows in size and complexity. Every individual can not be expected to be a specialist in every field;

(d)   allows subordinates to develop their skills, and to enrich their jobs by exercising greater responsibility. This will not only be useful in developing future generations of managers, but may have immediate effects in the morale and motivation of staff;

(e)   lets subordinates feel that they are trusted, and that their competence is recognised. This may again improve morale, job satisfaction, and relationships between subordinate and superior.

John should be advised, in particular instances where he might be able to delegate, to consider:

(a)   whether he requires the *acceptance* of subordinates - for morale, relationships, ease of implementation of the decision etc. If so, he would be advised at least to consult his subordinates, if acceptance is the primary need and the decision itself largely routine;

(b)   whether the *quality* of the decision is most important, and acceptance less so. Many financial decisions may be of this type and should be retained by the superior. If acceptance and quality are equally important, eg. for changes in work methods or the introduction of new technology, consultation may be advisable;

(c)   whether the *expertise or experience* of subordinates is relevant or necessary to the task or decision. If John is required to perform a task which is not within his own specialised knowledge, he should delegate to the appropriate person;

(d)   whether, being as objective as possible, he feels he can *trust* in the competence and reliability of his subordinates. As Handy notes, there is bound to be a 'trust/control dilemma' - and since John is accountable for the area of his authority, he should not delegate if he *genuinely* lacks confidence in his team;

(e) whether the task or decision requires tact and confidentiality, or, on the other hand, maximum exposure and assimilation by employees. Disciplinary action, for example, should not be delegated (ie. to a peer of the individual being reprimanded), whereas tasks involving new procedures (to which employees will have to get accustomed) may be delegated as soon as possible.

TEST YOUR KNOWLEDGE

(The numbers in brackets refer to paragraphs in this chapter)

1. Problems vary according to several factors. What are these factors? (1.2)

2. What are programmed decisions? (1.15)

3. Define discretion. What significance does discretion have for management decisions? (1.21)

4. Define authority, delegation, responsibility and accountability. (2.1, 2.2, 2.4, 2.6)

5. Drucker suggested that there are four characteristics of decisions which should influence the seniority or status of manager who should make the decisions. What are these four characteristics? (3.17)

6. How do appeal structures and pooled authority tackle the problem of delegating authority? (4.3, 4.4)

7. Why do organisations make use of committees? (5.5)

8. List the advantages of (a) centralisation and (b) decentralisation. (6.3,6.4)

9. What are the characteristics of a challenging management job?

Discussion point

Question 9
This question cannot be fully answered by the material in this chapter. A challenging management job must:

(a) provide a target or challenge for achievement;
(b) hold the job holder accountable for non-achievement;
(c) provide a personal challenge to the job holder;
(d) offer rewards for achievement.

The key factor in creating a challenge, however, is the ability to exercise *discretion*, and this will be a feature of the extent to which authority has been delegated within the organisation.

Chapter 7

DEGREES OF DELEGATION AND DECENTRALISATION

This chapter covers the following topics:

1. Scalar chain
2. Chain of command
3. Span of control
4. Federal and functional decentralisation
5. The contingency theory of delegation
6. Formal and informal delegation
7. Socio-technical systems view
8. Power and influence
9. Managers taking decisions

Purpose of this chapter

To consider how much delegation or decentralisation there should ideally be in any organisation.

To consider other influences on decision-making, apart from authority and 'position power', and to suggest that for non-programmed decisions, effective decision-making will be based on consensus.

1. SCALAR CHAIN

1. The scalar chain is the term used to describe the organisation's management hierarchy, ie the chain of superiors from lowest to highest rank. Formal communication is up and down the lines of authority, eg E to D to C to B to A in the diagram below. If, however, communication between different branches of the chain is necessary (eg D to H) the use of a 'gang plank' of horizontal communication saves time and is likely to be more accurate, as long as superiors know that such communication is taking place.

7: DEGREES OF DELEGATION AND DECENTRALISATION

Scalar chains:

ABCDE

ABJL

ABJM

AFGHI

AFKN

AFKOP

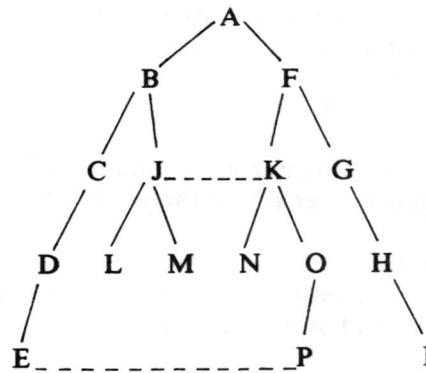

Gang planks:

CG

EP

1.2 Fayol criticised government departments for making insufficient use of the *gang plank*. By this, he means that the subordinates refer too many problems up the scalar chain to their boss because the problem involves a person in another section or department. Instead, the subordinate could contact the other person directly and ask for a joint solution to the problem. In the diagram here, if C has a problem with affects G, instead of referring it up to B (who might then refer it to A) C could cross the 'gang plank' - communicate horizontally - with G. The problem might then be solved jointly by C and G, provided that B and F are aware that this is happening.

2. CHAIN OF COMMAND

2.1 A chain of command in an organisation is a line of authority from the top of the management hierarchy down to employees at the very bottom. An organisation has many such 'scalar' chains of authority and command, but all of them originate at the topmost management authority which in a company is the board of directors. Managers at different levels in the hierarchy are all links in a chain of command.

2.2 One important problem for efficient and effective management is establishing the most suitable number of links in the chains of command.

(a) Townsend (*'Up the Organisation'*) estimated that the addition of each extra level of management into the hierarchy, adding one more link in the chain of command, reduces the effectiveness of communication within the organisation by about 25%.

Peter Drucker cites the Roman Catholic Church as a classic example of an organisation with a short chain of command. From Pope down to parish priest there is only one intermediary layer of management, the Bishops, so that a papal edict comes down to parish priests in just one step.

(b) In the years before World War II, the average churchgoer or factory hand was poorly educated and dependent on orders from above to know what to do. In such an environment it is relatively easy for a superior to give instructions and use a dictatorial manner, perhaps with coercion and threats, to win obedience.

The post-war years brought drastic changes: organisations are bigger and more complex, and employees are both better educated and also more protected from coercion by managers. Getting employees to do what is required of them is not easy in a diverse, complex business environment, where greater controls are necessary to protect investments. As a consequence, more managers have been introduced into organisations and chains of command have grown longer.

2.3 There might be a tendency for chains of command within a single organisation to get longer as the organisation grows older, and the length of the chains of command is a function of:

(a) the size of the organisation;
(b) the type and complexity of the products it makes or services it provides;
(c) the diversity of its products and services;
(d) its geographical spread;
(e) the number and complexity of controls required;
(f) the type of people it employs.

2.4 No rules have been (or can be) laid down for how chains of command should be structured, but a general observation is that chains of command should be kept as short as possible, consistent with sound management, and the factors in paragraph 2.3 (a) to (f) above.

(a) Management structure should be organised for business performance - converting all the business activities into 'drive'. Managers should fulfil valuable operational needs in a simple environment, and organisations should avoid a red-tape bureaucracy working on a mountain of paper or in a maze of procedures.

(b) Management structure should be organised so as to direct the organisation's efforts away from bad performance. Bad news should be communicated quickly so that problems can be rectified. Two damning indictments of long chains of command are:

(i) situations where trade unions can react to events much more quickly than a cumbersome slow-moving management;
(ii) situations where waste is encouraged because sectional managers have to spent up their full budgeted expenditure allocations before the year end, otherwise funds will be withdrawn and next year's budget cut.

Long chains of command create a tendency towards bad performance in both types of situation described.

(c) Short chains of command help managers to develop. Rosemary Stewart cited examples from nationalised industries as typical illustrations. Prior to nationalisation of the electricity industry, a power station manager reported to his managing director and saw him regularly: this direct and frequent contact gave the power station manager valuable insights into management problems and thinking 'at the top' which helped his own development as a manager. Similar direct relationships existed in the gas companies. After nationalisation, the direct contacts were replaced by tiers of intermediaries and specialists, so that top management became more remote, and a method of developing managers was lost.

(d) The chain of command and management structure should enable the organisation to train tomorrow's managers. Drucker has cited cases of well-known companies with as many as twelve links in the chain of command, which is far too excessive. Such a long chain makes promotion from the bottom to the top virtually impossible. To add to the problem, specialisation of skills in some management jobs (eg accountancy management) removes flexibility of appointments and restricts promotion prospects.

(i) As a consequence, many large companies turn divisions into 'independent' subsidiary and sub-subsidiary companies, to ensure that its bright young managers with potential to rise to senior positions are given a more direct experience of running a company (albeit a subsidiary) from an early stage in their career. Within their subsidiary, the chain of command is short, and general management experience more easily gained.

(ii) If large companies do not split their operations between subsidiary companies in this way, they will run the risk of losing their brightest management talents, because managers will be frustrated by delays waiting from promotion, and will instead move to smaller companies to gain their experience and make their mark more quickly.

2.5 In conclusion, chains of command should:

(a) reflect the business organisation, its environment, products, employees, diversity, spread and controls;
(b) be as short as possible consistent with efficiency and effectiveness;
(c) be short enough to provide a training ground for developing managers.

3. SPAN OF CONTROL

3.1 The 'span-of-control' or 'span-of-management' refers to the number of subordinates working to the superior official. In other words, if a manager has five subordinates, the span of control is 5.

3.2 Various writers of the classical school, such as Fayol, Graicunas and Urwick, argued that the managerial span of control should be limited to between 3 and 6. Their arguments were based on the twin beliefs that:

(a) there should be tight managerial control from the top of the organisation; and
(b) there are physical and mental limitations to any single manager's ability to control people and activities.

3.3 To ensure effective control, the number of subordinates and tasks over which a manager has supervisory responsibilities should therefore be restricted to what is physically and mentally possible. A narrow span of control offers:

(a) tight control and close supervision; better co-ordination of subordinates' activities;
(b) time to think and plan; managers are not burdened with too many day to day problems;
(c) reduced delegation; a manager can do more of his work himself;
(d) better communication with subordinates, who are sufficiently small in number to allow this to occur.

3.4 The French writer V A Graicunas (1937) devised a formula to show how the number of possible relationships between members of an organisation increases geometrically proportion to the number of members:

$$N = (2^{n-1} + (n-1))$$

Where N is the total number of possible relationships and n is the number of subordinates.

The greater the number of subordinates becomes, the supervisor finds himself managing a mushrooming number of organisational relationships (where n = 1, N = 1, and where n = 7, N = 490). This exploding complexity of larger and larger units must impose some limitations on the capabilities of management, ie the span of control is limited by the number of inter-relationships that one person can manage.

3.5 Urwick suggested a slightly different approach, in response to a report by James Worthy in 1950 that the policy of the American Sear Roebuck company was to have as wide a span of control as possible between stores managers and their subordinates, who were merchandising managers. A wide span of control forced stores managers to delegate authority, and the consequences, Worthy claimed, were improved morale and greater efficiency of merchandising management.

Urwick's counter-argument was that a wide span of control had been possible in this example of the American Sears Roebuck company because the work of the merchandising managers did not interlock, therefore the need for co-ordination and integration was not present. This reduced the burdens of supervision and made a wider span of control feasible. Urwick concluded that the maximum management span of control should be 6, when the work of subordinates interlocks.

3.6 A wide span of control offers:

(a) a greater decision-making authority for subordinates;
(b) fewer supervisory costs;
(c) less control, but perhaps greater motivation though job satisfaction.

Tall and flat organisations

3.7 The span of control concept has implications for the 'shape' of an organisation. A tall organisation is one which, in relation to its size, has a large number of management hierarchies, whereas a flat organisation is one which, in relation to its size, has a smaller number of hierarchical levels. A tall organisation implies a narrow span of control, and a flat organisation implies a wide span of control.

3.8 Some classical theorists accepted that a tall organisation structure is inefficient, because:

(a) it increases overhead costs;

(b) it creates extra communication problems, since top management is more remote from the 'actual work' done at the bottom end of the organisation, and information tends to get distorted or blocked on its way up or down through the organisation hierarchy;

(c) management responsibilities tend to overlap and become confused as the size of the management structure gets larger. Different sections or departments may seek authority over the same 'territory' of operations, and superiors may find it difficult to delegate sufficient authority to satisfy subordinates;

(d) the same work passes through too many hands;

(e) planning is more difficult because it must be organised at more levels in the organisation.

3.9 Behavioural theorists add that tall structures impose rigid supervision and control and therefore block initiative and ruin the motivation of subordinates.

3.10 Nevertheless, not all researchers favour flat organisation structures, and it can be argued that if work is organised on the basis of small groups or project teams, (therefore narrow spans of control and a tall organisation structure) group members would be able to plan their work in an orderly manner, encourage participation by all group members in decision-making and monitor the consequences of their decisions better, so that their performance will be more efficient than the work of groups in a flat structure with a wide span of control. D Vander Weyer (*'Management and People in Banking'*) suggested that in the case of large banking organisations 'it is virtually impossible for so complex an organisation as an international bank to work with less than five or six executive levels, and the writer's own bank (Barclays) has six'.

3.11 There is a trade-off between the span of control and the tallness/flatness of an organisation. The span of control should not be too wide, but neither should an organisation be too tall.

Tall organisations

Reasons in favour	*Reasons against*
1. Keeps span of control narrow.	1. A wide span of control means that more authority will be delegated to subordinates. Greater discretion leads to job enrichment and motivation.
2. A large number of career/promotion steps are provided in the hierarchical ladder. More frequent promotions possible.	2. With many rungs in the hierarchical ladder, the *real* increases in authority between one rung and another might not seem obvious to managers.
	3. Tall organisations are more expensive in management overheads costs.
	4. Tall organisations tend to suffer from worse communications.

3.12 It is reasonable to accept the view that there is a limit to a supervisor's capabilities and that the span of control should be limited. However, the span of control is now thought to be dependent on several factors.

3.13 The nature of the manager's work load is likely to influence the span of control he or she can deal with efficiently.

7: DEGREES OF DELEGATION AND DECENTRALISATION

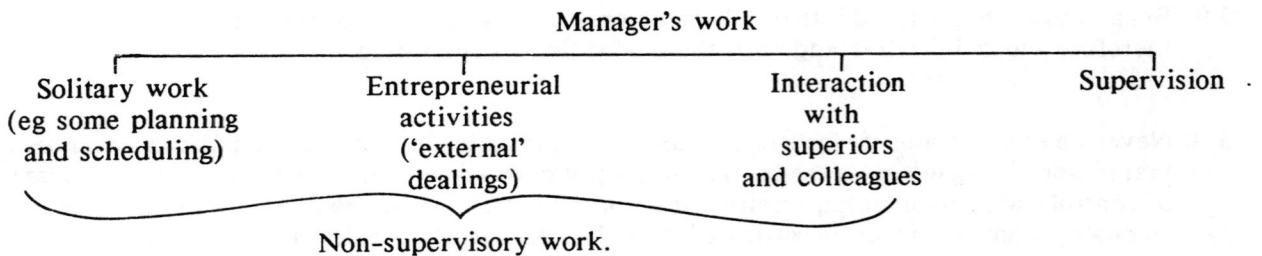

Manager's work

```
          Manager's work
 ┌──────────┬──────────────┬──────────────┬──────────────┐
Solitary work   Entrepreneurial   Interaction       Supervision
(eg some planning   activities        with
 and scheduling)   ('external'      superiors
                   dealings)      and colleagues
 └──────────────────────────────────────────┘
          Non-supervisory work.
```

The greater the proportion of non-supervisory work in a manager's work load,

(a) the narrower the span of control should be; or
(b) the greater the delegation of authority to subordinates should be.

3.14 Other factors influencing the width of the span of control are:

(a) the geographical dispersion of the subordinates;
(b) whether subordinates' work is all of a similar nature (wide span possible) or diversified;
(c) the nature of problems that a supervisor might have to help subordinates with;
(d) the degree of interaction between subordinates (with close interaction, a wider span of control should be possible);
(e) the competence and abilities of both management and subordinates;
(f) whether close group cohesion is desirable. Small groups will be more cohesive, with a better sense of team work. This would call for narrow spans of control;
(g) the amount of help that supervisors receive from staff functions (eg the personnel department).

3.15 The is no universally 'correct' size for the span of management, and no current writer on organisations would suggest that a 'correct' span exists, without considering the particular circumstances of any particular individual organisation or department.

4. FEDERAL AND FUNCTIONAL DECENTRALISATION

4.1 Drucker argued in favour of more rather than less decentralisation, in order to provide a spur to management for better performance. An organisation should be structured so as to facilitate efficient and effective management. Drucker listed three major requirements for structuring.

(a) The organisation must be one which is directed towards achieving business performance.

(b) The organisation should contain the least possible number of management levels, so that the chain of command is as short as possible. 'Every link in the chain sets up additional stresses, and creates one more source of inertia, friction and slack'. There is a tendency (identified by C Northcote Parkinson) for levels of management to increase in number, but this is both unnecessary and inefficient.

(c) The organisation structure should provide jobs in which young managers can be properly trained and tested for more senior management positions in the future. 'It must give people actual management responsibility in an autonomous position while they are still young enough to acquire new experience'.

4.2   The two structural principles which meet these requirements in classical organisation structures are:

(a)   functional decentralisation; and
(b)   federal decentralisation.

These are alternative organisation structures to greater centralisation of authority but with some functionally-organised or divisional-based decentralisation.

4.3   Of these, Drucker considered federal decentralisation much better where it could be applied but it can only operate at fairly senior management level and cannot go below a certain level in the management hierarchy. At lower management levels, functional decentralisation should be applied.

4.4   *Federal decentralisation* or *divisionalisation* is the division of a business into autonomous regions or product businesses, each with its own revenues, expenditures and capital asset purchase programmes, and therefore each with its own profit and loss responsibility. Each division of the organisation might be:

(a)   subsidiary companies under the head company; or
(b)   profit centres or investment centres within a single company.

4.5   The rules for federal decentralisation (divisionalisation) should be:

(a)   it must have properly delegated authority, but strong 'control' should be retained at centre by head office. In other words, management of federal units are free to use their authority to do what they think is right for their part of the organisation, but they must be held properly accountable to head office (eg for profits earned);

(b)   a decentralised unit must be large enough to support the quantity and quality of management it needs. It must not rely on head office for excessive management support;

(c)   each decentralised unit must have a potential for growth in its own area of operations;

(d)   there should be scope and challenge in the job for the management of the decentralised unit;

(e)   federal units should exist side-by-side with each other. If they deal with each other, it should be as an 'arm's length' transaction. 'Where they touch, it should be in competition with each other'. There should be no insistence on preferential treatment to be given to a 'fellow-unit' by another unit of the overall organisation'.

4.6   The advantages of federal decentralisation (divisionalisation) are:

(a)   it forces the attention of management below 'top level' on business performance and results;

(b)   it reduces the likelihood of unprofitable products and activities being continued;

(c)   it therefore encourages a greater attention to efficiency, lower costs and higher profits;

(d) management by objectives can be applied more easily. 'The manager of the unit knows better than anyone else how he is doing, and needs no one to tell him';

(e) it gives more authority to junior managers, and therefore provides them with work which grooms them for more senior positions in the future;

(f) it tests them in independent command early in their careers, and at a reasonably low level in the management hierarchy;

(g) it provides an organisation structure which reduces the number of levels of management. The top executives in each federal unit should be able to report direct to the chief executive of the holding company.

4.7 The limitations to federal decentralisation (divisionalisation) are that:

(a) in some businesses, it is impossible to identify completely independent products or markets. In the telecommunications system, for example:

(i) federal decentralisation by region or area is not properly possible because customers in one region make inter-regional calls;
(ii) federal decentralisation by service (eg telephones, data transmission, or local calls and trunk calls) is not properly feasible because different services use common equipment.

(b) federal decentralisation is only possible at a fairly senior management level, because there is a limit to how much independence in the division of work can be arranged. For example, every product needs a manufacturing function and a selling function. These functions cannot be separated into two federal units.

4.8 Where federal decentralisation is not possible, Drucker argues in favour of *functional decentralisation*. This should operate throughout some businesses and at lower management levels in others. Functional decentralisation exists when an organisation is structured on the basis of functional departments, and authority is decentralised as far as possible within each department.

4.9 Functional decentralisation sets up integrated units with maximum responsibility and authority for a major and distinct phase of the business process (eg departments for Machining, Assembly, Personnel, Accounting and Marketing and Sales etc). 'Otherwise functional managers will not have objectives of performance and measurements of results that are really derived from business objectives and really focus on business results'.

5.   THE CONTINGENCY THEORY OF DELEGATION

5.1 The contingency theory states that the degree of centralisation or decentralisation which would be most appropriate for an organisation will depend on the individual circumstances and the particular situation of that organisation. A number of factors which influence the appropriate degree of decentralisation can be listed.

5.2 *Cost:* there is a cost of centralisation or decentralisation, measurable in either qualitative or quantitative terms. For example, by delegating authority, there is a potential cost of mistakes which the subordinate might make. Senior managers should only delegate authority within acceptable limits, so that the costs of mistakes by subordinates are not more than the organisation can afford.

On the other hand, the failure to delegate sufficient authority has a hidden cost of low morale among subordinates.

5.3 *The history and growth of the organisation:* it has been suggested that when a company takes over smaller subsidiaries in order to diversify its operations, the organisational structure will undergo four phases of development:

(a) *Phase 1:* on taking over a subsidiary, a new management team must introduce a centralised management information system in order to impose financial control.

(b) *Phase 2:* once the acquisition settles down, much of the MIS for financial control becomes routine (budgets, variance reports etc).

(c) *Phase 3:* the subsidiary develops to a point where the links with head office strain; good financial control of an increasingly complex operation can no longer be centralised, therefore decentralisation becomes necessary.

The subsidiary sets its own financial targets, and standards are likely to vary between subsidiaries in the group. 'Goal congruence' for the group as a whole is more difficult to co-ordinate, and economies of scale will disappear.

(d) *Phase 4:* as the subsidiary continues to grow, the need to decentralise realises itself. The centralised support functions may now be limited to:

(i) treasury function;
(ii) legal services;
(iii) economic modelling;
(iv) long-range planning.

(e) *Conclusion:* decentralisation is inevitable under conditions of diversification. To recognise this fact and plan for it makes the process relatively painless.

5.4 A similar view of history and growth is that:

(a) in its early stages of development, an organisation will be entrepreneurial, relatively informally structured, and controlled by its senior managers (who are also the entrepreneurs);

(b) eventually, a formal organisation structure will develop, and authority will be centralised;

(c) the organisation will then continue to grow under a centralised management system;

(d) eventually, the formal organisation will be altered, to allow greater decentralisation;

(e) the organisation will then continue to grow under a decentralised management system;

(f) eventually, the size of the organisation will become so large that 'multiple structures' will be established (eg independent subsidiary companies within a conglomerate empire). Further growth of the organisation will occur within this multi-structured framework. .

5.5 *The status of the organisation's planning, control and information systems:* when an organisation has a well established system of planning (eg management by objectives), and when control information is reported regularly and efficiently to managers responsible for achieving results, there will be a greater tendency towards decentralisation.

5.6 *The nature of change in the organisation:* if the organisation is faced with rapid change and uncertainty in decision-making, there will be a greater reliance on local knowledge of events and 'on-the-spot' decisions, so that there should be greater decentralisation than in a relatively static organisation in a stable environment.

5.7 *Economic size:* up to a certain size of operations, there are likely to be economies of scale from centralisation (eg with specialisation of skills within a centralised management unit). Beyond a certain size of development, there may be diseconomies of scale if the centralised units are not broken up, and decentralisation will become economically desirable.

5.8 *The culture and personnel of the organisation:* the skill, knowledge and attitudes of subordinates will help to decide how much delegation will be wanted by the subordinates, and how far superiors will feel that they can trust the people below them. The culture of organisations, and its influence on structure, is the subject of a later chapter.

5.9 *Technology of the organisation:* it has been suggested that the technology of an organisation will help to determine its structure, and also the degree of centralisation of authority (the work of Eric Trist and Joan Woodward on this subject will be discussed in the later chapter on the structure and cultures of organisations). For example, it is possible to exercise better and cheaper central control by means of a centralised computer information system for management. However, developments in computer technology (eg micro-computers linked to a larger central computer or networked micros) may have made both centralised and decentralised management control easier and cheaper.

5.10 *Uniformity:* where a high level of uniformity is required throughout the organisation, and where effective co-ordination between different parts of the organisation is essential, there is likely to be more centralisation of authority. Examples of organisations requiring such uniformity might be the armed services, or some government departments (eg those dealing with the payment of social security, supplementary benefits, pensions etc).

5.11 *Management philosophy:* the philosophy of senior managers might favour either centralisation or delegation, and they will give authority to subordinates in accordance with these views.

5.12 *Environmental factors:* (eg geography, socio-cultural conditions, the legal and political environment etc) contribute towards the degree of centralisation in any organisation. These factors pull both ways (ie towards delegation and centralisation), for example:

(a) geographical dispersion of an organisation increases the pressure for decentralisation of authority to regional or area managers;

(b) on the other hand, the growth in the exercise of power by trade unions has resulted in a tendency to by-pass lower and middle management, and union representatives may insist on dealing with top officials. This creates greater centralisation of decision-making.

Exercise

In what ways will the extent of decentralisation in an organisation create impetus for greater accountability of individual departmental managers to the top management team?

Discussion points

This is an interesting question. The basis for any solution should be that:

(a) when authority is delegated, managers should be held responsible and accountable for how they have used their authority;

(b) greater decentralisation means that more managers, have some authority, and so more managers should be made accountable. Control systems and performance measurements become more widespread;

(c) discretion is thought to be motivating for managers, and decentralisation, by motivating managers, should make them *want* to be accountable;

(d) whenever authority is decentralised, it remains the task of top management to make other managers accountable.

---

6. FORMAL AND INFORMAL DELEGATION

6.1 *Formal delegation* refers to the division of authority among subordinates in a clear, structured manner. Organisation charts, procedure manuals and schedules of duties are examples of formal delegation (eg the budget manual is a formal statement of budgetary control procedures, including the authority and responsibility of individual managers to prepare different parts of the annual budget, the timescale for preparing the budget, the variances which will be reported, and who should be accountable for adverse variances and responsible for control action).

6.2 *Informal delegation* is usually associated with small companies in the 'entrepreneurial growth' stage of development. Formal authority is not given to subordinates because this would hamper the spontaneous and innovative nature of the decisions required to establish the organisation 'on its feet'. Informal delegation is more relaxed, easy-going and fluid and is often preferred by subordinates. Unfortunately, as organisations grow in size, the advantages of informality are outweighed by the need for clarity of individual functions and purpose; formality is introduced to provide a framework of rules and systems within which authority to make decisions can be delegated with reasonably predictable results (which contribute towards the achievement of organisational goals).

7. SOCIO-TECHNICAL SYSTEMS VIEW

7.1 Joan Woodward developed the so-called 'socio-technical systems' view that the structure of organisations and nature of management depended on the nature of the technology used within the organisation. In other words, organisations varied widely in character, and a major factor contributing to the variations was technology.

7.2 Woodward categorised the levels of technology into:

(a) unit production, or small batch production;
(b) mass production, or large batch production;
(c) process production, or continuous flow production.

This categorisation also describes a rising scale of technical complexity, ie process production is more complex than mass production, which is more complex than unit production. By 'technical complexity' she meant the extent to which the production process is controllable and its results predictable.

7.3 In *'Management and Technology'* (1958) Joan Woodward described the findings of a survey of firms in Essex.

"When the firms were grouped according to similarity of objectives and techniques of production, and classified in order of technical complexity of their production systems, each production system was found to be associated with a characteristic pattern of organisation. It appeared that technical methods were the most important factor in determining organisational structure and of setting the tone of human relationships inside the firms."

7.4 Elaborating further on the survey, she said that:

(a) different objectives of different firms controlled and limited the techniques of production they could use (eg a firm developing prototypes of electronic equipment cannot go in for mass production);

(b) analysing the firms into a continuum of ten levels of technical complexity (sub-divisions, slightly overlapping, of the three main levels described in paragraph 44) ranging from basically simple technology up to the complex, she found that firms using similar technical methods also had similar organisational structures. 'It appeared that different technologies imposed different kinds of demands on individuals and organisations and that these demands had to be met through an appropriate form of organisation.'

7.5 Specific findings were that:

(a) the number of levels in the management hierarchy increased with technical complexity, ie complex technologies lead to 'tall' organisation structures and simpler technologies can operate with a 'flat' structure;

(b) the span of control of first line supervisors was at its highest in mass production, and then decreased in process production; ie

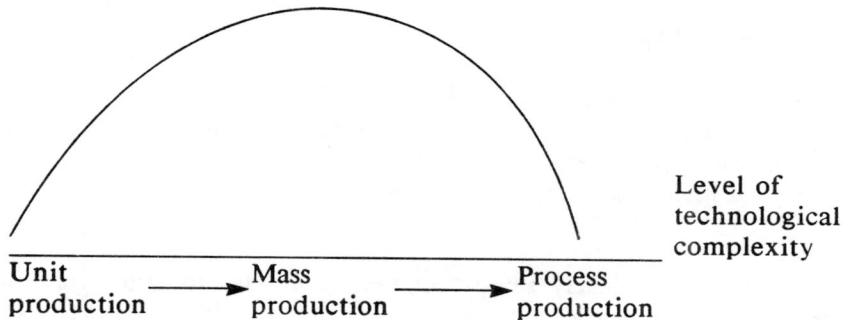

(c) labour costs decreased as technology advanced;

(d) the ratio of indirect labour to direct labour increased with technical advice;

(e) the span of control of the chief executive widened with technical advance;

(f) the proportion of graduates in supervisory positions increased with technical advance;

(g) the organisation was more flexible at both ends of the scale (simple unit production for customer orders at one end; continuous process production at the other)ie duties and responsibilities were less clearly defined. In mass production, duties and responsibilities are clearly set out, largely due to the nature of the technology, and this favours a formal, authoritarian structure;

(h) the amount of written, as opposed to verbal, communication, peaked with mass assembly line production; written communication is a feature of bureaucracy and formal structures;

(i) specialisation between the functions of management was most frequent in large batch and mass production companies; the clear cut demarcation (and resultant conflicts) between 'line' and 'staff' management was also most frequent here;

(j) the planning of production (ie the 'brainwork') and the actual supervision of production work are the most widely separated in large-batch and mass production companies;

(k) industrial and human relations were better at both extremes of the scale than in large-batch and mass production companies, possibly due to heavier pressure on all individuals in this type of organisation;

(l) the size of the firm was not related to its technical complexity, ie it is not possible to attribute the 'faults' of mass production to the size of the firm rather than to the nature of its technology;

7.6 The work of Shoshana Zuboff, mentioned in a previous chapter, indicates that information technology, if properly implemented, may have a major effect on the way businesses are managed. To recap:

(a) the work force has to be much better educated;
(b) information is shared leading to
(c) an erosion of managerial authority.

This might occur because information technology *automates* production, but also *informates*, by providing data about production that has not been previously available.

8. POWER AND INFLUENCE

8.1 Influence is the process by which one person in an organisation, A, directs or modifies the behaviour or attitudes of another person, B. Influence can only be exerted by A on B if A has some kind of power from which the influence emanates. Power is therefore the ability to influence, whereas influence is an active process.

8.2 Power and influence are clearly important factors in the structure and operations of an organisation. They help to explain how work gets done. In addition, it has also been suggested that:

(a) most individuals in an organisation would like to have more influence over their work;

(b) an individual who believes he exerts some influence is likely to show greater interest in his work. The research of writers, such as Likert, who support the principle of management by participation, suggests that employees may be more productive when they consider that they have some influence over planning decisions which affect their work;

(c) some individuals are motivated by the need for power (McClelland) and show great concern for exercising influence and control, and for being leaders.

8.3 C B Handy (*Understanding Organisations*) identified six types of power:

(a) *physical power* - ie the power of superior force. Physical power is absent from most organisations (exceptions are the prison service and the armed forces), but it is often evident as an under-current in industrial relations (eg violence on the picket line or bullying on the shop floor);

(b) *resource power* - ie the control over resources which are valued by the individual or group to be influenced. Senior managers may have the resource power to grant promotion or pay increases to subordinates; trade unions possess the resource power to take their members out on strike;

(c) *position power* - ie the power which is associated with a particular job in an organisation. A foreman has the position power to tell an employee to do a certain piece of work. Position power is usually associated with 'authority' - ie power that goes with the job - and must generally have the backing of physical power or resource power to be effective. Fiedler ('*A Theory of leadership effectiveness*' 1967) identified position power as a critical factor affecting the most efficient style of leadership for any particular manager, and said that a manager with clear, unambiguous position power is more easily capable of getting subordinates to do what he directs. Handy noted that position power has certain 'hidden' benefits:

(i) access to information: the ability to gather and disseminate information is associated with a manager's position. Information itself is a source of power and influence by providing knowledge and greater understanding to its recipients;

     (ii)   the right of access: holding a position often entitles managers to membership of committees which in turn act as a source of information and as a means of contact with other 'powerful' individuals in the organisation. A senior manager might have access to the ear of the managing director, but a junior manager will not have such access;

     (iii)   the right to organise: a position of power entitles an individual to organise conditions of working and methods of decision-making which in turn give him influence over the behaviour of subordinates;

(d)   *expert power* - ie the power which belongs to an individual because of his acknowledged expertise. This power can only belong to a person if others acknowledge him to be an expert. Many staff jobs in an organisation (eg computer systems analysts, organisation and methods analysts, accountants, lawyers or personnel department managers) rely on expert power to influence line management. If the expert is seen to be incompetent (eg if an accountant does not seem to provide sensible information) or if his area of expertise is not widely acknowledged (which is often the case with personnel department staff) he will have little or no expert power;

(e)   *personal power*, or *charisma* - ie the popularity of the individual. Personal power is capable of influencing the behaviour of others, and helps to explain the strength of informal organisations;

(f)   *negative power* is the use of disruptive attitudes and behaviour to stop things from happening. It is associated with low morale, latent conflict or frustration at work. A subordinate might refuse to communicate openly with his superior, and might provide false information; a colleague might refuse to co-operate; a typist might refuse to type an urgent letter because she is too busy; a worker might deliberately cause his machine to break down. Negative power is destructive and potentially very damaging to organisational efficiency.

Exercising influence

8.4   Influence, the act of directing or modifying the behaviour of others, stems from one or more sources of power.

   (a)   Brute force can be used by a person with physical power. Economic force can be applied by a person or group with resource power, eg a powerful trade union can force its employers or the government to accept its wishes by organising strike action.

   (b)   Rules and procedures can be established, which individuals are expected to obey. A person who enforces rules and procedures must have the position power and resource power to ensure that his wishes are obeyed.

   (c)   Bargaining and negotiation, and the art of compromise, provide a means of mutual influence. A person is in a weak bargaining position unless he has something worthwhile to offer in return for the favours he asks for. He must therefore have resource power or personal power to negotiate successfully.

   (d)   Persuasion (or even dictatorial command) is associated with resource power and personal power.

8.5 Handy identified two further, 'unseen' methods of influence.

(a) *Ecology* or the environment in which behaviour takes place. The *physical* environment can be altered by a manager, who may be able to regulate noise levels at work, comfort and security of working conditions, seating arrangements, the use of open-plan offices or segregation into many small offices, the physical proximity of departments as well as individuals, geographical dispersion of individuals, etc. The *psychological and sociological* environment can be altered by means of changing the size of committees or work groups, or encouraging participation by subordinates. 'The design of work, the work, the structure of reward and control systems, the structure of the organisation, the management of groups and the control of conflict are all ways of managing the environment in order to influence behaviour. Let us never forget that although the environment is all around us, it is not unalterable, that to change it is to influence people, that ecology is potent, the more so because it is often unnoticed.' (Handy)

(b) *Magnetism:* the unseen application of personal power. 'Trust, respect, charm, infectious enthusiasm, these attributes all allow us to influence people without apparently imposing on them.'

8.6 Handy argues, from the standpoint of contingency theory, that the method of influence which a person should use to direct or modify the behaviour of others will depend on various circumstances.

(a) The person exerting the influence must have a credible power base; for example, position power will not be adequate for person A to enforce rules or procedures on person B if B denies that A has the authority to direct him.

(b) Influence will be stronger if it is backed by several power sources instead of one.

(c) The method of being influenced will affect the manner in which an individual will respond to the influence:

(i) an individual might comply with instructions because of the threat of physical or economic force, or because of rules and procedures. Such compliance will be grudging, and with lack of commitment; the superior will probably need to check regularly and carefully that his instructions are carried out properly;

(ii) an individual might be influenced by a person because he is 'magnetised' by the personal power of the individual; equally, he will be influenced by the 'norms' of his work group if he identifies himself with the work group;

(iii) internalisation is the process by which an individual adopts an idea or proposal because he accepts it as his own. This is the form of influence which is most effective, efficient and long-lasting, but it is also most difficult to achieve. Various writers on motivation have attempted to suggest how such internalisation of corporate goals can be nurtured in subordinates by managers, and their views are described in the later chapter of this manual on motivation.

9. MANAGERS TAKING DECISIONS

9.1 Decisions are taken by managers, for matters which are within their sphere of authority. In a formal organisation structure, authority should be matched by responsibility and accountability. The extent to which authority is decentralised within an organisation is likely to vary according to circumstances.

9.2 The ability to use discretion in decision-making is a motivating feature of management work, and the exercise of discretion usually involves qualitative judgements.

9.3 However, managers cannot exercise discretion unilaterally, without regard to anyone else.

    (a) They should be accountable for what they do, and should be prepared to answer for the consequences of their decisions.

    (b) If they need cooperation from fellow-managers, they must seek to persuade colleagues to go along with what they want to do, and perhaps accept compromises or alternative suggestions that others make.

    (c) The willingness of subordinates to implement a decision will influence the success or otherwise of the decision. A manager must be able to carry his staff with him (or her), or face the consequences of resistance, hostility or apathy.

9.4 Although a manager should be able to use discretion, he or she should therefore only do so after having consulted with colleagues and subordinates, in an attempt to reach a consensus. The manager should accept responsibility for the consequences of the decision, and should lead the search for consensus; however, the most *effective decisions of a non-programmed* nature will be based on agreement, not managerial commands.

> If you disagree with this conclusion, you are adhering to the 'tells' style of management leadership, but a tells style is really only efficient where decision making is largely routine and programmed.

Exercise

Discuss the role and value of consensus in managerial decision-making.

Discussion points

The role of consensus is to get everyone affected by a decision to be involved in the decision-making process, at least to the point of being persuaded to agree to the decision. The *influence of others* on a manager should help towards reaching consensus.

The value of consensus is that:

(a) others will support the decision and be more likely to help with implementing it. Consensus might also provide better quality decisions, on the principle that 'two heads are better than one';

(b) the potential resistance, hostility, or apathy of others to the decision should be overcome, making the decision easier to implement.

TEST YOUR KNOWLEDGE

(The numbers in brackets refer to paragraphs in this chapter)

1. What factors affect the length of an organisation's chain of command? (2.3)

2. List the arguments in favour of and against 'tall' organisations. (3.11)

3. List the factors which influence the span of control and the tallness/flatness of an organisation's management structure. (3.13, 3.14)

4. What is federal decentralisation? What are its advantages? (4.4, 4.6)

5. What is the contingency theory of delegation? How did the findings of Joan Woodward lend support to this theory? (5.1, 7.5)

6. How can individuals influence decisions, other than by exercising authority and 'position power'? (8.4, 8.5)

7. What are the main organisational and environmental factors which limit the managerial discretion of the manager of a functional department in an organisation?

Discussion points

Question 7
A solution can be found in paragraphs 3.13 and 3.14, and by reference to the contingency theory of delegation.

Chapter 8

PLANNING AND CONTROL

This chapter covers the following topics:

1. Planning, control and accountability
2. Planning
3. Control
4. Designing a control system
5. Example of planning and control: manpower planning.

Purpose of this chapter

To look at the management functions of planning and control, and how they are interrelated parts of a management control system, which depends for its effectiveness on the quality of the organisation's management information system.

1. PLANNING, CONTROL AND ACCOUNTABILITY

1.1 Managers should be held accountable for what they do with their authority and the resources at their disposal. Making managers accountable is achieved through the processes of planning and control.

   (a) Planning is the process of deciding what should be done.

   (b) Control is the process of checking whether planned targets are being achieved, and if not, doing something about it.

   The combined processes of planning and control are known as a *control system*.

1.2 Accountability is a process whereby a manager's actual results and achievements are reviewed by his superiors. In other words, the consequences of a manager's planning and control decisions, and the manager's achievements with the resources at his disposal, are held up for inspection by his boss or bosses.

2. PLANNING

2.1 If individuals and groups within an organisation are to be effective in working for the achievement of the organisation's objectives, they need to know what it is that they are expected to do. This is the purpose of planning ie:

(a) to decide objectives for the organisation;
(b) identify alternative ways of achieving them, and
(c) select from amongst these alternatives for both the organisation as a whole, and also for individual departments, sections and groups within it.

2.2 Planning involves decisions by management about:

(a) what to do in the future;
(b) how to do it;
(c) when to do it;
(d) who is to do it.

The future cannot be foreseen with certainty, and even the best-laid plans will go wrong to a greater or lesser degree; nevertheless, plans give direction to an organisation. Without plans, events will be left to chance.

2.3 There are many managers in practice who are reluctant to make formal plans, and prefer to operate without them, dealing with problems only when and if they arise. The reason for their reluctance to plan might be any or all of the following.

(a) *A lack of knowledge (or interest) about the purpose and goals of the organisation*. However, unless a manager knows what the organisation's goals are, and how other departments and sections are trying to work towards those goals, his own efforts might well either:
  (i) duplicate the efforts of someone else, thereby causing a waste of time and resources; or
  (ii) conflict with the efforts of someone else.
  Good planning encourages the co-ordination of efforts within an organisation.

(b) *A reluctance to be committed to one set of targets*. Planning involves making a choice about what to do, from amongst many different alternative courses of action. A manager might want to keep his options open, which means that he will not want to have specific goals. Whereas this might be feasible in a very small organisation, it is unsatisfactory in any organisation where managers must co-ordinate their efforts and work together for the achievement of organisational goals. Freedom of choice could well be a recipe for lack of preparation for environmental changes, and a lack of co-ordinated response to economic, technological, social and political developments etc with which the organisation will be faced.

(c) *A fear of blame or criticism for failing to achieve planned targets*. By setting targets or plans, and later comparing actual performance against plans, it is possible to identify success or failure. When failure is 'punished' in any way (eg in the form of lower salaries or bonuses, or thwarted promotion prospects and career ambitions, or even the displeasure of superior managers) managers might resent planning, because planning is the start of a process by which they might later be labelled as failures.

(d) *A manager's lack of confidence in himself* to perform his job efficiently and effectively, or a lack of confidence in the organisation's senior management to provide him with the resources he needs to achieve his planned targets. For example, suppose that the manager of a retail store is asked to plan the target volume of turnover and profits for the store in the next two or three years.

The manager might lack confidence in the company's senior management to provide him with enough resources (staff, equipment, product ranges, money for sales promotion etc) to achieve a reasonable targeted performance; or if he did have sufficient resources, he might doubt his own ability to ensure that the targets are achieved. The manager would then prefer instead not to have any plans or targets at all.

(e) *A manager's lack of information* about what is going on in the 'environment'. Managers need to know about the needs of customers, the nature of their markets and their competition, the strength of public opinion or government pressures, the state of the economy etc. Without such information, they will be unable to make plans for the future which are achievable in view of environmental conditions. For example, when a government announces its intention to introduce legislation to ban lead in petrol, car manufacturers and oil companies must know about the timing and nature of such legislation before they can plan properly for its consequences.

2.4 A further problem in planning is that some managers have plans imposed upon them without any prior consultation at all. If a manager is told what he must do and what his targets are, he is likely to resist the plan, and find reasons why it is unachievable.

2.5 The barriers to good planning must be overcome.

(a) All levels of staff should be involved (to a greater or lesser degree) in the planning process. Imposing plans on staff without their participation perhaps, or without their opinions being sought, is a barrier to successful planning.

(b) Planners must be provided with the *information* they need (and access to sources of future information, when it arises) to plan properly. The source of information might be:
(i) from outside the organisation and concerning environmental factors;
(ii) from inside the organisation, concerning facts about the organisation itself. This information is called 'feedback'.

(c) A system of rewards for successful achievement of plans might be beneficial. However, a system of rewards is also a system of punishment for those managers who fail to earn rewards. The motivational problems of rewards and punishments are not easily overcome, and are likely to be a continual barrier to good planning.

(d) Managers should be taught the virtues of planning, and the techniques of good planning. For example, managers should learn the value of co-ordinating the efforts of all staff in the organisation for the achievement of common goals; and the managers should also learn that a subordinate can only be expected to achieve certain targets if he is given sufficient resources to do his job properly etc.

2.6 There are four major aspects to planning.

(a) The purpose of every plan (and of every subsidiary plan within the framework of an overall plan) is to make it easier for management to achieve a goal or objective.

Planning allows managers to identify:
 (i)   what actions will serve towards achieving a stated objective;
 (ii)   what actions will be counter-productive and serve to obstruct the achievements of an objective; and
 (iii) what actions will irrelevant to the achievement of an objective.

(b) Planning precedes all other management functions. An organisation must have an idea of its objectives and what actions must be performed to achieve them before management can:
 (i)   provide a formal organisation structure to carry out the activities;
 (ii)   identify the style and qualities of leadership necessary to get the best out of the staff; and
 (iii) set standards and targets of performance for groups and individuals, by which control can be exercised.
 Planning therefore precedes organisation, staffing, commanding and leading, and control as management functions, and planning is also an essential feature of co-ordination.

(c) Planning is a function of all managers. Some managers do more planning than others, but all managers, even first-line supervisors and foremen, do some planning.

(d) Plans enable managers to decide whether the achievement of certain targets is worth the cost of putting the plan into operation. An efficient plan is one whose costs of implementation are less than the benefits obtained from its contribution to the organisation's goals and objectives. The planning process enables managers to evaluate the efficiency (or cost effectiveness) of their proposed actions and intended targets.

Types of plan

2.7 There are a number of different types of plans, which might be classified as follows.

(a) *Objectives* for the organisation as a whole. This might be to earn a profit, or provide a certain service. It might also be possible to distinguish between a mission for the organisation (eg to provide a certain type of product in order to satisfy a certain type of customer need or need of society) and an objective (eg to make a profit whilst accomplishing the organisation's mission).

 An objective is an end goal towards which all activities should be aimed.

(b) Objectives might be identified for individual departments or divisions within the objectives for the organisation as a whole. For example, within an international company organisation, separate objectives might be identified for the domestic division and the international division.

(c) *Strategies* follow on from the determination of long-term goals and objectives. They are plans of activity (mainly long-term) and plans for the allocation of resources which will achieve the organisation's goals and objectives. There are different types of strategy. For example:

 (i)   a product/market strategy is a plan about the types of product or service an organisation should provide (in order to obtain a sufficient volume of customer demand) and about the types of market in which it should be trying to sell those products or services. A product/market strategy is also a plan for competition against other producers of the same products in the same markets;
 (ii)   a manpower strategy is a plan about the number and types of staff which will be required in the long term to achieve the organisation's goals.

166

(d) *Policies* are general statements or 'understandings' which provide guidelines for management decision making. Company policies might be, for example:

(i) to offer 5 year guarantees on all products sold and give money back to customers with valid complaints;

(ii) to promote managers from within the organisation, wherever possible, instead of recruiting managers to senior positions from 'outside';

(iii) to encourage all recruits to certain jobs within the organisation to work towards obtaining an appropriate professional qualification;

(iv) to be price-competitive in the market;

(v) that employees in the purchasing department should decline gifts from suppliers (subject, perhaps, to certain exceptions or purchase limits).

Policy guidelines should allow managers to exercise their own discretion and freedom of choice, but within certain acceptable limits.

(e) *Procedures* are a chronological sequence of required actions for performing a certain task. Procedures exist at all levels of management (eg even a board of directors will have procedures for the conduct of board meetings) but procedures become more numerous, onerous and extensive lower down in an organisation's hierarchy.

The advantages of procedures for routine work are set out below.

(i) *Efficiency*. Procedures should prescribe the most efficient way of getting a job done.

(ii) The absence of any need for the exercise of discretion in routine tasks;

(iii) *Familiarity*. Staff will find jobs easier to do when they are familiar with established procedures.

(iv) *Standardisation* of work. Prescribed procedures ensure that a task of a certain type will be done in the same way throughout the organisation.

(v) *A written record* of required procedures can be kept in a procedure manual. People unfamiliar with how a job should be done can learn quickly and easily by referring to the manual.

(vi) They reduce the likelihood of inter-departmental friction. For example, work done by the warehousing department of a factory will affect the work of the sales force, delivery and distribution department, and production department. The warehousing department will require documentation from production giving details of goods put into store, and documentation about sales orders from the sales force. It will issue delivery instructions to the delivery crews. By having established procedures, disputes between departments about who should do what, and when, and how, should be avoided.

(f) *A rule* is a specific, definite course of action that must be taken in a given situation. Unlike a procedure, it does not set out the sequence or chronology of events (but a procedure is a chronological sequence of rules). For example, the following are rules but not procedures:

(i) employees in department X are allowed 10 minutes exactly at the end of their shift for clearing up and cleaning their work-bench;

(ii) employees with access to a telephone must not use the telephone for personal calls.

Rules allow no deviations or exceptions , unlike policies, which are general guidelines allowing the exercise of some management discretion.

(g) *Programmes* are co-ordinated groups of plans (goals, policies, procedures, budgets) for the achievement of a particular objective. A company might undertake an expansion programme; in the USA, the government's space agency has a number of programmes, such as the Space Shuttle programme. A programme of any importance is usually a complex of plans which stands by itself and has a clear, separate identity within the organisation and its planning structure.

(h) *A budget* is a formal statement of expected results set out in numerical terms, and summarised in money values. It is a plan for carrying out certain activities within a given period of time, in order to achieve certain targets. The budget indicates how many resources will be allocated to each department or activity in order to carry out the planned activities.

The budget is usually prepared on a company-wide or organisation-wide basis, so that all the activities of the organisation are co-ordinated within a single plan. In order to compare the plans and targets of each department, section, group and individual manager, budgets are expressed in money terms as well as in terms of physical quantities.

Budgets are numerical statements, and as such, tend to ignore *'qualitative' aspects of planning and achievement.*

The steps in planning

2.8 The steps in a planning decision are as follows.

(a) Recognise an opportunity to be exploited or a problem to be dealt with.

(b) Establish goals or objectives as the end result of exploiting the opportunity or solving the problem.

(c) Obtain forecasts of relevant information (eg about products, markets, competition, prices, wage rates, technology etc). Some planning premises should be established which are agreed and used by managers throughout the organisation. An accepted set of premises about the environment in which the organisation will operate, and the resources it will have at its disposal, will provide guidelines for planning decisions.

For example, suppose that a forecast is made that the market for product Z has reached saturation, and prices are likely to fall in the future because of over-supply. Costs are expected to rise, and the profitability of the product will go into decline for reasons outside management control. Given these planning premises, management's plans for dealing with the problem of product profitability, or any opportunities provided by spare production capacity, would not be to spend on advertising to sell more of the product, or to use the spare capacity to make more of the product and introduce more price competition into the market! Planning decisions would be channelled towards different solutions for the company's problems.

(d) Alternative 'realistic' courses of action for the achievement of the objectives should then be considered.

(e) The alternative courses of action should be compared, and the best course selected.

(f) Detailed plans should then be formulated for carrying out the chosen course of action. These plans consist of:

(i)   supporting plans for the provision of the required resources (materials, equipment, trained labour, finance etc);

(ii) numerical plans or budgets, indicating targets for achievement, sales prices, budgeted sales and production quantities, expenditure budgets etc.

2.9 These steps in planning apply to:

(a) 'one-off' plans or projects, but also to routine plans or budgets; and
(b) planning at senior management, middle management and junior management levels.

2.10 Planning should cover the long term as well as the short term.

(a) There is a planning period or 'time horizon' which is the length of time between making a planning decision and the implementation of the decision. For example, a decision to build new premises has a time horizon of many years, a decision to develop and launch a new product might take several years, a normal capital budget might span a five year period, and an operating budget a one-year period, whereas a production schedule might be produced weekly.

Plans of varied duration will be made within an organisation, although the longer the planning horizon, the more senior the management planner is likely to be.

(b) Long term planning indicates a commitment by an organisation to a certain course of action. In other words, plans are tangible evidence of a commitment to decisions already taken. The length of a planning period should be long enough for the commitment to these past decisions to be reflected in the determination of objectives, strategies and resource allocations.

(c) Long term objectives might conflict with shorter term plans, and a feature of planning should be to reconcile the needs of the long and short terms. For example, if a company has a short term problem of resource availability, and has only limited funds for expenditure, it might be tempting to devote all the resources to maintaining a current profitability. However, if longer term spending on capital investment or research and development are ignored, the company's profitability in the long term might be sacrificed.

(d) In the short term, a company might consider profitability as the major objective. In the longer term, profitability will also be important; however other qualitative considerations such as social responsibility, employee welfare, corporate image, standards of service and reputation etc might also take on added importance. If long term planning recognises non-profit goals, there will be a greater likelihood of short term planning also making some concessions to these goals.

(e) Plans, once formulated, should not be rigid, because the future is uncertain and plans should be changed whenever necessary to meet unforeseen circumstances which arise. The need for flexibility in planning is an argument in favour of having shorter planning periods, and so avoiding wasted time on long term plans which will inevitably change.

A compromise should be found between the need for flexibility (keep plans short term) and the need for commitment to decisions already made (make plans as long as the planning horizon requires). The best compromise is that perhaps that plans should be reviewed regularly, and redrawn if necessary.

3. CONTROL

3.1   It was suggested in the previous chapter that decision making is often constrained by the influences of other people, and that decisions can be improved by consensus. Littler and Salaman (1982) have argued that control decisions should both deal with conflict and achieve consensus.

> 'Control must be seen in relation to conflict and sources of conflict *and* in relation to the potential terrain of compromise and consensus.'

3.2   Direct instructions and commands might resolve some problems, but not others, and the nature of control decisions might vary between commands and consensus.

3.3   In this chapter, we are concerned mainly with *formalised* systems of control, although the principles apply to more informal and 'one-off' control measures - for example, a supervisor telling off a subordinate who is not performing as he should (eg taking too much time off at lunchtime, or working too slowly etc).

3.4   The management function of control is the measurement and correction of the activities of subordinates in order to make sure that the goals of the organisation, or planning targets, are achieved. 'In an undertaking, control consists in verifying whether everything occurs in conformity with the plan adopted, the instructions issued and the principles established.

It has for object to point out weaknesses and errors in order to rectify them and prevent recurrence. It operates on everything; things, people, actions'.(Henri Fayol).

Control is a necessary management function at all levels in the management hierarchy.

3.5   In order to carry out their control functions, managers must have:

(a)   plans, which indicate the targets or goals which the efforts of themselves and their subordinates should be directed towards achieving and the rules and procedures for achieving them;

(b)   an organisation structure; in particular a clear indication of the managers responsible for the actual results achieved and deviations from plan (and the managers who should therefore have the authority to investigate corrective action).

3.6 The basic control process or control cycle in management has six stages:

> (a) making a plan; deciding what to do and identifying the desired results. Without plans there can be no control;
>
> (b) recording the plan formally or informally, in writing or by other means, statistically or descriptively. The plan should incorporate standards of efficiency or targets of performance;
>
> (c) carrying out the plan, or having it carried out by subordinates; and measuring actual results achieved;
>
> (d) comparing actual results against the plans. This is sometimes referred to as the provision of 'feedback';
>
> (e) evaluating the comparison, and deciding whether further action is necessary the ensure the plan is achieved;
>
> (f) where corrective action is necessary, this should be implemented.

3.7 Control is dependent on the receipt and processing of *information*. Within organisations, information may be received from:

(a) formal sources within the organisation;
(b) informally from sources within the organisation;
(c) formal sources outside the organisation, ie from the environment;
(d) informally from environmental sources.

3.8 Examples of information requirements are as follows.

Activity in control cycle	Information required
Make plan	Resources available, value to the company if the plan is successfully carried out, compared with alternative plans which could be carried out.
Record the plan	The way in which the plan will fit into the company's operations as a whole, so that other people/departments affected by the plan can be informed.
Carry out the plan	Details of the quantity and quality of resources for the job: specifying time and place.
Comparison of actual against plan	What happens?
Evaluation and control plan	Changes which have taken place since the original action outside the framework of the plan itself; the goal of the original plan may need to be amended and control action should be adjusted accordingly.

Control systems

3.9 The arrangements within a business organisation for exercising control over the business can be referred to as a management control system.

3.10 A business must be controlled to keep it steady or enable it to change safely, ie each business must have its control system. Control is required because unpredictable events occur so that actual results deviate from the expected results or goals. Examples of unplanned and unforeseen events would range, in a business, from the entry of a powerful new competitor into the market, an unexpected rise in labour costs, or the failure of a supplier to deliver promised raw materials, to the tendency of employees to stop working in order to chatter or gossip. A control system must ensure that the business is capable of surviving these 'disturbances' by dealing with them in an appropriate manner.

Feedback

3.11 *Feedback* for management control is information which is measured from business operations and reported as control information to the managers responsible for those operations.

3.12 A business organisation uses feedback for control; however, external influences are not ignored. A management information system must be designed to provide both proper feedback and also sufficient environmental information to optimise the control system.

3.13 *Negative feedback* is information which indicates that results are deviating from its planned or prescribed course, and that some re-adjustment is necessary to bring it back on to course. This feedback is called 'negative' because control action would seek to reverse the direction or movement of the system back towards it planned course.

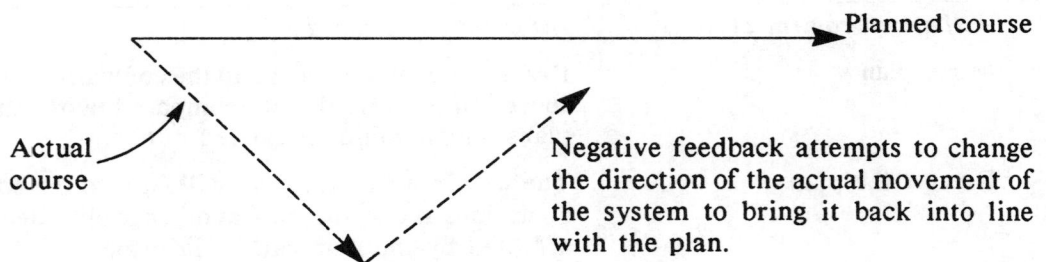

Planned course

Actual course

Negative feedback attempts to change the direction of the actual movement of the system to bring it back into line with the plan.

Thus if the budgeted sales for June and July were £100,000 in each month, whereas the report of actual sales in June showed that only £90,000 had been reached, this negative feedback would indicate that control action was necessary to raise sales in July to in order to get back on the planned course. Negative feedback in this case would necessitate July sales exceeding the budget by £10,000 because June sales fell short of budget.

3.14 A control system might be drawn as a 'black box' diagram, in which the system being controlled is shown simply as a box, and the input resources, outputs, feedback and control actions are shown.

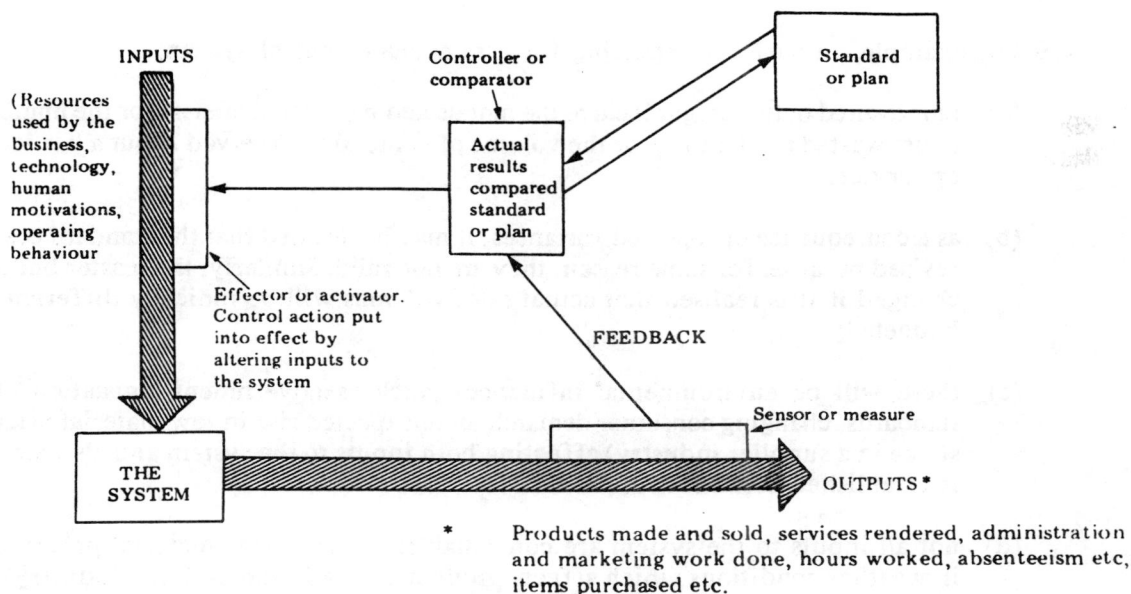

* Products made and sold, services rendered, administration
and marketing work done, hours worked, absenteeism etc,
items purchased etc.

3.15 This control system can be said to consist of four key elements:
   (a) the plan for the system - ie the 'condition to be controlled';
   (b) the measure or 'sensor' of results;
   (c) the comparison of actual results against plan ('the comparator');
   (d) putting any control action into effect (the 'effector' or 'activator').

3.16 This diagram is as yet incomplete, but it may be helpful at this stage to relate this control system to a practical example, such as monthly budgetary control variance reports.

   (a) Standard costs and a master budget are prepared for the year. Management organises the resources of the business (inputs) so as to achieve the budget targets.

   (b) At the end of each month, actual results (output, sales, costs, revenues etc) are reported back to management. The reports are the measured output of the control system, and the process of sending them to the managers responsible provides the feedback loop.

   (c) Managers compare actual results against the plan and where necessary, take corrective action to adjust the workings of the system, probably by amending the inputs to the system. Where appropriate the standard may be revised.

3.17 In this example, however, we have not allowed for several factors, ie:

   (a) the influence of the environment on both plans and system inputs;

   (b) whether control action is possible. For example, a manager might not be able to do anything about the effect of inflation on the costs of his department;

   (c) how much information should be measured and fed back to the managers responsible for the activities. Not all output is measured, either because it would not have any useful value as information, or because the system does not provide for its measurement.

3.18 It is also important to bear in mind that the standard or plan might need to be changed and a comparison of actual results against the existing plan might be invalid. Environmental influences could be responsible for the need to change the standard.

3.19 For example, in variance reporting for a budgetary control system:

(a) unmeasured output might include the morale and motivation of staff, or the number of labour · hours wasted as idle time, or the volume of complaints received about a particular product or service.

(b) as a consequence of reported variances, it may be decided that the standard costs should be revised because, for some reason, they are not valid. Similarly, the master budget might be changed if it is realised that actual sales volumes will be radically different from those budgeted;

(c) there will be environmental influences (such as government legislation about safety standards, changing consumer demand, an unexpected rise in raw material prices, or a long strike in a supplier industry) affecting both inputs to the system and also how the budget is established or amended;

(d) not all inputs to the system are controllable; a rise in raw material prices, or a change in weather conditions which affects production (eg in the building industry) or sales (eg ice creams, soft drinks) are outside the scope of management control. Other inputs might be controllable, but are not controlled due to lax or inattentive management (eg poor labour morale and a high labour turnover, or difficulties in recruiting staff which might be controllable by improving the quality of job content, training or pay).

Double loop feedback

3.20 Higher level feedback or double loop feedback, is control information transmitted to a higher level in the system. In a business system, higher level feedback is reported to a more senior level of management. Whereas single loop feedback is concerned with 'task control', higher level feedback is concerned with 'multiple (overall) task control'. The term 'double loop' feedback indicates that the information is reported to indicate both divergencies between the observed and expected results where control action might be required, and also the need for adjustments to the plan itself, perhaps in response to changing environmental conditions. The scale of control action at a higher level will be wider than at the level of single loop feedback - ie there will be larger variances requiring control measures. Higher level feedback consists of information gathered from measuring outputs of the system itself, but also *environmental information*.

3.21 It must therefore be concluded that an important feature of any control system is the *timeliness* of control information. In a formal management reporting system, for example, there ought to be established feedback periods, which are "the frequency of transmitting feedback information to the control function, which will be determined by such factors as the likelihood of the process going out of control, availability of information and cost of collection." (CIMA Official Terminology).

Feedforward control

3.22 With feedback control, *historical* actual results are measured and reported, so that control action can be taken where necessary. As we have seen, there can be a *control delay*, and the time lag in reporting or taking action could damage the effectiveness of the control system.

3.23 Where some control delay is inevitable with feedback reporting, management might be able to use feedforward control instead.

3.24 Feedforward control is based on *trying to anticipate what will happen in the future*, unless something is done to correct or change matters now, and *comparing this anticipated outcome with the planned outcome.*

If the anticipated outcome does not match up adequately to the plan, control action can be taken now, before it is too late to do anything effective to put matters right. By providing control information sooner (ie before an event happens rather than after it has happened), a feedforward control system can prevent control delay that might be harmful and unavoidable in some circumstances.

3.25 This might seem confusing as an explanation, and an example might help to make feedforward control clearer to you.

One example of feedforward control is network analysis, using a critical path chart. A critical path chart shows a sequence of activities and events in a project, the expected duration of each activity, and the expected completion dates of each activity and of the project as a whole. The chart can be used as a plan for the scheduling and completion of work.

3.26 To take a very simple example of a project with four activities, A, B, C and D, which must be carried out one after the other. A critical path chart, showing estimated times (in weeks) is shown below:

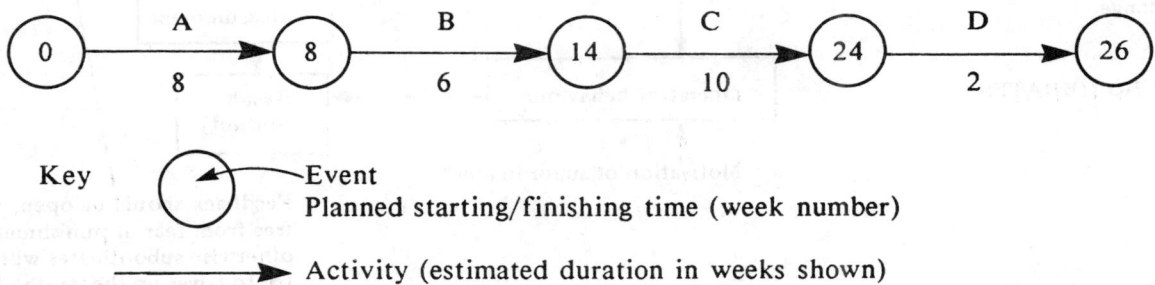

3.27 A plan might be established to complete the project in 26 weeks.

Suppose that at the end of week 4, once the project is under way, a report is given to the project manager that activity A is now likely to take 10 weeks to finish, instead of eight as planned. This increase in the time needed for A has been notified to the manager before it has actually happened, and it is an example of feedforward control. It gives the manager time to take control action before it is too late. For example, he might be able to acquire extra men to help with activity B, and so reduce the time needed for B to 4 weeks; this would keep the overall completion time for the project down to the planned 26 weeks.

3.28 If the delay in completing A had been left until the delay had already happened - ie until week 8 or even week 10, the manager might not have had time to get more men to help with B. The feedforward control information in week 4 gives him more time to take control measures, and so avoid the damage of control delay.

3.29 To maintain an effective feedforward control system, management must:

(a) identify all the critical activities or events;
(b) develop an overall plan, including targets for these critical activities or events;
(c) keep the model updated, as events or circumstances change;
(d) report deviations in anticipated results from the planned (model) results as soon as they become apparent.

The process of management control

3.30 Child has developed the control cycle to suggest how the process of *management* control operates.

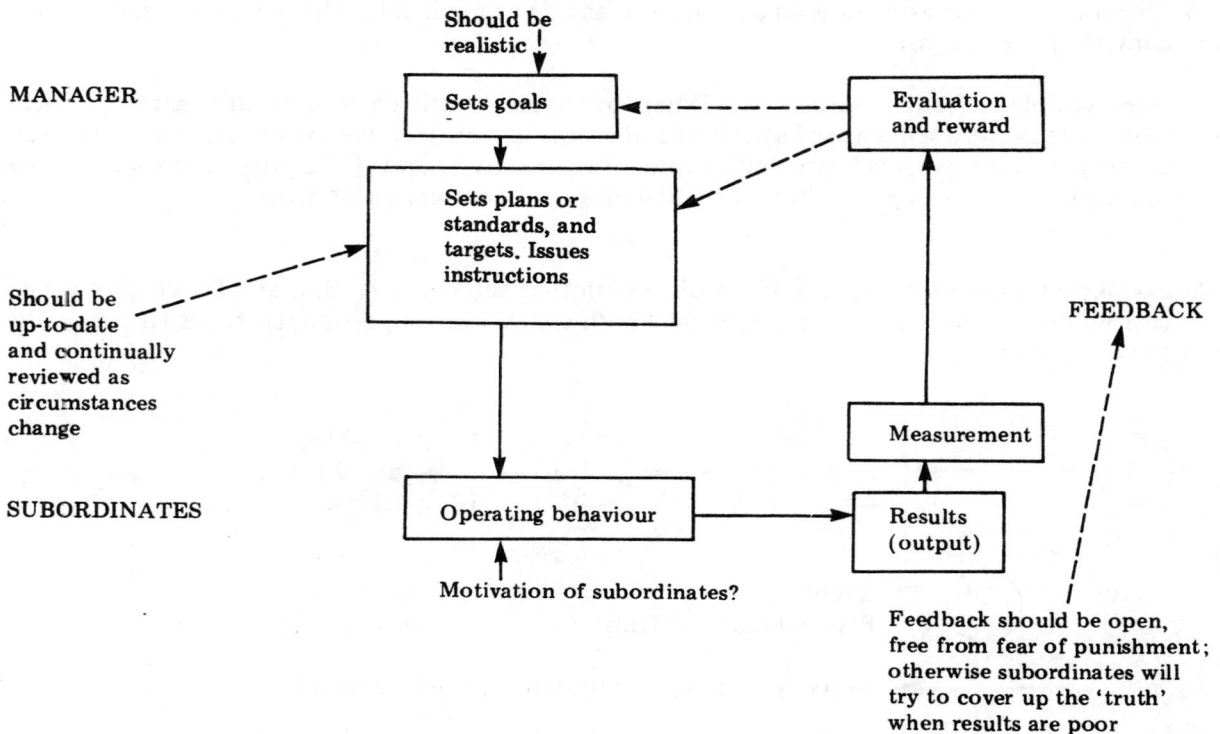

3.31 Child has suggested that there are three main design choices in the structure of a control system:

(a) the degree of centralisation or decentralisation of decision-making;

(b) the degree of formality or informality in control. Organisation growth sets up pressures for decentralisation but also for greater formality in control. The disadvantage of decentralisation and formality in control systems is that rules, procedures and bureaucracy can take over;

(c) the degree of personal supervision that managers exercise over subordinates. This is the issue of *span of control*.

3.32 Child goes on to suggest that there are four alternative strategies for control in an organisation.

---

1. *Personal centralised control*

> Centralised decision making.
>
> Personal leadership; direct supervision.
>
> Often a feature of small owner-managed companies.

---

2. *Bureaucratic control*

> Based on rules and procedures, budgets and budgetary control.
>
> As much programmed decision-taking as possible.
>
> Control is based on the principles of scientific management - ie specialisation of work, simplification of work methods, and standardisation of procedures.

---

3. *Output control*

> The organisation of work is structured so as to identify groups that can be made responsible for a particular output. Systems of *'responsibility accounting'* are operated. Authority for operational matters regarding the output is delegated to the operational managers. Divisional organisation structures fall into this category.

---

4. *Cultural control*

> Cultural control is achieved where all employees develop a strong personal identification with the goals of the organisation. There is often semi-autonomous working, with few formal controls. Employees are motivated by prospects of career progression; selection, training and development of staff are important features of management policy.
>
> Examples of organisations where cultural control exists are firms of chartered accountants, and companies such as Japanese corporations, in which a strong composite identity is built up, and which Ouchi and Price (1978) have called the 'industrial clan' mentality.

3.33 The most appropriate control strategy, Child argues, will depend on contingent factors, such as

		Control strategy likely to be suitable
Market demand for the organisation's output	Strong	Output and/or cultural
	Weak	Centralised and/or bureaucratic
Employee skills and education	High	Output and/or cultural
	Low	Centralised and/or bureaucratic
Change	Rapid	Output and/or cultural
	Slow	Centralised and/or bureaucratic
Size of organisation	Small	Centralised
	Not small	Any other

4. DESIGNING A CONTROL SYSTEM

4.1 We are now in a position to consider the qualities of a good system of management control. These are discussed in the following paragraphs, and include:

(a) good quality of information;
(b) relevant and objective information;
(c) attention to critical control points;
(d) cost-effectiveness; and
(e) flexibility.

Good quality of information

4.2 The term 'Management Information System' or MIS is used to describe the data and information that is provided to management for planning, control purposes and decision making. The information provided in control reports should have the qualities of good information.

(a) The information should be *accurate*. Inaccurate control information will either misdirect management's attention and make them overlook matters requiring control action, or else it will make management take incorrect and inappropriate control decisions.

(b) The information should be *timely*, so as to avoid control delay and encourage prompt control action. Information for control should therefore ideally be reported at the earliest opportunity.

(c) The information should be *clear*, so that a manager receiving a control report will understand what the report is telling him. One way of making control reports more clear is to highlight *exceptional items* which might call for particular attention: this is known as reporting by exception and can be used to make control reports more concise. For example, if a manager receives a performance report every month consisting of several sheets of computer printout, much of the information on the printout might simply show that actual results compare reasonably well with the planned results. It might be fairly easy, however, for the manager to overlook exceptional items in the middle of the large quantities of unexceptional data provided. If exceptional items are highlighted in the report, the manager's control responsibilities will be made more immediately clear.

(d) The information should nevertheless be *comprehensive (complete)*. Unless a manager has a complete picture of events, he might use the inadequate and insufficient information to make an inappropriate control decision.

4.3 Control reports should be sent to the manager who has the authority and responsibility for control action. This might seem an obvious point, but it is all too easy to compile reports containing information which is inappropriate to a particular manager.

(a) Information should have a purpose, and it should be relevant to that purpose. For example, the manager of department A should receive control information about the performance of department A. It would not be useful for him to receive reports about other departments in the organisation because he could not use such information (which would therefore be worthless).

(b) There should be a hierarchy of control reports, so that each manager in the organisation is made responsible for the activities over which he has authority. The diagram below might help to illustrate the hierarchical nature of such reports.

DIVISION A REPORT, JUNE 19X5

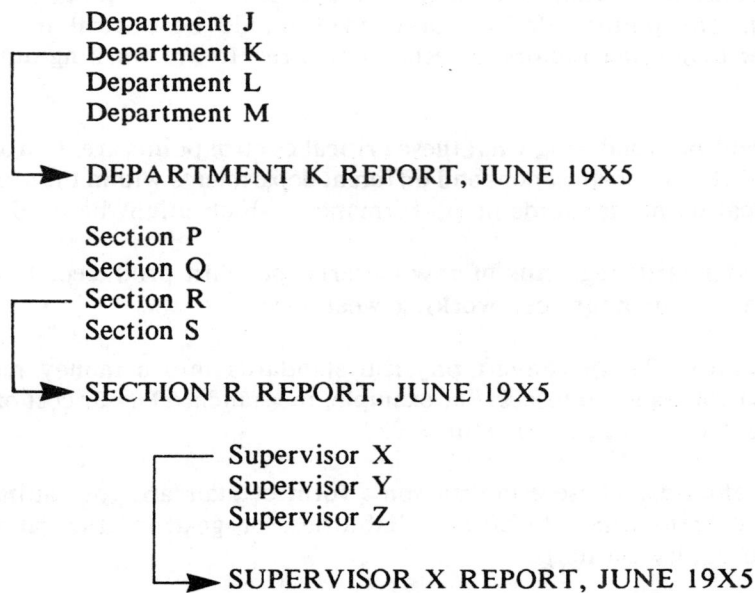

Department J
Department K
Department L
Department M

DEPARTMENT K REPORT, JUNE 19X5

Section P
Section Q
Section R
Section S

SECTION R REPORT, JUNE 19X5

Supervisor X
Supervisor Y
Supervisor Z

SUPERVISOR X REPORT, JUNE 19X5

Controls should therefore be tailored to positions in the organisation. Clearly, the information required by a divisional manager will differ enormously from the information for a supervisor. Similarly the control information required by a production department will be different from the sort of control data required by the marketing department.

179

4.4 Control reports and control information should be 'objective' and should avoid subjective judgements. Subjective measurements (eg on the morale of staff, or the goodwill of customers) might be disbelieved by the manager receiving the report, so that he will take no control action, or at best, make only half-hearted efforts at control.

4.5 Objective standards can be either:

(a) quantitative (eg costs, labour hours per unit, completion dates for a job etc); but also

(b) qualitative (eg the value of a training scheme can be measured by specific characteristics of the matters being taught or skills learned; the quality of service might be measured by the number of complaints received etc).

Whether quantitative or qualitative, it is important that standards should be determinable and measurable.

4.6 It is worth stressing the point that control measurements can relate to qualitative factors as well as to quantifiable factors. However, there should be *targets* for qualitative performance (eg ethical standards of behaviour) because unless there is a standard or target, it will be impossible to establish whether or not actual achievements have been satisfactory.

4.7 Control information should draw management's attention to critical control points - ie points about performance that require special attention because they are judged critical to the success of operations. The points selected for control should be critical in the sense that they indicate better than other factors whether actual results are working out according to plan.

4.8 You will perhaps be wondering what these critical control points are. Unfortunately, they will vary between different organisations and different departments within the same organisation. The types of critical point standards of performance which might be used are:

(a) physical standards (eg units of raw material per unit produced, labour hours per unit produced, labour hours per working week etc);

(b) cost standards. These convert physical standards into a money measurement by the application of standard prices. For example, the standard labour cost of making product X might be 4 hours at £5 per hour = £20;

(c) capital standards. These establish some form of standard for capital invested (eg the ratio of current assets to current liabilities, or gearing (the ratio of fixed interest capital to equity capital)).

(d) revenue standards. These measure expected performance in terms of revenue earned, such as turnover per square metre of shelf space (in a supermarket) or value of sales orders per salesman, or revenue per passenger-mile (for transport services) etc;

(e) standards for programme completion. Performance might be measured in terms of actual completion dates for parts of a project compared against a budgeted programme duration;

(f) the achievement of stated goals;

(g) intangible standards. These may be difficult to measure objectively, but they should only be used if objectivity can be achieved. Intangible standards might relate to employee motivation, quality of service, customer goodwill, corporate image, product image etc.

The consequences of an inadequate MIS

4.9 The importance of a good quality management information system can perhaps be appreciated more fully by asking what would happen if an MIS were of a poor quality.

The table on the next page illustrates the possible consequences of various inadequacies in an MIS.

Quality of information	Consequences of planning	Consequences of control
1. Information is inaccurate	Planning decisions might be misguided.	Managers won't be told about what is really going on, and so won't take control action when it is needed.
2. Information is too late	Decisions will be taken without all the necessary facts being available – decisions could be misguided.	Managers won't be told what is going on until too late, or until after unnecessary damage has been done.
3. Information is not clear	Managers might misunderstand what they have been told, and so make misguided decisions.	Managers might overlook or misunderstand what they have been told, and so be unaware that control action is needed.
4. Information is incomplete	Decisions will be taken without all the facts being available.	Decisions will be taken without all the facts being available.
5. Information is irrelevant	Managers might be confused by data which is irrelevant to decisions they have to take, and waste time with it unnecessarily.	Managers might be confused by data which is irrelevant to their needs, and waste time unnecessarily.
6. Information is subjective	Managers might refuse to accept subjective opinions, or worse still, might make decisions based on subjective opinions that other people might resent and resist.	Managers might refuse to accept the subjective opinions given to them.
7. Control information is not directed at critical points	–	Managers will not have their attention directed towards key issues, and might overlook them. Control action that should be taken might therefore be missed.

Cost-effectiveness of control

4.10 Controls should be economical - worth their cost in terms of the benefits obtained. Large organisations can probably afford a larger control system because its potential benefits or savings are higher. Control will probably be economical if it is tailored to:

   (a) the critical points of the organisation's work; and
   (b) the size of the organisation.

4.11 It could be argued, however, that although large scale organisations can afford more complex control systems, the organisations themselves are so large and complex that they have:

   (a) more control problems, of a greater magnitude than small organisations;
   (b) more problems of efficient communication;
   (c) a wider area of planning, and therefore
   (d) greater problems of communication.

   A large organisation therefore needs a more complex control system to avoid its 'in-built' organisational inefficiencies, so that an argument can be put forward that smaller organisations are easier to control, even with a less complex control system.

4.12 A guiding principle of control economy is that controls are efficient when they identify and explain the causes of important differences between actual performance and planned results with the minimum of costs.

Control flexibility

4.13 Controls should continue to be workable even when events show that original plans are un-achievable (and should therefore be changed) perhaps due to unforeseen circumstances which arise. In other words, controls must be flexible and adaptable to new circumstances.

4.14 Perhaps the most clear example of the need for flexibility is the budget. Suppose that a company has an annual marketing costs budget of £500,000 and a distribution costs budget of £300,000. These budgets were based on expected sales demand of £6,000,000 per annum, or £500,000 per month. Now if actual sales turn out to be much higher than expected, and start running at, say £750,000 per month, it would be reasonable to expect marketing and distribution costs to exceed the original budget. This means that a monthly or weekly comparison of actual costs against budgeted costs, as the year progresses, will be pointless, because the control information will merely indicate overspending which might reasonably be expected.

   To overcome this problem, it is possible to prepare a flexible budget, which adjusts planned spending to a level which ought to be expected in view of the increase in sales. Actual spending is then compared against expected spending in the flexible budget, and any deviations and variances would then provide more meaningful control information about over-or underspending.

4.15 Other features of a good control system include the following.

(a) The control system should be acceptable to the organisation's members.

    (i) Employees who are used to a rigid, disciplinarian management will perhaps accept strict measures of control and procedures or rules for investigating exceptional variations between actual results and plans.

    (ii) Employees who are accustomed to participating in planning decisions, and are encouraged to use their initiative, will react unfavourably to rigid controls 'imposed' on them by senior management.

The purpose of control information is to stimulate control action, and it must therefore be tailored to the 'culture' of the organisation or the department etc within the organisation.

(b) Controls should be tailored to the capabilities and personalities of individual managers. If a manager cannot or will not understand control information given to him, he will not trust it, and if he does not trust it, he will not use it. Some managers (eg accountants, statisticians) might prefer numerical reports of some complexity, whereas other managers might prefer simpler reports (perhaps with charts or diagrams). The providers of information might compile long reports in a computer printout, which managers will not use because of their length and complexity.

(c) Controls should not be too sophisticated, either, using techniques of measurement and analysis which only a statistical or accounting 'expert' might understand. Non-technical managers are easily put off by technical reports, and would react more favourably to a control system which is more crude, but nevertheless more comprehensible.

(d) A control system will serve no useful function at all unless it leads management into taking corrective action.

Exercise

What are the main managerial issues to be faced by a functional manager wishing to achieve effective control over *one* of the following:

(a) a production or operations department;
(b) a marketing department;
(c) a research and development department;
(d) a sales department *(either* in manufacturing *or* service *or* retail); or
(e) a service department in *either* the private *or* the public sector (for example, a social services department, a community health unit)?

Discussion points

Your solution should be based on just one of the management functions, and examples ought to be used. However, any solution ought to have certain common ingredients, which are:

(a) there must be a clear plan or target for achievement. The planning targets must be realistic;

(b) there must be regular feedback of actual results as they occur, to allow managers to compare actual achievements against the plan. (In some situations, feedforward control might be used);

(c) there must be a good Management Information System. The qualities of good information should be explained (accuracy, completeness, timeliness, relevant, clarity, objectiveness). Control information should be directed at critical control points;

(d) the control system should be flexible, and allow for changing circumstances should the need arise.

---

5. EXAMPLE OF PLANNING AND CONTROL: MANPOWER PLANNING

5.1 The value of good planning for effective management control can be illustrated with an example. The example that will be used here is manpower planning, partly because it is related to the syllabus topic of management training and development, and partly because it has featured in an examination question in the past. As you read through the example, however, notice in particular that:

(a) plans are made for the future, but future events are uncertain. However, uncertainty does not make planning a waste of time. Rather, plans should recognise uncertainty, and state clearly the assumptions on which they are based;

(b) planning targets can be both quantitative (numbers to be recruited) and qualitative (targets for training, industrial relations, working conditions etc);

(c) by setting clear targets based on specified assumptions, the comparison of actual results against the plan and the control requirements will be clear. Rational control decisions can be taken.

5.2 Labour is one of the resources of an organisation which management must plan and control. Compared to machines, materials and money, labour is a relatively unpredictable and uncontrollable resource for these reasons.

(a) Environmental factors such a government decisions or the state of the markets create uncertainties in the demand for labour, whereas other factors (such as education or the demands of competitors for labour) create uncertainties in the supply of labour.

(b) Employees as individuals may have their own personal goals, and make their own decisions about, for example, whether to leave the organisation, whether to co-operate with management strategies and whether to undertake further training. When large numbers of individuals are involved, the pattern of behaviour which emerges in response to any change in strategy may be hard to predict for reasons such as local culture and attitudes and industrial relations in the local area or plant.

Management and employees may be capable of adapting to change by accepting changes in job content, work organisation or retraining. However, it may be necessary to negotiate rather than imposes changes and to accept the consequences of changes for labour turnover and employee motivation.

(c) Legislation as well as social and ethical values constrain the ways in which labour may be used, the controls which may be placed over labour, the ease with which labour may be replaced, the criteria which may be used in recruitment or promotion, and in some cases, the rate of pay.

5.3 The purpose of manpower planning in both the short and the long term is therefore:

(a) to estimate the (uncertain) demand for each grade and skill of employee;
(b) to estimate the (uncertain) supply of labour for the appropriate grades and skills;
(c) where there is a discrepancy between demand and supply to take measures which will reduce demand or improve supply. Attention must be given to pay, productivity, labour turnover, training, career structure, job enrichment etc.

This purpose can perhaps be stated more simply as being the objective of having the right people in the right jobs at the right time.

5.4 The process of manpower planning may be described in general terms as follows:

(a) obtaining information on current manpower analysed by grades, skills, ages and retention rates, on which to base estimates of future manpower;

(b) forecasting manpower requirements, by grades and skills, to meet the long term and short term needs of the organisation;

(c) devising a strategy to meet the projected manpower requirements by grades and skills;

(d) acquiring manpower and controlling its 'flow' through the organisation, ie. the personnel functions of conditions of employment, pay, training, welfare, recruitment, promotion etc;

(e) developing the skills of individuals so that with experience, they will become more productive and effective (eg management development);

(f) attempting to persuade employees to adapt to changes in technology, organisation structure, the social habits of co-workers etc;

(g) attending to the human relations factor so that corporate goals are achieved in a manner acceptable to and approved by the workforce.

5.5 Manpower planning should be applied to all jobs in an organisation - managerial as well as non-managerial. For *manager* and *technical* manpower planning:

(a) a short-term plan (say 2 years ahead) is largely concerned with *promotion* planning;

(b) the longer term plan (say 5-10 years ahead) is more important, because it forces management to plan what organisation structure it wants, and what skills and age structure of management are needed to achieve organisational goals.

Manpower planning as demand and supply forecasting

5.6 Manpower planning, as stated earlier, involves manpower demand and supply forecasting.

'Rapid technological change is leading to a requirement for manpower which is both more highly skilled and more adaptable, while social changes, including changes in the education system, are altering the pattern of the supply of human resources in ways which are not always in gear with technological requirements.' (Hughes 1971) A problem faced by many companies in the UK today is the severe shortage of skilled workers, whilst many unskilled school-leavers are unwanted and unemployed. The skilled labour shortage acts as a constraint on industry's production capabilities.

'The general aim of corporate manpower planning is to reduce the risk of either surplus or shortage of particular kinds of manpower, because any imbalance between personnel and other resources or corporate needs is likely to involve waste.' (Smith 1971)

5.7   The demand for labour must be forecast by considering:

(a)   the objectives of the organisation, and the long and short term plans in operation to achieve those objectives. Where plans are changed, the effect of the change must be estimated;

(b)   manpower utilisation - ie. how much labour will be required, given the expected *productivity* or work load of different types of employee. Improvements in productivity might be estimated on the assumption that concessions will be made on pay to the employees concerned.

5.8   Planning future manpower requires accurate forecasts of turnover and productivity. Suppose for example, a company employing 3,000 people (of whom 20 are mechanics) estimates that in five years time turnover will be doubled and productivity increased by 50%. Thirty mechanics would therefore be needed to meet the requirement in five years time. In fact, turnover may be three times greater and labour productivity unchanged so that the calculations will be inaccurate, and sixty mechanics would really be needed.

5.9   The supply of labour will be forecast by considering:

(a)   forecasts of wastage (turnover through resignations, retirement etc), promotion and absentee and productivity levels etc;

(b)   the existing work force structure (age distribution, grades, location, sex, skills, hours of work and rates of pay);

(c)   the potential supply of new labour with the relevant skills from the 'environment' ie. the labour market.

5.10 Demand and supply must be compared in a review we could call a *manpower position survey*. Forecasts of discrepancies between them in the numbers required/available, their grade, skills or location can be removed through the application of an integrated manpower strategy. Short-term adjustments of manpower to requirements may be made and consultation concerning the long-term strategy continued.

5.11 Manpower strategy requires the integration of policies for:

    (a)   pay and conditions of employment;
    (b)   promotion;
    (c)   recruitment;
    (d)   training;
    (e)   industrial relations.

5.12 Because all these factors are inter-related, an integrated approach is necessary, for example:

    (a)   job/rate evaluation should be carried out in large companies to avoid unfairness; a serious problem is the narrow pay differential in the UK between skilled and unskilled workers, and between middle management and other workers;

    (b)   the costs of recruitment include intensive training if personnel move quickly between companies and labour turnover is high;

    (c)   for management development, a strong policy is required to ensure that junior management is given sufficient training for senior management positions. If this is not implemented there will be a vacuum when senior managers retire or resign;

    (d)   in industrial relations, problems may occur because of a lack of communication between unions and management. Schemes of employee participation which have occasionally proved successful in Europe may also eventually be effective in Britain following EEC measures aimed at increasing employee participation.

5.13 Tactical plans can then be made, within this integrated framework, for:

    (a)   pay and productivity bargaining;
    (b)   physical conditions of employment;
    (c)   management and technical development and career development;
    (d)   organisation and job specifications;
    (e)   recruitment and redundancies;
    (f)   training and retraining;
    (g)   manpower costs.

5.14 If it is not possible, through manpower planning, to close the gap between the forecast demand for labour and forecast supply, it follows that labour will be a resource acting as a constraint on the ability of the organisation to achieve its planned goals. The constraint may be long or short term.

5.15 We have so far discussed manpower planning in very general terms. It might help to clarify matters if we look at an approach to manpower planning in some more detail.

5.16 To begin with, the manpower structure of the organisation should be drawn, and 'entry points' or 'recruitment points' identified. In the following simplified example of a regional branch banking manpower system, entry points are confined to recruitment at the lowest level and transfers from other regions at clerical levels. For simplicity, six levels of staff are assumed, plus an administrative staff grade.

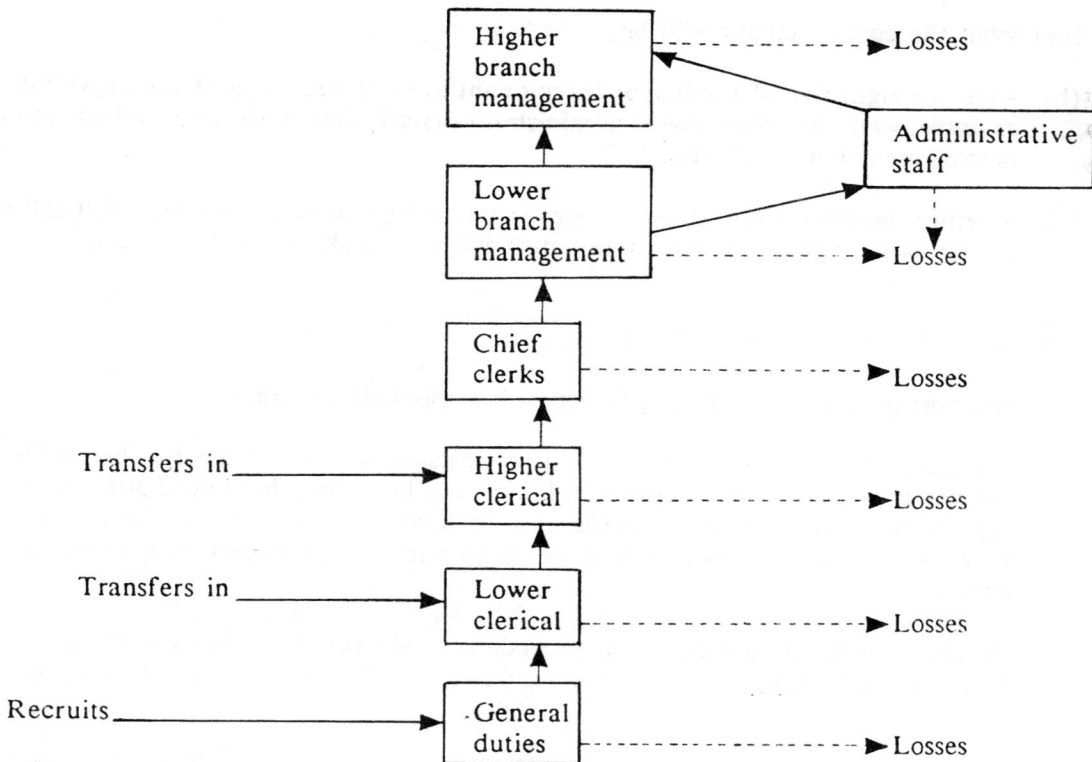

The policy of recruitment, transfers and promotion must be specified, so that 'entry points' into the manpower structure can be identified. In this example, the policy of external recruitment only into general duties work and inter-regional transfers only into clerical duties has been specified as organisation policy.

Losses are brought about by retirement, resignation or dismissal (as well as by promotion).

5.17 The next stage in planning is to estimate the demand for manpower. As we have already seen, this is a very difficult task, because the planner must estimate:

(a) what rate of growth (if any) the organisation will have;

(b) how its business might diversify into new operations;

(c) what productivity will be. This in turn depends on how much capital expenditure will be undertaken, what new technologies are available, how work will be organised, and what the motivation of staff will be;

(d) social factors such as the desire for more leisure time and holidays. This might mean a change in the length of the working week or the number of weeks holiday each year;

(e) external factors, such as economic slump or boom, which will influence the organisation's planned rate of growth.

5.18 Other factors affecting the demand for manpower, which must be allowed for in the demand forecast, are:

(a) what the cost of labour will be;

(b) what the right size of the labour force ought to be in each part of the organisation. For example, what should the size of administrative (staff) departments be, and what should the management/employee ratio be?

(c) whether there are likely to be changes in technology or markets which will call for new labour skills, and if so, how many staff with these skills will be needed.

5.19 Estimates of staff losses will also be necessary:

(a) retirement figures can be predicted with reasonable accuracy;

(b) 'natural wastage' due to resignation, dismissals, or retirement for health or family reasons is more difficult to predict. It appears, however, that the likelihood of wastage is greatest amongst young employees, and employees who have been in their job for a fairly short time. An age profile of employees might therefore be necessary in order to calculate losses;

(c) the rate of natural wastage is also dependent on whether there are alternative jobs in the external job market: not many people want to make themselves unemployed!

5.20 A promotion policy will also be required to estimate the percentage numbers of staff at one grade (of given age and experience) who might expect promotion to a higher grade within a given period of time.

Example: manpower demand forecasting

5.21 A simple numerical example might help to illustrate how demand forecasting, and estimates of losses and promotions can be used to decide the number of new recruits required.

Suppose that a company has 1,000 staff in clerical grade 1, the lowest clerical grade in the company, with the following age structure:

Under 20	600
20 - 30	300
Over 30	100
	1,000

Wastage rates and promotion prospects in the next two years are expected to be:

Age	Wastage	Promotion
Under 20	30%	10%
20 - 30	10%	40%
Over 30	5%	20%

The demand forecast shows that 1,200 clerical grade 1 staff will be required in two years' time.

5.22 The manpower plan will show:

Opening staff		1,000
Wastage (30% of 600) + (10% of 300) + (5% of 100)	(215)	
Promotions to higher grade		
(10% of 600) + (40% of 300) + (20% of 100)	(200)	
Promotions from lower grades	N/A	(415)
Existing staff in the same grade in 2 years' time		585
Staff required in the grade in 2 years' time		1,200
Estimated recruitment requirements over 2 years		615

5.23 The same calculations can be made for 1 year's time, and 3, 4, 5 years etc; and once the number of promotions from grade 1 are estimated, similar manpower estimates can be made for higher grades in the organisation.

Control over manpower

5.24 Once a manpower plan has been established, regular control reports should be produced.

(a) Actual numbers recruited, leaving and being promoted should be compared with planned numbers. If actual manpower levels seem to be getting too high, control action can be taken by stopping recruitment temporarily. If actual manpower levels seem to be getting too low, recruitment, promotions or retraining activity should be stepped up.

(b) Actual pay, conditions of employment and training should be compared with assumptions in the manpower plan. Do divergences explain any excessive staff turnover?

(c) Periodically (perhaps once a year) the manpower plan itself should be reviewed and brought up to date.

The control systems in an organisation provide a basis for senior management to assess the performance of their subordinates, and hold them accountable for how they have used their authority and the resources at their disposal. Making managers responsible for their actions - performance measurement - is the subject of the next chapter.

TEST YOUR KNOWLEDGE

(The numbers in brackets refer to paragraphs in this chapter)

1. List the possible barriers which prevent or discourage managers from making plans. How might these barriers be overcome? (2.3-2.5)

2. What types of plan are there? (2.7)

3. What is feedback? (3.11-3.13)

4. Sketch a control system. (3.14, 3.30)

5. Child identifies four strategies for control. What are they? Suggest what types of organisation for which each of these strategies might be appropriate. (3.32, 3.33)

6. What are the qualities of good control information? (4.2-4.4, 4.7)

7. How important is effective Management Information for planning, control and decision-making? (4.9)

8. Discuss the application of manpower planning to an organisation preparing for the introduction of a major new technology to its operations.

Discussion

Question 8

Manpower planning has been fully described in the example in this chapter. A particular feature of this old ICSA examination question, however, is that the organisation is planning to introduce major new technology. The consequences of this might be fewer jobs - and so redundancies - and also a need for new labour skills. The new skills might be obtained by retraining existing staff. Conceivably though, existing staff might be made redundant and new staff with different skills recruited from outside. These factors must be taken into account in the manpower plan, and measures should be taken (eg retraining, negotiations with trade unions, pay, working conditions) to minimise staff unrest.

Chapter 9

ASSESSING PERFORMANCE

This chapter covers the following topics:

1. Assessing performance by comparison
2. Performance indicators
3. Value for money
4. Organisational effectiveness

Purpose of this chapter

To consider how management should be held responsible and accountable for their achievements, by means of performance appraisal.

1. ASSESSING PERFORMANCE BY COMPARISON

1.1 The performance of a manager or a unit of an organisation is assessed by means of comparison. In most cases, actual results are compared with one or more of the following:
   (a) planned (targeted) results;
   (b) a standard or norm for achievement;
   (c) the results achieved by a similar manager, unit or organisation (comparison with others);
   (d) progress over time (comparison with results in the past).

1.2 The comparisons should be reported to the manager who is responsible for the operations, and also to his superiors, who should appraise the manager's performance, reward him (or her) for successful results and hold him accountable for disappointing results.

2. PERFORMANCE INDICATORS

2.1 Performance indicators are the factors or measurements by which actual performance is assessed. These might be *quantitative* measures or *qualitative* measures.

Quantitative measures

2.2 Quantitative measures of performance include:

   (a) number of units or transactions processed;
   (b) number of people served;
   (c) completion dates;
   (d) efficiency or productivity measurements (eg output per manhour, output per machine hour);
   (e) sales revenue;
   (f) costs;
   (g) profits;
   (h) profits compared with assets employed to achieve those profits (return on investment).

EXAMPLES OF QUANTITATIVE MEASURES OF PERFORMANCE

Performance indicators	Example	Method of assessing and controlling performance
1. *Sales*	A sales manager might be given a sales target of £1 million in the first six months of the year. He might be given a staff of 4 sales representatives. Sales discounts must not exceed, say, 30%. An advertising or sales promotion campaign will back his sales effort.	Performance would be monitored monthly (or weekly) by comparing actual sales to date against budget. If sales to date are too low, control measures should be taken, but the manager will be constrained by the resources at his disposal (4 men, fixed advertising), and the contstraint of the discount limit of 30%.
2. *Costs*	A manager responsible for the running of an office building might be given an annual budget for running costs of £250,000, to include cleaning, repairs, maintenance, heating and lighting etc.	Performance would be monitored monthly by comparing actual costs to date against budget. The manager might have quite wide discretionary powers - eg to employ or dismiss cleaning and maintenance staff. he could also reduce costs by turning down the heating, reducing the frequency of window cleaning etc. His performance should also be measured, however,in terms of how well the building functions - is it open when staff want to get in; is is it kept clean and tidy; is it secure from intruders; is it well lit and well heated, or are there complaints from users of the building?
3. *Profits*	A manager for a division (profit centre) may be required to achieve a target profit for the year of £2m.	Performance should be monitored monthly, by comparing actual profits with target profits. Divisional managers should be allowed wide discretionary powers to take control action should actual profits be too low.
4. *Completion dates*	A project manager might be required to complete a contract for a customer by 30 June, within a budget limit of £150,000.	Performance would be assessed on the basis of whether the job was completed in time and within its cost limit.

This list is by no means comprehensive, and you should try as an exercise to think of a few more, perhaps from your own work experience.

2.3 At middle and senior management level in an organisation, performance is often measured by comparing actual results against a budget, and monthly performance indicators relate to sales, costs and profits.

Qualitative measures

2.4 Qualitative measures of performance include:

(a) the quality of output;

(b) the quality of service;

(c) the morale of the work force;

(d) the flexibility of the organisation in response to change;

(e) the timeliness of planning decisions (eg are managers making decisions later than they should, thereby wasting opportunities to steal a march on competitors?)

2.5 Some qualitative factors can be monitored by quantitative measures of performance. For example:

(a) the quality of output could be measured by the number of production items rejected on inspection, or the number of items returned after sale as faulty by customers;

(b) the quality of a service could be measured by the level of complaints or by favourable reaction. The quality of a training course, for example, could be monitored by asking trainees to complete an assessment form when the course has finished. The training manager's performance could assessed on the basis of the responses;

(c) the morale of the work force could be monitored by measuring changes in the rate of labour turnover, absenteeism or time lost through stoppages caused by industrial action by staff.

2.6 As a very general rule, it could be suggested that quantitative indicators of performance pinpoint matters where control action can often be taken in the short term to improve results, whereas qualitative indicators of performance might indicate more deep-seated problems of poor organisation and leadership, where more fundamental, and perhaps longer term, corrective measures need to be taken.

Exercise

What factors should be considered in assessing the performance of the following:

(a) a department store;
(b) a non-profit-making hospital;
(c) a bank;
(d) a manufacturing company?

Discussion points

To monitor the effectiveness of any organisation, we need to establish what its objectives are. These should be measurable, and an organisation will be effective if it succeeds in achieving its objectives. Objectives vary from organisation to organisation, and may be both long term and short term, quantitative and qualitative. As brief suggestions:

(a) *Department store.* Profits, return on capital. Annual increase in turnover/number of sales (ie number of customers).

(b) *Hospital (non-profit-making).* Number of patients treated. Length of waiting list. Quality and range of treatment. Possibly, training for medical students and nurses. Constraints of expenditure budget.

(c) *Bank.* Profits, return on capital. Range of financial services successfully provided. Comparison with other banks/building societies. Growth rate.

(d) *Manufacturing company.* Profits, return on capital. Range and quality of products. Up-to-dateness of products.

Qualitative objectives that apply to all four organisations should include ethical standards of behaviour, flexibility (ability to adapt to change) and good morale amongst the workforce.

---

3.   VALUE FOR MONEY

3.1   A term that is quite often used in the context of performance measurement is value for money, or VFM. There are three elements in value for money, and these are known as the '3 Es':

(a)   economy - doing things cheaply;
(b)   efficiency - doing things well and right;
(c)   effectiveness - doing the right things.

Economy

3.2   A system or operation should be economical, which means that it ought to acquire its resources (eg manpower, equipment, materials) of a *suitable quality* and in *sufficient numbers* to do the work properly, *but at the lowest cost.* Economy does not mean skimping and saving, because too much cost-cutting and expenditure control could result in the work not getting done properly. It is perhaps better to think of economy as avoiding waste and unnecessary spending.

3.3   Performance indicators to measure economy will be concerned with matters such as 'Did the manager spend more than he needed to on the resources he used? Could be have done exactly the same job, but with less money?' For example:

(a)   if a manager paid external consultants £1,000 to do a job, was the price too high? Should he have been able to negotiate a lower fee?

(b)   if a manager buys an office microcomputer for £10,000, could he have bought a smaller, less powerful but much cheaper micro to do the same job? Is the machine he bought too powerful for its planned use?

Efficiency

3.4   A system or operation should be efficient, which means that it should use its input resources to good effect to produce its outputs. Efficiency can be measured by ratios of outputs to inputs, or quantity of output produced per £1 spent, and so on. Greater efficiency results in lower unit costs.

3.5   Performance indicators to measure efficiency will be concerned with matters such as: 'Were the resources at the manager's disposal used efficiently? Was there a satisfactory ratio of outputs produced per unit of resource input?'. Examples of productivity measurements are:

(a)   units produced or transactions processed per labour hour;
(b)   average time per transaction;
(c)   sales revenue per employee;
(d)   cost per employee;
(e)   profit per employee;
(f)   units produced or transactions processed per machine per day.

Effectiveness

3.6   A system or operation should be effective, which means that it should be successful in accomplishing the targets that were set for it. Targets for a service are targets for outputs, and these might be expressed in terms of quantity or quality, and there could well be multiple targets.

3.7   Performance indicators to measure effectiveness are concerned with matters such as 'has the manager achieved the short term targets that were set by him (or for him)? Does he appear to be achieving the longer term targets that were set?'. Targets for achievement include:

(a)   reaching a budgeted sales target;
(b)   achieving a budgeted profit figure;
(c)   achieving a planned weekly output target.

3.8   These examples of targets for monitoring effectiveness are all quantitative and fairly short term targets. Some targets will be quantitative and qualitative performance indicators relate to effectiveness rather than to efficiency or economy.

3.9   As another example, targets for a hospital might be set in terms of:

(a)   treating a target number of patients;
(b)   reducing the percentage of total time that beds are empty;
(c)   speeding up the treatment of patients;
(d)   handling more of one type of case (eg heart surgery) and less of others;
(e)   keeping within budgeted limits for spending.

An assessment of effectiveness must ask the question 'has this area of operations achieved the targets that were set for it, and if not, by how much did it fall short, and why?'

3.10 A relationship between the 3 Es can be illustrated as follows:

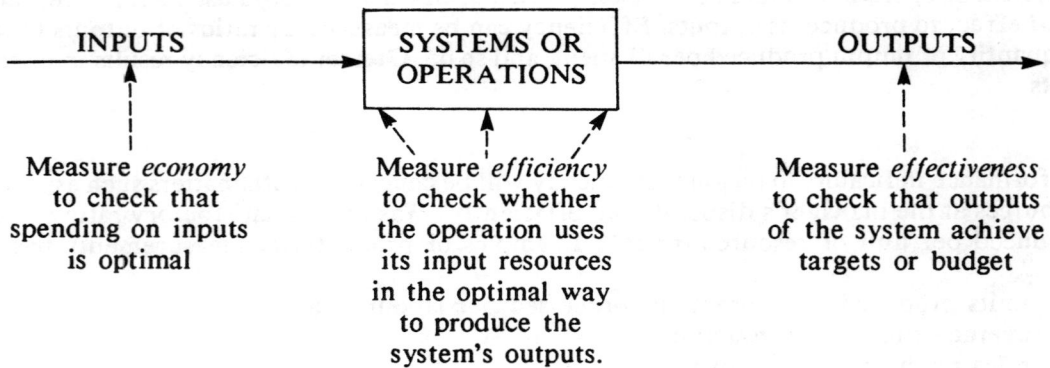

```
INPUTS ──────────▶  ┌──────────────┐ ───────────▶  OUTPUTS ──────────▶
                    │ SYSTEMS OR   │
          ▲         │ OPERATIONS   │                      ▲
          ┊         └──────────────┘                      ┊
          ┊          ↖    ↑    ↗                          ┊
```

| Measure *economy* to check that spending on inputs is optimal | Measure *efficiency* to check whether the operation uses its input resources in the optimal way to produce the system's outputs. | Measure *effectiveness* to check that outputs of the system achieve targets or budget |

4. ORGANISATIONAL EFFECTIVENESS

4.1 Senior management should be accountable for the effectiveness of the organisation as a whole. An effective organisation is one where:

(a) financial objectives are met;

(b) objectives for providing a product or service are met.

4.2 There are also qualitative symptoms of an effective organisation, namely:

(a) the morale and motivation of employees are high;

(b) management decisions are taken promptly, as soon as the need for decisions arises;

(c) there is no conflict between different units of the organisation, whose activities are well co-ordinated;

(d) there are good responses to changing circumstances, and a readiness to adapt to these changes;

(e) the administration costs of the management team are kept under control.

4.3 The *performance indicators* of a struggling organisation are therefore both *quantitative* (profits, revenues, products or services provided to customers) and *qualitative*. The reasons why an organisation might be struggling will be largely attributed to senior management.

4.4 The *causes* of organisational ineffectiveness are mainly poor management, poor control systems or poor organisation, as the following table suggests:

Symptom of struggling organisation	Possible causes
1. *Failure to achieve financial objectives.*	1.1 Unrealistic planning: unattainable objectives.
	1.2 Poor control actions by operational management.
	1.3 Weak organisation.
	1.4 Environmental factors (eg fall in customer demand) making targets unattainable. Failure to adapt to change.
2. *Low motivation and morale* (industrial unrest, high staff turnover, high absenteeism etc).	2.1 Inconsistent and arbitrary rules by management. No 'standard rules'.
	2.2 Little responsibility/authority for subordinates and no chance for achievement, recognition or reward. Close supervision and narrow spans of control.
	2.3 Employees are not clear about what they are supposed to do, nor how their performance will be measured.
	2.4 Work pressures are high, to get things done, but there is a lack of priorities.
	2.5 There are unrealistic expectations of what employees should be able to do, and staff are overworked.
3. *Late or poor decisions.*	3.1 Poor management information system, possibly because the organisation is tall, and information does not pass well between the different hierarchies of management.
	3.2 Poor co-ordination between groups. Decisions taken by one group leader are inconsistent with decisions taken by another group.
	3.3 Not enough delegation. Decision-makers are overloaded with decisions to make.
	3.4 No procedures for evaluating results, and so both planning and control decisions late or poor.

4.	*Conflict and lack of co-ordination*	4.1	Conflicting goals of different divisions, departments or groups in the organisation. No hierarchy of organisational objectives.
		4.2	Poor liaison between departments or groups. Lack of teamwork.
		4.3	Separation of planning from operational management, because operational managers are not involved in planning decisions.
5.	*Poor response to change.*	5.1	No specialist jobs in the organisation for responding to change (eg no forecasting jobs, no environmental studies, little or no R and D work).
		5.2	Change and innovation are not mainstream activities, when they ought to be.
		5.3	Poor co-ordination between market research and technological R and D.
6.	*Rising costs of management administration.*	6.1	The organisation is top-heavy with 'chiefs'.
		6.2	Excessive paperwork needs more and more managers to handle.
		6.3	Organisational problems referred to earlier call for more and more managers to try to handle them.

Summary

4.5 The key points to be aware of about performance measurement and accountability are:

(a) performance is measured by indicators, which can be quantitative or qualitative;

(b) the usual way of assessing performance is to compare actual results against a target, against results achieved by other groups or organisations, or against results in the past;

(c) performance can be assessed on the basis of value for money - economy, efficiency and effectiveness;

(d) measuring effectiveness can be done with quantitative measures, but qualitative measures might be very important too. The performance of senior management can be measured by organisational effectiveness, not just by profits and return. Measures of organisational effectiveness are largely qualitative.

TEST YOUR KNOWLEDGE

(The numbers in brackets refer to paragraphs in this chapter)

1. List as many quantitative measures of performance as you can. (2.2)

2. List as many qualitative measures of performance as you can. (2.4)

3. What are the 3 Es of value for money? (3.1)

4. What are the symptoms and causes of an ineffective organisation, for which senior management ought to be accountable? (4.4)

5. To what extent does general management have a responsibility for ensuring 'value for money' from all expenditure? What can general managers do to encourage and sustain such a discipline?

6. Can we measure the effectiveness of an organisation through quantitative indicators such as profit, cost and turnover or should we pay attention, also, to qualitative indicators such as employee attitudes and flexibility? How important are these qualitative indicators as measures of future effectiveness?

Discussion points

Question 5
A solution to this question ought to define VFM, and make the point that general management have a responsibility for achieving organisational objectives efficiently and economically. This is true in non-profit-making organisations as well as profit-making ones.

To encourage and sustain a VFM discipline, general management should try to establish control systems whereby managers:

(a) are given clear targets for achievement (quantitative and qualitative);

(b) are given sufficient resources to achieve those targets;

(c) are given regular feedback about performance;

(d) have sufficient authority to take control decisions on their own initiative;

(e) should be made responsible for their achievements. This can be done by making them accountable to senior management, through performance reporting. The control system provides the discipline. General management should also provide the discipline by setting an example for others.

Question 6
The wording of this question virtually answers itself. The question is much the same as question 4 above. An organisation is effective if it achieves the objectives that are set for it, and if each manager achieves the objectives set for him or her. More will be said about objective setting in the next chapter.

Chapter 10

OBJECTIVE SETTING AND MANAGEMENT BY OBJECTIVES

```
This chapter covers the following topics:

1.    Categories and examples of objectives
2.    The purpose of setting objectives
3.    The hierarchy of objectives
4.    Converting objectives into planning targets: problems with budgets
5.    Management by objectives
```

Purpose of this chapter

To consider what objectives might be set for an organisation and for individual managers within it, and how a system of control and performance measurement might be set up to monitor effectiveness.

1.   CATEGORIES AND EXAMPLES OF OBJECTIVES

1.1 It was suggested in the previous chapter that the effectiveness of an organisation and its management can be monitored by checking whether objectives have been achieved. Objectives should be set for the organisation as a whole, and where possible expressed as quantitative targets (eg target return on investment of x% pa). Objectives could also be set for individual managers, throughout the management hierarchy, within a system of management by objectives or MBO.

1.2 Objectives could be listed under the following broad headings:

(a) *financial*: eg. profitability, return on capital employed, return on shareholders' equity, return on trading assets employed, earnings per share;

(b) *market position*: eg. total market share of each market segment, growth of sales, customers or potential customers, the need to avoid relying on a single customer for a large proportion of total sales, what markets should the company be in;

(c) *product development*: ie. to bring in new products, develop a product range, spend money on research and development, to provide products of a certain quality at a certain price level (eg. to provide products of a certain reliability at a cheap price);

(d) *technology*: eg. to acquire the latest technology in equipment for production, to improve productivity and reduce the cost per unit of output;

(e) *employees and management*: eg. to pay employees a wage above the industry's average, to provide job satisfaction and career development, to look after staff welfare, to train employees in certain skills, to reduce labour turnover;

(f) *organisation*: eg. to create an organisation where much authority is delegated and employees, lower and middle management have a greater degree of participation in planning and decision-making;

(g) *public responsibility*: eg. to acknowledge the social responsibilities of the company to protect the environment and support their local communities.

1.3 Alternatively, Drucker suggested that objectives should be identified and quantified under eight headings.

(a) *Market standing*. This must be measured against the total market potential, and the market standing of competitors. The goals which should then be established are:

  (i) the desired standing of existing products in existing markets (£ turnover and % market share);

  (ii) the desired standing of existing products in the new markets;

  (iii) the products which should be abandoned because they will no longer be profitable enough;

  (iv) the number of new products required in existing markets, their necessary characteristics, and their desired standing;

  (v) the number of new products (and their desired market standing) in new markets;

  (vi) the distribution organisation needed to accomplish these marketing goals, and the pricing policy required;

  (vii) a customer service objective (ie. a measure of how well the customer should be supplied with 'value for money').

(b) *Innovation*. Innovation objectives should attempt to forecast future technological developments, and how the organisation should adapt:

  (i) its products and services; or

  (ii) its methods of working;

to the changes. However, innovation in products or services are necessary even in industries where technological change is not significant. Changes in consumer demand will render many existing products and services obsolete, and create marketing opportunities for new ones.

(c) *Productivity and added value.* Productivity targets are a measure of the desired efficiency with which resources should be utilised (eg. output per man hour, output per metre of cloth, output per machine hour). Added value is the difference between the revenue from a product and the material costs of production and sales. Targets for performance might therefore be that:

    (i)   the company should earn added value of £x per employee;

    (ii)   employees should earn in total wages or salaries equal to y% of added value.

(d) *Physical and financial resources.* Every business uses physical resources and money, and it must be sure of its supply. Objectives should be set for obtaining sufficient resources to enable the business to achieve its goals for market standing and innovation.

(e) *Profitability.* Profitability targets must be set. These may be 'satisficing' profit targets; however, Drucker argued that they should be *minimum* profit targets that will ensure survival and the provision of funds for re-investment in future innovation for expansion.

(f) *Manager performance and development.* These objectives are considered in the later chapter on management by objectives.

(g) *Worker performance and attitudes.* Objectives should be set for worker performance and should not be left in the initiative of trade unions. However, there is a problem, as we shall discuss later in this text, that there is no clear link between workers' attitudes and their performance. Setting objectives for absenteeism, labour turnover, safety, grievances or attitudes will not necessarily ensure that worker performance is at all satisfactory.

(h) *Public responsibility.* It is management's job to cover the demands placed on an organisation by public opinion and attitudes, and legal and political pressures, into opportunities for future growth and innovation.

2.   THE PURPOSE OF SETTING OBJECTIVES

2.1   'Objectives are needed in every area where performance and results directly and vitally affect the survival and prosperity of the business' (Drucker). Objectives in these key areas should enable management:

    (a)   to organise and explain the purpose and direction of the business in a small number of general statements about goals;

    (b)   to test the validity of these goals as a means of achieving the organisation's purpose;

    (c)   to predict behaviour;

    (d)   to appraise the validity of decisions about strategies and budgets (by assessing whether these are sufficient to achieve the stated objectives);

    (e)   to assess and control actual performance.

2.2 It will be useful to list a few examples of possible objectives. These are fairly broad objectives, for an organisation, division or department as a whole:

(a) *market position*: eg. to increase export sales, increase the share of the total market or market segments;

(b) *product and market development*: **eg.** to introduce new products, extend an existing product range, find new markets, develop new technologies, spend money on R & D;

(c) *profitability*: eg. to increase **earnings, profits**, return on capital employed (ROCE) etc;

(d) *customers*: eg. to eliminate all **order sizes below** £x, to avoid reliance on individual large customers;

(e) *productivity and output*: to increase productivity and achieve a certain capacity level of output;

(f) *finance*: to achieve a capital gearing structure of x%;

(g) *management development*: to provide a career structure for managers, use management by objectives, and delegate authority to lower levels of management;

(h) *industrial relations*: eg. to secure productivity/pay agreements with trade unions;

(i) *organisation*: eg. to create a new subsidiary to deal with a new product range and to rationalise several head office departments into a single office etc.

3. THE HIERARCHY OF OBJECTIVES

3.1 It is generally accepted that there is a *hierarchy* of objectives, with one prime corporate objective (restricted by certain constraints on corporate activity) and a series of subordinate strategic objectives which should combine to ensure the achievement of the overall objective.

3.2 There has been considerable disagreement about the choice of the overall corporate objective, although it is often agreed that for a *company* it must be a financial objective.

Various financial objectives would include:

(a) profitability;
(b) return on capital employed; (ROCE)
(c) survival, ie. the avoidance of loss;
(d) (growth in) earnings per share (EPS);
(e) (growth in) dividends to shareholders;
(f) a target price earnings (P/E) ratio;
(g) return on shareholders' capital with an allowance for the element of risk.

These objectives all differ in some respects, although it is perhaps sufficient to note that they are all concerned with financial achievements (even (c) - survival).

3.3 In many organisations, especially large ones, managers do not operate on the principle of *maximising* profits. They are content to achieve a level of profits or return on capital which will appear acceptable and realistic to all managers in the organisation, shareholders, employees, government and public opinion! In other words, they will seek a satisfactory or satisficing level of profits.

3.4 Although many writers agree that there should be an overall financial objective, expressed as a quantified target, they acknowledge **that there are** certain social or ethical obligations which a company must fulfil. More will be **said about** this topic in a later chapter.

3.5 After the overall financial objective has been identified and quantified as a target and similarly, after the ethological objectives have been identified, it is necessary to identify objectives for sub-divisions of the company:

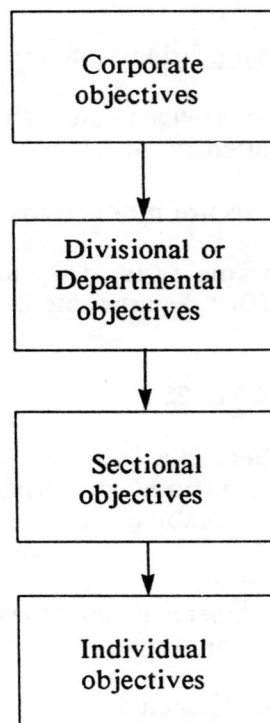

```
        ┌──────────────────┐
        │    Corporate     │
        │   objectives     │
        └──────────────────┘
                 │
                 ▼
        ┌──────────────────┐
        │  Divisional or   │
        │  Departmental    │
        │   objectives     │
        └──────────────────┘
                 │
                 ▼
        ┌──────────────────┐
        │    Sectional     │
        │   objectives     │
        └──────────────────┘
                 │
                 ▼
        ┌──────────────────┐
        │    Individual    │
        │   objectives     │
        └──────────────────┘
```

4. OBJECTIVES AND BUDGETS

4.1 One way of converting objectives into action plans and targets is to prepare budgets. There are a few major problems with budgets, however:

(a) they might be too short term in outlook, and place too much emphasis on financial objectives;

(b) budgets often fail to win the commitment of managers.

4.2 Although *budgets* are an important feature of management control, they are not sufficient on their own to provide a link between company objectives and strategic plans on the one hand, and shorter-term, management decisions on the other. In other words, there is the problem of converting strategic plans into management action plans.

4.3 The main need is to obtain the support of management. This cannot be done simply by issuing budgets and instructing managers to use them, or telling managers what their objectives are. The system will only be effectively supported when the managers who will be held responsible for achieving the targets actually participate in their framing. Managers must be fully aware of the rationale behind their objectives and targets, and the company's requirements for effective planning and control. The management author, Bill Reddin, has conducted considerable research to prove that targets are only really effectively fulfilled when the manager concerned is involved in the preparation of the target and is supplied with prompt, valid feedback of performance figures.

4.4 'The real difficulty lies indeed not in determining what objectives we need, but in deciding how to set them. There is only one fruitful way to make this decision; by determining what shall be measured in each area and what the yardstick of measurement should be.' (Drucker).

5. MANAGEMENT BY OBJECTIVES

5.1 Management by objectives (MBO) is a more 'comprehensive' approach to setting objectives, targets and plans. MBO is a scheme of planning and control which provides co-ordination, ie:

(a) co-ordination of short-term plans with longer-term plans and goals;
(b) co-ordination of the plans (and commitment) of junior with senior management;
(c) co-ordination of the efforts of different departments.

'Management by objectives requires effort and special instruments. For in the business enterprise managers are not automatically directed towards a common goal. On the contrary, business, by its very mature, contains three powerful factors of misdirection: in the specialised work of most managers; in the hierarchical structure of management; and in the difference in vision and work and the resultant insulation of various levels of management'. (Drucker).

5.2 Successful achievement of organisational goals requires that:

(a) each job is directed towards the same organisational goals. Each managerial job must be focused on the success of the business as a whole, not just one part of it;

(b) each manager's targeted performance must be derived from targets of achievement for the organisation as a whole;

(c) a manager's results must be measured in terms of their contribution to the business as a whole;

(d) each manager must know what his targets of performance are;

(e) a manager's superior must know what to demand from the manager, and how to judge his performance.

'Each manager, from the big boss down to the production foreman or the chief clerk, needs clearly spelled-out objectives.' (Drucker).

5.3 Another writer who became a leading advocate of MBO in the 1960s was John Humble (in *Improving Business Results* and *Management By Objectives*). Humble argued that against a background of long-term corporate plans, the operating and functional units of a company (branches, regions, marketing department etc.) should clarify their own objectives.

(a) Both team objectives and individual managers' objectives must be identified; therefore key tasks must be analysed and performance standards agreed.

(b) These key tasks will be fused together into individual plans, prepared each year by divisional managers, and expressed in strategic terms rather than in short-term budgets.

(c) The divisional plans are reviewed centrally and amended by company or group headquarters, in consultation with divisional managers. Any imbalance between divisional objectives can be adjusted at this stage - ie. is one division attempting to do too much and another attempting too little? Are the divisional plans consistent with each other, or is there sub-optimality? If resources are scarce and the demand by divisions for resources exceeds the supply, how should a fair allocation be made between them?

(d) Having agreed annual plans for each division, with key tasks identified and performance indicators established for each team and individual manager within the division, managers identify:

(i) *policies*: ie, guides to making decisions which are in keeping with corporate objectives;

(ii) *financial budgets*: ie. a statement in money terms of a plan to achieve certain objectives. Financial budgets *are not the objectives themselves*.

Humble said that each of these three devices (policies, procedures and financial budgets) were necessary to sound management control.

(e) Each division should make a monthly operating report, measuring actual results against key performance indicators. There should also be similar quarterly and annual reviews, after which new divisional plans would be prepared.

5.4 One of the most difficult problems for top management is finding the right balance between the conflicting claims of long-term and short-term results. Shareholders expect dividends every year, and will not be content to wait for the long term to receive their returns. On the other hand, large capital-intensive companies are forced to take the long view because they do not have the flexibility to change plans and direction quickly:

(a) 'since any attempt to interlock different levels of objectives in detail is bound to fail, great concentration must be made on selecting a limited number of priorities which *must* be linked from top to bottom of the business' (Humble);

(b) interlocking these key objectives must be not only vertical, but horizontal, ie. the objectives of the production function must be linked with those of sales, warehousing, purchasing, R & D etc;

(c)   short-term objectives can be regarded as intermediate 'staging-posts' on the road towards long-term objectives.

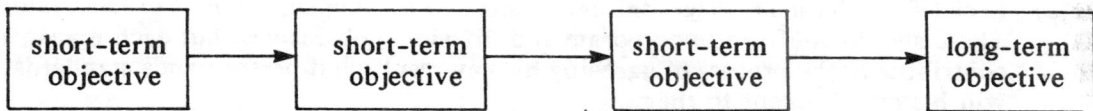

```
┌─────────────┐     ┌─────────────┐     ┌─────────────┐     ┌─────────────┐
│ short-term  │ ──▶ │ short-term  │ ──▶ │ short-term  │ ──▶ │ long-term   │
│ objective   │     │ objective   │     │ objective   │     │ objective   │
└─────────────┘     └─────────────┘     └─────────────┘     └─────────────┘
```

5.5   The hierarchy of objectives which emerges is as follows:

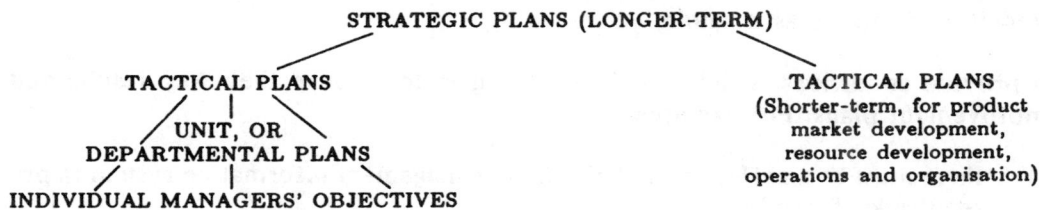

STRATEGIC PLANS (LONGER-TERM)

TACTICAL PLANS

UNIT, OR DEPARTMENTAL PLANS

INDIVIDUAL MANAGERS' OBJECTIVES

TACTICAL PLANS (Shorter-term, for product market development, resource development, operations and organisation)

5.6   There are two approaches to establishing this hierarchy of objectives:

(a)   Senior managers (perhaps the managing director himself) can tell managers what to do and set up control procedures. Humble comments that 'this apparently sensible and logical approach often misses the spark of vitality, challenge and involvement on which the real use of human being depends'. It is 'top-down' management.

(b)   Develop the contribution and motivation of each manager in the business by involving him in the planning process. This approach, which Humble called 'improving management performance', introduces an element of 'bottom-up' management, organised within the framework of corporate objectives and strategic plans.

5.7   Advocates of MBO (Drucker, Humble etc) argue that managers will only be committed to their objectives if they are allowed to assume responsibility for setting their own objectives for their unit of the business. Higher management should:

(a)   reserve the right to approve or disapprove the manager's objectives set by himself;

(b)   help the manager to set his objectives by communicating to him the goals and broad strategies of the organisation over the corporate planning period.

5.8   Management development is a key feature of MBO and it will only be successful if managers are given the responsibility for setting their own objectives (in consultation perhaps with their superiors).

5.9   Each manager should be given the information he needs to control his own performance, as soon as the information can be made available (economically) for him to use. The control information should go directly to him, and not to his boss. Control should not be seen to come down from above, because this will reduce managers' commitment to their objectives.

5.10 The essential features of Humble's recommended approach are:

(a) to clarify with each manager the *key results* and *performance standards* he should achieve. These should conform to corporate and divisional objectives, but each manager should contribute to the process of agreeing his key results and performance standards, so as to win his commitment to them;

(b) to agree, with each manager, a *job improvement plan* for himself, which will make a quantifiable and measurable contribution to achievement of the plans for the department, branch or company as a whole;

(c) to provide conditions which will help managers to achieve their key results and job improvement plans. For example:

    (i) there must be an efficient and effective management information system to provide feedback of results;

    (ii) there must be an organisation structure which provides managers with sufficient flexibility and freedom of action;

    (iii) there should be a sense of 'team spirit and corporate purpose' within the organisation;

(d) to have a systematic *performance review* of each manager's results;

(e) to hold a regular *potential review* for each manager so as to identify the individuals with potential for advancement within the company;

(f) to develop *management training plans* to improve management skills;

(g) to motivate managers by effective *salary, selection and career development plans.*

5.11 It is essential that management control procedures should be properly integrated with corporate objectives, and Humble argues that this control cannot be done 'mechanistically' but depends on the contribution of a flexible and skilled management team. Managers who get results should be encouraged, and these men are not necessarily the ones who stand out for their personalities. The only way to get the best out of managers is to identify and develop their potential (through training) and win their co-operation and commitment (through participation in planning decisions, salaries and career prospects).

5.12 Humble described the typical sequence of events for the introduction of a scheme of management by objectives as follows:

(a) The direction must come from the chief executive. A corporate plan and corporate strategies must be identified, and the involvement of the chief executive is essential.

(b) The objectives of the 'sub-units' of the organisation (subsidiaries, departments, sections etc) must be clarified.

(c) An analysis must be prepared of the key results expected from each manager. These key results are agreed in consultation between the manager himself, his boss (and his boss' boss) and a staff 'advisor'.

(d) Top management assesses the 'unit' objectives and the key results for each manager. Since resources will no doubt be scarce, priorities for improvements will need to be decided.

(e) Top management expresses these priorities formally in a 'unit' improvement plan. From this, 'job improvement plans' for individual managers are agreed.

(f) Each manager must be given sufficient authority and opportunity to achieve his job improvement plan. A timescale for achievement must be decided.

(g) There must be a systematic performance review of each manager's results, together with a performance review for the 'unit' as a whole.

(h) There must be a continuing management development programme (ie. potential reviews, training, career development, selection etc.)

(i) There must be a continuity or cycle in the revision of the unit and job improvement plans. Annual budgets provide one method of continuity, although at a lower level of management a shorter cycle might be more appropriate.

5.13 Unit objectives are required for all departments. They must be set first of all in terms of primary targets, relating to:

(a) profitability;
(b) level of activity, or turnover;
(c) achievement of production schedules and delivery dates;
(d) the quality of output or services;
(e) safety;
(f) efficiency in the use of resources (labour, productivity, material usage);
(g) plant utilisation; ... and so on.

5.14 For each of these primary targets, secondary targets (or sub-targets) will be set. For example:

(a) profitability: the contribution required from each individual product, and the method of fixed overhead allocation;

(b) quality of output: the acceptable level of rejected units at inspection should be specified for each type of work and product, the acceptable standards of workmanship identified, target requirements for after-sales service and customer complaints might be set out.

5.15 Once the unit objectives have been identified, it is then necessary to identify which individual managers within the unit are in a position to influence the achievement of each of them.

Key results analysis

5.16 At the same time that unit objectives are formulated, a key results analysis is prepared for each individual manager. As the term suggests, the analysis attempts to identify *key* results, and does not list all the tasks of each manager. For example, the key results of the data processing operations manager might be:

ITEM	KEY RESULT
(a) Service to users	To ensure that users get immediate access to processors through on-line terminals, and all batch processing must be done within agreed turn-round schedule.
(b) Use of resources and efficiency levels	Mainframe computers must operate at more than 80% capacity within a 2-shift day, 6-day week. Breakdown time must not exceed 5%.
(c) Costs	The cost per operating hour must not exceed £60 which is the standard cost.
(d) Quality	There must be no irretrievable corruption of files, and complaints from users must be restricted to an acceptable level (this level must be quantified, if possible).

5.17 Identifying and establishing *performance standards* is an important feature of management control (note: and also of operational control). Performance standards may be:

(a) *quantitative*: eg. volume of output or sales, market shares, levels of scrap and inventory, cost levels, timescales etc. Quantities can be expressed in terms of volumes, quality, time, costs and profits;

(b) *qualitative*: eg. attitudes of employees and customers.

At middle management level, any quantitative performance standards will be largely expressed in terms of money (costs, revenues, profits).

5.18 Performance standards provide a means of both planning and control. Where they are quantitative, control will be initiated by the preparation of a report of control document (eg. monthly operating statement, profit and loss account etc.).

5.19 Top management must integrate the unit objectives of each department, and the key results analysis of individual managers. The purpose of this critical analysis will be:

(a) to ensure that unit objectives are consistent with each other and with overall corporate objectives;

(b) to identify common areas for improvement and ensure that the best joint approach is being taken to deal with them;

(c) to assign priorities for improvement schemes and objectives;

(d) to check whether every key area of business performance is the responsibility of one manager, and that there are no gaps where control is non-existent;

(e) to check whether there is unnecessary duplication of control work by more than one manager.

Unit improvement and job improvement plans

5.20 Top management will now make a unit improvement plan for each 'unit' of the business, setting out specifically the objectives for improvement, the performance standards and the timescale. Although many of these plans will be given a one-year duration so as to fit within a scheme of budgetary control, some aspects may be longer-term.

5.21 Each unit improvement plan must be approved by the senior manager with overall responsibility for the unit (eg. departmental manager, profit centre manager, or managing director of a subsidiary).

5.22 The unit improvement plan is then broken down into a series of results required from the various individual managers within the unit, expressed as job improvement plans:

(a) the job improvement plan tells the manager what he must do within given time periods;

(b) key results analysis tells the manager how his achievements can be gauged;

(c) performance standards for each key result will provide a means of measuring actual results against the plan in each key area.

'Once it is agreed and issued, the job improvement plan is vitally important. The manager is committed to achieving the results and his boss is committed to providing any agreed resources and information.' (Humble)

Performance review

5.23 A performance review must be a formal and disciplined review of the results achieved by each manager, carried out regularly on pre-determined dates. Performance standards in key results areas provide the means of comparison for actual results achieved.

5.24 Failure to achieve satisfactory results should initiate control action by the manager himself, with prompting from his superior.

5.25 As an important feature of management by objectives, Humble recommends a management development programme. The role of management development has been described already in a previous chapter.

Advantages and disadvantages of MBO

5.26 The advantages of MBO may be summarised briefly as follows:

(a) better managing through better planning and control;

(b) clarification of organisational goals within the framework of a long-term plan;

(c) it is a scheme for converting strategic plans into management action plans and budgets;

(d) the co-ordination of individual management targets into the overall scheme, so that each individual manager knows what is expected of him;

(e) it commits individual managers to their targets;

(f) it encourages better communication and co-ordination within the organisation;

(g) it helps to identify the need for change in organisational goals or individual managers and provides a system for making such changes.

5.27 The disadvantages of MBO are, briefly:

(a) it is not as effective as it should be if strategic plans have not been properly established; ie. MBO should be used within the structure of an overall corporate planning system;

(b) some targets may be long-term whereas managers may prefer short-term targets and tangible results. If a person expects to be transferred to a different job after, say, 2 years, he will not be satisfied with targets for a 3 or 4 year period;

(c) there is a danger of inflexibility, ie. individual objectives, once set, are not changed because the overall plan is rigidly adhered to. There must be flexibility and a willingness to accept amended objectives in the light of changing circumstances;

(d) it can be a time-consuming exercise which might not justify the benefit achieved;

(e) it might call for a significant change in the attitudes of senior managers, the style of leadership and the organisation structure if it is to function effectively as a system;

(f) it requires considerable inter-personal skills by managers throughout the organisation (in setting objectives and in reviewing performance with subordinates);

(g) it might overstress the need for individual achievements at the expense of teamwork.

5.29 A company has a prime economic objective. This is expressed as a quantified target. A target is not a forecast of what will happen, but it is a goal towards which planning must be directed.

5.30 To convert an organisation's objectives into practical planning targets, budgeting could be used. An alternative and probably more effective system would be MBO, although to establish a system of MBO calls for a lot of effort and a participative approach to decision making by senior management.

TEST YOUR KNOWLEDGE

(The numbers in brackets refer to paragraphs in this chapter)

1. What broad categories of objective are there? (1.2, 1.3, 3.2)

2. Why do managers set objectives? (2.1)

3. Describe a typical hierarchy of objectives. (3.5)

4. What are the deficiencies of budgets when it comes to achievement of strategic plans? (4.2, 4.3)

5. How does Management by Objectives seek to improve the achievement of organisational goals? (5.2)

6. Describe the key features of an MBO approach. (5.10)

7. What are (a) key results analysis and (b) performance standards? (5.16, 5.17)

8. What are the advantages and disadvantages of MBO? (5.26)

SECTION C

ORGANISATION

Chapter 11

ORGANISATION STRUCTURE AND DESIGN

This chapter covers the following topics:

1. The broad aspects of organisation structure and design
2. Job design
3. Work structuring
4. The primary work group and the research of Trist
5. Departmentation
6. Matrix organisation
7. The culture of organisations
8. The cultures approach to organisation structure
9. The adaptive organisation
10. Organic and mechanistic organisations
11. Contingency approach to organisation structure.

Purpose to this chapter

To consider different approaches to designing an organisation structure, and the relative merits and drawbacks of each, and whether there is any particular structure which is likely to produce a more efficient and effective organisation.

1. THE BROAD ASPECTS OF ORGANISATION STRUCTURE AND DESIGN

1.1 Organisation structure can be designed or rearranged to make an organisation function as effectively and efficiently as possible. There are three broad aspects of organisation design.

(a) *Structure*. Structure refers to matters such as the tasks and responsibilities assigned to each jobholder, discretion and authority, specialisation, hierarchies of authority, spans of control, formal reporting systems, monitoring and control systems, performance appraisal and reward systems.

(b) *Operating mechanisms*. These are concerned with how the work gets done within the organisation.

(c) *Decision mechanisms*. These refer to how decisions are taken, and the management information systems that are available to provide assistance to decision-makers.

11: ORGANISATION STRUCTURE AND DESIGN

1.2 There are a number of choices or options for organisation design.

> **For example:**
>
> 1. Should jobs be specialised and focus on a narrow aspect of work, or should jobs have a broader scope?
>
> 2. How much discretion should be allowed to individuals to do their job?
>
> 3. Should the organisation structure be tall or flat?
>
> 4. How should tasks be grouped? Should there be a 'federal' structure of operating divisions, or should there just be a functional (departmental) structure?
>
> 5. How much formality should there be in control systems?
>
> 6. Should there be a common culture throughout the organisation, or not? Culture is discussed later in this chapter.
>
> 7. What reward systems (pay etc) should be used?
>
> 8. How should the organisation recognise *change*, and adapt accordingly?
>
> 9. What might be the effect of *new technologies* on the organisation, and how should it change accordingly?

1.3 Some of these issues have been discussed already in earlier chapters, and we needn't go into them again. In particular, authority, responsibility, delegation, discretion, span of control, centralisation and decentralisation, tall and flat organisations, control systems and performance appraisal have all been covered. In this chapter, we shall go on to consider some of the further issues about organisation structure and culture.

2. JOB DESIGN

2.1 Job design is the structuring of tasks and responsibilities into individual jobs. The two basic features of job design are:

(a) how much specialisation should there be in a job?
(b) how much authority and discretion should each job holder be allowed?

2.2 Scientific management theory is that work can be divided into a series of small tasks, and each individual job should focus on a narrow, specialised task. The specialist job holder will carry out repetitive standard procedures and will do the work more efficiently than if jobs had a wider scope and less specialisation.

2.3 The counter-argument against scientific management theory is that a narrow specialisation of jobs results in boredom and apathy among employees. Significant improvements in performance can be achieved by creating interesting jobs which motivate the job holder. A motivation job is one which provides job enrichment, and enrichment is obtained by:

(a)   giving more discretion to the job holder;

(b)   to some extent, by job enlargement - ie less specialisation and a wider scope of responsibilities.

2.4 The issues of job enrichment and job enlargement were discussed in the earlier chapter on motivation in practice.

3.   WORK STRUCTURING

3.1 There is a view that the organisation of work should not concentrate on individual jobs, *except at supervisory and management level*, but should concentrate instead on work groups, and the work that is done by the group as a unit. This approach to work design is called work structuring.

3.2 The advantages of work structuring for an *organisation*, which has been used successfully by some Japanese companies, are as follows.

---

1.   Operational work is often group-based, not individual-based, and it is often possible to identify 'primary work groups' of about 4 to 20 people.

2.   By allocating tasks to a group instead of to individuals, the way that the work is shared out within the group can be adapted to suit the individual preferences of the group members.

3.   It promotes team work.

4.   It is better for training and learning the job.

---

4.   THE PRIMARY WORK GROUP AND THE RESEARCH OF TRIST

4.1 One of the first proponents of work structuring was Eric Trist, who argued that organisations should be structured on the basis of the *primary work group*. In their studies into coal mining organisations, Trist and Bamforth wrote 'It is difficult to see how these (organisation) problems can be solved efficiently without restoring responsible autonomy to primary groups throughout the system and ensuring that each of these groups has a satisfying sub-whole as its work task, and some scope for flexibility in work-pace. Only if this is done will the stress of the deputy's role be reduced and his task of maintaining the cycle receive spontaneous support from the primary work groups.'

4.2 It is interesting to study in more detail the research work of Trist and his colleagues into the coal mining operations.

4.3 The Coal Board had been trying to introduce new mechanical processes into coal mining in order to increase productivity, but the innovation provoked severe industrial unrest. Trist and his colleagues were invited to study the problem and to come up with a solution.

4.4 Prior to the technical innovations by the Coal Board, miners had been used to working in small autonomous groups or teams. Each team had its own place at the coal seam and was responsible for hewing coal with a pick or drill, loading it into tubs for transportation out of the mine and propping up the roof as they advanced. Each miner in the team was an all-rounder and did not have to specialise in any single activity within the overall task of the group. Each team was paid as a group and the pay was shared out equally between its members.

4.5 The Coal Board decided to change the work organisation in order to introduce new coal-cutting equipment capable of cutting a long stretch of wall at a time. Their new organisation (known as the *conventional longwall* system) divided the mining work into three separate tasks or shift:

(a) one group of miners did the cutting;

(b) a second group of miners loaded the loose coal onto a moving conveyor which took it away from the coal face;

(c) a third group moved the coal cutting equipment and conveyor forward, and propped up the roof.

4.6 The new arrangements proved unsuccessful. Within each specialised task there were some miners more willing and more able than others to carry out the specialised work. There were also problems in co-ordinating the work of the three different groups or shifts. As a result, it was found that closer supervision was required by management to ensure that the work was done properly and that every individual did his fair share.

4.7 Trist and his colleagues concluded that close managerial supervision was unsuitable to mining work, which was carried out in dangerous conditions. They agreed that the technical equipment used in operations must influence the type of work organisation for employees. In the case of coal mining, the new cutting equipment and conveyor belts made working in small groups no longer practicable. However, a work group has social and psychological properties and the work organisation should not be arranged in such a way that the advantages of technological improvements are thrown away by employee resistance and unrest.

4.8 They argued that an organisation is a socio-technological system which must attempt to balance:

(a) the economic advantages;
(b) the technological advantages; and
(c) social and psychological advantages

from work organisation. Their solution to the coal mining problem was to recommend a *composite longwall* method of working.

4.9 Under the composite longwall method the new technology was retained but the workforce was no longer split into three separate tasks. Instead, the whole task was to be completed by the entire group. The team as a whole was given the responsibility for assigning individuals to particular tasks or jobs. By this means, the work group was given autonomy, self-regulation, multi-skilled roles and a complete task to perform. As far as possible, the social conditions of the traditional system of mining were thereby restored. The 'three-task' group was thus defined as the new primary work group for coal mining operations.

4.10 Trist's work provides an early example of the systems approach to organisation. He argued that it is not sufficient to introduce the **most up-to-date** technology if a cheaper older technology is available or if the new work **organisation** will create serious employee unrest.

4.11 Similarly, it is not sufficient to create worker satisfaction if this entails inefficiency and uneconomic working which could be improved by better technological equipment.

4.12 A balance needs to be drawn between economic, technological and social/psychological advantages available. The work organisation should be seen as a whole, and the influence of one factor upon another (ie the inter-relationship between sub-systems in an organisation or an organisation and its environment) must be considered in setting up work organisation.

4.13 Primary groups are important in an industrial company because they form the smallest units within it, because they are the immediate social environment of the individual worker and because the methods and team-spirit which prevail there will determine the efficiency and relationships within the whole company.

4.14 The optimum size of a primary working group is important; the intimate, face to face relationships on which a primary group depends cannot be formed among more than, say, a dozen people. Anthony Jay (*Corporation Man*) identifies a group of ten - a 'ten group' - as the linear descendant of the primeval hunting-band, balancing the individuality necessary for generating new ideas, with the support and comradeship necessary for developing them.

4.15 In the sense that most industrial work falls into small groups of up to a dozen or so, primary groups are commonly found in industry. In the sense that these groups are provided for in the plan of organisation and provided with *official* leaders, primary groups are rarely found. Too often, the official organisation of a company comes to an end well above the primary group level.

4.16 Whenever the official organisation of a company fails to provide for the primary groups, unofficial primary groups will spring up. These will usually have a self-protective purpose and they will offer roles to unofficial leaders whose aims will not necessarily be in harmony with the official aims of the organisation.

4.17 Most industrial work falls naturally into primary groups and there are a number of roles such as those of setters, overlookers, and the like which are in effect leadership roles. In many cases, however, these are recognised only for their technical content and not for their human content. If such people were held responsible for the whole of their leadership role - for relationships and team spirit among the group as well as for its technical working - management organisation would extend to the primary working groups.

4.18 John Child summarised the advantages *for employees* of work structuring for *operative work*, based on primary groups, as follows.

Requirements of employees	*Achieved by*

1. Social interaction
Recognition
Discipline, leadership
Chance for development
  of employees.
	Team working in
	  primary groups of
	  4 to 20.

2. Use of skills and abilities
Variety
Challenge
Sense of completeness in
  work done.
	Work groups to
	  perform a whole
	  task.

3. Responsibility Discretion.	Work group to plan its own work.

4. Achievement
Identifiable objectives
Knowledge of results achievement
	Work group to be able
	  to evaluate performance
	  against targets, by
	  receiving regular feedback.

5. Individual needs within a
  group for fair treatment
  and flexibility.
	Common methods of
	  payment and conditions
	  of service.

Notes

1. Supervisors' work will now have less emphasis on 'firefighting' and progress chasing, and more emphasis or co-ordinating and developing team members.

2. Work structuring won't be effective if the work culture is wrong - eg if the workers have a deep suspicion of management's intentions. For example, proposals for work restructuring by the Ford Motor Company in the UK (1988) were resisted by strike action, with skilled workers fearful of loss of status and a general belief that the new system would put all workers at more risk by increasing their responsibility. Work restructuring, as in the example of Fords, will probably have to be 'sold' to workers with the offer of more pay all round.

3. Work structuring might not be applicable to management jobs, where the issues of individual job design (job enrichment, discretion etc) are likely to be more significant factors.

5. DEPARTMENTATION

5.1 Departmentation is an aspect of organisation structure and design which is concerned with the grouping of activities. Here, we are not looking at work structuring for primary work groups, but at the ways in which lines of authority are established and responsibilities are divided up - the horizontal differentiation between divisions, departments, groups and jobs.

5.2 **As an organisation grows in size:**

(a) it is able to take advantage of economies of scale, which in turn may call for the establishment of departments of specialists or experts (eg research and development, management scientists etc);

(b) the number of levels in the organisation hierarchy increases, so that problems of delegation of authority and control arise;

(c) specialist support teams (eg service and maintenance, quality control, corporate planning, organisation and methods, data processing etc) are created to ease the burdens and complexities of line management. Such support teams need to be slotted into the hierarchical structure;

(d) separate groups and departments continue to be formed as specialisation extends; new problems of communication and co-ordination (or integration) now arise.

5.3 When an organisation diversifies its activities into different products and markets, it is common for the structure to be 'divisionalised'. Large divisions of a company may in turn be sub-divided into smaller units.

5.4 The creation of departments and divisions is known as *departmentation*. Different patterns of departmentation are possible, and the pattern selected will depend on the individual circumstances of the organisation. Various methods of departmentation are:

(a) *by numbers:* when menial tasks are carried out by large numbers of workers, supervision can be divided by organising the men into gangs of equal size. Departmentation by numbers alone is rare; an example might be the organisation of a conscript army of infantrymen into divisions, and battalions etc;

(b) *by shifts:* with shift-working employees organised on the basis of 'time of day';

(c) *by function:* this is a widely-used method of organisation. Primary functions in a manufacturing company might be production, sales, finance, and general administration. Sub-departments of the production function might be manufacturing (machining, finishing, assembly etc) production control, quality control, servicing and purchasing. Sub-departments of sales might be selling, marketing, distribution and warehousing. Government departments include the Treasury, Home Office, Foreign Office, Department of Trade, Department of Industry, Ministry of Defence, etc.

Functional organisation is logical and traditional and accommodates the division of work into specialist areas. Apart from the problems which may arise when 'line' management resents interference by 'staff' advisors in their functional area, the drawback to functional organisation is simply that more efficient structures might exist which would be more appropriate in a particular situation;

(d) *by territory:* this method of organisation occurs when similar activities are carried out in widely different locations. The telecommunications service, for example, is presently divided into regions which in turn are sub-divided into Telephone Areas. Some authority is retained at Head Office (organised, perhaps, on a functional basis) but day-to-day service problems are handled on a territorial basis. Within many sales departments, the sales staff are organised territorially.

The *advantage of territorial departmentation* is better local decision-making at the point of contact between the organisation (eg a salesman) and its customers. Localised knowledge is put to better use and in the right circumstances it may be less costly to establish area factories/offices than to control everything through Head Office (eg costs of transportation and travelling may be less).

The *disadvantage of territorial departmentation* might be the duplication of management effort. For example, a national organisation divided into ten regions might have a customer liaison department at Head Office. If the organisation did all customer liaison work from head office it might need fewer managerial staff. In a similar way, there would be a tendency for regions to duplicate planning management, personnel and training management, accountancy management etc, thus increasing overhead costs and problems of co-ordination and integration.

(e)   *by product:* some organisations group activities on the basis of products or product lines. Some functional departmentation remains (eg manufacturing, distribution, marketing and sales) but a divisional manager is given responsibility for the product, product line or brand, with authority over personnel of different functions.

Advantages of product departmentation are that:

(i)   individual managers can be held accountable for the *profitability* of individual products;

(ii)   specialisation can be developed. For example, some salesmen will be trained to sell a specific product in which they may develop technical expertise and thereby offer a better sales service to customers and for the company. Service engineers who specialise in a single product should also provide a better after-sales service;

(iii)   the different functional activities and efforts required to make and sell each product can be co-ordinated and integrated by the divisional/product manager.

The disadvantage of product departmentation is that it creates a new form of management and therefore increases the overhead costs and managerial complexity of the organisation;

(f)   *by customer or market segment:* a manufacturing organisation may sell goods through wholesalers, export agents and by direct mail. It may therefore organise its sales, marketing and distribution functions on the basis of types of customer, or market segment. Departmentation by customer is commonly associated with sales departments and selling effort, but it might also be used by a jobbing or contracting firm where a team of managers may be given the responsibility of liaising with major customers (eg discussing specifications and completion dates, quality of work, progress-chasing etc);

(g)   *by equipment specialisation:* the most obvious example of departmentation based on equipment specialisation is provided by the data processing departments of large organisations. Batch processing operations are conducted for other departments at a computer centre (where it is controlled by DP staff) because it would be uneconomical to provide each functional department with its own large mainframe computer.

5.5   The various patterns of departmentation fall into three broad types:

(a)   *functional groupings* - dividing work by functions such as production, marketing, personnel, accounting and finance, etc. Managers are given tasks and responsibilities with a particular 'specialist' function;

(b) *product or market groupings* – dividing work by products or markets. A division of the organisation is made responsible for producing and selling a particular product item or product range, or for selling the organisation's product range to a particular market of market segment;

(c) *a mixture of functional and product groupings*, in a matrix organisation structure.

5.6 The distinction between functional and product groupings was described in the earlier chapter on decentralisation, but it is illustrated in the diagram below.

(a) *Functional groupings*

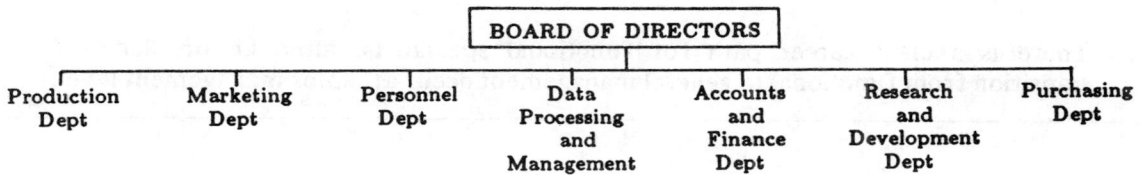

```
                        ┌─────────────────────┐
                        │ BOARD OF DIRECTORS  │
                        └─────────────────────┘
    ┌──────────┬──────────┬──────────┬──────────┬──────────┬──────────┐
Production  Marketing  Personnel    Data      Accounts   Research   Purchasing
  Dept        Dept       Dept     Processing     and        and        Dept
                                      and       Finance  Development
                                   Management     Dept       Dept
```

(b) *Federal groupings*

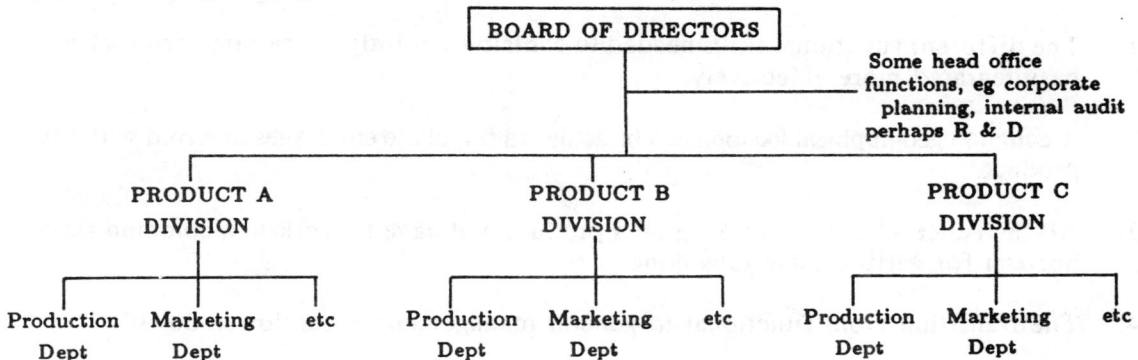

```
                        ┌─────────────────────┐
                        │ BOARD OF DIRECTORS  │
                        └─────────────────────┘
                                                Some head office
                                                functions, eg corporate
                                                planning, internal audit
                                                perhaps R & D

        ┌───────────────────────┬───────────────────────┐
     PRODUCT A               PRODUCT B               PRODUCT C
     DIVISION                DIVISION                DIVISION

  ┌──────┬──────┐        ┌──────┬──────┐        ┌──────┬──────┐
Production Marketing etc Production Marketing etc Production Marketing etc
  Dept     Dept          Dept      Dept          Dept      Dept
```

Notes

1. The 'etceteras' represent other functional groupings within each product division, such as purchasing, personnel, accounting, perhaps R & D and so on.

2. Each product division has its own divisional HQ.

5.7 The factors that should influence the choice between functional and divisional (product) groupings, or matrix organisation, are the ability of each to provide:

(a) effective information processing;
(b) potential for mutual learning;
(c) economy of staffing; and
(d) ease of control.

The advantages of functional departmentation

1. There is a grouping of skills, equipment, etc under the same management.

2. Co-workers share the same 'technical' or 'skills' experience.

3. When different products undergo common processes (eg if different products undergo processing on the same machines) it is likely to be more efficient to have a functional department for the common processes (eg a single manufacturing department, rather than several manufacturing departments, one in each of a number of product divisions).

4. There is a clear career path for functional specialists, although problems of transition from functional to general management occur at senior management level.

The advantages of product divisionalisation

1. The different functional skills needed to contribute jointly to the same product can be integrated more effectively.

2. A common geographical location can be achieved for all the employees involved with the product.

3. All the functional staff working on a product will have to work to a common time horizon for getting their jobs done.

4. The transition from functional to general management starts 'lower down'.

5. Advantages of decentralisation.

6. Divisional structures are particularly suitable for organisations with diverse products and markets.

5.8 With product divisions, there are several choices for organisation design.

(a) How broad should each division's coverage be? How many products should one division be responsible for? How wide a geographical area should one division cover?

(b) How much independence should each product division have for specialist functions, and to what extent should they rely on support departments at central HQ? As an example, an engineering and electronics group might have several product divisions, and a choice would have to be made about where to locate research and development resources. Each division could have its own R & D unit, or there might instead be a central R & D unit at head office. A mixture of a central R & D unit and divisional R & D units is also possible, with central R & D concentrating more on longer term research and divisional R & D concentrating more on shorter term product development.

(c) How much control should central HQ exercise over its divisions. The planning, co-ordinating and information systems could vary, with central HQ being involved to a greater or lesser extent in these matters.

5.9 The problems of *co-ordination* are discussed in the next chapter.

6. MATRIX ORGANISATION

6.1 Matrix organisation is a structure which provides for the formalisation of management control between different functions, whilst at the same time maintaining functional departmentation. It is a mixture of functional and product departmentation.

6.2 A golden rule of classical management theory is *unity of command:* one man should have one boss. (Thus, staff management can only act in an advisory capacity, leaving authority in the province of line management alone.)

6.3 Matrix management may possibly be thought of as a reaction against the 'classical' form of bureaucracy by establishing a structure of dual command.

6.4 Matrix management first developed in the 1950s in the USA in the aerospace industry. Lockheed-California, the aircraft manufacturers, were organised in a functional hierarchy. Customers were unable to find a manager in Lockheed to whom they could take their problems and queries about their particular orders, and Lockheed found it necessary to employ 'project expediters' as customer liaison officials. From this developed 'project co-ordinators', responsible for co-ordinating line managers into solving a customer's problems. Up to this point, these new officials had no functional responsibilities.

6.5 Owing to increasingly heavy customer demands, Lockheed eventually created 'programme managers', with authority for project budgets and programme design and scheduling. These managers therefore had functional authority and responsibilities, thus a matrix management organisation was created. It may be shown diagramatically as a management *grid*; for example:

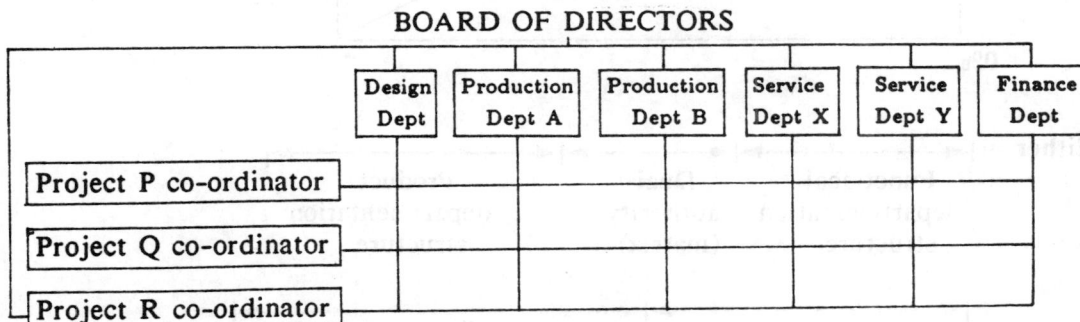

BOARD OF DIRECTORS

	Design Dept	Production Dept A	Production Dept B	Service Dept X	Service Dept Y	Finance Dept
Project P co-ordinator						
Project Q co-ordinator						
Project R co-ordinator						

6.6 Authority would be shared between the project co-ordinators and the heads of the functional departments. Functional department heads are responsible for the organisation of the department, but project co-ordinators are responsible for all aspects of the project itself. An employee in a functional department might expect to receive directions/commands from a project co-ordinator as well as from the departmental head - ie there may be dual command.

6.7 Departmentation by product has already been described, but it is possible to have a product management structure superimposed on top of a functional departmental structure in a matrix; product or brand managers may be responsible for the sales budget, production budget, pricing, marketing, distribution, quality and costs of their product or product line, but may have to co-ordinate with the R & D, production, finance, distribution, and sales departments in order to bring the product on to the market and achieve sales targets, ie:

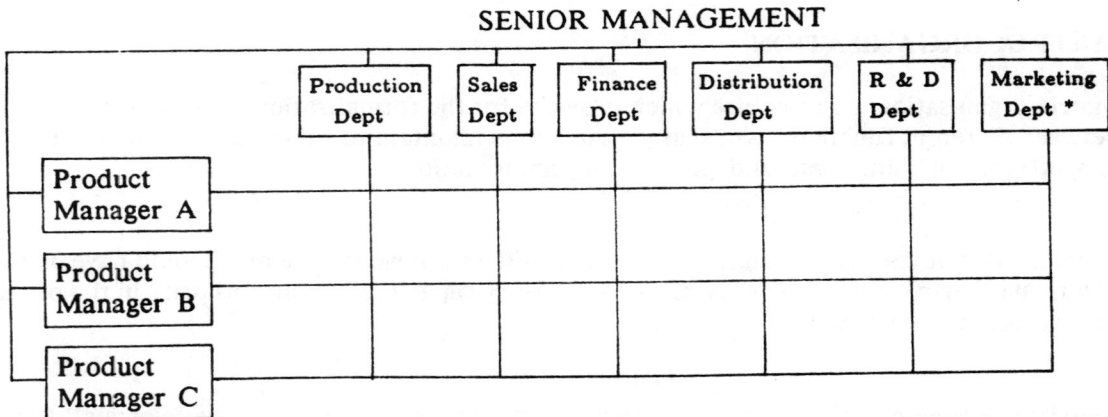

SENIOR MANAGEMENT

	Production Dept	Sales Dept	Finance Dept	Distribution Dept	R & D Dept	Marketing Dept *
Product Manager A						
Product Manager B						
Product Manager C						

* The product managers may each have their own marketing team; in which case the marketing department itself would be small or non-existent.

6.8 The authority of product managers may vary from organisation to organisation. J K Galbraith drew up a range of alternative situations:

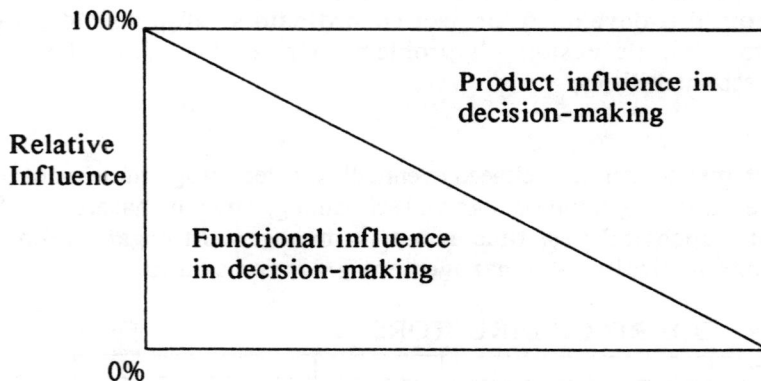

100%

Relative Influence

Product influence in decision-making

Functional influence in decision-making

0%

Either

Functional departmentation structure

Dual authority (matrix)

Product departmentation structure

Or: (matrix structure)

Functional authority with product managers or departments having some influence

Product authority structure with functional managers or departments having some influence

Once again, the division of authority between product managers and functional managers must be carefully defined.

6.9 Project teams are another example of a simple matrix structure. A project may be inter-disciplinary, and require the contributions of an engineer, a scientist, a statistician and a production expert, who would each be appointed to the team from their functional department, whilst still retaining membership and status within the department, ie:

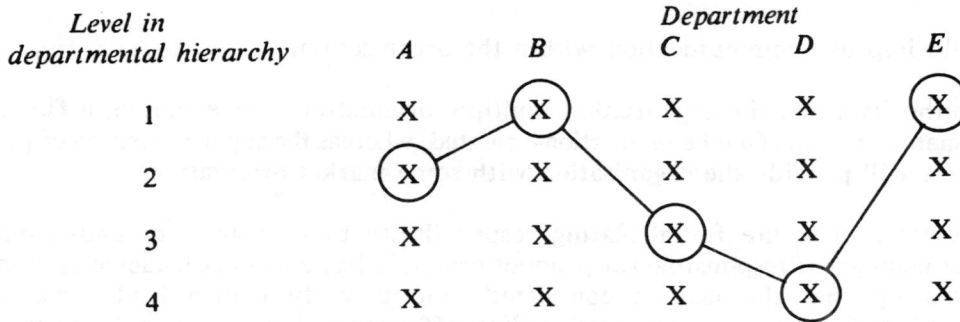

Level in departmental hierarchy	Department				
	A	*B*	*C*	*D*	*E*
1	X	Ⓧ	X	X	Ⓧ
2	Ⓧ	X	X	X	X
3	X	X	Ⓧ	X	X
4	X	X	X	Ⓧ	X

Members of the project team (circled) would provide formal lateral lines of communication and authority, superimposed on the functional departmental structure. Leadership of the project team would probably go to one of the more senior members in the hierarchy, but this is not a requirement of the matrix structure.

6.10 Matrix management thus challenges classical ideas about organisation in two ways:

(a) it rejects the idea of one man, one boss;
(b) its subverts the bureaucratic ethic of authority based on status in the formal hierarchy.

6.11 Matrix organisation means that subordinates have two (or more) 'bosses', in the sense that they must *report* to both a functional boss and a project boss.

6.12 However, a subordinate *cannot* easily *take orders* from two or more bosses, and so an arrangement has to be established whereby either:

(a) a subordinate takes orders from one boss (the functional manager) and the second boss (the project manager) has to ask the first boss to give certain instructions to the subordinate; or

(b) a subordinate takes orders from one boss about some specified matters and orders from the other boss about different specified matters. The authority of each boss would have to be carefully defined. Even so, good co-operation between the bosses would still be necessary.

6.13 The *advantages* of a matrix structure are said to be that:

(a) it offers greater flexibility:

(i) of people. Employees adapt more quickly to a new challenge or new task, and develop an attitude which is geared to accepting change;

(ii) of tasks and structure. The matrix structure may be short-term (as with project teams) or readily amended (eg a new product manager can be introduced by superimposing his tasks on those of the existing functional managers).

Flexibility should facilitate efficient operations in the face of change;

(b) it should improve communication within the organisation;

(c) dual authority gives the organisation multiple orientation. For example, a functional departmentation will often be production-oriented, whereas the superimposition of product managers will provide the organisation with some market orientation;

(d) it provides a structure for allocating responsibility to managers for end-results. A product manager is responsible for product profitability, a project leader is responsible for ensuring that the task is completed, and a study course leader has direct responsibility for the provision of a complete, efficient and effective course to students;

(e) it provides for inter-disciplinary *co-operation* and a mixing of skills and expertise;

(f) arguably, it motivates employees to work harder and more efficiently by providing them with greater participation in planning and control decisions.

6.14 Argyris praised matrix organisations because they break down departmental monopolies and foster participative management styles based on teamwork, which he hoped would eliminate the traditional subordinate-superior relationships.

6.15 A matrix organisation is most suitable in situations where:

(a) there is a fairly large number of different functions, each of great importance;

(b) there could be communications problems between functional management in different functions (eg marketing, production, R & D, personnel, finance);

(c) work is supposed to flow smoothly between these functions, but the communications problems might stop or hinder the work flow;

(d) there is a need to carry out uncertain, interdependent tasks. Work can be structured so as to be *task centred*, with task managers appointed to look after each task, and provide the communications (and co-operation) between different functions;

(e) there is a need to achieve common functional tasks so as to achieve savings in the use of resources - ie product divisions would be too wasteful, because they would duplicate costly functional tasks.

6.16 The *disadvantages* of matrix organisation are said to be as follows.

(a) Dual authority threatens a conflict between functional managers and product/project managers. Where matrix structure exists it is important that the authority of superiors should not overlap and areas of authority must be clearly defined. A subordinate must know to which superior he is responsible for a particular aspect of his duties.

(b) One individual with two or more bosses is more likely to suffer role stress at work.

(c) It is sometimes more costly - eg product managers are additional jobs which would not be required in a simple structure of functional departmentation.

(d) It may be difficult for the management of an organisation to accept a matrix structure. It is possible that a manager may feel threatened that another manager will usurp his authority. (Where authority is not clearly defined, this is likely to happen. The decision-making process would also be expected to slow down.)

7. THE CULTURE OF ORGANISATIONS

7.1 An organisation's culture may be defined as the complex body of shared values and beliefs of an organisation.

> Peters and Waterman, in their study *(In Search of Excellence)* found that the 'dominance and coherence of culture' was an essential feature of the 'excellent' companies they observed. A 'handful of guiding values' was more powerful than manuals, rule books, norms and controls formally imposed (and resisted). They commented: 'If companies do not have strong notions of themselves, as reflected in their values, stories, myths and legends, people's only security comes from where they live on the organisation chart.'

7.2 Handy sums up 'culture' as 'that's the way we do things round here'. For Schein, it is 'the pattern of basic assumptions that a given group has invented, discovered, or developed, in learning to cope with its problems of external adaption and internal integration, and that have worked well enough to be considered valid and, therefore, to be taught to new members as the correct way to perceive, think and feel in relation to these problems.'

> 'I believe that the real difference between success and failure in a corporation can very often be traced to the question of how well the organisation brings out the great energies and talents of its people. What does it do to help these people find common cause with each other? And how can it sustain this common cause and sense of direction through the many changes which take place from one generation to another?...I think you will find that it owes its resiliency not to its form of organisation or administrative skills, but to the power of what we call *beliefs* and the appeal these beliefs have for its people.'
>
> Watson (IBM) quoted by
> Peters and Waterman

7.3 All organisations will generate their own cultures, whether spontaneously, or under the guidance of positive managerial strategy. The culture will consist of the following.

(a) *Basic, underlying assumptions* which guide the behaviour of the individuals and groups in the organisation, e.g. customer orientation, or belief in quality, trust in the organisation to provide rewards, freedom to make decisions, freedom to make mistakes, the value of innovation and initiative at all levels etc.

(b) *Overt beliefs expressed by the organisation and its members.* which can be used to condition (a) above. These beliefs and values may emerge as sayings, slogans, mottos etc. such as 'we're getting there', 'the customer is always right', or 'the winning team'. They may emerge in a richer mythology - in jokes and stories about past successes , heroic failures or breakthroughs, legends about the 'early days', or about 'the time the boss...'. Organisations with strong cultures often centre themselves around almost legendary figures in their history. Management can encourage this by 'selling' a sense of the corporate 'mission', or by promoting the company's 'image'; it can reward the 'right' attitudes and punish (or simply not employ) those who aren't prepared to commit themselves to the culture.

One way by which management try to establish a culture is by drawing up a *mission statement*. A mission statement is a declaration of an organisation's aims, objectives and values. For example, J Sainsburys plc's mission statement states that the company's aim is:

"...to discharge the responsibility as leaders in our trade by acting with complete integrity, by carrying out our work to the highest standards and by contributing to the public good and quality of life." (Financial Times, 11/1/1989)

Such statements generate high levels of cynicism if they are at variance with reality, and so for a mission statement to mean anything at all, it must be an expression of a sense of mission already existing. When defining what an organisation's mission is, management needs to consider four issues:

(i)   the organisation's *purpose* (eg maximise shareholder value);
(ii)   the organisation's *strategy* (ie the business it is in, its intentions for the future);
(iii)   the *values* that determine the treatment of employees, suppliers, customers etc;
(iv)   whether the organisation does in fact *behave* in accordance with its stated mission.

It is not always clear to whom a mission statement is likely to be addressed, but mission statements are generally meant to encourage loyalty by giving employees motives for working other than pay and job security by providing a context of shared values.

(c)   *Visible artifacts* - the style of the offices or other premises, dress 'rules', display of 'trophies', the degree of informality between superiors and subordinates etc.

7.4   A culture takes shape and colour in wide variety of ways, such as:

(a)   the extent of formalisation of the structure;

(b)   whether the decisions are made by committees or individuals;

(c)   the degree of freedom allowed to subordinates to show initiative (and the degree of freedom which subordinates expect to be given);

(d)   whether junior employees feel free to talk to senior managers;

(e)   the formalisation of clothing and office layout;

(f)   the kind of people employed (eg their education, age, ambition).

A supermarket has a different culture from a university, which in turn has a different culture from the armed services or a coal mine.

8.   THE CULTURES APPROACH TO ORGANISATION STRUCTURE

8.1   The cultures/structures approach is that the ideal organisation structure in any particular situation is dependent on the culture which exists within it.

8.2   Handy, following a 1972 article by Roger Harrison, discusses four cultures. An organisation might have a structure which reflects a single culture; on the other hand, different structures reflecting different cultures might exist in separate parts (or departments) of the organisation. (For example, the organisation structure of the field engineering division, and the computer systems design department might differ, because the culture in the two departments are not the same.)

(a)   *Power culture:* power and influence stem from a central source, perhaps the owner-directors. The degree of formalisation is limited, and there are not many rules and procedures. Important decisions are made by key people, and other employees tend to rely on precedent in the absence of other guidelines as to what to do. Other characteristics of the power culture are:

(i)   the organisation, since it is not rigidly structured, is capable of adapting quickly to meet change; however, the success in adapting will depend on the luck or judgement of the key individuals who make the rapid decisions;

(ii)   personal influence decreases as the size of an organisation gets bigger. The power culture is therefore best suited to smaller organisations, where the leaders have direct communication with all employees.

(b)   *Role culture:* or bureaucracy. These organisations have a formal structure, and operate by well-established rules and procedures. Job descriptions establish a definite task for each person's job, and procedures are established for many work routines, communication between individuals and departments, and the settlement of disputes and appeals. The organisation structure defines authority and responsibility to individual managers, who enact the role expected of their position. Individuals are required to perform their job to the full, but not to overstep the boundaries of their authority. Line management will accept advice from specialist staff experts only when such advice seems necessary or appropriate. Since a wide variety of people of different personalities are capable of doing the same job, the efficiency of this organisation depends on the structuring of jobs and the design of communications and formal relationships, rather than on individual personalities. Individuals who work for such organisations tend to learn an expertise without experiencing risk; many do their job adequately, but are not over-ambitious.

The bureaucratic style can be very efficient in a stable environment and when the organisation is of a large size. Thus the Civil Service, insurance companies and many large well-established companies with long-term products are associated with bureaucratic organisations and the role culture. Unfortunately, bureaucracies are very slow to adapt to change and when severe change occurs (eg an economic depression) many run into financial difficulties or even bankruptcy (eg BL cars, the British Steel Corporation);

(c)   *Task culture* as reflected in a matrix organisation or else in project teams and task forces. In such organisations, there is no dominant or clear leader. The principal concern in a task culture is to get the job done; therefore the individuals who are important are the experts with the ability to accomplish a particular aspect of the task. Each individual in the team considers he has more influence than he would have if the work were organised on a formal 'role culture' basis.

Such organisations are flexible and constantly changing; for example, project teams are disbanded as soon as their task has been completed. Project teams and task forces are useful in helping an organisation adapt to change; for example, if a large department were to change from an existing method of working to a new, real-time computerised system of operations, a task force of data processing experts and departmental managers would probably be created to implement the change.

Since job satisfaction tends to be high owing to the degree of individual participation and group identity, 'behavioural' management theorists might recommend this type of organisation structure as being the most efficient available. Handy would argue that this type of structure might only be successful if the nature of the work is suited to matrix organisation or project work, and the employees of the organisation belong to the task culture and therefore want the work organised in this way;

(d) *Person culture*, formed in an organisation whose purpose is to serve the interests of a person or the individuals within it. These organisations are rare, although an example might be a partnership of a few individuals who do all the work of the organisation themselves (with perhaps a little secretarial or clerical assistance). It is quite common, however, for individuals to use an organisation to suit their own purposes; for example:

(i) studio artists look on their job as a means of expressing themselves artistically;
(ii) university lecturers might use their official position as a springboard from which to launch a wider career.

8.3 We must now consider the implications of cultures/structures theory for organisational design, and begin by recognising the factors which help to determine, in any situation, what the predominant culture and therefore organisation structure will/should be.

(a) *Size:* large organisations are more likely to favour a bureaucracy (role culture) as a means of organising the complexity of work.

(b) *People:* some people like to be told what to do, and would favour an organisation structure based on power culture or role culture. Others enjoy the challenge of a complex job and 'ambiguity' and would therefore prefer (task-culture) project work. People with strong need for security tend to prefer bureaucracies. Personal ambition is perhaps more associated with power culture and person culture, though it should be said that many bureaucracies are intensely 'political' with much energy spent on personal rivalry.

(c) *The age of the organisation:* many businesses and other organisations begin to grow through the efforts of a few individuals (eg owner-directors, or the founder of a political pressure group) and tend to be highly centralised (power culture). As the organisations get older, and the former leaders are replaced by a new 'generation' of managers, systems tend to formalise and bureaucracy develops.

(d) *The predominant goals or objectives of the organisation:* if the main purpose of an organisation is service to the community (eg hospitals, local government, railways, public utilities), a bureaucratic organisation will probably be most suitable for providing, monitoring and controlling the required level of service. If the predominant goal is growth or survival, an organisation based on power culture or task culture would be more efficient and successful.

(e) *The technology of the organisation:* an important school of thought best known through the works of Eric Trist and Joan Woodward suggests that the most efficient structure of an organisation will be one which is suited to the technological conditions of the work (ie the equipment, methods of working, the nature of automation etc).

(f) *The environment (economic, competitive, socio-cultural, legal, geographical etc):* examples of environmental influences are:

   (i) economic and market changes. Efficient organisations which adapt best are those structured according to a task culture or power culture;

   (ii) an organisation which is spread over a wide geographical area is likely to decentralise authority on a regional basis, so that different cultures might predominate in different regions;

   (iii) the appointment of worker-directors to the board of a company might betoken a change of attitudes towards decision-making within an organisation, from bureaucracy towards teamwork and group decisions (ie from a role culture to a task culture).

9. THE ADAPTIVE ORGANISATION

9.1 Most organisations exist in a changing environment and must adapt in order to survive. Although formalisation and bureaucratic organisation helps a small company to develop into a large one, it may be insufficient to enable the organisation to survive continuing environmental changes. Handy states that an organisation adapts to change in one of three ways:

(a) *by deliberation:* the organisation 'seeks to reinforce the formal structure by more formal structures'. Companies or governments might establish committees with powers to investigate, recommend or even to make decisions. Special project teams might be created, or new departments established (eg corporate planning department or economic advisory section);

(b) *by reproduction:* large national organisations might delegate authority ('decentralise') to regional headquarters. Unfortunately, decentralisation of this nature usually results in regional organisation structures which duplicate the former national structure. Bureaucracy remains in the same form, but on a smaller scale. Unless the environment is fairly stable, such organisational adaptation is likely to be inefficient;

(c) *by differentiation:* the organisation employs different structures with different cultures, in separate parts of the organisation, using a contingency approach - ie choosing the most suitable structure for each particular situation:

   (i) stable, routine work will be performed in a formalised bureaucratic manner (role culture);

   (ii) adaptation to change (development of new products and new markets, or meeting environmental 'threats') should be organised on a task basis;

   (iii) any sudden crisis might have to be dealt with by key individuals with emergency powers (power culture);

   (iv) overall policy decisions of the organisation should be set by a ruling body of key individuals (board of directors, the Cabinet of government ministers, or the supreme policy-making councils of other organisations) (power culture).

9.2 'One culture should not be allowed to swamp the organisation' (Handy). However, where differentiation, on a contingency basis, is applied in an organisation structure, there is a potential for conflict. Project teams might resent policy decisions of senior managers because they believe them to be inappropriate to the problems of the organisation; line managers might resent 'free-wheeling' 'undisciplined' members of project teams. The management of an organisation must be capable of reconciling differences and integrating the work of all employees towards a common aim.

10. ORGANIC AND MECHANISTIC ORGANISATIONS

10.1 Burns and Stalker contributed significant ideas about managing organisation growth and change. They identified the need for a different organisation structure when the technology of the market is changing, and innovation is crucial to the continuing success of any organisation operating in the market.

10.2 They recommended an *organic structure* (also called an 'organismic structure') which has the following characteristics.

(a) There is a 'contributive nature' of specialised knowledge and experience to the common task of the organisation.

(b) Each individual has a realistic task which can be understood in terms of the common task of the organisation.

(c) There is a continual re-definition of an individual's task, through interaction between the individual and others.

(d) There is a spread of commitment to the concern and its tasks.

(e) There is a *network* structure of authority and communication.

(f) Communication tends to be *lateral* rather than vertical.

(g) Communication takes the form of information and advice rather than instructions and decisions.

10.3 Burns and Stalker contrasted the organic structure of management, which is more suitable to conditions of change, with a *mechanistic* system of management, which is more suited to stable conditions. A mechanistic structure has the following characteristics.

(a) Authority is a hierarchical formal scalar chain.

(b) Communication is *vertical* rather than lateral.

(c) Individual tasks are not clearly related to the goals of the organisation, owing to specialisation of work.

(d) Individuals regard their own tasks as something distinct and divorced from the organisation as a whole.

(e) There is a precise definition of duties in each individual job (eg rules, procedures, job definitions).

10.4 Mechanistic systems are unsuitable in conditions of change for three reasons:

(a) the *ambiguous figure system:* in dealing with unfamiliar problems authority lines are not clear, matters are referred 'higher-up' and the top of the organisation becomes over-burdened by decisions;

(b) *mechanistic jungle:* jobs and departments are created to deal with the new problems creating greater problems;

(c) *committee system:* committees are set up to cope with the problems. The committees can only be a temporary problem-solving device, but the situations which create the problems are not temporary.

11. THE CONTINGENCY APPROACH TO ORGANISATION STRUCTURE

11.1 The main question we should be asking about organisation structure is: 'can we identify one type of structure that is more effective and efficient than any other?'.

11.2 Contingency theory, which is now the generally-held view, is that there isn't a universally-best organisation structure, but that there could well be a best structure for each individual organisation, which will depend on 'contingent factors'.

11.3 Essentially, it takes the view of 'different horses for different courses' - what managers should do in practice will depend on the particular circumstances or situations he is in; similarly, the optimal organisational structure will depend on the individual circumstances or situation of the organisation. This approach is an important one because it rejects the belief, which is inherent in scientific management especially, that there is a universally correct answer to a given problem in every case whenever and wherever it crops up.

11.4 Conclusions may be drawn from a study of general principles, about what type of organisation or style of management appears to be best for different situations, but specific conclusions should be reached with care and caution.

John Child wrote: 'Institutions in many fields of business, public service, trade unionism and so forth have grown steadily larger, with the aim of expanding their field of activity, taking advantage of economies of large-scale operations and supporting the overheads of advanced research and development or a wider range of specialist support services. As the number of levels of management increases, bringing additional problems of delegation and control at each level. The increase in size makes it economically possible to utilise specialist support services which must be slotted into the organisation structure, The spread of separate groups and departments across the organisation also increases with growth. Additional procedures are then required for co-ordination and communication between these different units, while the contribution of new specialists has to be integrated with the activities of line management'.

11.5 Size is not the only factor which will affect the optimal structure of the organisation. Handy identified history and ownership, technology, goals ad objectives, the environment and the people involved as other contributory factors.

11.6 The contingency approach states that there is a structure which would improve the efficiency of an organisation, but that this ideal structure will vary in type according to the situation or circumstances of each particular individual organisation.

11.7 The structure which is actually selected is likely to be a 'compromise' between pressures which pull in opposite directions.

(a) There are pressures for *uniformity:*
    (i) standardisation of methods, rules and procedures might result in economies of scale;
    (ii) where uniform procedures exist, it is easier to impose centralised control;
    (iii) the interchangeability of personnel from one part of an organisation to another is made easier;
    (iv) specialised skills can be developed and applied throughout the organisation.

(b) There are also strong pressures for *diversity*. Differences in regional characteristics, markets, customers or products, differences in the technology used in various aspects of the organisation's work, the greater readiness of individuals to identify with smaller work groups than with an entire organisation, and the desire of subordinates to have more authority (ie for 'decentralisation') are all factors which shape diversity in different parts of an organisation.

11.8 The contingency approach suggests that the following factors help to determine the optimal structure in any particular situation.

(a) *The environment.* The organisational structure most conducive to high performance depends on whether the environment is stable and simple, or changing and complex. In a stable environment, the pressures for uniformity are strong; any unforeseen events will be rare and can be dealt with by top management. Lawrence and Lorsch compared the structural characteristics of a 'high-performing' container firm, which existed in a relatively stable environment, and a 'high-performing' plastics firm which existed in a rapidly changing environment. They concluded that:

    (i) in a stable environment (ie the container firm) the most efficient structure was one in which the influence and authority of senior managers were relatively high and of middle managers low;

    (ii) in a dynamic environment (ie the plastics firm) the most efficient structure was one in which the influence and authority of senior managers were somewhat less, and of middle managers correspondingly greater.

(b) *Diversity.* Lawrence and Lorsch referred to 'differentiated' organisations, ie organisations in which work practices, goods and planning time horizons varied widely between different parts of the organisation.

Successful firms will employ an organisation structure which reduces uncertainty:

    (i) 'staff' experts will be employed to act as an interface between the organisation and its environment, and to gather information from the environment;

    (ii) there may also be pressure to delegate decisions to the line manager 'on the spot';

    (iii) there will be less formalisation and a greater emphasis on discussions, participation in decision-making, co-ordination and dissemination of information.

For example, in an environment of rapid change, some managers (eg in research and corporate planning) concentrate on longer-term goals and time horizons; development engineers and sales staff might be more conscious of changes in the short term, and production management might be steeped in problems of day-to-day manufacture. Lawrence and Lorsch argued that the more widely differentiated an organisation becomes, the greater will be the pressures for a diversified organisation structure. A more obvious example might be 'conglomerate' companies, which are commonly organised on a decentralised, divisionalised basis.

(c) *Size*. It has already been suggested that as an organisation grows larger, its systems tend to formalise into a bureaucracy. Contingency theory suggests that although an informal structure is more efficient for smaller firms, in large organisations formalisation and bureaucracy is often the most efficient type of structure available.

(d) *Type of personnel*. Some employees like to be told what to do and prefer a standardised, uniform structure of organisation with authoritarian leadership; other employees (often those with a broader and greater education) prefer to be given responsibilities and to work in teams, and to make decisions in their own ways.

(e) *the 'culture' of the organisation*. This has been described in this chapter;

(f) *Technology of the organisation*. The socio-technical systems approach to organisation structure has been described in an earlier chapter.

11.9 Contingency theory does have its critics, such as John Child: 'One major limitation of the contemporary contingency approach lies in the lack of conclusive evidence to demonstrate that matching organisational designs to prevailing contingencies contributes *importantly* to performance.'

11.10 Lawrence and Lorsch suggested in their research that poor-performing companies have an inappropriate organisation structure for their particular circumstances. However, it could be argued that an organisation is badly structured because it is poorly managed, and even if it were re-structured, poor management would continue to depress the organisation's performance - performance may be attributable to management and not to structure.

11.11 Similarly, other factors might contribute more importantly to organisational performance, such as planning and control methods, information systems, leadership and employee motivation.

11.12 Well established organisations might be able to perform successfully with *any* type of organisation structure because they are secure within their environment and can ignore contingency factors (eg the Civil Service, perhaps).

Conclusion

In this chapter, our concern has been the design of an optimal organisation structure. However, for any organisation to be effective and efficient, there must be co-operation between the different people and departments within it. This is the subject of the next chapter.

TEST YOUR KNOWLEDGE

(The numbers in brackets refer to paragraphs in this chapter)

1. List six or seven choices or options in organisation design. (1.2)

2. What is work structuring? (3.1) What are its advantages for the organisation and for employees in work structuring of operative work? (3.2, 4.18)

3. Sketch two organisation charts, one in which there are functional groupings of work and the other in which there are product groupings. (5.6)

4. What are the relative advantages of (a) functional departmentation and (b) product divisionalisation? (5.7)

5. Describe what you understand by the phrase 'Matrix Organisation'. In what situations do you think Matrix Organisation is appropriate? (6.1, 6.11-6.15)

6. How important is the organisational climate or 'culture' for employee attitudes and commitment to the organisation? (7.1, 7.2, 8.2)

7. How did Burns and Stalker distinguish between organisations and organisation structures, in the context of responding to a changing environment? (10.1-10.4)

8. What is meant by the contigency appproach to organisation structure? (11.2, 11.3, 11.8)

Chapter 12

COMMUNICATION, CO-ORDINATION AND CONFLICT

This chapter covers the following topics:

1. Communication
2. Informal communication channels
3. Communication and MIS design
4. Co-ordination (integration)
5. Line and staff management
6. Conflict
7. Improving co-ordination and integration
8. Programmed decision making

Purpose of this chapter

To consider the need for communication by and for management, and to suggest that good communication is an essential ingredient of co-ordination.

To consider problems of co-ordination within an organisation, including conflict, and to identify the symptoms, causes and remedies for poor co-ordination.

1. COMMUNICATION

1.1 In any organisation, the communication of information is necessary:

(a) for management, to make the necessary decisions for *planning, co-ordination* and *control;* managers should be aware of what their departments are achieving, what they are not achieving and what they *should* be achieving;

(b) between departments, so that all the interdependent systems for purchasing, production, marketing and administration can be synchronised to perform the right actions at the right times to *co-operate* in accomplishing the organisation's aims;

(c) by individuals. Each employee should know what is expected from him. Otherwise, he may be off-target, working without understanding, interest or motivation, and without any sense of belonging and contributing to the organisation. Effective communication gives an employee's job meaning, makes personal development possible, and acts as a motivator, as well as oiling the wheels of labour relations.

Communication *for* and *by* management is particularly important.

12: COMMUNICATION, CO-ORDINATION AND CONFLICT

1.2 Communication in the organisation may take the form of:

(a) giving instructions;
(b) giving or receiving information;
(c) exchanging ideas;
(d) announcing plans or strategies;
(e) comparing actual results against a plan;
(f) laying down rules or procedures;
(g) job descriptions, organisation charts or manuals, ie. communication about the structure of the organisation and individual roles.

1.3 Communication is passed *vertically* between superiors and subordinates and *horizontally* between employees at the same level of the organisation. It can be written, verbal, visual or electronic.

1.4 One of the functions of communication is to ensure that each individual in the organisation knows what he/she is expected to be doing at work to further the the goals of the organisation. Good communication is therefore necessary to *co-ordinate* the activities of individuals, groups and departments.

> Without good communication, there will be poor co-ordination.

1.5 Regular causes of poor communication are:

(a) interpersonal conflicts, especially between superior and subordinates;
(b) inter-departmental conflicts;
(c) serious difficulties in communication owing to different social, racial, educational backgrounds, age differences and personality differences;
(d) an adequate system of providing information, especially an inadequate *management* information system.

1.6 Rosemary Stewart reported a survey of 160 managers in British companies (1967) in which it was found that 78% of their time was spent communicating (talking took up 50% and reading and writing 28% of their time).

1.7 Good communications are essential to getting any job done because co-operation is impossible without it. Difficulties occur, however, because of:

(a) distortion or omission of information by the sender;
(b) managers not realising that what they say may be misunderstood;
(c) verbal misunderstandings, owing to lack of clarity or technical jargon;
(d) a general tendency to distrust a message in its re-telling from one person to another, to another etc;
(e) a subordinate mistrusting his superior, and looking for hidden meanings in whatever he is told;
(f) people from different jobs or specialist backgrounds (eg accountants, marketing managers, engineers) having difficulty in talking on the same wavelength;
(g) people having different senses of values so that one person places greater or less emphasis on a situation than another;

(h) subordinates giving superiors incorrect or incomplete information (eg to protect a colleague, to avoid bothering the superior); also a higher manager can only handle edited information because he does not have time to look at detail;

(i) 'overload' - ie a person is given too much information to digest;

(j) a frequent lack of opportunities, formal or informal, for a subordinate to say what he thinks or feels;

(k) managers who are prepared to make decisions on a 'hunch' without proper regard to the communications they may have received;

(l) non-verbal signs contradicting a verbal message, so that the truth of the communication is in doubt;

(m) perceptual bias by the receiver of information. A person may hear what he wants to be told;

(n) the relative status in the hierarchy of the sender and receiver of information. A senior manager's words are listened to more closely and a colleague's, perhaps, discounted;

(o) conflict in the organisation. Where there is conflict between individuals or departments, communications will be withdrawn and information withheld;

(p) information which does not have immediate use tending to be forgotten.

Barriers to communication

1.8 The barriers to good communication arising from differences in social, racial or educational backgrounds, compounded by age differences and personality differences, can be particularly severe.

(a) Male employees with sexist attitudes may resent working for women, as they do not feel such a situation conforms with their prejudices as to what is 'natural'. Alternatively, a woman's views may be ignored simply because she is female. Communication is therefore impeded by the persistence of traditional gender stereotyping.

(b) A young person might be resented by an older person of the same grade or status in the organisation. The young person might look down on the older one as someone who has failed to advance his career, and is therefore second-rate. Difficulties in seeing each other's point of view might be compounded by different methods of expression (slang words and phrases etc).

(c) Personality differences might occur where one person appears fairly happy-go-lucky, and another is more serious in his application to work and his outlook on life. Frustration may occur in communication between the two because their different values give them conflicting views about what is important and what is less so.

1.9 Differences in background might result in:

(a) failure to understand the other's point of view and sense of values and priorities;

(b) failure to listen to the information the other person is giving. The information is judged according to the person who gives it;

(c) a tendency to give the other person ready-formulated opinions (which the other does not accept) instead of factual information which will enable the other person to formulate his own opinions;

(d) personal dislike, jealousies and conflict.

1.10 Personal conflict or antagonisms will cause further communication problems:

(a) Emotions (anger, fear, frustration) will creep into communications and further hinder the transmission of clear information.

(b) The person responsible for transmitting information will speak to the recipient as rarely as possible, so messages may be delayed.

(c) The recipient of information will tend to:

(i) hear what he wants to hear in any message;
(ii) ignore anything he does not want to accept in a message;
and blame it on the other person if problems arise later on.

1.11 To achieve good communications, managers must:

(a) express themselves effectively and simply, both verbally and in writing;

(b) obtain the co-operation of subordinates in what they are doing. The willing co-operation of a subordinate is essential to proper communication and effective action because:

(i) it avoids suspicion of management intentions;
(ii) it encourages subordinates to say what they think or to say when they do not understand what they have been told.

2. INFORMAL COMMUNICATION CHANNELS

2.1 The formal pattern of communication in an organisation is *always* supplemented by an informal one, which is sometimes referred to as the 'grapevine' or 'bush telegraph'. People like to gossip, and talk about rumours and events, on the telephone, over a cup of tea in the office, on the way home from work, in the corridor, at lunch, and so on.

2.2 The danger with informal communication is that it might be malicious, full of inaccurate rumour or half-truths, or full of wild speculation. This type of gossip can be unsettling to people in an organisation, and make colleagues mistrust one another or act cautiously.

2.3 For example, suppose that you work for a company in London, and your friend from another department telephones to say that he has heard from someone who knows someone else in the personnel department that your office is going to be moved to Cardiff, and anyone refusing to go will be given the sack. This sort of news would be certain to upset you for a while, even if it turns out eventually to be wrong.

2.4 Formal communication systems need the support of a good - and accurate - informal system, and some ideas have been put forward about how this might be done.

(a) One idea is to set up 'official' corporate communications that will feed information into the informal system. House journals or briefings groups can be used to provide accurate bits of information, which individuals can pick up and gossip about,

(b) Another idea, put forward by Nancy Foy (1985), is that an organisation should encourage 'networking'. *Networking* describes 'a collection of people, usually with a shared interest, who tend to keep in touch to exchange informal information'.

2.5 The *grapevine* is one aspect of informal communication. A well-known study into how the grapevine works was carried out by K Davis (1953) using his 'ecco-analysis' technique, ie the recipient of some information, A, was asked to name the source of his information, B. B was then asked to name his source, C etc until the information was traced back to its originator. His research findings were that:

(a) the grapevine is fast;

(b) the working of the grapevine is selective: information is not divulged randomly;

(c) the grapevine usually operates at the place of work and not outside it;

(d) perhaps surprisingly, the grapevine is only active when the formal communication network is active: the grapevine does not fill a gap created by an ineffective formal communication system;

(e) it was also surprising to discover that higher level executives were better communicators and better informed than their subordinates. 'If a foreman at the sixth level had an accident, a larger proportion of executives at the third level knew of it than at the fourth level, or even at the sixth level where the accident happened';

(f) more staff executives were in the know about events than line managers (because the staff executives are more mobile and get involved with more different functions in their work).

2.6 Davis concluded that since the grapevine exists, and cannot be got rid of, management should learn both to accept it and to use it, ie harness it towards achieving the objectives of the organisation.

2.7 Fostering *creativity* (new ideas and innovations) is a function of management which relies heavily on good communication. Organisations must be creative to survive and the characteristics of a creative organisation are that:

(a) it has 'ideas men' and open channels of communication;
(b) it has sub-units or committees to deal with or to generate new ideas and suggestions;
(c) it encourages contact with outside sources;
(d) it hires a variety of personality types, including eccentrics;
(e) it evaluates ideas on their merit, not on the status of the originator;
(f) promotion is on merit only;
(g) it invests in basic research, and has flexible long-range planning;
(h) it is decentralised;
(i) it tolerates mistakes, and is prepared to take risks;
(j) it does not follow the market leader, but sets objectives independently;
(k) it keeps the creative functions (R and D) separate from and not responsible to the production function.

2.8 An argument of Nancy Foy and others is that the *rate of change* in an organisation is sometimes so fast that people need continual information to keep them aware of what might be happening, and how it could affect them. This will help them to adapt, and to preserve their loyalty to the organisation and commitment to work. Formal information channels might be inadequate for keeping people aware of change, and efficient informal communication, such as networking, could play a key role.

2.9 *Brainstorming* sessions are problem-solving conferences of 6-12 people who produce spontaneous 'free-wheeling' ideas to solve a particular problem. Ideas are produced but not evaluated at these meetings, so that originality is not stifled in fear of criticism. Brainstorming sessions rely on the ability of conference members to feed off each other's ideas. They have been used in many organisations and might typically occur, for example, in advertising agencies to produce ideas for a forthcoming campaign.

2.10 In the 1950s W J Gordon of the Arthur D Little company, a consulting firm in Massachussets, developed the *Gordon technique*. The company offered, among its other business lines, the services of an invention design group which could invent a product to order. The Gordon technique relies on brainstorming sessions with the unique difference that only the conference leader knows the nature of the problem and it is his task to steer the ideas of the group towards a solution 'in the dark.' This prevents any member from getting addicted to a single idea, which is an inherent danger in a normal brainstorming session.

3. COMMUNICATION AND MIS DESIGN

3.1 Information is the material that is communicated, and the formal sources of information for *managers* are what we call the organisation's management information system or MIS.

> The importance of a good quality MIS was discussed in the earlier chapter on planning and control. Planning and control, remember, are the management functions through which much of the task of co-ordination should be achieved.

4. CO-ORDINATION (INTEGRATION)

4.1 Co-ordination is the process of integrating the work of different sections and departments of an organisation towards the effective achievement of the organisation's goals. There are various reasons why co-ordination might be difficult to achieve.

> *Signs of inadequate integration are*
>
> 1. Persistent conflict between departments
> 2. Fudging integration issues through a proliferation of committees
> 3. An overloading of top management with problems to resolve
> 4. The use of 'red tape' to try to ensure that integration does take place
> 5. Empire-building by co-ordinators
> 6. Complaints by clients, customers and other external parties (eg customers being told different things by different departments).
>
> (Derek Pugh, 1979)

Reasons for lack of co-ordination

1. Poor communications

2. Inadequate system of planning and objective setting

3. Different groups work under different time pressures

4. Differences in leadership style

5. Weak organisation structure

6. Inter-departmental or inter-personal dislikes and rivalries - ie conflicts

7. Problems of integrating 'line' and 'staff' departments

8. Difficulties in creating an effective management team with people from different disciplines - eg a production management team must bring together people with technical skills (engineering, quality control), financial skills (budgetary control, cost reduction), personnel skills (recruitment and training) and planning skills (production planning).

9. In an organisation which must be innovative in response to environmental changes, there may be problems in promoting innovation - ie integrating innovation specialists into the mainstream of the organisation.

4.2 Let's now look at some of these reasons for lack of co-ordination in some detail.

4.3 There might be *poor communications* both horizontally and vertically within the organisation:

(a) different departments might fail to communicate with each other properly;
(b) superiors and subordinates might communicate badly.

Poor communications are a symptom of conflict. This is described later in this chapter.

4.4 Management might *fail to provide a plan* for the organisation which is acceptable to everyone within the organisation. Different departments, for example, might have different views about how the goals of the organisation will best be achieved. The sales department might wish to satisfy customers by providing a wide range of products on time and adjusted to customer specifications, whereas the production department might seek economies of scale through standardisation of products, a limited production range and longer production run; the accounting department might emphasise the paramount importance of cost control etc. The goal of the sales department (high sales and customer satisfaction) the goal of the production department (lower unit costs) and the goal of the accounting department (keeping within budget) would then be difficult to reconcile.

4.5 It is difficult to co-ordinate the work of different departments and groups which work under *differing time pressures*.

(a) The operational departments of a business have to produce output quickly and regularly. Decisions need to be taken for a speedy implementation. In contrast, a research and development department will carry out much of its work on projects which might take years to finish, so that the time pressures are not as great, planning and control might be very flexible, and the concern of the department will be for long-term profitability of the business rather than the short term.

(b) Sometimes, it might be necessary to integrate the work of two groups which work to different time pressures. An example would be the implementation of a new computer system into an operational department, where the system has been designed by a project group over a number of years. The project group might be responsible for supervising the introduction of the system into operational working, and there might be problems of co-ordination because the project group will be used to working without severe time pressures, whereas the operational department will be concerned that the implementation of the system should not disrupt its work schedules and efficiency. Staff in the operational department might even claim that they do not have time, because of work pressure, to learn the new system adequately, and cannot afford to 'waste time' listening to members of the project group.

4.6 Co-ordination problems might be aggravated by *differences in leadership style*. If the manager of department X is strictly authoritarian, whereas the manager of department Y is democratic and encourages the interest and participation of subordinates in decision-making, it might be difficult for members of department X to co-operate efficiently with members of department Y. They will be used to different ways of doing things, and different timescales for getting a job done: these differences might well cause breakdowns in communication and therefore a failure to achieve a properly co-ordinated effort.

4.7 Co-ordination also depends on the design of the *organisation structure*. It will be easier for section A to co-ordinate its efforts with section B if they are in the same department, with the same immediate superior. Where close organisational ties within the scalar chain of command are not practicable, methods of promoting co-ordination between different functional groups include:

(a) a matrix management structure. For example, a product manager might be responsible for co-ordinating the efforts of functional groups dealing with development and design, production, manpower, purchasing, sales, marketing, distribution and warehousing;

(b) the use of inter-disciplinary project teams - groups of staff drawn from different departments or regions;

(c) the use of committees - representatives of the different departments whose efforts must be co-ordinated.

5. LINE AND STAFF MANAGEMENT

5.1 There are two ways of looking at the distinction between line and staff management.

(a) Line and staff can be used to denote functions in the organisation. Line management consists of those managers directly involved in achieving the objectives of an organisation (ie all production and sales managers in a manufacturing company). Every other manager is staff (eg accounting, marketing, research and development). Rosemary Stewart wrote that 'Line functions are those which have direct responsibility for achieving the objectives of the company. Staff activities are those which primarily exist to provide advice and service.'

(b) As an alternative definition, line and staff can be used to denote relationships of authority. A line manager is one who has relatively unlimited authority over a subordinate to whom he gives orders. By this definition, any manager, no matter what department he works in (an operations department or an advisory department) will have line authority over his subordinates. Thus if the personnel department is a staff department, the manager in charge of recruitment and training will be subordinate in a line relationship to the personnel director. In other words, line authority can be a term used to describe the scalar chain of command in the management hierarchy.

5.2 Another popular distinction between line and staff is that:

(a) staff managers are thinkers and advisors;

(b) line managers are doers.

5.3 Staff departments exist in many organisations where there is a need for specialisation of management. Accountants, personnel administrators, economists, data processing experts and statisticians are all experts in a specialised field of work. Where this expertise is 'syphoned off' into a separate department, the problem naturally arises as to whether:

(a) the experts exist to *advise* line managers, who may accept or reject the advice given; or

(b) the experts can step in to *direct* the line managers in what to do - ie to assume line authority themselves.

5.4 Unfortunately, this is an aspect of organisation which causes enormous friction. Line managers are thought of as 'first class citizens' and staff are relegated in status to the second rank as expensive 'overheads', who are not contributing anything of worth to the organisation. Staff managers are therefore constantly trying to acquire line functions.

5.5 The conflict between line management, who may resent specialist advice, and staff management, who may be frustrated when their advice is ignored, has no organisational solution. The problem can be lessened, however, if:

(a) all vital activities of the business are line management functions;

(b) staff management are kept in close proximity (either physically or by communications links) to the line management they advise.

5.6 There are situations where some 'staff' management have become highly specialised in areas of work which form a fundamental part of the line management positions. Examples are usually found in the fields of industrial relations and capital expenditure. In these areas the line manager would allow the staff manager to assume some of his responsibilities while still retaining final authority and responsibility. A typical example would be where the personnel manager specifies the rules for training or recruitment of employees. The line manager recognises that the staff manager has greater knowledge and expertise on this subject and agrees to do what the staff manager decides.

5.7 There are drawbacks to using staff; a knowledge of the problems should enable management to deal with them, and thus use staff functions more effectively. These drawbacks are as follows.

(a) There is a danger that staff experts may, intentionally or not, undermine the authority of line managers. Subordinates might respect the 'expert power' of the staff man, and show a lesser willingness to accept the judgement of their line boss.

(b) Friction may also occur when staff managers report to a higher authority in the scalar chain of command. For example, a management accountant may submit reports about a line manager's performance to the production director or the managing director. The line manager might look on such reporting as 'telling tales' and resent the interference.

(c) Staff managers have no line authority and therefore no responsibility for what actually happens. If they give advice which is acted on, but fails to achieve desired results, staff men can blame the line managers for not acting on their advice properly.

(d) Because staff managers are 'thinkers' they may have their head in the clouds. Their ideas may be unrealistic and impracticable; line managers, having received poor advice from one staff expert, might tar all staff managers with the same brush and resist all future expert help.

(e) Staff managers may attempt to usurp line authority. Any change in the boundaries of authority should be the result of conscious planning, and not surreptitious empire-building.

5.8 The solutions to these problems are easily stated, but not easy to implement in practice.

(a) Authority must be clearly defined, and distinctions between line authority and staff advice clearly set out (eg in job descriptions).

(b) Senior management must encourage line managers to make positive efforts to discuss work problems with staff advisors, and to be prepared to accept their advice. The use of experts should become an 'organisational way of life'.

(c) Staff managers must be fully informed about the aspects of the business on which they are experts. By providing them with detailed information they should be less likely to offer impractical advice.

(d) When staff advisors are used to plan and implement changes in the running of the business, they must be kept involved during the implementation, monitoring and review of the project. Staff managers must be prepared to accept responsibility for their failures and this is only really possible if they advise during the implementation and monitoring stages.

5.9 There has to be a balance between operations managers (line) and managers of support functions (staff). The problem for organisation is seen, typically, as follows:

(a) If operational managers had a superhuman ability to learn all the specialist skills necessary for management, there would be no need for support functions.

(b) It is only because specialist support is essential (eg accountants, computer specialists) or advisable (eg personnel specialists) - that is, because operational managers would on their own be unable to make well-informed decisions - that the problem arises of finding a balance of authority or influence between line and staff.

5.10 The argument of the classical school of management in favour of clear lines of authority is a valid one (although of course it is debatable whether a 'one boss for one subordinate' scalar chain of command is necessarily the only suitable way of establishing a clear authority structure).

5.11 Drucker argues that the traditional view of staff specialists as 'advisors with some authority' is a poor approach to organisation design. He suggested that 'as far as I have been able to grasp the concept, to be 'staff' means to have authority without having responsibility. And that is destructive'. It is much better that (support) functional departments, which are necessary in any large organisation:

(a) should have their own clear objectives;
(b) should have clearly stated areas of authority;
(c) should be responsible and accountable for their exercise of that authority.

5.12 Staff management, Drucker argued, should not be allowed to impede the performance of operational (line) managers. However, a counter-argument to Drucker's views is that operational management and staff management will have overlapping areas of interest, and frequently conflicting views. The problem remains that authority must be divided between line and staff, and to the extent that operational managers retain authority over certain aspects of work, they might still need to rely on specialist advice from functional staff. Nevertheless, the need to clarify areas of authority is an important principle of sound organisation structure.

6. CONFLICT

6.1 As a co-ordinator and integrator, a manager should be able to reconcile differences of opinion. Handy identified three ways in which differences are expressed:

(a) by *argument*: this is the constructive exchange of ideas with the positive intention of reaching an agreement;

(b) by *competition*:

    (i) constructive competition between individuals or groups has the beneficial effect of:
      1 setting or improving standards of achievement;
      2 stimulating activities;
      3 sorting out the good, successful employees from the bad, unsuccessful ones;

    (ii) harmful competition occurs when one person or group can only do well at the expense of another; this is known as 'zero-sum' competition, because if one person gains, another loses an equal amount. Competition for resources, recognition and better results, if zero-sum, will degenerate into conflict;

(c) by *conflict*.

6.2 There are three ways of looking at organisations in terms of the way conflict exists in them. These ways are known as the 'happy family' view, the conflict view and the evolutionary view.

The 'happy family' view

6.3 This view presents organisations as:

(a) co-operative structures, designed to achieve agreed common objectives, ie. with no systematic conflict of interest; and

(b) harmonious environments, where conflicts are exceptional and arise from:

(i) misunderstandings;
(ii) personality factors;
(iii) the expectations of inflexible employees; or
(iv) factors outside the organisation and its control.

6.4 Drucker (*The Practice of Management*) writes that "Any business must mould a true team and weld individual efforts into a common effort. Each member of the enterprise contributes something different, but they must all contribute towards a common goal. Their efforts must all pull in the same direction, without friction, without unnecessary duplication of effort".

6.5 This kind of view is reasonably common in managerial literature, which attempts to come up with training and motivational techniques for dealing with conflicts which arise in what are potentially 'conflict-free' organisations.

Conflict is thus blamed on bad management, lack of leadership, poor communication, or 'bloody-mindedness' on the part of individuals or interest groups that impinge on the organisation. The theory is that a strong culture, good two-way communication, co-operation and motivational leadership will 'eliminate' conflict.

6.6 The 'happy family' view starts from a belief in 'social order' or 'industrial peace': conflict is a threat to stability, and must be avoided or eradicated.

The conflict view

6.7 In contrast, there is the view of organisations as arenas for conflict on individual and group levels. Members battle for limited resources, status, rewards, professional values etc. Organisational politics involve constant struggles for control, and choices of structure, technology and organisational goals are part of this process. Individual and organisational interests will not always coincide.

6.8 Some writers have regarded conflict as an inevitable feature of organisational life, as organisations merely reflect the conflicts of interest in society as a whole. Adam Smith, for example, in *The Wealth of Nations* (1776) writes the following about the relationship between employers and employees.

> "What are the common wages of labour, depends upon the contract made between those two parties [workmen and masters] whose interests are by no means the same. The workmen desire to get as much, the masters to give as little as possible...We rarely hear, it has been said, of the combinations [trade unions] of masters, though frequently of those of the workmen...Masters are always and everywhere in a sort of tacit, but constant and uniform combination not to raise the wages of labour above their actual rate...[and]... sometimes enter into particular combinations to sink the wages of labour even below this rate. These are always conducted with the utmost silence and secrecy...Such combinations, however, are frequently resisted by a contrary defensive combination of workmen...They are desperate, and act with the folly and extravagance of desperate men who must either starve or frighten their masters into immediate compliance."

6.9 These views are also associated with Marxism which holds that the basic interests of capitalists and workers are necessarily antagonistic.

(a) Organisations provide some of the arenas for class struggle.

(b) "Industrial relations", "participation" and so forth are therefore cynical exercises in tacit social control by the bourgeoisie, as the question of the ultimate ownership and control of the means of production, distribution and exchange is not addressed.

(c) Conflict, in the right circumstances, is desirable if it advances change.

> "The history of all hitherto society is the history of class struggles. Freeman and slave, patrician and plebeian, lord and serf, guildmaster and journeyman, in a word, oppressor and oppressed, stood in constant opposition to one another, carried on an uninterrupted, now hidden, now open fight ..."   Marx and Engels. *The Communist Manifesto* (1888)

6.10 This view must be distinguished from trade union activities, which are basically concerned with improving "terms and conditions" of the current employment situation (eg health and safety, equal opportunities, working hours, wages).

The 'evolutionary' view

6.11 This view regards conflict as a means of maintaining the status quo, as a useful basis for evolutionary - rather than revolutionary - change. Conflict keeps the organisation sensitive to the need to change, while reinforcing its essential framework of control. The legitimate pursuit of competing interests can balance and preserve social and organisational arrangements. A flexible society benefits from conflict because such behaviour, by helping to create and modify norms, assumes its continuance under changed conditions.

6.12 This 'constructive conflict' view may perhaps be the most useful for managers and administrators of organisations, as it neither:

    (a) attempts to dodge the issues of conflict, which is an observable fact of life in most organisations; nor

    (b) seeks to pull down existing organisational structures altogether.

6.13 Ideology apart, managers have to get on with the job of managing, maintaining society as a going concern, and upholding organisational goals with the co-operation of other members. We will therefore look more closely at the idea of 'managing' conflict.

Constructive and destructive conflict

6.14 Given that conflict is inevitable, and assuming that organisational goals are broadly desirable, there are two aspects of conflict which are relevant in practice to the manager or administrator.

    (a) Conflict can be highly desirable. It can energise relationships and clarify issues. Hunt suggests that conflict is constructive, when its effect is to:

        (i) introduce different solutions to problems;
        (ii) define power relationships more clearly;
        (iii) encourage creativity, the testing of ideas;
        (iv) focus attention on individual contributions;
        (v) bring emotions out into the open;
        (vi) provide opportunity for catharsis - ie. the release of hostile feelings etc that have been, or may be, repressed otherwise.

    (b) Conflict can also be destructive, or negative (injurious to social systems, which the radical perspective regards as desirable). Hunt suggests that conflict of this kind may act in a group of individuals to:

        (i) distract attention from the task;
        (ii) polarise views and 'dislocate' the group;
        (iii) subvert objectives in favour of secondary goals;
        (iv) encourage defensive or 'spoiling' behaviour;
        (v) result in disintegration of the group;
        (vi) stimulate emotional, win-lose conflicts, that is, hostility.

6.15 Tjosvold and Deerner researched conflict in different contexts. They allocated to 66 student volunteers the roles of foremen and workers at an assembly plant, with a scenario of conflict over job rotation schemes. Foremen were against, workers for.

One group was told that the organisational norm was to 'avoid controversy'; another was told that the norm was 'co-operative controversy', or *trying* to agree; a third was told that groups were out to win any arguments that arose, or 'competitive controversy'. The students were offered rewards for complying with their given norms. Their decisions, and attitudes to the discussions, were then monitored.

Where controversy was avoided, the foremen's views dominated.

Competitive controversy brought no agreement - but brought out feelings of hostility and suspicion.

Co-operative controversy brought out differences in an atmosphere of curiosity, trust and openness: the decisions reached seemed to integrate the views of both parties.

But can *real* managers and workers be motivated to comply with useful organisational 'norms' in this way?

6.16 Charles Handy redefined the term 'conflict' to offer a useful way of thinking about destructive and constructive conflict and how it might be managed.

(a) Organisations are political systems within which there is competition for scarce resources and unequal influence.

(b) *Differences* between people are natural and inevitable. Differences emerge in three ways:

    (i)   argument;
    (ii)   competition; and
    (iii) conflict - which alone is considered wholly harmful.

Argument and competition are potentially beneficial and fruitful; both may degenerate into conflict if badly managed.

6.17 *Argument*

Argument means resolving differences by discussion; this can encourage integration of a number of viewpoints into a better solution. Handy suggests that in order for argument to be effective:

(a) the arguing group must have shared leadership, mutual trust, and a challenging task; and

(b) the logic of the argument must be preserved - ie. the issues under discussion must be classified, the discussion must concentrate on available information, and the values of the individuals must be expressed openly and taken into account.

Otherwise, argument will be frustrated. If this is so, or if the argument itself is merely the symptom of an underlying, unexpressed conflict, then conflict will be the result.

6.18 *Competition*
Competition can:

    (a)   set standards, by establishing best performance through comparison;
    (b)   motivate individuals to better efforts; and
    (c)   sort out the 'men from the boys'.

6.19 In order to be fruitful, competition must be *open*, rather than *closed*; or, rather, must be *perceived* by the participants to be open, rather than closed. 'Closed' competition is a win-lose (or 'zero-sum') situation, where one party's gain will be another party's loss. One party can only do well at the expense of another, in competition for resources, recognition etc. 'Open' competition exists where all participants can increase their gains - eg. productivity bargaining.

6.20 If competition is perceived to be open, the 'rules' are seen to be fair, and the determinants of success are in the competitor's control, competition can be extremely fruitful. The observations of Peters and Waterman on the motivational effect of comparative performance information supports this view. If these preconditions are not met, competition may again degenerate into conflict.

Causes, symptoms and tactics of conflict

6.21 Conflict may be caused by differences in the *objectives* of different groups or individuals. It is a function of management:

    (a)   to create a system of planning whereby individual or group objectives are formulated within the framework of a strategic plan. A poor planning structure leaves the door open for conflict to enter where formal objectives, roles, authority relationships etc overlap or are unclear; and also

    (b)   to provide leadership, and to encourage individuals to accept the goals of the organisation as being compatible with their personal goals. Poor leadership might also lead to conflict, with the goals of individuals of groups diverging and at odds with each other.

6.22 Conflict may also be caused by disputes about the *boundaries of authority*. For example:

    (a)   staff managers may attempt to encroach on the roles or 'territory' of line managers and usurp some of their authority;

    (b)   one department might start 'empire building' and try to take over the work previously done by another department.

6.23 Personal differences, as regards goals, attitudes and feelings, are also bound to crop up. Ideologies - which we discuss below - may also effect the objectives of individuals and interest groups, and may render 'co-operative controversy' impossible.

6.24 According to Handy, the observable symptoms of conflict in an organisation will be:

(a) poor communications, in all 'directions';
(b) interpersonal friction;
(c) inter-group rivalry and jealousy;
(d) low morale and frustration;
(d) proliferation of rules, norms and myths; especially widespread use of arbitration, appeals to higher authority, and inflexible attitudes towards change.

6.25 The tactics of destructive conflict may be as follows:

(a) One manager will withhold information from another. A manager who lacks some important information will be in a weak position for making decisions or urging his own views. Keeping information away from a 'rival' manager is a very effective tactic for increasing influence and extending the boundaries of one's own authority and influence.

(b) Information might be presented in a distorted manner. This will enable the group or manager presenting the information to get their own way more easily. For example, if the engineering department wants to introduce a new item of equipment into service, they might give biased information about likely 'teething troubles' with the equipment's technology or the expected costs of maintenance, or breakdown times.

(c) A group (especially a specialist group such as accounting) which considers its influence to be neglected might seek to impose rules, procedures, restrictions or official requirements on other groups, in order to bolster up their own importance.

(d) A manager might seek to by-pass formal channels of communication and decision-making by establishing informal contacts and friendships with people in a position of importance. A departmental manager might establish informal contacts with the managing director's personal assistant, and so get 'one up' on other departmental managers, by having a friend close to the managing director's ear.

(e) Line managers might refuse to accept the member of a staff department to fill a vacancy in their department. Similarly, line managers might refuse to accept the recommendations of staff department experts. This attitude of conflict by line towards staff management is more likely to occur where staff departments use tactics of their own to obtain more influence over line department operations.

(f) Conflict might also take the form of fault-finding in the work of other departments: eg. Department X might duplicate the work of department Y - hoping to prove department Y 'wrong' - and then report the fact to senior management.

Managerial response to conflict

6.26 Hunt identifies five different management responses to the handling of conflict - not all of which are effective:

(a)   Denial/withdrawal, or 'sweeping it under the carpet'. If the conflict is very trivial, it may indeed 'blow over' without an issue being made of it, but if the causes are not identified, the conflict may grow to unmanageable proportions.

(b)   Suppression - or 'smoothing over', to preserve working relationships despite minor conflicts. As Hunt remarks, however: "Some cracks cannot be papered over".

(c)   Dominance - or the application of power or influence to settle the conflict. The disadvantage of this is that it creates all the lingering resentment and hostility of 'win-lose' situations.

(d)   Compromise - or bargaining, negotiating, conciliating. To some extent, this will be inevitable in any organisation made up of different individuals. However, individuals tend to exaggerate their positions to allow for compromise, and compromise itself is seen to weaken the value of the decision, perhaps reducing commitment.

(e)   Integration/collaboration. Emphasis must be put on the task, individuals must accept the need to modify their views for its sake, and group effort must be seen to be superior to individual effort. Not easy.

6.27 Handy suggests two types of strategy which may be used to turn conflict into competition or argument, or to manage it in some other acceptable way.

(a)   *Environmental ('ecological') strategies*. These involve creating conditions in which individuals may be better able to interact co-operatively with each other: they are wide-ranging, time-consuming, and unpredictable, because of the sheer range of human differences. Such strategies involve:

   (i)   agreement of common objectives;

   (ii)   reinforcing the group or 'team' nature of organisational life, via culture;

   (iii) providing feedback information on progress;

   (iv)   providing adequate co-ordination and communication mechanisms;

   (v)   sorting out territorial/role conflicts in the organisational structure.

(b)   *Regulation strategies*. These are directed to control conflict - though in fact they make it so much a part of the formal structure of the organisation that they tend to legitimise and even perpetuate it. Possible methods include:

   (i)   the provision of arbitration to settle disputes;

   (ii)   the establishment of detailed rules and procedures for conduct by employees;

   (iii) appointing a person to 'manage' the area of conflict - ie. a liaison/co-ordination officer;

   (iv)   using confrontation, or inter-group meetings, to hammer out differences, especially where territorial conflicts occur;
   (v)   separating the conflicting individuals; and

260

(vi)   ignoring the problem, if it is genuinely likely to 'go away', and there is no point in opening fresh wounds.

7.   IMPROVING CO-ORDINATION AND INTEGRATION

7.1   Co-ordination can be improved by the following.

(a)   Good communication (formal and informal).

(b)   Controlling conflict.

(c)   An organisation structure which is designed so that where there will be a need for two departments to integrate their activities, a co-ordinating level of management exists to ensure that their work harmonises properly. By delegating responsibility for co-ordination, conflicts which escalate up to head of department or board level should be avoided.

(d)   The organisation structure might provide for the appointment of liaison or integration officers. One example is the product manager in a matrix management structure, who co-ordinates the efforts of different departments so as to ensure the profitability and successful performance of the product or product range for which he is responsible.

(e)   Co-ordination might be achieved through the appointment of:
(i)   committees, or
(ii)   project groups,
which include representation from all departments whose work needs to be co-ordinated.

(f)   Friendly, informal communication between managers of different departments should be built up. This might enable managers to co-ordinate their activities more effectively in the absence of any formal system or procedures for the integration of efforts.

(g)   The system of planning and control within the organisation should recognise the need for integration of different departmental interests in the pursuit of organisational goals. In the preparation of a formal plan (eg a budget) managers should try to reach an understanding and agreement on how their efforts should be formally co-ordinated towards a common purpose.

Methods of encouraging integration

7.2   In *A behavioural theory of the firm* Richard M Cyert and James G March described and explained how business decisions came to be made. They based their studies on the large multi-product organisation operating under imperfect competition.

7.3   Classical theory tends to view a firm as run by an entrepreneur who has perfect knowledge of the market and whose goal is profit maximisation.

7.4 Cyert and March believe a firm is a system adapting and responding to a variety of internal and external constraints in arriving at decisions. The firm is not monolithic. Its organisation is composed of a number of departments with diverse interests. The people concerned with the firm include managers, workers, shareholders, suppliers, customers, lawyers, auditors, tax collectors etc all of whom have differing interests. Decisions cannot be made without all their respective interests being taken into account, ie management must recognise the need to integrate the work and goal-direction of many different people and groups.

7.5 It has already been suggested that management must act to provide an adequate communication system and to reduce conflict within the organisation. It is also possible to improve the co-ordination of efforts by the creation of *teams*. For example:

(a) *Planning* within the organisation is more likely to be properly integrated if there is a long-term corporation plan. A corporate planning team acting in an advisory role, and as communicators, should help to co-ordinate this planning effort.

(b) *Innovation*: project teams (often inter-disciplinary) may be created to introduce changes into the organisation. Such teams should have a liaison manager (or several managers) whose job is to 'sell' the change to other members of the organisation and to act as a bridge between the team and the people who will be affected by the change.

A further feature of project teams may be that membership will vary throughout its life; new members will be brought in to lend temporary expertise, and released back to their department when their part of the task is done.

Some managers 'specialise' in change and new ideas - eg operational researchers, and systems analysts. These people should be trained to deal with the human aspect of innovation, and must be aware that their job includes the task of integration, so that their ideas are accepted by the people who must put them into practice.

(c) *Production*: a frequent problem for foremen is uncertainty about the authority of 'staff' experts, such as quality control managers, production planning and control management, work study engineers, the storekeeper, the management accountant etc. Many specialist functions are involved in production - production managers themselves, and also planning, finance and personnel departments. To co-ordinate the efforts of the different specialists, an organisation might use a production committee.

(d) *Professional services*: in local government, there are sometimes difficulties in co-ordinating the activities of different professional services, such as doctors, psychiatrists and social workers. A team or committee of professional experts might be established for the purpose of integrating their efforts.

7.6 James Thompson *(Organisations in Action)* listed three types of integration:

(a) standardisation;
(b) plans and schedules;
(c) mutual adjustment.

Both (a) and (b) are used by bureaucracies. While policy and procedure manuals co-ordinate the day-to-day work of staff there is also a need for written communication of operating goals and objectives. The larger and better organised companies ensure that objectives and goals are clearly defined and quantified in respect of every manager in the organisation (eg in a system of management by objectives).

7.7 Mutual adjustment (c), which involves the exchange of information and a mutual response to these communications, is not commonly used, but Thompson argued that this method of integration is perhaps best for dealing with complex problems.

7.8 Thompson's ideas were supported by J Galbraith *(Designing Complex Organisations)* who argued that with the increasing complexity of organisations and management decisions, the systems of bureaucracy become less efficient. The choices open to management are:

(a) to accept the reduction in efficiency, or to employ more staff;

(b) to split up the organisation into autonomous divisions. This solution may be expensive because there will be some duplication of resources in each division;

(c) to improve vertical communication up and down through the organisation, with improved (computerised) information systems;

(d) to improve *lateral* (horizontal) communications by organising the interchange of ideas and co-operation of efforts between employees in different departments, but at the same level in the management hierarchy. This method of integration was preferred by Galbraith, as being likely to promote better decision-making at a lower cost.

8. PROGRAMMED DECISION-MAKING

8.1 It is interesting to compare the ideas of Thompson and Galbraith with those of Herbert Simon. Simon is a leading writer of the so-called 'Carnegie' approach to management (the approach which focuses on the procedure of decision-making).

8.2 Simon (eg in *The New Science of Management Decision)* believed that 'management' is equivalent to 'decision-making' and his major interest has been an analysis of how decisions are made and of how they might be more effective. He describes three stages of making a decision:

(a) intelligence activity, finding occasions for making a decision;
(b) design activity, finding possible courses of action;
(c) choice activity, choosing the preferable option.

8.3 Simon considered that there is a range of decision types, from the highly repetitive routine to the new and most unusual (from *programmed* to *non-programmed)*. An organisation should attempt to programme most decisions to reduce the areas of uncertainty. Different problem-solving techniques apply to programmed and to non-programmed types of decision.

8.4 Simon's arguments imply that a bureaucracy is capable of improving its decision-making at least at lower levels in the organisation hierarchy, by programming (and computerisation).It is only at senior levels that complexities occur and where the problems of communication, integration and efficiency might therefore arise.

9. CONCLUSIONS ABOUT CO-ORDINATION

9.1 There is no easy solution to the problems of integration; indeed, it could be suggested that this entire text is concerned with aspects of improving integration and therefore the efficiency of an organisation. This chapter has merely focused on the problem, and suggested a few of the 'solutions' which can be attempted.

9.2 From earlier paragraphs in this chapter it might also be suggested that integration can only occur if communications are good between managers and subordinates and also laterally within the organisation.

(a) Managers must develop a relationship of trust with their subordinates.

(b) Co-operation is a common cultural belief, and one that is basic to any economic system. In work organisations it is universally believed that co-operation is a Good Thing, and achieve greater productivity than lack of co-operation. For most tasks, this is proven by experience.

(c) Co-operation is a set of shared values, to the extent of submission of individual needs and differences to the needs of the 'team'.

(d) Co-operation has a rational appeal. It is demonstrable that a suitable number of people co-operating on a task will achieve a better result than one person doing the same task.

(e) Co-operation has an emotional appeal. It incorporates values about unity, teamwork, comradeship, insiders (versus outsiders).

(f) Methods of encouraging co-operation include reinforcing cultures, communication, team cohesiveness and the control of conflict. (Remember that co-operation itself may even involve a certain amount of argument or competition.)

TEST YOUR KNOWLEDGE

(The numbers in brackets refer to paragraphs in this chapter)

1. Why do we need communication in organisations? (1.1)

2. What is informal communication, and what is the main danger with it? (2.1, 2.2)

3. What are the symptoms of and reasons for inadequate integration? (4.1)

4. Distinguish between line and staff management. (5.1, 5.2)

5. What are the problems of having specialist staff functions? (5.7) How can these problems be resolved? (5.8)

6. What are the consequences of (a) constructive conflict and (b) destructive conflict? (6.14)

7. What are the tactics of destructive conflict? (6.25) How might co-ordination be improved? (7.1, 7.5, 7.6, 8.3)

Chapter 13

CORPORATE AND STRATEGIC PLANNING

This chapter covers the following topics:

1. Corporate planning
2. Strategic planning
3. Setting a prime corporate objective
4. SWOT analysis
5. Strategy identification, evaluation and selection
6. Product life cycle
7. Competitive advantage
8. Product/market strategies
9. Synergy
10. Forecasting models
11. Corporate planning: a summary
12. The role of the board of directors

Purpose of this chapter

To describe the corporate planning process, and to suggest its role in planning for future change.

1. CORPORATE PLANNING

1.1 Every business enterprise must plan ahead to survive. Increasingly, nowadays, plans must be made for the longer term as well as for the immediate future. Some businesses do not have an organised planning system and so tend to carry out their planning and control decisions in a disorganised and haphazard manner. However, in businesses where the scale and complexity of operations is so large and diverse, corporate planning can be an invaluable aid to management.

1.2 Corporate planning and strategic planning are two terms which can be taken too mean the same thing.

1.3 Corporate planning has been variously described as follows.

(a) 'Corporate planning is a comprehensive, future oriented, continuous process of management which is implemented within a formal framework. It is responsive to relevant changes in the external environment. It is concerned with both strategic and operational planning and through the participation of relevant members of the organisation, develops plans and actions at the appropriate levels in the organisation. It incorporates monitoring and control mechanisms and is concerned with both the short and the long term.'

(b) It is 'a systematic and disciplined study designed to help identify the objective of any organisation or corporate body, determine an appropriate target, decide upon suitable constraints, and devise a practical plan by which the objective may be achieved.'

(Argenti 1968)

2. STRATEGIC PLANNING

2.1 Prof. John Higgins (University of Bradford Management Centre) has defined *strategic planning* as 'comprehending the environment, and ensuring that the organisation adapts to that environment.'

2.2 Strategic planning is a complex process, which involves taking a view of (a) the organisation, and (b) the future that it is likely to encounter, and then attempting to organise the structure and resources of the organisation accordingly. To that end, strategic planning therefore embraces (a) strategy and policy formulation, and (b) the development of a set of plans.

2.3 Higgins describes the strategic planning process as embracing:

(a) setting the corporate/strategic *objectives* which need to be expressed in quantitative terms with any *constraints* identified;

(b) from (a), establishing the corporate performance required;

(c) internal appraisal, by means of assessing the organisation's current state in terms of resources and performance;

(d) external appraisal, by means of a survey and analysis of the organisation's environment;

(e) forecasting future performance based on the information obtained from (c) and (d), initially as purely passive extrapolations into the future of past and current achievements;

(f) analysing the *gap* between the results of (b) and (e);

(g) identifying and evaluating various strategies to reduce this 'performance gap' in order to meet strategic objectives;

(h) choosing between alternative strategies;

(i) preparing the final corporate plan, with divisions between short term and long term as appropriate;

(j) evaluating actual performance against the corporate plan.

2.4 There are two different approaches to strategic planning:

(a) one approach is that strategic planning must be a disciplined, structured and continuous planning exercise;

(b) alternatively there is the view that strategic planning should be an 'ad hoc' exercise, so planning should be done at the corporate level only when opportunities arise for implementing a new business strategy.

2.5 The large majority of writers favour a disciplined approach, for many reasons.

(a) Many organisations are large, have a complex structure and operate in many different markets. Conglomerates and multinationals are among the most complex. Without discipline, planning would be unmanageable and in the case of multinationals or conglomerates, a failure to impose the discipline of strategic planning would result in the fragmentation of the organisation into separate unco-ordinated parts.

(b) The rate of change in production, technologies and markets is very fast. A manager must be able not only to deal with change when it occurs, but to be able to foresee changes before they happen in order to be better prepared to meet them. Unless planning is disciplined, managers will think in the short term and not far enough into the future.

(c) Because of the complexity of many business decisions, there is a need for an information system which provides information of a sufficient quality to enable better decisions to be made. A formal information system, drawing from external sources as well as internal feedback, should be linked to a formal system for corporate planning and control.

(d) There is still a growing tendency for managers to be less authoritarian in style and to allow subordinates a greater scope of authority. Management objectives to subordinates have therefore, in many instances, become more generalised and longer term.

(e) If there is discipline in budgeting, we should expect to find discipline at the higher level of strategic planning. Planning itself is a discipline which focuses attention on significant issues which might otherwise be ignored.

(f) A disciplined approach to strategic planning should ensure that:

(i) all the stages in the planning process are carried out;
(ii) it is a continuous system, not an occasional 'one-off' exercise, so that there is a monitoring and review process;
(iii) the entire organisation is co-ordinated, from the decisions of top managers to those of factory foremen and other front-line supervisors.

2.6 The second approach to strategic planning is to operate a system whereby opportunities are exploited as they arise, judged on their individual merits and not within the rigid structure of an overall corporate strategy. This approach contrasts with the generally accepted principles of disciplined strategic planning and is called *freewheeling opportunism.*

2.7 The advantages of this approach are that:

(a) opportunities can be seized when they arise, whereas a rigid planning framework might impose restrictions so that the opportunities are lost;

    (b)   it is flexible and adaptable. A formal corporate plan might take a long time to prepare and is fully documented. Any sudden, unexpected change (eg. a very steep rise in the price of a key commodity) might cause serious disruption, so that the process of preparing a new components plan would be slow. A freewheeling opportunistic approach would adapt to the change more quickly;

    (c)   it might encourage a more flexible, creative attitude among lower-level managers, whereas the procedures of formal planning might not.

2.8   Professor Bernard Taylor in his paper *New Dimensions in Corporate Planning* reiterates the fact that the way strategic planning is practised will vary with circumstances. Fitting the planning 'mode' to the situation will require a good deal of skill and experience.

    (a)   In a large bureaucratic organisation, this will probably require the introduction of a formal planning system.

    (b)   In circumstances where growth or innovation are required, it will be important to organise for new projects.

    (c)   In an uncertain situation with many interest groups involved, it may be advisable to use an organisational 'learning' process - to improve mutual understanding, to explore the problem, and possibly to evolve a consensus.

    (d)   If it is necessary to influence decisions in other organisations there may be a need for special arrangements to improve formal and informal contacts, eg. through joint committees, liaison officers etc.

    (e)   Where there is a 'crisis of identity' in the organisation (eg. if it is not thought to be socially valuable or if the future of the enterprise is tied up with the creation of a new technology with important social implications) it may be particularly important to re-examine the future role of the enterprise in society.

3.   SETTING A PRIME CORPORATE OBJECTIVE

3.1   The process of setting corporate objectives, and expressing these objectives as targets for achievement within a designated time span, was described in an earlier chapter. Setting an overall objective is the first step in the corporate planning process.

3.2   The next aim of the planning process should be to select strategies which should enable the organisation to achieve its main objectives. In order to select these strategies, and to set strategic objectives for each of them, the organisation must first of all think about what it is good at, and what it is bad at, and about what dangers and opportunities it is likely to face in the future.

4.   SWOT ANALYSIS

4.1   This internal appraisal of the organisation's strengths and weaknesses, and external appraisal of the opportunities and threats facing the organisation, is known as SWOT analysis.

```
S  -  strengths
W  -  weaknesses
O  -  opportunities
T  -  threats
```

Internal appraisal of strengths and weaknesses

4.2 The purpose of a strengths and weaknesses analysis is to express, quantitatively or qualitatively:

(a) which areas of the business have strengths that should be exploited by suitable strategies;

(b) which areas of the business have weaknesses for which strategies should be developed to improve them.

4.3 The strengths and weaknesses analysis is internal to the company and intended to shape its approach to the external world. For instance, the identification of shortcomings in skills or resources could lead to a planned acquisition programme or staff recruitment and training.

The strengths and weaknesses part of the SWOT analysis involves looking at the findings of the position audit.

4.4 Typically, the analysis would consider information in the following areas.

(a) *Marketing*
   (i) Fate of new product launches - have these a good success record or not, and so is the organisation developing new products successfully?
   (ii) Success or failure of advertising campaigns - is the organisation using advertising to good effect?
   (iii) Market shares and market sizes - is the organisation in a strong or weak position?
   (iv) Company's standing in growth markets - is the organisation well-placed in growth markets, or does it rely on mature or declining markets?
   (v) Skills of the sales force and selling techniques used - how good is the success rate of the sales team in winning orders?

(b) *Products*
   (i) Analysis of sales by market, area, product groups, outlets etc.
   (ii) Profit margin and overall profit contribution - are profits for each product good or not?
   (iii) Age and future life of products - does the company have a good balance between old and new products, and rising, mature and declining products?
   (iv) Price elasticity of demand of products - is demand price sensitive, and so are prospects for putting up prices poor?

(c) *Distribution*

   (i) Delivery service standards - what are delivery lead times, and how do they compare?
   (ii) Warehouse delivery fleet facilities - can the delivery fleet cope with demand?

(iii) Geographical availability of products - is the distribution network poor/adequate/excellent?

(d) *Research and development*

(i) Are R & D projects relevant to future marketing plans?
(ii) The costs of R & D - is R & D spending too little/too much?
(iii) Benefits of R & D in new products/variations on existing products - how good has R & D been?
(iv) R & D workload and schedules. Will we beat our competitor to the new launch?

(e) *Finance*

(i) Availability of short term and long term funds, cash flow - is the organisation in a strong or weak position for further borrowing or cash flow?
(ii) Contribution of each product - how is each product contributing to cash flow?
(iii) Returns on investment.
(iv) Accounting ratios - ratio analysis should help to identify areas of strength or weakness in performance (eg. asset turnover ratios, liquidity ratios etc).

(f) *Plant and equipment and other facilities*

(i) Age, value, production capacity and suitability of plant and equipment.
(ii) Valuation of all assets.
(iii) Location of land and buildings, their value, area, use, length of lease, current book value.

Are assets inadequate? too old? well kept? technologically advanced? Does the organisation have freehold or long leasehold property? If not, does renting or holding short leases on property indicate a potential danger/weakness?

(g) *Management and staff*

(i) Age spread, succession plans.
(ii) Skills and attitudes.
(iii) State of industrial relations, morale and labour turnover.
(iv) Training and recruitment facilities.
(v) Manpower utilisation.

In general, is the management team strong or weak, and what ways?

(h) *Business management: organisation*

(i) Organisation structure - is this properly suited to the organisation's needs? Is the organisation based on functional divisions (eg. production, marketing, finance etc) or product/market profit centres?
(ii) Management style and philosophy - does the management style seem well-suited to the businesses the organisation operates in?
(iii) Communication links - are these adequate?

(i) *Raw material and finished goods stocks*

(i) The sources of supply - is there a single supplier or can supplies be obtained from numerous sources?
(ii) Number and description of items.

      (iii)   Turnover periods – long or short?
      (iv)   Storage capacity – adequate? Is there spare capacity?
      (v)   Obsolescence and deterioration.
      (vi)   Pilfering etc.

4.5 The purpose of the analysis is to express, qualitatively or quantitatively, which areas of the business have strengths to exploit, and which areas have weaknesses which must be improved. Although every area of the business should be investigated, only the areas of significant strength or weakness should warrant further attention.

Example: strengths and weaknesses analysis

4.6 A strengths and weaknesses analysis might come up with the following results:

(a) *Strengths:*

      (i)   marketing, products and markets:
          - products A, B and C are market leaders;
          - product D, new product launch, high profit potential;
          - good brand images;
          - good relations with suppliers and dealers;
          - good packaging and advertising appeal;

      (ii)   production:
          - new factory in North West, fully operational for next year;
          - thorough quality inspection standards;

      (iii) finance:
          - £0.5 million cash available from internal resources;
          - further £2.0 million overdraft facility, so far unused;

      (iv)   management and staff:
          - high skills in marketing areas of packaging, sales promotion, advertising and sales generally;
          - good labour relations, except at one plant which has low productivity.

(b) *Weaknesses:*

      (i)   marketing:
          - products X, Y and Z contribute no profit;
          - products P, Q and R are declining and will lose profitability in 3 years;
          - sales of product D are dependent upon a high level of sales of complementary products (eg. razor blades and razor);
          - no new products, except for D, have been successfully launched in the last two years;

      (ii)   research and development:
          - no major new products have been derived from R & D for two years. Becoming too dependent on acquisition for additions to product range;
          - little control over R & D budget;

      (iii) production:
          - plant at most factories has an average age of 8.7 years;

- new developments could threaten ability to compete;
- high level of spoiled goods on lines 3, 7, 9 at one location;
- low productivity on all lines at one plant;

(iv) management and staff:
- poor labour relations at plant with low productivity;
- senior executives approaching retirement with no clearly recognisable successor;
- success of the organisation too dependent on senior executive charisma.

External appraisal of opportunities and threats

4.7 The internal appraisal highlights areas within the company which are strong and which might therefore be exploited more fully, and weaknesses where some 'defensive' planning might be required to protect the company from poor results. Strengths and weaknesses show up inherent *potential*.

4.8 An external appraisal is required to identify profit-making opportunities which can be exploited by the company's strengths and also to anticipate environmental threats (a declining economy, competitors' actions, government legislation, industrial unrest etc) against which the company must protect itself. The external appraisal is the opportunities and threats analysis part of SWOT analysis.

4.9 For *opportunities* it is necessary to decide:

(a) what opportunities exist in the business environment;

(b) what is their inherent profit-making potential;

(c) what are the internal strengths/weaknesses of the organisation, and whether it is capable of exploiting the worthwhile opportunities and still achieve its social and ethical objectives;

(d) what is the comparative capability profile of competitors and whether these competitors are better placed to exploit these opportunities;

(e) what is the company's comparative performance potential in this field of opportunity.

The opportunities might involve product development, market development, market penetration or diversification. No realistic opportunity should be ignored.

4.10 For *threats* it is necessary to decide:

(a) what threats might arise, to the company or its business environment;

(b) how competitors will be affected;

(c) how the company will be affected. Does it have strengths to deal with the threat or do weaknesses need to be corrected so as to survive the threat? Are contingency strategies required?

4.11 The opportunities and threats which might be identified include the following.

(a) *Economic:* at a local or national level, threats and opportunities would relate to unemployment, the level of wages and salaries, increases in local government rates and fuel costs, the expected total market behaviour for products, total customer demand, the growth and decline of industries and suppliers, general investment levels etc. At an international level, world production and the volume of international trade, demand, recessions, exchange controls, etc. must be considered.

(b) *Government:* legislation may affect a company's prospects through the threats/ opportunities of pollution control or a ban on certain products. A law to ban lead in petrol would be a threat to petrol producers and car makers, but at the same time an opportunity for selling lead-free petrol and making cars that use it. Pollution controls offer opportunities for companies that make equipment to prevent or limit pollution. Taxation incentives, rent-free factory buildings, or investment grants might be available for exploitation or under threat of withdrawal. Government policy may be to increase expenditure on housing, defence, schools and hospitals or roads and transport and this gives opportunities to private companies and the relevant government organisations alike. Political attitudes may threaten the nationalisation of companies' assets, or nationalised industries may face the threats/opportunities of privatisation. Political upheaval might damage market and investment prospects, especially overseas.

(c) *Competitors:*

(i) Possible competitors' actions in the future must be considered and their comparative strengths and weaknesses evaluated. In Britain, it is especially important to identify where competitors are weak in export markets, and where foreign competitors might threaten the industry with cheaper or better imports. British industry in fairly recent years has called at some time or another for protection against Japanese cars, foreign textiles and imported fish, having been unable to meet the external threat successfully and therefore requiring external assistance from the government. In contrast, manufacturers of lawn mowers successfully identified a threat from Japanese importers and developed competitive new products of their own.

(ii) The company must also decide whether it is under threat of a takeover bid by any other company. A comparison of internal strength and weakness and potential buyers is needed.

(d) *Technology:* technological changes must be forecast so as to identify the possibility of new products appearing, or cheaper means of production or distribution being introduced. The underdeveloped potential of the microchip has far-reaching effects for producers (eg. the use of robots), service industries (eg. the communications and information services), and markets (eg. the new products that will be made available for consumers).

(e) *Social:*

(i) Social attitudes will have a significant effect on customer demand and employee attitudes. Attitudes to work are changing, and employees are increasingly unwilling to work in 'dirty' jobs or menial work. Hours of work are shortening, holidays getting longer, and the age of retirement may be lowered. Voluntary early retirement has been a feature in recent years. Inflation in the 1970s and credit cards in the 1980s appear to have encouraged a switch of attitudes to 'spend now, pay later'. This important shift in social attitudes explains the growing interest by many companies in exploiting the leisure and health industry - eg. golf clubs and driving ranges, squash, home computers, gambling, holiday items, fitness centres etc;

(ii) Society is also applying pressure to improve the environment, and to reduce noise and pollution. The government in Britain is also making early efforts to protect the employment rights of women and encourage racial equality;

(iii) Population trends must also be considered. Britain currently has an ageing population so that in future, an increased market will exist among retired people, with limited spending power. There are recognised opportunities for growth in the personal pensions market, reinforced by prospects of new legislation in this area.

(iv) Permanently high unemployment figures will influence the available total spending power of consumers, especially in some of the more depressed regions of the UK.

Example: opportunities and threats analysis

4.12 Some years ago, an analysis of opportunities and threats in its industrial environment would have been of some value to strategic planners in the UK paint industry. From 1980, four pressures built up on the industry:

(a) the economic recession;
(b) rising costs of production and marketing;
(c) the fragmentation of the markets for paint products; and
(d) new technology.

4.13 As raw material costs rose, paint prices were kept down by intense competition between paint manufacturers, so that profit margins were squeezed. New market segments combined with new technology have forced paint manufacturers to spend heavily on product development - paints for plastics, paints for painting steel coils or aluminium coils on automated production lines, one-coat paints, non-drip paints, and all-weather woodstains are examples of product changes based on new technology. With low profit margins, companies need to have a 15% - 20% share of a market segment to be profitable, but there are still about 10 big paint manufacturers in the UK.

4.14 The threats and opportunities in the environment might suggest that:

(a) there are threats of being taken over by a UK or foreign competitor or opportunities to take over a rival;

(b) some manufacturers should plan to 'divest' and get out of certain segments of the market. Indeed, ICI, the overall market leader, pulled out of the market for heavy duty paints for agricultural, construction and earth-moving equipment, leaving Macpherson as the dominant market leader in this market segment.

The changes in the paint industry are no doubt still far from over.

5. STRATEGY IDENTIFICATION, EVALUATION AND SELECTION

5.1 The internal and external appraisals will be brought together, and perhaps shown in cruciform chart, so that potential strategies can be identified.

5.2 A cruciform chart is simply a table listing the significant strengths and weaknesses, and opportunities and threats. For example:

STRENGTHS	*WEAKNESSES*
£10 million of capital available	Heavy reliance on a small number of customers
Production expertise and appropriate marketing skills	Limited product range, with no new products and expected market decline. Small marketing organisation.
THREATS	*OPPORTUNITIES*
A major competitor has already entered the new market	Government tax incentives for new investment.
Growing demand in a new market, although customers so far relatively small in number.	

5.3 In this example, it might be possible to identify that the company is in imminent danger of losing its existing markets and must diversify its products, or its products and markets. The new market opportunity exists to be exploited, and since the number of customers is currently small, the relatively small size of the existing marketing force would not be an immediate hindrance. A strategic plan could be developed to buy new equipment and use existing production and marketing to enter the new market, with a view to rapid expansion. Careful planning of manpower, equipment, facilities, research and development etc. would be required and there would be an objective to meet the threat of competition so as to obtain a substantial share of a growing market. The cost of entry at this early stage of market development should not be unacceptably high.

5.4 In this example, one individual strategy has been identified from our simplified cruciform chart. In practice, a combination of individual strategies will be required with regard to product development, market development, diversification, resource planning, risk reduction etc.

5.5 Once a company has defined its business and analysed strengths and weaknesses, taking regard of external factors, it is in a position to develop its strategy and define a range of strategic objectives. To define the range of objectives does not, of itself, bring about their attainment. The company will need to identify opportunities for growth and profit improvement that will enable it to achieve its objectives.

5.6 Drucker tells us that 'successful planning is always based on maximising opportunities' and he cites the example of Marks and Spencer who are consistently asking themselves – 'which are the opportunities where doing something new and different is likely to have the greatest economic results?' Drucker goes on to outline (*Management for results*) three main approaches to improving business effectiveness:

(a) The executive can define 'the ideal business' which would produce best results from the available market knowledge and opportunities.

(b) He can try to maximise opportunities by focusing the available resources on the most attractive possibilities to obtain greatest results.

(c) He can maximise resources so that those opportunities are found – if not created – that give the available best resources the greatest possible impact.

5.7 Individual strategies should be tested against a list of criteria for acceptance, namely:

(a) to what extent will the strategy contribute towards the organisation's financial objectives or other prime objectives in both the short and long term?

(b) is the strategy consistent with the social and ethical objectives of the organisation?

(c) does the strategy conform to other strategies pursued by the organisation, or is it a completely new direction? (eg. conglomerate diversification, or investment in pure research might be proposed strategies which are currently not pursued by the organisation);

(d) the element of risk attached to a proposed strategy should not be too high compared with the potential rewards. If the strategy can only be successful under the most favourable conditions, then the risk is probably too great;

(e) is the strategy capable of succeeding in spite of the likely reaction by competitors?

(f) will there be adequate control techniques? A new strategy needs a careful check on performance to put any necessary remedial steps into effect, particularly in the early decision-making;

(g) is the strategy preferable to other, mutually exclusive strategies? Is there an option to combine two separate strategies into one action? 'While it is often sufficient to solve problem A by taking action A and to solve problem B by taking action B, great economy in effort and in cost would be achieved if one could take action C to solve both problem A and problem B at the same time – two birds with one stone, as it were' (Argenti). Argenti used the example of one department buying a computer for £50,000 for accounting work, and a second department buying a £30,000 computer for scientific work, when a £60,000 computer would be capable of handling the workloads of both departments;

(h) are the technology and resources available to carry out the strategy? The time span within which a strategy is expected to achieve its purpose must not be so short that the company suffers from severe 'indigestion' during this period. Time must be allowed for new organisational and communication patterns to develop and operate freely, and for personal abilities and relationships to mature;

(i) is the new strategy flexible and capable of adjusting to change in the business environment?

5.8 The diagram below shows how a company progresses through the sequence of defining its business, formulating objectives, assessing external factors, analysing its strengths and assessing its weaknesses through to evaluation of alternative courses of action.

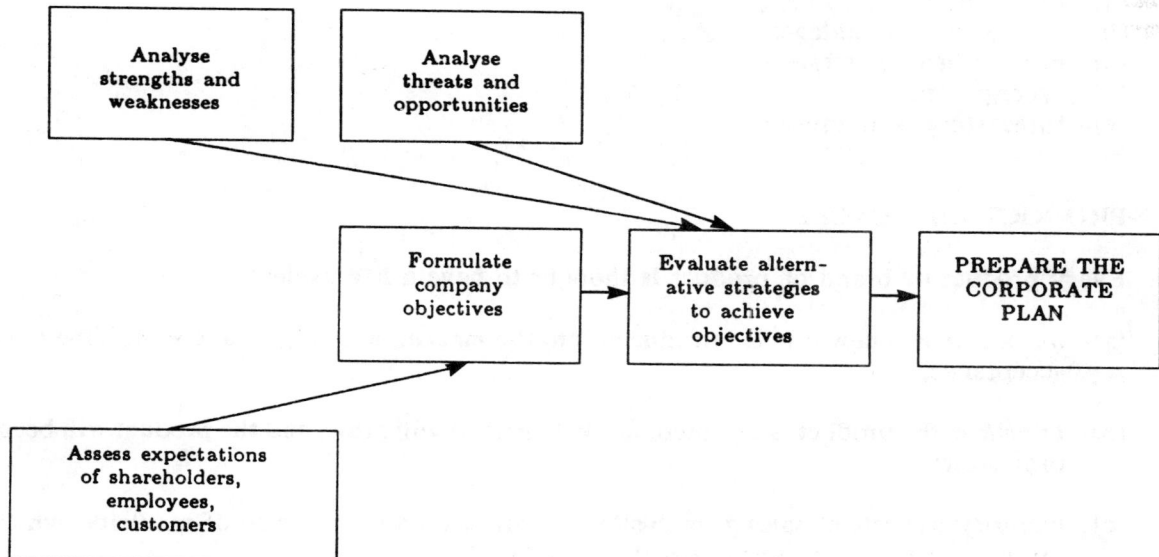

```
┌──────────────────┐      ┌──────────────────┐
│     Analyse      │      │     Analyse      │
│   strengths and  │      │   threats and    │
│   weaknesses     │      │  opportunities   │
└──────────────────┘      └──────────────────┘
          │                        │
          └──────────┐   ┌─────────┘
                     ▼   ▼
┌──────────────┐   ┌──────────────┐   ┌──────────────┐
│  Formulate   │   │ Evaluate altern-│ │ PREPARE THE  │
│   company    │──▶│ ative strategies│▶│  CORPORATE   │
│  objectives  │   │   to achieve    │ │    PLAN      │
└──────────────┘   │   objectives    │ └──────────────┘
       ▲           └──────────────┘
       │
┌──────────────────┐
│ Assess expectations │
│  of shareholders,   │
│     employees,      │
│     customers       │
└──────────────────┘
```

5.9 The task of selecting a suitable 'portfolio of strategies' is a very complex one because of the wide variety of options available.

5.10 Ansoff commented that the selection of a portfolio 'at first glance ... would appear to be quite simple; the portfolio which offers the best performance for the firm's objectives is the one to choose. In practice this turns out to be a difficult process. Each portfolio is measured by three ratings, one each in proximate (up to 3 - 10 years), long-term (beyond 3-10 years) and flexibility objectives. These are in the nature of apples, pears and oranges. Each contributes to a different aspect of the firm's performance; each is measured by a different yardstick and an increase in one usually involves decreases in the others. There is no obvious way in which they can be combined to produce a single figure of merit for each scope.'

5.11 The choice is so complex that Argenti recommends that the corporate plan should exclude as much detail as possible, and provide only a 'coarse-grained' strategic structure for the long-term future, leaving the detail of new product selection, new markets, diversification opportunities (in detail), R & D projects, resource management etc. in the hands of executive managers. He wrote: 'A corporate plan, then, will specify both the strategic structure towards which the company is to move and the individual strategic actions that will bring it about. The depth of detail required in the corporate plan should be sufficient to allow the management to judge their confidence in it; if more than this depth of detail is present then the scope for opportunism and initiative by individual managers may be needlessly curtailed. Deciding how much to decide is an important part of all planning.'

5.12 We have now considered how strategic plans might be decided. There are a few concepts in corporate planning which we have not yet discussed, but which are relevant to an understanding of the corporate planning process. These are:

(a) the product life cycle;
(b) competitive advantage;
(c) product/market strategies;
(d) synergy; and
(e) forecasting techniques.

6. PRODUCT LIFE CYCLE

6.1 Every product or brand of product is thought to have a life cycle:

(a) *introduction*: a new line is introduced into the market, and might take some time to gain acceptance;

(b) *growth*: if the product is accepted, market demand will grow, and the product will become profitable;

(c) *maturity*: the rate of sales growth slows down, and enters a period of maturity, which is the longest period of a successful product's life;

(d) *decline*: eventually, sales will decline. The product will become unprofitable, and will then be removed from the market.

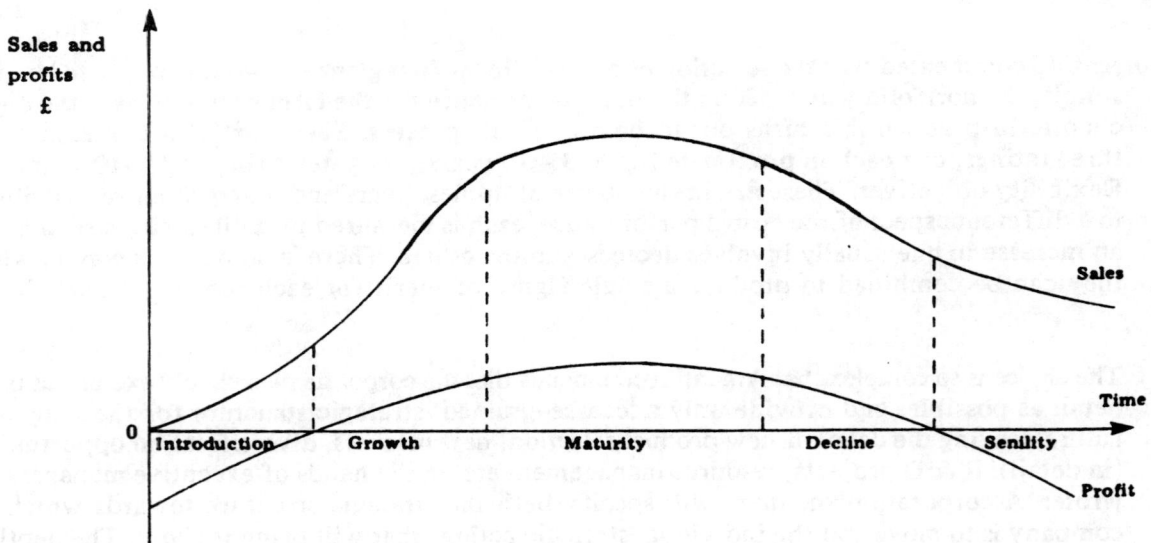

6.2 A company should ideally have a range of products at differing stages in their life cycle. Since some products are 'yesterday's breadwinners' and will not continue to be profitable for ever, *innovation* - the development of new products or brands - is essential for a firm's continued (long-term) survival.

7. COMPETITIVE ADVANTAGE

7.1 A company will be more successful in its markets if it gains a *competitive advantage* over its competition. This means that strengths of the company should be exploited to secure an advantage. A competitive advantage (which can perhaps be protected by patents) might be provided by the following categories of product:

(a) breakthrough product: completely new products or services which offer a radical performance advantage over competition, at a drastically lower price, or products which have no competition (yet) at all;

(b) improved product: products which are not radically different from competitors' products, but which have an obvious superiority in terms of quality or price;

(c) competitive product; products which offer 'value for money' by providing an appealing balance between quality and price.

8. PRODUCT/MARKET STRATEGIES

8.1 The structure of competitive advantage is determined by the firm's overall product-market mix, that is a combination of current and new products in current and new markets, described as:

(a) *market penetration* in which the firm seeks to increase its share of current markets with current products, eg. through competitive pricing, advertising, sales promotion, spending more on distribution or direct selling etc;

(b) *market development* in which the firm seeks new markets for its current products, such as exporting if the firm has previously served only the domestic market;

(c) *product development* in which the firm seeks to create new products to replace existing products, for current markets; and

(d) *diversification* in which the firm seeks to develop new products in new markets.

8.2 These four options are shown in the following table:

	PRODUCT OR SERVICES	
	Present	*New*
Present market:	Market penetration	Product/service development
New market:	Market development	Diversification

9. SYNERGY

9.1 Synergy is the advantage to a firm gained by having existing resources which are compatible with new products or markets that the company is developing, ie. new 'product-market entries'. It can be described as the 2 + 2 = 5 effect, where a firm looks for combined results that reflect a better rate of return than would be achieved by the same resources used independently as separate operations. The combined performance, therefore, is greater than the sum of its parts.

9.2 The various types of synergy may be categorised as:

(a) sales synergy;
(b) operating synergy;
(c) investment synergy; and
(d) management synergy.

9.3 *Sales synergy* for products is obtained through use of common facilities such as distribution channels, sales administration, warehousing. Supplying a range of complementary products increases the productivity of the sales force, an obvious example of which is the range of both dairy and non-dairy products carried by milk deliverymen. Common advertising, sales promotion and corporate image can generate much higher return than average, per pound spent.

9.4 *Operating synergy* results from better use of facilities and personnel, bulk purchasing, greater spread of fixed costs and advantages of common learning curves.

9.5 *Investment synergy* can be achieved from joint use of plant, common raw material stocks, transfer of research and development from one product to another.

9.6 *Management synergy* is the advantage to be gained where management skills concerning current operations are easily transferred to new operations because of the similarity of problems encountered in the respective industries. The converse is true in that synergy aspects of top-level management could be counter-productive in situations where the problems inherent in new ventures are unrelated to current operations and attempts to solve them in the familiar way lead to incorrect or even disastrous decisions.

9.7 Synergy is gained by exploiting the strength within the company, and is closely associated with 'economies of scale'. Although synergy might be acquired by developing the internal resources of a company, it is more commonly sought through mergers and acquisitions.

9.8 Corporate planners will seek to develop strategic plans which provide synergy, yet there is a severe danger of misguided optimism. Argenti wrote: 'It should be noted that synergy is unlikely to occur, or even to be negative, when a company attempts a new activity that is not related to a strength. A company with a poor distribution channel for Product A may court disaster by attempting to sell Product B through it as well. Synergy is popularly described as the "2 + 2 = 5" effect. This equation may be correct for strengths, but for weaknesses, it must be "-2 - 2 = -5".'

10. FORECASTING MODELS

10.1 Forecasting models and forecasting techniques are often used to obtain planning information.

10.2 There are some *subjective methods* of forecasting including:

(a) individual assessment. Individuals are asked to assess what they think will happen. Typically, salesmen might be asked to make a sales forecasting for their area, based on their opinion of what they think they will be able to sell;

(b) Delphic method of forecasting. This is a method which experts are asked to give their independent opinions about long term developments in the future, which are eventually refined into a consensus view of the future, on which strategic planning decisions might be based;

(c) surveys - eg market research surveys.

10.3 There are some *statistical forecasting models*, based on extrapolating historical results into the future. Examples of statistical forecasting models are:

(a) *Moving averages and trend analysis.* An example is the computer models used by the so-called 'chartists' - eg investment analysts in the world's major financial centres - to forecast the movement of share prices. Computers can help with the analysis of trends, especially when there is a mixture of long-term, medium-term and short-term trends.

(b) *Exponential smoothing.*

10.4 Models and computers will often be used. Higgins cites the case of an insurance company that made extensive use of computers in its corporate planning and control systems. In addition to its basic 'essential' information system the company developed computer-based financial, taxation and econometric models.

(a) The financial model was found to be particularly useful for the quick appraisal of the effects on the business of inflation.

(b) The taxation model was used in developing arguments for negotiations with the Inland Revenue authorities.

(c) The econometrics model found employment in making the company's management aware of the impact of economic trends on the company's activities, and in producing 'initial scenarios' in its planning processes.

Strategic planning models

10.5 Strategic planning models are sometimes referred to as business planning models. Forecasting what will happen in the future calls for data about the organisation itself and its resources, that is, internal data, and also external environmental data. Large quantities of data are needed to make reasonably reliable forecasts, and the value of computer databases might seem obvious in this context.

Scenario building

10.6 Scenario building is another name for strategic or long-range planning. It can be described as the process of identifying alternative futures, ie. constructing a number of distinct possible futures permitting deductions to be made about future developments of markets, products and technology. Such models include simple surprise-free extrapolations, creative thinking such as brainstorming, systems models such as the MIT World Model, and the Delphi model.

10.7 The Delphi model involves a panel of experts providing views on various events to be forecast such as inventions and breakthroughs, or even regulations or changes over a time period into the future. Within the context of the time period, probability weightings are then applied to the possible outcome of events. While this is little more than quasi-quantified informed opinion, it is nonetheless helpful in strategic planning when an organisation is endeavouring to define objectives and constraints over specific time scales.

10.8 From a more general standpoint, McNamee has outlined a seven point approach to scenario building.

(a) *Develop a data base.* Any modelling must have access to a sufficient database. Let it suffice to say here that it should include data about both the organisation itself and the environment.

(b) *Develop a strategic profile of the organisation:* establish its culture and style of leadership etc. Strengths and weaknesses analysis and gap analysis may be an element of this exercise. Much of the data will be highly quantitative; financial values, physical resources in terms of raw materials, skilled headcount, market share, cash and potential for increased gearing etc.

(c) *Develop a profile for the environment.* The Delphi technique is one way of doing this. Much of the UK public sector has been faced with greater competition from private sector organisations, against a background of government policy that has been alien to traditional public sector thinking and culture. Privatisation has emerged as a strategy for many public sector organisations to develop.

(d) *Test the impact of the environmental element upon the organisational element.* Essentially this means bringing the environmental factors and internal strengths and weaknesses together in order to assess strategies that are under review.

(e) *Analyse further the elements revealed by the analysis in step (d).* For example, a power supply company in a sunshine state of the USA may identify the growth of the population in its territory. This may need further analysis as to the population's profile, and what its requirements might be. Population growth may just be the result of older people migrating towards the sunshine on retirement, or else it might be part of a more general population movement towards the sunshine states, bringing with it a growth in commercial and industrial customers. The nature of the population growth would have implications for the power supply company in terms of planning capacity, eg. how long can the company continue to use imported power from a neighbouring state? When is the latest time to take decisions about capacity expansion? Most important, how may this capacity expansion be undertaken bearing in mind environmental lobby groups and resistance to the use of coal (sulphur emissions) and nuclear power.

(f) *Repeated testing of the information revealed by the first analysis.* Plans are rarely finalised at the first attempt, and it is not unreasonable to assume that this process may have to be repeated several times.

(g) *Select the final strategy* subject perhaps to the constraints of suitability, acceptability and feasibility.

Econometric models for medium-term forecasting

10.9 Econometrics is the study of *economic variables* and their interrelationships, using computer models. Short-term or medium-term econometric models might be used for forecasting. Such models, incorporating mathematical techniques such as regression analysis, may well be more accurate for medium-term forecasting than long-term trend projections based on scenario building.

10.10 Barometric techniques of forecasting are those which predict changes in market demand (or demand for a company's products), just as a barometer predicts changes in the weather.

10.11 This method of forecasting depends on:

(a) the firm's ability to identify key 'indicators' of change, in advance of the change actually occurring; and

(b) the ability to predict the span of time between a change in the indicator and a change in market demand. 'Change' in an indicator is especially useful for demand forecasting when they reach their highest or lowest points (when an increase turns into a decline or vice versa).

10.12 There are three types of indicator, but only one of these is useful for demand forecasting.

   (a) *Leading indicators* are indicators which change *before* market demand changes. For example, a sudden increase in the birth rate would be an indicator of future demand for children's clothes. Similarly, a fall in retail sales would be an indicator to manufacturers that demand from retailers for their products will soon fall.

   (b) *Lagging indicators* are indicators which show a change *after* market demand has changed. For example, the level of stocks held by manufacturers will probably fall after the national economy has fallen into a recession. Stockholding levels would therefore confirm that a recession has begun, and would be a lagging indicator of falling demand.

   (c) *Coincident indicators* are indicators which reach a peak or trough value at the same demand that demand peaks or reaches a bottom.

10.13 Lagging indicators and coincident indicators do not provide information to help in forecasting demand. Leading indicators may be useful, but the 'lead time' must be sufficiently long to give firms time to plan for the change.

10.14 The use of barometric techniques has so far been applied mainly to the prediction of upturns or downturns in a nation's economy. Leading indicators in this area of forecasting may include industrial profits, interest rates, the money supply, industrial production, the Stock Market All-Share Index or FT-SE Index, and retail sales etc.

Judgement and intuition

10.15 The future is difficult to predict with certainty. The more distant the planning horizon, the greater is the uncertainty. With corporate planning, where plans might cover a period of 5 years, 10 years or conceivably even longer, the uncertainty is such that managers will have to use their judgement, based on experience, and even intuition, to:

   (a) recognise significant longer term threats and opportunities for business development;
   (b) assess whether the numerical forecasts seem reasonable;
   (c) *make* forecasts (eg the Delphi method);
   (d) select strategies which might be successful in the future.

10.16 The difference between judgement and intuition is that:

   (a) judgement should be well *reasoned*, perhaps based on experience, and so a manager should be able to explain why he has come to a certain judgement;

   (b) intuition is not a reasoned opinion, but inspired guesswork, or a hunch. When the future is very uncertain, planning decisions might be based on intuition. The manager thinks he is right, but he can't tell you why.

11. CORPORATE PLANNING: A SUMMARY

11.1
> Corporate planning is the task of identifying the organisation's objectives, and preparing quantified targets of achievement in a long-term plan. Strategic plans and objectives are also selected, which will enable the overall goals of the organisation to be achieved.

11.2 The major obstacles to corporate planning can be listed as follows:

(a) senior management might fail to specify clear objectives and goals for the organisation on which to base realistic strategic plans. This in turn means that divisions and departments cannot set clear goals and objectives for themselves;

(b) if a business exists in a rapidly-changing environment, planning becomes extremely difficult because there are so many unforeseen or unpredictable events which might quickly invalidate plans. It has been suggested, for example, that the current state of technological change in the banking industry makes it extremely difficult to foresee what new competition might enter the banking market, and what customer demand for 'new-technology' services (eg. electronic funds transfer at the point of sale, cash management systems, home banking) might be;

(c) time scale. The longer a (corporate) planning period is, the greater will be the likelihood of unforeseen events occurring, which will make the plan invalid. This factor and also (b) above inevitably discourage managers from attempting detailed long-term plans;

(d) lack of information. An organisation's information system might be inadequate and unable to provide the information from the business environment which is necessary for long-term planning;

(e) inflexibility. Management might fail to provide for periodic reviews of the corporate plan, and for adapting it to changing circumstances as they arise or as they are foreseen. An inflexible corporate plan will quickly become out-of-date;

(f) it is difficult to reconcile all the long-term and short-term, financial and non-financial interests of an organisation (eg. see paragraph 10.4). This is a problem which has several adverse consequences.

   (i) It might be difficult to obtain the agreement of all managers in the organisation to a set of objectives and strategies in the corporate plan.

   (ii) Strategic plans might be too generalised so that sub-units of the organisation are unable to convert these plans into action plans.

   (iii) Corporate planning objectives are long-term as well as short-term, so that it might be difficult to communicate them to lower levels of management in such a way that they are not soon forgotten. Commitment to the objectives is necessary, and a system of continual reminders or performance appraisal will be necessary.

   (iv) Managers not involved in preparing the corporate plan might be hostile or unenthusiastic about it.

(g) Managers will only be committed to a set of objectives if their performance is measured against a set of quantified targets for achievement. It is a failure of many long-term plans that they do not provide quantified targets. It is more convenient to judge management performance against a budget, and all too often, budget targets are concerned with achieving revenue or profit targets, or keeping within budget cost limits. Non-profit factors (such as public responsibility and employee welfare) are not often budgeted for.

Furthermore, if budgets are prepared independently of the corporate plan, and are not treated as a short-term part of it, management will be working towards budget goals which are not necessarily consistent with the corporate plan. In other words, there might be a problem of co-ordinating the corporate plan with budgets.

(h) Corporate planning can be an expensive exercise. Large organisations have a corporate planning department advising the board of directors. The benefits from corporate planning must exceed the costs if the exercise is to be justified.

(i) Corporate planning might be a paper exercise. Senior management might pay lip service to certain objectives, but in practice their actual behaviour might belie their intentions and interests. For example, objectives about public responsibilities and employee welfare might soon be forgotten when profit margins are tight. Similarly, plans for innovation through research and development might be the first to suffer in a round of budget cuts.

11.3 The problems in corporate planning can be overcome if management organises its planning processes correctly.

(a) Corporate objectives must be defined clearly.

(b) Quantified corporate plans should be prepared for a period within which changes in the business environment can be foreseen with some realism. A planning period of five years might be appropriate, in which plans are quantified in some detail.

(c) Plans should be reviewed regularly, typically once each year (so that there will be, say, a rolling five year plan).

(d) Within the corporate plan, very detailed short-term plans (budgets) should be prepared. The link between long-term plans and budgets is critically important for the successful implementation of the corporate plan.

(e) The information system of the organisation should be developed so that it is capable of providing sufficient information from the environment for the preparation of realistic plans.

(f) Ideally, management throughout the organisation should participate in the corporate planning process (perhaps in a scheme of management by objectives). This will:

(i) encourage the commitment of management to corporate plans; and

(ii) make easier the conversion of strategic plans into detailed action plans for every section and manager in the organisation.

Factors to consider in corporate planning

11.4 Examination questions in the past have often asked about the factors to take into account when developing corporate plans or long range plans for a *particular* organisation. These questions are very broad-ranging in their scope, and it will be useful to begin with a list of what these factors might be, for *any* type of organisation.

Factors to consider in corporate planning
A checklist

1. Establishing the main objective of the organisation.

2. Establishing ethical 'constraints' which the organisation should be bound by.

3. How formal should the planning process be?

4. How can the planning process be co-ordinated and made effective?

5. There is likely to be a need to encourage innovative thinking. How can this be achieved?

6. Should corporate planning involve departmental and functional management? Should planning be confined to a small corporate planning team at central HQ? In a divisionalised organisation, should divisions prepare their own corporate plans, subject to approval by central HQ? A key issue is getting the *commitment* of all management to the plans.

7. What information is needed for planning? Where will it come from? Who will provide it? How good will it be?

8. What forecasting methods should be used?

9. To what extent will forecasts be reliable, and how much uncertainty is there in the future?

10. What areas of the organisation and its environment should be investigated in SWOT analysis? Nothing of potential significance should be overlooked.

11. Will there be any constraints on the development of strategies for the future (eg a shortage of finance, or a shortage of key resources, such as skilled labour?)

12. It is always important to keep *change* in mind when planning for the longer term future - eg changes in technology.

13. How often should plans be reviewed to assess whether they are still valid?

14. How can objectives be set for management for which they can be made responsible and accountable? Control through performance appraisal is essential in corporate planning, just as in other systems of planning and control.

Exercise

In the exam, you might be asked to discuss the main issues which must be addressed when developing a corporate plan for a particular type or organisation, such as

(a) a college or university
(b) a bank
(c) a building society
(d) a national charity
(e) a local authority
(f) an insurance company
(g) a retail store
(h) a manufacturing company.

Pick two of these and try to develop a corporate plan for it. The factors to consider are broadly the same, regardless of the type of organisation it is, as the list above has tried to suggest. However, you should try to relate the factors to the circumstances of the particular organisation.

---

12. THE ROLE OF THE BOARD OF DIRECTORS

12.1 At the top of the chain of command in any organisation is a body of people with decision-making powers. A local council, a Board of Trustees or a Board of Directors all have powers delegated to them by another body - the voting population, the settlor and beneficiaries and the shareholders in each case. The quality of this body's decisions is therefore subject to review but for practical purposes a board should 'run' the organisation. Whether this is so or not depends largely on the relations between the board and the executive managers who take day-to-day decisions.

12.2 Legally, the Board of Directors is the representative of the owners of a company, that is its ordinary shareholders. Drucker argued, however, that 'it is perhaps not too much to say that it has become a shadow king. In most of the large companies, it has in effect been deposed and its place taken by executive management...The board may have become a mere showcase, a place to inject distinguished names, without information, influence or desire for power'.

12.3 The reasons for what Drucker saw as the decline of power in the Board of Directors (and the rise of the 'managerial corporation') were:

(a) the much-publicised divorce of ownership from control which makes it absurd that the business enterprise should be directed by the representatives of the shareholders;

(b) the complexity of modern business operations; and

(c) perhaps most important, the difficulty of finding good people with the time to sit on Boards and take their membership seriously.

12.4 The Board of Directors should, however, have a function and, if it is not to be a rubber stamp for executive management, it must include non-executive directors with real influence. The task of the Board might be to:

    (a) approve the executive's decision about what business the organisation should be in;

    (b) approve the executive's choice of objectives and targets;

    (c) appraise the company's profit-planning and profit performance;

    (d) appraise its capital expenditure policy and its revenue expenditure budget;

    (e) act as a 'Supreme Court' in respect ot organisation problems and the relationships between the organisation and its environment;

    (f) select the chief executive, or approve nominations of top managers.

12.5 Drucker stated that:

    (a) the chief executive should be the governing organ of a business; and

    (b) the Board of Directors should be an 'organ of review, appraisal and appeal'.

The Board should only become an organ of action when the existing executive management has failed, at which time it is the duty of the Board to step in and replace the executive with new people.

12.6 Another way of stating the role of the board of directors would be to analyse its functions into three categories.

    (a) *Legal*: the legal functions and duties of directors are laid down by company law, which varies from country to country. They will include:

        (i)   preparing an annual profit and loss account and directors' report and making an annual return to the government authorities;

        (ii) calling meetings of members;

        (iii) declaring a dividend;

        (iv) safeguarding the company's assets (a duty of '*trusteeship*');

        (v)   having regard to the interests of employees, customers, the environment etc;

        (vi) having a legal duty to manage the company.

    (b) *Managerial*: the board of directors will take certain management decisions collectively in meeting – such as decisions to raise new capital or to decide what proportion of the company's income should be paid to employees, paid as dividends or held as retained profits.

        Other management functions will be delegated to committees or lower-rank managers. The directors can decide how much authority should be delegated, and what the formal organisation structure should be. When authority is delegated to junior managers in the organisation structure, executive directors will retain responsibility (and will also have some authority) as heads of divisions or departments, eg companies might have a production director, marketing director, finance director, personnel director etc.

        The board might also appoint a director and confer on his or her 'any of the powers exercisable by them upon such terms and conditions and with such restrictions as they may think fit'.

    (c) *Planning*: the board of directors is the ultimate planning authority within a company. Planning is a management function, of course, but it is itemised separately here. Planning functions might include:

        (i)   authorising the preparation of a budget and corporate plan, including the establishment of basic business objectives;

        (ii) approving the budget;

        (iii) approving the corporate plan;

        (iv) reviewing actual progress against plan (although much of the control work will be delegated).

> "Directors, by establishing corporate objectives and formulating major policies, are of course doing basic planning. But this is not enough. Being responsible for seeing that the company is well managed, the board should assure itself that the operating managers are making adequate plans. Thus a board should review and approve, or be informed of, management programs in such areas as new products, marketing approaches, personnel, organisation, management development and finance....
>
> A board should also see that results are being accomplished in accordance with plans.... Too often, boards of directors approve planning programs and then forget them."
>
> *Koontz, O'Donnell and Weihrich*

12.7 Many companies employ individuals from outside the organisation to act as non-executive members of the board of directors. Such non-executive directors are expected to contribute their skills and experience to the supreme decision-making body of the company without having to get involved in its day-to-day affairs. They are also able to take an independent, 'broad' view of a situation which executive directors, worried by their day-to-day problems, might be too narrow-minded to see by themselves. In terms of organisation structure, non-executive directors may be thought of as 'staff' management but their votes on the board are effectively a contribution to the line authority of decisions by the board.

12.8 The inexperience of non-executive directors in the detailed affairs of the company should not be a disadvantage, provided that they are well informed and properly guided by the executive members of the board. If a board member is a representative of a consumer group, the function of the member may be to remind the board (eg of a nationalised industry) of its duties towards the organisation's customers.

12.9 Some non-executive directors may add a quality of dependability or trustworthiness to a company in the eyes of outsiders. This is another reason why the boards of nationalised industries might benefit from including a representative of consumers' interests. It is also possible that a company might hire a non-executive director in order to obtain the prestige of adding his or her name to the company notepaper!

12.10 Drucker argued that: 'The Board must be detached from operations. It must view the company as a whole. This means that working executives of the company should not dominate the Board. In fact, the Board will be stronger and more effective if it is genuinely an 'outside' Board, the bulk of whose members have never served as full time officers of the company'.

12.11 A Code of Recommended Practice on Non-Executive Directors was published in April 1987 by PRO NED, and its adoption 'warmly recommended' by The Stock Exchange. The aim of the code is to achieve a proper balance between independent non-executive directors and other directors.

> "Effective Boards are essential to the success of British business. In quoted companies, Boards are more likely to be fully effective if they comprise both able Executive Directors and strong, independent Non-Executive Directors."

12.12 Among other points, the code states that:

(a)   an independent Non-Executive Director is one who:

   (i)   has not been employed in an executive capacity by the company on whose Board he or she sits, within the last five years;

   (ii)   if a professional advisor, is not retained by the company (whether personally, or through his or her firm) on a continuing or regular basis; and

   (iii) is not (whether personally or through his or her employer) a significant customer of or supplier to the company;

(b)   in larger quoted companies where the turnover is £50million or more or whose employees number 1,000 or more, the board should normally include at least three independent Non-Executive Directors (who should comprise about one-third of the Board). In smaller quoted companies, or in large companies with small boards, the number of non-executive directors should be appropriate to the size of the board and the company's resources;

(c)   the main tasks of the Non-Executive Director are to:

   (i)   contribute an independent view to the Board's deliberations;

   (ii)   help the board provide the company with effective leadership;

   (iii) ensure the continuing effectiveness of the Executive Directors and management; and

   (iv)   ensure high standards of financial probity on the part of the company;

(d)   in order to succeed in these tasks, the Non-Executive Directors will need to enjoy the full support of the Chairman, and will need to be provided with the necessary information, in sufficiently good time for them to consider it properly;

(e)   Non-Executive Directors should be consulted on major issues of audit and control and on the appointment, dismissal and renumeration of directors. Where appropriate committees are established (Audit committee, Appointments and Remuneration Committee), these should be composed mainly of Non-Executive Directors;

(f)   Non-Executive directors should normally be appointed for a specific term, subject to election by rotation as for other directors.

12.13 The Code recommended that listed and USM companies not yet complying with it should do so within a 'reasonable period of time'. By 1990 many large UK companies have still not complied, despite Stock Exchange pressure to do so. The EEC and institutional investors (insurance companies, pension funds etc) also want to see more use made of non-executive directors, particularly in the light of some recent very public disasters among listed companies which may have been avoided if cool, independent views were held on the Board.

TEST YOUR KNOWLEDGE

(The numbers in brackets refer to paragraphs in this chapter)

1. What are the steps in strategic planning? (2.3)

2. What is SWOT analysis? (4.1) What areas of manufacturing business should SWOT analysis cover? (4.4)

3. Suggest what opportunities and threats might face an organisation in the future. (4.11)

4. What is a product life cycle? (6.1) (Note: a product life cycle applies to services too.)

5. What is competitive advantage? (7.1)

6. What are the four basic product/market strategies that an organisation might select for developing its future business? (8.1)

7. What is synergy? (9.1) Give examples. (9.3-9.6)

8. What is scenario building? (10.6) Give an example. (10.7)

9. What is the difference between judgement and intuition in planning decisions? (10.16)

10. List the major obstacles to corporate planning. (11.2)

11. List the main factors to consider when preparing a 5 year corporate plan. (11.4)

12. What are the functions of a company's Board of Directors? (12.4, 12.6)

Chapter 14

LARGE AND SMALL BUSINESSES

This chapter covers the following topics:

1. Bureaucracy
2. Parkinson's Laws
3. The problems of large organisations
4. The management of small businesses

Purpose of this chapter

To review the problems of large organisations and, in contrast, to consider the management of small businesses.

1. BUREAUCRACY

1.1 A bureaucracy exists when the officials of an organisation are physically separated from the 'real work' of an organisation. To a layman, the word 'bureaucracy' has unpleasant associations; however, the German writer, Max Weber (1864–1920) was inclined to regard bureaucracy as the ideal form of organisation, which is 'from a purely technical point of view, capable of attaining the highest degree of efficiency and is in this sense formally the most rational means of carrying out imperative control over human beings'.

1.2 It is wrong to confuse bureaucracy with large organisations, because the features of bureaucracy can be found in some small and medium-sized organisations too. Nevertheless, many (if not all) large organisations are bureaucratic, and it will be useful to start by listing what the characteristics of bureaucracy are.

1.3 Weber regarded an organisation as an authority structure. He specified several general characteristics of bureaucracy, which he described as 'a continuous organisation of official functions bound by rules':

(a) *hierarchy*: each lower office is under the control and supervision of a higher one;

(b) *specialisation and training*: there is a high degree of specialisation of labour. Employment is based on ability, not personal loyalty;

(c) *impersonal nature*: employees work full time within the impersonal rules and regulations and act according to formal, impersonal procedures;

(d) *professional nature of employment*: an organisation exists before it is filled with people. Officials are full-time employees, promotion is according to seniority and achievement; pay scales are prescribed according to the position or office held in the organisation structure;

(e) *rationality*: the 'jurisdictional areas' of the organisation are determined rationally. The hierarchy of authority and office structure is clearly defined. Duties are established and measures of performance set;

(f) *uniformity* in the performance of tasks is expected, regardless of whoever is engaged in carrying them out;

(g) officials are technically competent, and their competence is rarely questioned within the area of their expertise;

(h) *stability*: the reward for employees who do their jobs well is stability, regular pay, a retirement pension, the chance of promotion etc.

Criticisms of large bureaucratic organisations

1.4 A bureaucratic organisation structure can be efficient and effective, but there is a tendency, especially in large organisations, for inefficiencies to creep in.

1.5 The following list of typical complaints may be familiar to you.

(a) It is debatable whether large organisations give talented top management a chance to exercise their abilities to the full, or whether top management is inefficient because the calibre required for large organisations is so high that no one can be found to do the job successfully.

(b) Employees feel no sense of identification with the organisation, and no personal loyalty towards it or their boss.

(c) Line managers resent the interference of large numbers of staff managers.

(d) Staff managers feel frustrated when their advice is not taken.

(e) There is too much specialisation and not enough management with broad company experience. Specialists cannot identify with the organisation as a whole.

(f) Junior and middle management feel a long way from authority and cannot get decisions because of the long chain of command.

(g) Workers, to get things done, strike rather than go through lengthy chains of negotiation with junior and middle managers.

(h) Low morale causes higher rates of:
   (i)   absenteeism;
   (ii) strikes; and
   (iii) accidents.

(i) There is too much inflexibility and delay, red tape, empire building and poor communications.

2. PARKINSON'S LAWS

2.1 Although not all of his ideas are confined to criticisms of bureaucracy, it is useful at this stage to mention the wasteful organisational practices which were formulated by C Northcote Parkinson into 'Parkinson's Laws'. These include:

(a) work expands so as to fill the time available for its completion;

(b) the 'law of triviality', which means the time spent on any item of the agenda will be in inverse proportion to the sum involved;

(c) the 'co-efficient of inefficiency' - the larger the committee, the more inefficient it becomes;

(d) injelitis - a disease caused by incompetence and jealousy which is related to injelitance; the head of a department who is incompetent makes sure that his subordinates are just as incompetent;

(e) appearance can be used as a guide to a company's standing. The neater, more efficient and perfect an office appears, the nearer it is to collapse;

(f) 'expenditure rises to meet income' a theory we all know too well in practice.

2.2 There is also his law of multiplication of subordinates: Parkinson suggested that when an official, A, is overworked, he has the choice of resigning, halving the work with colleague B, or asking for two subordinates, C and D. In the Civil Service at least, A would invariably ask for two subordinates because:

(a) to resign would affect his pension;

(b) to share the work with B would involve loss of status, and B would be a rival for promotion;

(c) two subordinates (not one!) will add to his standing.

In time, C will complain of overwork, and subordinates E and F will be appointed to work under C and to keep D happy, he too must be given two subordinates, G and H. Seven officials, A, C, D, E, F, G and H are now doing the work that A alone did before.

2.3 Finally there is the law of multiplication of work: continuing from the law of multiplication of subordinates, Parkinson suggested that these seven officials would be kept more busy than A alone has been before. By drafting reports, correcting drafts, writing memos to each other, dealing with personal and health problems of subordinates etc more work is done to achieve the same end result.

2.4 The validity or otherwise of Parkinson's laws may be checked from your own experience or observations!

The organisational multiplier

2.5 Following the ideas of Parkinson, Hicks and Graves suggested that there is an organisational multiplier which is similar in nature to an economic multiplier, so that an addition to personnel in one part of an organisation will spark off a series of additions to personnel (or other resources) throughout the organisation. One extra manager, for example, will create extra volumes of reports and letters (which must be read and answered), attend meetings (someone else is required to meet with him) and require services from the payroll office, personnel office etc. 'The organisational multiplier, then, is that factor by which a primary change in a particular sector of the organisation is multiplied to determine the total change in the whole organisation'.

2.6 In its extreme form, an organisation might grow and multiply by 'feeding on itself', so adding nothing to corporate objectives and creating no extra external output. Hicks and Graves cited instances of fund-raising organisations which spent 90% of the money they collected on their own internal administration. They suggested that wasteful multiplication:

(a) is more likely to occur in non-profit making organisations;

(b) is more likely to occur in large organisations;

(c) is often overlooked, and is rarely costed when the decision to increase personnel in one department is taken.

3. THE PROBLEMS OF LARGE ORGANISATIONS

3.1 A large organisation is one which has a large amount of resources at its disposal and so, typically, employs a lot of people.

3.2 The problems of large organisations, which are hinted at in the criticisms listed above, stem mainly from the difficulties of getting a lot of people to work well together. How can large numbers of people share the work that has to be done, and how can their work be properly planned, co-ordinated and controlled?

3.3 These problems have been discussed already in this text, but it will be useful here to draw them together into a summarised list.

PROBLEMS OF LARGE ORGANISATIONS

1. Organisation structure

1.1 Sharing out tasks and responsibilities. Who does what?

1.2 How much specialisation/functionalisation should there be?

1.3 What span of control is suitable? And so how tall/flat will the organisation be? There is a tendency for the management hierarchy to develop too may levels. The more management levels there are, the greater the problem of communication between top and bottom, and the greater the problems of control and direction by management at the top.

1.4 To what extent should authority be delegated? How much centralisation/decentralisation should there be? Can junior/middle managers be trusted to exercise discretion and make decisions? How should managers be trained and developed?

2. Planning and control

2.1 How should the organisation identify its objectives and set targets for achievement? In the case of large diversified 'conglomerate' corporations, can the organisation have a major objective other than a financial one (eg. profit maximisation)?

2.2 Developing formal management information systems to enable managers to plan and control properly. Communication problems.

2.3 The problem of making managers accountable, monitoring performance and setting up effective control systems.

2.4 The difficulties of co-ordinating the efforts of managers: problems of conflict (line versus staff; interdepartmental rivalries etc).

2.5 Difficulties of setting up a system of rewards that is directly linked to performance appraisal and the achievement of objectives.

3. Adapting to change

3.1 Large organisations might be slow to adapt to change because of a bureaucratic system of operating and decision-making that stifles ideas for innovation.

4. Motivation

4.1 It is difficult for individuals to identify themselves with the objectives of a large organisation. The organisation's objectives and their personal objectives will differ.

4.2 Difficulties for individuals to see how their efforts contribute to achieving the organisation's objectives (due to narrow specialisation of jobs etc).

4.3 Possible problems in getting employees to enjoy working in a large organisation, where a bureaucratic 'role culture' predominates.

4.4 Decision-making might be slow, with managers not allowed the authority and discretion they would like.

3.4 An organisation might become so widely diversified in the range of products or services it offers that it becomes difficult, if not impossible, for management to integrate all of the organisation under a common objective and within a single 'management philosophy' and 'organisation spirit'. The different parts of the organisation will not complement each other, and might tend to pull the organisation in different directions. Drucker argued that 'this danger is particularly great in the business that originated in a common technology, such as chemistry or electrical engineering. As the technology unfolds, it creates more and more diversified products with different markets, different objectives for innovation and ultimately even with different technologies... The point may be reached where objectives and principles that fit one business (or group of businesses) endanger another'.

3.5 The sheer size of an organisation provides both top management and more junior management with problems of co-ordination, planning, effective control and therefore the achievement of economies of scale and versatility in the range of products and services offered. For example, a junior manager might find the organisation so large that he has relatively little influence. Decisions which he regards as important must be continually referred up the line to his superiors, for inter-departmental consultations etc. At the same time, the top management might find the organisation so large and complex to understand, and changes in policy and procedures so difficult and time-consuming to implement, that they also feel unable to give direction to the organisation. The organisation is therefore a 'monster' which operates of its own accord, with neither senior nor junior managers able to manage it effectively.

3.6 In a large organisation, many of the 'specialised' tasks for junior functional managers, and many day-to-day tasks of junior operational management are routine and boring. Even middle management might be frustrated by the restrictions on their authority, the impersonal nature of their organisation, the inability to earn a just reward for their special efforts (owing to the standardisation of pay and promotion procedures) and the lack of information about aspects of the organisation which should influence their work. These problems are likely to result in:

(a) poor motivation amongst managers;
(b) consequently, poor motivation amongst their junior staff;
(c) a reluctance to accept responsibility.

Overcoming the problems of large size

3.7 These difficulties of large organisations can, to some extent, be overcome by:

(a) decentralisation and delegation of authority, in particular in a policy of federal decentralisation plus functional decentralisation within federal units. This was described in an earlier chapter. However, the aim of decentralisation should be to encourage decision-making at lower levels of management 'closer to the action'. Management motivation, but also management efficiency in target-setting, planning and control should improve;

(b) a pay policy which provides for just rewards (individual or team bonuses) for outstanding efforts and achievements;

(c) the introduction of comprehensive management and employee *information systems* which enable all managers and employees:
   (i) to understand their planned contribution towards achieving organisational objectives;
   (ii) to compare their actual achievements against their targets;

(d) a task structure within the organisation which, through job enrichment, stimulates employee motivation towards better performance.

4. THE MANAGEMENT OF SMALL BUSINESSES

4.1 The management of small businesses contrasts directly, in many ways, with the problems of management of large organisations.

4.2 *Ownership and top management*
The top manager (or managers) of a small organisation is usually the founder and owner of the business. As such, he or she will often want to take a close and detailed interest in many management decisions that are taken, and the organisation will be characterised by centralised decision-making, and so be strongly influenced by the character and personality of the owner-leader.

4.3 The centralised control and decision-making by the owner-manager could eventually act as a constraint on the growth of the organisation because eventually, as the organisation gets bigger, the burdens of authority will become too great for one individual, or just a handful of individuals.

4.4 Other features of the management of small businesses could be summarised as follows.

---

1. **Organisation structure, planning and control**
1.1 Less rigid definition of jobs than in large organisations, and less specialisation.
1.2 Authority often centralised, although the management hierarchy will be small and all managers should feel quite close to the decision-making process.
1.3 Planning, control and communication (management information systems) will be less formal than in larger organisations.
1.4 Fewer people than in large organisations, and so lesser problems of co-ordination. Greater sense of teamwork.
1.5 Not so much bound by formal rules and procedures as large organisations.
1.6 Decision-making procedures are relatively fast. Decisions can be taken quickly.
1.7 Individual managers have a better idea of the overall objectives of the business, and of how their sections and tasks relate to them.

2. **Adapting to change**
2.1 Small organisations are usually staffed by individuals who are more innovative in their ideas, and more responsive to change. Ideas for innovation and adapting to change are more accepted.

3. **Motivation**
3.1 Individuals have a wider range of duties, and are often able to contribute more to the achievements of the organisation, compared with the achievements of individuals in large organisations.
3.2 Individuals might develop a closer sense of identity with the organisation - eg. through personal association with the owner-managers.
3.3 Pay and reward systems are usually more personalised than in large organisations.
3.4 Management training and development are not encouraged as much as in large organisations. How many managers of small businesses are capable of stepping into a management job in a large organisation, and doing it well?
3.5 The 'culture' in small organisations is unlikely to be bureaucratic.

4.5 Small businesses have limited resources, and this restriction imposes very serious constraints on what the organisation can do. A task of management is to achieve as much as possible within the limitations that a small size imposes.

4.6 *Finance*
Small businesses are considered risky investments, and lending organisations such as banks will be reluctant to lend much money without security. A small company's borrowing capability might therefore limited to a small unsecured bank overdraft, plus a secured loan for which the assets of a company or the personal guarantees of its owners provide the security.

4.7 Small companies will also have difficulty in raising share capital. Many such companies are owner-managed, and the owners will only want to put in a certain amount of their own cash, and no more.

(a) Retained profits can be a very important source of extra shareholder funds, but the company must be profitable in order to have access to extra funds from this source.

(b) If the existing shareholders are willing to allow other shareholders into the company, it might be possible to raise more finance by issuing new shares.

4.8 In the UK, there is a tax incentive scheme called the Business Expansion Scheme (BES) which tries to encourage investors to buy new shares in unquoted companies. BES capital is a form of venture capital, and there are other organisations which specialise in providing venture capital for small companies either as a loan or in exchange for shares. The 3i group is the most well-known example in the UK. Another route to raising new finance from a share issue is a launch on to one of the stock markets for small companies, which in the UK are the Unlisted Securities Market (USM) and the Third Market.

4.9 Small companies will be restricted in what they can do because of their finance constraints, but the financial challenge for managers is to:

(a) create a profitable company;

(b) achieve a financially stable company (with good liquidity, and a good debt capital/share capital ratio etc);

(c) develop attractive plans for the future which will encourage investors to want to put money into the company, or to be willing to lend to it.

4.10 *Product/service development*
Small firms are often innovative and creative. Some are founded on the strength of their owner's original idea for a new product. A major problem for such small firms is the shortage of resources for developing new product ideas.

4.11 The small firm which succeeds in developing a new product with good commercial prospects will often need the support of a big company after a while. To develop a successful product, a high technology company will need:

(a)   more capital than it can probably raise;
(b)   cash for more R & D;
(c)   more management skills to develop, produce, finance and market the new product;
(d)   a marketing organisation through which to sell the product.

These are requirements which only a large company can usually satisfy.

4.12 A major challenge to management in small firms is therefore:

(a)   to obtain the resources to maintain an effective product research and development unit, capable of producing a continual flow of new product ideas; and at the same time

(b)   to avoid being taken over by a larger 'predator' company.

4.13 Further risk, especially in innovative (usually high-technology) product areas, is entailed by the comparative inability of small businesses to *diversify*. In theory, therefore, the small organisation may have 'all its eggs in one basket': loss or failure of one activity or product will not be 'covered' by the success of other areas - the company cannot spread the risk.

4.14 *Training and development*
All organisations need to recruit good, effective managers, and managers are likely to seek employment in organisations which offer:

(a)   career development; and
(b)   a satisfying job; as well as
(c)   good remuneration.

4.15 Training and management development were discussed in an earlier chapter, but the problem for small companies is again one of limited resources.

(a)   Can they spare an individual's time to let him or her attend external training courses? (Small companies will usually be unable to provide in-house training of their own).

(b)   Do they have enough management tasks to provide a development programme for their managers? Or will all the key decisions be taken by one or two owner-managers, leaving little else for other managers?

(c)   Are there any trained 'understudies' to take over active managment if someone leaves: are there the resources for a management succession plan?

4.16 In more general terms, according to Koontz, O'Donnell and Weihrich (*Management*), 'a small corporation may not be able to afford specialised talent, mangerial and technical, and yet its problems are the same, except in degree and scope, as those of a large corporation. The owner-manager of the typical small corporation frequently has severe limitations, both in education and experience.'

4.17 Koontz et al suggest that small business managers have particular problems of 'short-sightedness':

(a) neglecting basic policy-making as they get bogged down in recurring operating problems;

(b) failing to plan, particularly for sales and production fluctuations, unexpected expenses, drains on working capital etc. Small businesses are often tempted to accept orders without properly considering the capital required to meet them;

(c) neglecting to review company objectives in the light of changes in technology, or the political, economic or legal environment.

Summary

Small businesses often encounter problems with:

- Raising finance
- Developing new products - without being taken over
- Inability to diversify and spread risks
- Management development and succession
- Management and staff expertise and experience
- Lack of economies of scale, marketing advantages etc arising from larger size and resources
- Strategic decisions neglected in favour of operational ones

---

Conclusion

4.18 The discussion in this chapter of large and small organisations has probably touched on ideas which are familiar to you from your own experience.

4.19 As a concluding comment, you should try to reflect how the management features of large organisations are different from those of small organisations, and the organisation and management structure that is best suited to any business or operation will depend to some extent on the organisation's age and size.

TEST YOUR KNOWLEDGE

(The numbers in brackets refer to paragraphs in this chapter)

1. How did Weber define bureaucracy and what did he identify as its key characteristics? (1.3)

2. Describe five of Parkinson's Laws. (2.1–2.3)

3. How does the organisational multiplier work? (2.5)

4. Describe four ways in which the problem of large size can be overcome in an organisation. (3.7)

5. How are small businesses typically financed? (4.6–4.8)

6. What are the specific problems of short-sightedness which can prove disastrous for small businesses? (4.17)

**SECTION D
THE MANAGEMENT
OF CHANGE**

Chapter 15

THE MANAGEMENT OF CHANGE

This chapter covers the following topics:

1. The meaning of change
2. Innovation
3. Management of growth and stability
4. Management of contraction (divestment)
5. Growth and structural reorganisation
6. Planning for change

The purpose of this chapter

To consider why changes are necessary and to look at various aspects of change - growth, stability, contraction and structural reorganisation.

Also to consider the need for careful planning of changes, and the possible role of external consultants or a Management Services Division in assisting the process of change.

1.   THE MEANING OF CHANGE

1.1   Change, in the context of organisation and management, could relate to any of the following.

(a) *Changes in the 'environment'*

These could be changes in what competitors are doing, what customers are buying, how they spend their money, changes in the law, changes in social behaviour and attitudes, economic changes, and so on.

(b) *Changes in the products the organisation makes, or the services it provides*

These are made in response to changes in customer demands, competitors' actions, new technology, and so on.

(c) *Changes in how products are made, or who makes them. Changes in working methods.*

These changes are also in response to environmental change - eg new technology, new laws on safety at work etc.

(d) *Changes in management and working relationships*

For example, changes in leadership style, and in the way that employees are encouraged to work together. Also changes in training and development.

(e) *Changes in organisation structure or size (growth)*

These might involve creating new departments and divisions, greater delegation of authority or more centralisation, changes in the way that plans are made, management information is provided and control is exercised, and so on. Organisation re-structuring will be made in response to changes in (a),(b),(c) or (d) above.

1.2 The point being made here is that when we discuss change, we might be discussing:

(a) the original source of change - usually, an environmental change; or
(b) a change within the organisation which is made in response to another change.

In other words, one change can lead on to another and another and another.

1.3 *Buckley and Perkins (1984)* made a distinction between:

(a) change, which is gradual and small; and
(b) transformation, which is change on a significant scale.

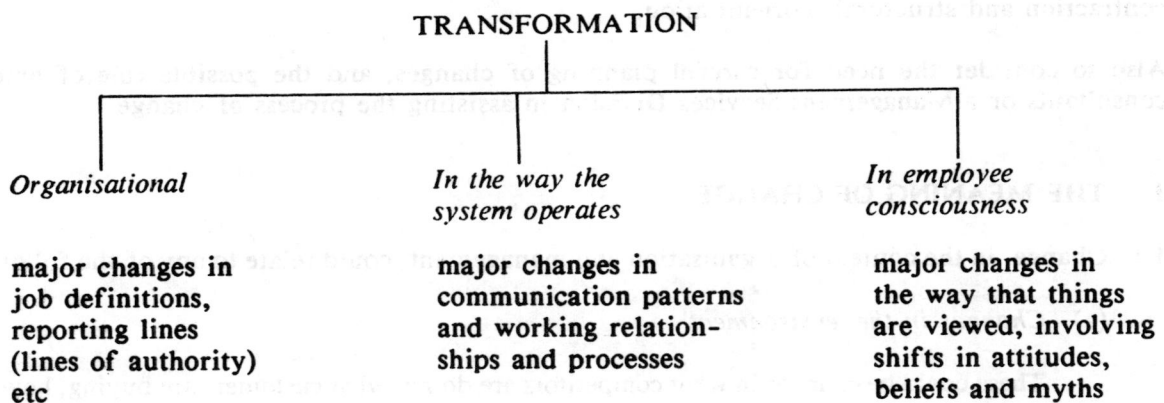

TRANSFORMATION

Organisational	*In the way the system operates*	*In employee consciousness*
major changes in job definitions, reporting lines (lines of authority) etc	major changes in communication patterns and working relationships and processes	major changes in the way that things are viewed, involving shifts in attitudes, beliefs and myths

1.4 *Innovation* is a term that is often associated with change. Innovation, quite simply, is something completely new. Some changes might result in going back to something that was done before: change doesn't necessarily mean doing something entirely new. Innovation creates change, but change isn't always innovative.

The nature of changes

1.5 Changes can be brought about in a variety of different ways.

	Nature of change		Examples
1.	New technology (*Remember:* the effects of new technology on organisation and management were described in an earlier chapter.)	(a) (b) (c) (d)	Computerisation New products New working methods Better management information systems
2.	Reorganisation	(a) (b) (c) (d)	Company taken over, having to adopt the organisation policies of the new parent company Growth, causing reorganisation into divisions, or more specialist functional departments Divestment of businesses - ie getting smaller Drive to keep costs down, leading to cost cutting measures (job losses etc)
3.	Working conditions	(a) (b) (c) (d) (e)	New offices Shorter working week More varied work times More 'outplacement' of work, ie giving work to outsiders Greater emphasis on occupational health
4.	Personnel policies	(a) (b)	Changes in rules and procedures - eg about smoking at work Promotions, transfers, separation of employees, training and development, problems perhaps growing in complexity
5.	Philosophy of management. Relations between management and employees	(a) (b) (c) (d)	New senior manager introduces new style of leadership Attitudes of managers and employees change over time - eg with greater participation of subordinates in decision-making Communications with employees less paternal Greater collaboration between management and trade unions in labour relations

At this point you should refer back to the earlier chapter where we looked at Burns and Stalker's theories on mechanistic and organic organisations. Clearly the nature of the organisation in this sense will affect its success or failure when dealing with change.

2. INNOVATION

2.1 *Innovation* is a term that is often associated with change. Innovation, quite simply, is something completely new. Some changes might result in going back to something that was done before: change doesn't necessarily mean doing something entirely new. Innovation creates change, but change isn't always innovative.

2.2   The rate of change might be fast or slow, depending on the organisation's circumstances, and the environment in which it operates.

Organisations which operate in a rapidly-changing environment need to be innovative, and responsive to change, if they are to survive and grow (cf. Burns and Stalker's ideas about organic and mechanistic structures, mentioned in Chapter 19).

2.3   Very few organisations operate in a static environment. You might argue that Western society is geared up for change, and all organisations within such a society must innovate continually just to survive.

> "Organisations must breathe new life into procedures and management styles; if not, established organisations will lose ground to more vibrant, smaller or newer enterprises. For innovation to succeed, corporate culture - the missing link in moving forward in today's world - must be managed, and all the strategies for managing complex organisations implemented."
> *Tom Attwood,*
> Management Accounting, January 1990

2.4   To encourage innovation the objective for management should be to create a more outward-looking organisation.

● Emphasis should be placed on self-reliance and vigorous iniative.

● People should be encouraged to look for new products, markets, processes, designs. People should seek ways to improve productivity.

2.5   Thomas Attwood suggests the following steps for creating an innovative culture from one which has previously existed in a cosy, unthreatening world:

(a)   ensure management and staff know what innovation is and how it happens;
(b)   ensure that senior managers welcome, and are seen to welcome, changes for the better;
(c)   stimulate and motivate management and staff to think and act innovatively;
(d)   understand people in the organisation and their needs; and
(e)   recognise and encourage potential 'intrapreneurs' (see below).

2.6   The chief object of being innovative is to ensure the organisation's survival and success in a changing world. It can also have the following advantages:

(a)   improvements in quality of product and service;

(b)   a leaner structure - layers of management or administration may be done away with, and the need for specialist support may be reduced;

(c)   prompt and imaginative solutions to problems (through use of project teams);

(d)   less formality in structure and style - leading to better communication; and

(e)   greater confidence inside and outside the organisation in its ability to cope with change.

2.7 One of the necessary corollaries of innovation is increased delegation. Part of the creed is to give subordinates more authority so they can 'have their head' and act on creative ideas. In itself delegation has great value - morale and performance are improved, top management is freed for strategic planning and decisions are made by those 'on the ground' and therefore more 'in the know'. Most importantly the organisation benefits from the imagination and thinking of its highflyers.

2.8 Warning bells ring, however, when delegation is confused with lack of control.

> "The line between efficient corporate performance through delegation and anarchy resulting from a loss of total control is a very fine one."
> *Alec Reed*
> MD, Reed Accounting

2.9 The logical consequence of being continuously innovative and involving all personnel in initiative-taking amidst consistent change would indeed seem to be anarchy and chaos. Chaos is seen as a positive thing by Tom Peters in his 1987 book, *Thriving on Chaos*. He suggests that a company which reacts proactively with chaos will thrive; it is 'a source of market advantage, not a problem to be got round'.

2.10 The dilemma then is between the need to be innovative so as to deal with a chaotic environment and the need to retain control over employees so as to prevent anarchy. This can be done simply by giving employees and managers parameters within which discretion can be exercised, and by ensuring that they know they are accountable for their actions.

Entrepreneurship and intrapreneurship

2.11 Koontz, O'Donnell and Weihrich mention the 'entrepreneurial' aspects of managing as comprising:

- profit maximisation
- innovation, and
- risk-taking.

> We usually think of an entrepreneur as existing only in business - as a person who sees a business opportunity, obtains the needed capital, knows how to put together an operation successfully, and has the willingness to take a personal risk of success or failure. But in a real sense we see entrepreneurial ability also as an important input in most non-business operations.'
> *Koontz et al*

2.12 Charles Garfield (*Peak performers: the new heroes in business*) writes of the change in ethos which now celebrates innovation and adaptability, opportunism and flair - the attributes of the entrepreneur.

> "Entrepreneurs and intrapreneurs (the internal entrepreneurs who pull together diverse strengths within their organisations to promote innovation) are the new stars."

2.13 Garfield quotes the example of 3M (Minnesota Mining and Manufacturing) in America (a favourite of Peters and Waterman too). "It is company policy to measure the results of innovation, and actually to *require* it. At least 25 percent of sales in every 3M division each year must come from products introduced within the last five years. Toward that end, employees can spend 15 percent of their office time on independent projects."

2.14 Peters and Waterman, in their influential anecdotal study of successful American companies - *"In Search of Excellence"* - define 'excellent' as *'continually innovative'*. They, too, note that the promotion of exploration, experimentation, willingness to change, opportunism and internal competition create an entrepreneurial 'culture' or 'climate' in organisations that keeps them adaptive to their environment and enables consistent success. Excellence is discussed in more detail in a later chapter.

2.15 In 1982 Macrae developed the idea that a company should consider several different ways of doing the same thing by creating separate intrapreneurial groups consisting of a small number of people, each group being in competition with the others. Together each group would seek the best way of doing something to maximise productivity.

2.16 Macrae used the example of a small typing pool as an intrapreneurial group within a large pool, each person being paid for what he or she produced rather than merely for turning up at work. Each group was autonomous in its organisation. He identified great differences in the groups' operations compared with classical structures.

	Role (Classic) organisation	Intrapreneurial organisation
Emphasis	Bureaucracy	Enterprise
Control	Exercised by managers down	Internal within group by members
Size orientation	Single large unit	Many small units
Inter-unit relation	Co-ordination	Competition
Relationship to centre	Strictly controlled	Independent
Work flexibility	Low	High
Sphere of operation	Company	Company but can also take on outside work
Leadership	Appointed by management	Group's choice of leader accepted by management
Work design	Done by experts and managers	Done by group members themselves

Encouraging innovation

2.17 An innovation strategy calls for a management policy of giving encouragement to innovative ideas. This will require:

(a) giving financial backing to innovation, by spending on R & D and market research and risking capital on new ideas;

(b) giving employees the opportunity to work in an environment where the exchange of ideas for innovation can take place. Management style and organisation structure can help here:

    (i) management can actively encourage employees and customers to put forward new ideas. Participation by subordinates in development decisions might encourage employees to become more involved with development projects and committed to their success;

    (ii) development teams can be set up and an organisation built up on project team-work;

(c) where appropriate, recruitment policy should be directed towards appointing employees with the necessary skills for doing innovative work. Employees should be trained and kept up to date;

(d) certain managers should be made responsible for obtaining information from outside the organisation about innovative ideas, and for communicating this information throughout the organisation;

(e) strategic planning should result in targets being set for innovation, and successful achievements by employees should if possible be rewarded.

2.18 Creative ideas can come from anywhere and at any time, but if management wish to foster innovation they should try to provide an organisation structure in which innovative ideas are encouraged to emerge.

(a) Innovation requires creativity. Creativity may be encouraged in an individual or group by establishing a climate in which free expression of abilities is allowed. 'Hot water thought sessions' (brainstorming etc) could be used. The *role of the R & D department* will be significant in many organisations.

(b) Creative ideas must then be rationally analysed (in 'cold water thought sessions') to decide whether they provide a viable (commercial etc) proposition.

(c) A system of organisation must exist whereby a viable creative idea is converted into action through effective control procedures.

3. MANAGEMENT OF GROWTH AND STABILITY

3.1 An organisation will usually seek to grow - by increasing its range of products and markets, its sales turnover and its profits - or, at the least, it will seek stability with a secure and stable level of sales turnover and profits.

3.2 Companies might seek to grow organically, by developing their own internal resources, or else to grow by merger and acquisition (in takeover). Many companies seek growth through a combination of the two strategies.

3.3 If a company operates in a market with a good prospect for growth, it can grow organically either by exploiting existing product-market opportunities or by diversifying. However, because existing products have a finite life, a strategy of organic growth must include plans for *innovation* - developing new products.

3.4 Kotler wrote (1972):

> 'Business firms are increasingly recognising that the key to their survival and growth lies in the continuous development of new and improved products. Gone is the confidence that established products will maintain strong market positions indefinitely. There are too many competitors with fast-moving research laboratories, sophisticated marketing strategies and large budgets standing ready to woo away customers'.

3.5 Stability calls for innovation too. An organisation cannot rely on its existing products and markets for ever, because products have a finite life, and customer demands change. An organisation which wants to maintain its sales and profits must therefore develop new or improved products, or new markets, to replace the old ones in decline. It is a case of having to keep on running just to stand still.

3.6 Product development involves:

(a) expenditure on R & D. Even if a company chooses to copy the products already developed by competitors, and so never be first in the market with a new product, it must be prepared to follow the innovations of others. Innovation is crucial to organic growth in the long term;

(b) often, heavy capital expenditure to set up a new product or new market operation.

3.7 An innovation strategy should take a broad view of what sorts of innovation should be sought. A product might be completely new, or just a different quality version of an existing product. A new product is not necessarily much different from existing products; rather, the essential characteristic is that it should be distinguishable from its predecessors in the eyes of its customers. The car industry provides a very good example of the different types of product innovation. Some years ago, the hatchback was a fairly major innovation. Different quality versions of basically the same model are a common feature of the car market. Modifications to existing models are made regularly, to keep consumers interested and wanting to buy.

Example of organic growth/innovation strategy: Courtaulds

3.8 Courtaulds is one of the world's largest textiles-to-clothing businesses, but competition from low cost producers in the Far East and Eastern Europe ate into its market for 'run of the mill' commodity fibres, so that Courtaulds' output was nearly halved within a few years in the 1980s.

3.9 All fibre producers in the Western world such as Courtaulds, ICI, duPont and Hoechst etc reacted by changing their strategy, and looking for new high quality fibres. These have the advantage of selling at prices that give a higher added-value than commodity fibres.

3.10 This change of strategy meant:

(a) Relying on innovation through R & D to develop new high quality fibres. Courtaulds developed a new generation of cellulose fibre, under the project name Genesis.

(b) Combining this with a switch in marketing effort, from the Third World markets and other 'long distance' markets to the economically sophisticated markets of Western Europe. Courtaulds, which used to sell 50% of its output outside Western Europe, now sells 90% of its output inside Western Europe.

3.11 Some firms lead the way with technological innovation, and actively seek new products for their markets. Other firms react to what the leaders do - ie they follow-my-leader. Either approach can be a successful strategy for innovation. Imitation might even be a more successful approach than leadership in innovation, because the leader will make mistakes that the followers can learn from and avoid.

New product strategies

3.12 Innovation can mean creating new markets as well as new products - creating extra demand from existing customers in a 'strengthened' market, or creating new demand from new customers. A matrix of new product strategies and new market strategies can be set out as follows. (The analysis was first presented by Johnson and Jones in 1957.)

	Product		
	No technological change	*Improved technology*	*New technology*
Market unchanged	-	*Reformulation* A new balance between price/ quality has to be formulated	*Replacement* The new technology replaces the old
Market strengthened (new demand from same customers)	*Remerchandising* The product is sold in a new way – eg by re-packaging	*Improved product* Sales growth to existing customers sought on the strength of product improvements	*Product line extension* The new product is added to the existing product line to increase total demand
New market	*New use* By finding a new use for the existing product, new customers are found	*Market extension* New customers sought on the strength of product improvements	*Diversification*

Motives for growth

3.13 W H Starbuck suggested various motives for organisational growth:

(a) Organisations may pursue *self-realisation* by attempting to realise their ultimate objective. This may involve providing a more complete service to customers, eg by expanding geographically or by vertical integration.

(b) Executives might like the *challenge and adventure* of a new gamble. Boredom with the existing situation might prompt changes.

(c) The *power* of individuals, and their job security may be enhanced by growth.

(d) Executive *salaries* are likely to rise as a result of increasing turnover (rather than by increasing profits).

(e) Growth may lead to *profit maximisation*.

(f) Growth may lead to *economies of scale*.

(g) Large organisations tend to more *stable* than small ones; the desire for stability may lead to growth.

---

4. THE MANAGEMENT OF CONTRACTION (DIVESTMENT)

4.1 Change might involve a *contraction* of the organisation and its business, rather than growth. This is often known as divestment, or getting rid of something. In strategic planning terms, it means selling off a part of a firm's operations, or pulling out of certain product-market areas (closing down a product line).

4.2 One reason for divestment is de-growth. A more common reason is to rationalise a business as a result of a strategic appraisal. A company might decide:

(a) to concentrate on its 'core' businesses and sell off fringe activities;
(b) to sell off subsidiaries where performance is poor, or where growth prospects are not good.

Examples: Beecham and Cadbury Schweppes

4.3 From 1982 to 1985, the profits of Beecham, the pharmaceuticals and consumer products company, had been fairly constant, with little or no growth. A diversification by the group into the home improvements business in 1983 failed to have the desired effect on growth and profits. Rumours began to circulate in financial and investment circles that Beecham might be the prey for a takeover bid by a predator. In a strategy review in 1986, Beecham's board of directors announced its intention of restoring growth into the group by means of selling off 'non-core' businesses, and concentrating on the 'core' businesses of health and personal care. Proposed sell-offs included:

(a) the home improvements division;
(b) the Findlater, Mackie Todd wines and spirits business;
(c) Germaine Monteil, the US cosmetics company.

4.4 These divestments, it was announced, would be the first Beecham had made in *20 years* - an indication of the radical re-think in strategic planning that the group had made with its new policy of divestment.

4.5 Cadbury Schweppes provides another example of a company that decided to divest itself of some non-core businesses in order to concentrate on core businesses as a strategy for improving profitability. The Chairman's statement in the company's 1985 accounts commented:

> 'In 1985 Cadbury Schweppes took a number of strategic decisions .... Cadbury Schweppes is concentrating its efforts behind its strengths in its international confectionery and soft drinks businesses and your Board is confident that the 1986 results will confirm that the right strategic course has been taken ....
>
> With the objective of concentrating on our core international health businesses, we have sold the Health & Hygiene Division and announced the sale of the Beverages & Foods Division. The sale of these companies at a premium over their asset value will free resources for investment in the Group's mainstream businesses, which earn a higher rate of return on capital employed. Your Board continues to monitor the changing structure of the food industry in its major markets and to look for opportunities to strengthen the Group's presence in them, in line with the strategic objectives ....'

4.6 The main advantages of divestment are that:

(a) by selling off parts of the business that are not performing as well as others, a firm can concentrate on areas of its business that provide better results;

(b) selling off a subsidiary will bring in funds that can be invested in other projects;

(c) it might be more profitable to demerge than to expand.

4.7 If a firm goes into a product-market area and finds that it has made a mistake, or that after some years of good returns, the market is declining, it makes good commercial sense to pull out at a suitable time. There is no point in carrying on with an operation just through reluctance to let things go. However, divestments will probably mean significant redundancies among staff, which might meet strong resistance from employees and their trade union officials.

4.8

Growth, stability and contraction: summary

Many companies pursue a growth objective - growth in turnover, profit, EPS (earnings per share), share price and market capitalisation (total market value).

Growth can be achieved

(a)   organically (internally), or
(b)   by means of a merger or takeover.

Growth can be pursued in existing markets and products, or by *diversifying* into new products and new market areas, depending on the product-market strategy selected.

Some companies do not pursue a growth strategy, but instead:

(a)   opt to divest some of their operations, perhaps to concentrate on core products in which they have a major competitive advantage;

(b)   in some cases, simply to survive or remain stable. Survival and stability, like growth, call for continual innovation and change.

---

5.   GROWTH AND STRUCTURAL REORGANISATION

5.1   When an organisation grows in size to the point where further growth within the same organisation structure would create inefficiencies and ineffectiveness, there should be a structural reorganisation.

5.2   Just what the new organisation structure ought to be will depend on the circumstances and situation in which the organisation operates (contingency theory). However, Child has suggested that there are typically four stages of development in organisation structure, as the organisation grows and diversifies.

	Product/market status	*Organisation structure*
Stage 1	Single product	1. No significant differentiation in production or transactions.
		2. Little or no formal structure. Led by owner-bosses.
Stage 2	Single product	1. Stages in production now differentiated, but integrated transactions in the organisation's selling markets.
	Function A Function B Function C → Produces product X → Market	2. Specialisation based on *function* or process develops.
Stage 3	Multiple products, *or* multiple markets	1. Differentiation between product lines (eg product A, product B, product C manufacture separated completely) or between markets (eg selling to market X and selling to market Y are separately organised and operated).
	Either	
	Functions A1 A2 A3 → Product A Functions B1 B2 B3 → Product B → Market	2. Specialisation based either on products or on geographical areas – ie *divisionalisation*.
	or	
	Function A Function B Function C → Product P → Market X / Market Y	
Stage 4	Multiple products *and* multiple markets	1. Non-integrated product and market transactions.
		2. Matrix organisation structure based on both products and geographical areas.

5.3 Changes in what an organisation does - eg the products and services it provides, the number of people it employs etc - could lead to a need for a restructuring of the organisation, to maintain its efficiency in the face of change.

The need for reorganisation might be caused by:

1. Changes in the 'environment' of the organisation.

For example, greater competition might create pressures for cost-cutting, and so staff cuts.

2. Diversification into new product-market areas.

There is a need for better lateral and vertical integration as an organisation becomes more complex and differentiated. Possible role for special co-ordinators. Also the problem of when to switch from a functional to a divisional organisation structure.

3. Growth

Employing more people creates problems of extended management hierarchies and poor communication.

4. New technology

5. Changes in the capabilities of personnel employed.

Changes in education levels, the distribution of occupational skills, employee attitudes to work etc.

5.4 Initially, there is a problem of *identifying the need to reorganise*. The need for restructuring might become apparent:

(a) when the existing organisation shows signs of weakness and strain, eg

   (i) management overload;
   (ii) poor integration and co-ordination;
   (iii) insufficient innovation;
   (iv) weakening control.

These are common management problems, but made worse by deficiencies in the organisation structure;

(b) by anticipating that reorganisation will be beneficial, and planning the structural changes in advance before the deficiencies have time to develop.

5.5 Restructuring isn't always necessary every time that changes take place in an organisation's circumstances. When a problem arises with an organisational deficiency, management has to analyse and diagnose the fault.

(a) What is the scope of the problem?

(b) What is the source of the problem? (It's relatively easy to spot *personal* problems, when a manager isn't doing his job properly, or there are personal rivalries and conflicts, but it isn't so easy to diagnose faults in organisational structure.)

(c) Is the problem temporary or permanent, unique or recurrent?

(d) At what level in the management hierarchy and organisation structure is the problem located? This is the point where restructuring will be needed.

6. PLANNING FOR CHANGE

6.1 For an organisation to be innovative, and continually responsive to the need for change, a systematic approach should be established, for planning and implementing changes.

6.2 A step-by-step model for change is shown below.

Step

1 Determine need or desire for change in a particular area.

2 Prepare a tentative plan.
   • Brainstorming sessions a good idea, since alternatives for change should be considered *(Lippitt 1981)*

3 Analyse probable reactions to the change

4 Make a final decision from the choice of alternative options
   • Decision taken either by group problem-solving (participative) or by manager on his own (coercive)

5 Establish a timetable for change

   • 'Coerced' changes can probably be implemented faster, without time for discussions.

   • Speed of implementation that is achievable will depend on the likely reactions of the people affected (all in favour, half in favour, all against etc).

   • Identify those in favour of the change, and perhaps set up a pilot programme involving them. Talk with the others who resist the change.

6 Communicate the plan for change
   • This is really a continuous process, beginning at Step 1 and going through to Step 7.

7 Implement the change. Review the change.
   • Continuous evaluation and modifications

6.3 Organisational changes need careful planning. This is true of all but the smallest changes, and it is especially true of major changes.

6.4 Major organisational changes should usually originate during the corporate planning process. You will recall from the earlier chapter on corporate planning that the first stages in corporate planning are:

(a) to establish the organisation's major objectives;

(b) to carry out an analysis of the strengths and weaknesses of the organisation, and of the opportunities and threats in its environment.

6.5 An assessment of the organisation's major objectives will occasionally reveal a need for a substantial change in what the organisation is trying to achieve. Two questions of particular importance are:

(a) 'What business are we in?' and
(b) 'What business should we be in?'

6.6 If an organisation is planning to expand its business, it should decide how it ought to be growing, and what product or market areas will be best suited to it. A well-documented example is the case of the Hollywood film industry, which was threatened with extinction in the 1960s and 1970s by the competition from home entertainment, such as television and video. The eventual response of the film industry was to reassess its objectives.

(a) We are in the business of making films for the cinema.
(b) We ought to be in the business of providing entertainment.

6.7 Hollywood decided to move into the production of programmes for television, and to encourage the video market, rather than resist it. This was a major change brought about initially by a reassessment of corporate objectives.

6.8 Similar examples might be found in the public sector. In education, a reassessment of objectives might be:

(a) we are in the business of providing mainly academic education to children up to the age of 16;

(b) we ought to be in the business of providing technical education, and education in day-to-day skills, as well as a minimum examinable standard of academic education, up to the age of 16.

6.9 A SWOT analysis of strengths and weaknesses, and opportunities and threats should enable an organisation's management to plan major internal changes in response to changes in the environment. The corporate planning process gives management the chance:

(a) to identify significant developments in the environment - eg new technological developments;
(b) to consider their potential implications for the organisation's future;

(c)   to consider how the organisation should adapt in response.

6.10   Changes in strategic policies should be developed - eg to develop new products or new markets, to sell off or close down some businesses, to introduce new production methods, recruit employees with different skills, alter the organisation structure, and so on.

6.11   Having formulated strategies for the future, and set targets for achievement, the strategies must be converted into action.

(a)   Because major changes have many ramifications, for products, services, production methods, working procedures, organisation structure etc, they ought to be thoroughly planned, and an action plan produced.

(b)   Because changes often meet with resistance from the employees affected, the planning process should also take account of how such resistance might be overcome, and changes accepted.

6.12   Two further reasons for needing to plan changes carefully are that management must make sure that:

(a)   they have the resources to make the change:

(i)   they have the money to buy the new equipment or premises or other assets they will need;
(ii)   they have the staff, properly *trained in advance* to deal with the new systems;

(b)   the change is worth doing. The major test of whether a change is worthwhile is a cost-benefit analysis. The benefits from the change - which might be non-money benefits as well as money-benefits - must justify the costs of making the change. The costs of change include the time and effort it takes, as well as the money cost.

'Training and personal development requirements connected with the change should be satisfied before rather than after the event. The staff concerned with carrying through the change should be adequately educated and equipped. Not least, senior management should be given an understanding of the problems and duration of change so that it appreciates what is likely to happen, and can be quite clear as to the probable costs as well as benefits.'

(Child)

6.13   A further reason for needing to plan changes is to obtain the support and co-operation of the employees who will be affected. These individuals should be involved in discussions about work problems and how to overcome them, and their participation in the decision to change could be a key factor in overcoming their resistance. This calls for planning, on an informal basis perhaps for small groups, but with some formality when large numbers of people are involved. The 'human' aspects of change are discussed in the next chapter.

Organisation development programmes

6.14 To adapt to the increasing complexities of modern business life, an organisation cannot afford to be a sluggish bureaucracy.

    (a) Individuals should be motivated to welcome change, and to co-operate with other members of an organisation in achieving change and adapting to it.

    (b) Management and leadership styles must be such as to make change and adaptation (development) possible.

    (c) An organisation must react to its environment. 'A management which takes its environment as given and concentrates on organising internally is pursuing a dangerous course. This does not mean that top management should not be involved in internal problems, but that such involvement must be oriented to the environment opportunities and demands.'

6.15 To be adaptive, employees and management of an organisation must learn the 'new' technologies and ideologies and how to relate them to their own work situation. This is the reason why organisation development must be a process of educating.

6.16 This education process might not generate itself within an organisation which lacks innovative employees and a willingness to change, and it is therefore sometimes necessary to provide the impetus towards organisation development by means of some external agency.

6.17 *Margulies and Wallace (1973)* suggested that managing change is not a matter of learning techniques, or applying standard solutions to standard problems.

    (a) Successful change relies on well-informed and well-motivated individuals, if results are to be maintained.

    (b) No single technique or method will give the best way to make changes every time. *Diagnosis* of a situation is the key to deciding what changes will be best.

6.18 The basic stages of an organisation development programme might be as follows.

    (a) An organisation's management must first become aware of deficiencies and faults in its method of operations and take the decision to hire a consultant. An organisation development programme therefore begins with a recognition of a problem at work which 'scientific' methods of management (or techniques) cannot cure.

    (b) A full disclosure of the objectives of the programme must be given. It is vital that all employees should know the purpose of the exercise. It is also important that a mutual confidence should be quickly established between the consultant and the employees of the organisation with whom he will be dealing. At this stage (the 'entry' stage of the programme) the consultant must attempt to win over employees to his views on the relevance of individual attitudes, leadership styles and the environment etc.

    (c) Having established the required mutual trust, the consultant may then proceed with a data gathering and diagnostic exercise, ie collecting the 'facts' and analysing them to discover the causes of deficiency or fault.

Data gathering can be time-consuming. Although it is possible to use questionnaires, it is common to collect data by interviewing individuals. The various methods of data gathering which can be used may be summarised as:

(i) collection of documented data (job descriptions, organisation charts, procedure manuals, personnel records eg for individual performance reports). Information which compares objectives and targets against actual performance, and records of the control action taken (and its effect) should also be gathered;

(ii) questionnaires (possibly as an initial step towards interviewing);

(iii) individual or group interviews. Group interviews may be used to save time or to resolve conflicting facts or opinions which emerged during personal interviews.

Diagnosis should be made by:

(i) encouraging individuals to say what they think is wrong and how it should be put right;

(ii) cross-checking and comparing all the collected data;

(iii) questioning and making suggestions about the causes of problems and deficiencies. In this way, the consultant may be able to lead employees to discover for themselves what is at fault.

(d) The conclusions from the diagnostic exercise should be fed back to higher management in order that a strategy for organisation development may be agreed.

(e) The consultant should suggest a choice of objectives (ie what changes might be made) to senior management, and possibly to recommend the option he considers the most preferable. Once the objective has been agreed, the support and knowledge of the employees concerned must be secured.

(f) The consultant then has the task of formulating a strategy to enable the declared objective to be achieved. Implementing the changes will generally necessitate teaching employees to change their attitudes, and to overcome the difficulties of convincing individuals requires the expertise of the consultant.

(g) The implementation of any such change will require monitoring. The actual effects on the faults at work must be gauged to decide whether the aims of the programme have been achieved. It is also likely that new problems will emerge, and that these in turn will require diagnosis and educative, corrective action.

6.19 The diagnosis of problems and of the need for change could be provided by 'specialists' or experts. These might be:

(a) specialists from the management services division of the organisation; or
(b) external consultants.

15: THE MANAGEMENT OF CHANGE

The use of external consultants

6.20 There are substantial *benefits* in using external consultants.

1. They will use analytical techniques and specialist knowledge, in which internal staff do not have the training.

2. They bring experience from dealing with similar problems in other organisations.

3. They can help with the resolution of internal conflicts within the organisation, by acting as an 'independent referee'.

4. In theory they are 'neutrals', outside departmental politics.

5. They are not tied by status or rank, and can discuss problems freely with the people involved, at all levels within the organisation.

6. They can look at problems objectively, and unlike internal managers don't have to worry about the consequences of their recommendations for their jobs or career prospects.

6.21 But there are also *disadvantages* to the use of consultants.

1. They might be seen as top management's 'poodles', or 'outside meddlers'.

2. They are sometimes brought in as a weapon in internal political battles.

3. They might show an inclination to bring a standard solution to a unique problems, and fail to resolve the problem properly.

4. They might be too academic, and lack experience in 'actual' management.

5. They will need time to learn about an organisation, and 'acclimatise' themselves. The client organisation will have to pay consultancy fees for this learning process!

6. They are very expensive, and may not always give value for money.

6.22 To be effective, a consultant must be capable of building a positive relationship with his client organisation.

6.23 Top management should give its wholehearted support to the consultant's efforts, once the decision to hire him has been taken. His abilities should not be questioned during the course of his work and he should be offered full co-operation in setting about his task.

6.24 The style of leadership in the organisation (eg authoritative, consultative, participative) is likely to affect the approach which the consultant is able to take to his job. Good motivation of employees should act in favour of positive change and against negative conservatism (supposing, that is, that conservatism is negative in a particular situation).

6.25 Winning over middle and lower managers and lower grade staff to the consultant's project is vital:

(a) Personality clashes must be avoided.

(b) Any official might feel threatened in his job security, or might fear criticism in the results of any investigations.

(c) A willingness to accept change might need to be taught.

(d) Co-operation will be most effective when it is based on giving clear information about the nature and purpose of the research to employees involved in the project. Regular feedback about the progress of the project should also be given.

6.26 A consultant is unlikely to be effective unless the reasons why he has been called in have been properly and clearly defined. There must be a problem in order to have a solution.

6.27 The problem may be one which requires a long-term solution; in such cases, the success of a consultant will not be apparent until much later.

6.28 The consultant may offer a range of possible solutions and give the organisation's management the final choice itself.

A solution might be the 'correct' one, but difficult to implement in practice.

6.29 A positive relationship with the client has a different meaning where a problem is scientific or technical, compared to a situation where the problem requires a 'human' or social/organisation solution.

6.30 The more widespread the problem, the more difficult it might be to establish a proper relationship - a 'local' problem involving fewer employees might be easier to solve.

A Management Services Division

6.31 A Management Services Division (MSD) is a department of an organisation which specialises in providing support services for management. The nature of the support services that it provides will vary between organisations, and not all organisations have an MSD. Typically, however, the MSD will be staffed by managers who are trained in the techniques of management consultancy, eg

(a) in organisation and method study (O & M);
(b) in computer technology and software systems (eg networking and databases).

6.32 The function of the MSD is to help management in other divisions and departments to:

(a) analyse and diagnose problems they are having;
(b) discuss how to resolve the problems and help the management to plan how to implement their solution;
(c) act as advisers when major changes are introduced as a solution to the problem.

6.33 The role of the MSD could be described as that of 'internal consultants' - bringing skills and experience of handling management problems, to assist the 'line' managers who cannot find a solution to their problems themselves.

6.34 The role of the MSD, like that of external consultants, will usually be associated with *change*, because radical solutions might be needed for the problems they provide consultation for.

   (a) O & M studies often result in major changes in the way that work is organised, and the methods that are used to get work done.

   These could involve:

   (i)   changes in organisation structure, such as more or less delegation;
   (ii)   changes in the decision-making process - eg greater participation by subordinates;
   (iii) more formalised planning systems, management information systems and performance appraisal and control systems;
   (iv)   changes in work procedures and technology - eg more computerisation, flexible working hours, job losses, more 'outworking'.

   (b) Studies into information technology (IT) systems could result in major changes in:

   (i)   how work is done;
   (ii)   what work is done;
   (iii) information systems;
   (iv)   the labour skills required, and so in staff training programmes.

6.35 As we have seen, instead of having an in-house MSD an organisation could use external consultants to do the same job. The choice between one or the other will depend on:

   (a) *relative cost*. It is only worth having an MSD if there is a continual flow of work to do. External consultants are more suitable for 'one-off' investigations;

   (b) *relative quality of service*.

   (i)   External consultants should have the benefits of broader experience. In contrast, it might be difficult to recruit and train good staff for an in-house MSD, and give them sufficient experience to be accepted as 'realistic' and 'common-sensical' by the departmental managers they advise.

   (ii)   However, in-house MSD staff should have a better in-depth knowledge of their organisation's business, which an external consultant might have to learn as best he can in the time available. For example, a large telephone company could have an MSD, with staff who are familiar with how telephone systems operate and what operating difficulties there could be, and such background knowledge might give them an advantage over external consultants, whose consultancy experience might range from financial services companies to fast-food restaurants or government departments.

Summary and conclusion

6.36 Organisations operate in a changing environment, and must change or transform themselves. Change often calls for innovation, and management should therefore foster creativity and innovative ideas. Innovation is needed for an organisation seeking either growth or stability. Occasionally an organisation might adopt a strategy of contraction.

6.37 Growth and other changes may eventually create the need for a restructuring of the organisation.

6.38 Change should be planned and monitored. Planning changes should start with the corporate planning process, and a reassessment of the organisation's objectives and strategies.

6.39 The need for change might be diagnosed with the help of external consultants or a management services division.

TEST YOUR KNOWLEDGE

(The numbers in brackets refer to paragraphs in this chapter)

1. What are the various types of organisational change? (1.5)

2. What are the advantages of innovation? (2.6)

3. How do intrapreneurial groups compare with classical structures? (2.16)

4. Suggests various motives why managers might want their organisation to grow. (3.13)

5. Child identifies four stages in an organisation's restructuring as it grows in size. What are they? (5.2)

6. What, apart from growth, might create inefficiencies in an organisation which restructuring would cure? (5.3)

7. What are the steps in a model for planning change? (6.2)

8. What are the advantages and disadvantages of using external consultants to help with organisational change or development? (6.20, 6.21)

9. What is the function of a management services division? (6.32-6.34)

10. Discuss the impact of changing technology on an organisation and its employees.

11. What contribution may a Management Services Division make to the introduction of a computerised management information system into an organisation?

15: THE MANAGEMENT OF CHANGE

Discussion points

Question 10
The effect of changing technology on an organisation and its employees was described in an earlier chapter. New technology might be used to reduce operating costs, introduce new products or services, increase operational flexibility, improve management control and integration, or improve the quality of a product or service. Consequences for an organisation and its staff might include fewer jobs, continuous shift work on expensive new plant, a need for new employee skills and so re-training, more working at home or contracting work to outsiders, degrading old skills, less need for middle managers due to improved databases, improved communications etc.

Question 11
The contribution of an MSD would be similar to the contribution that external consultants could make. MSD staff would also act in the role of computer specialists, with an understanding of the hardware and software, and how to make it operate most effectively. They could be used to train staff in the new system. They would also act as advisers and consultants whenever operational staff need help in sorting out problems in using the new system.

Chapter 16

CHANGE: THE LEADER'S ROLE AND EMPLOYEE ATTITUDES

This chapter covers the following topics:

1. The role of leadership in change
2. The individual and change
3. Resistance to change at work
4. The keys to successful change
5. Acceptance of change
6. Changes and group norms
7. The pursuit of excellence

Purpose of this chapter

To consider the possible attitudes of employees to change, and the role of the manager in overcoming their resistance to change and encouraging a positive approach towards change. We finish the chapter by looking at how innovation and change can be used by all the people in an organisation in the pursuit of *excellence*.

1. THE ROLE OF LEADERSHIP IN CHANGE

1.1 "Those who are in charge must know how to decide on changes and implement them effectively or they will fail. The principles for doing it are quite simple. The application of the principles is not so easy." (Donald Kirkpatrick *'How to manage change effectively')*

The role of managers should be:
- (a) to encourage innovative ideas, from subordinates, colleagues, themselves etc, and to encourage a willingness amongst employees to accept changes;
- (b) to evaluate ideas for change;
- (c) to make the decision about what changes to make;
- (d) to plan the change;
- (e) to implement the change;
- (f) to review the consequences of the change, over time.

1.2 Bennett (1961) suggested that:
- (a) the leader needs to have ways of thinking about change. The creation of problem-solving processes should help with both the conception and the implementation of change;
- (b) the leader must have clear goals and objectives, towards the achievement of which any change should be intended to contribute;

(c)   the leader should begin the effort to change at the point where he has most control, and can make the most reliable predictions about the consequences of his decision;

(d)   the leader should recognise the knock-on effects of any decision to make changes - a change in one part of the organisation can affect other parts of the organisation.

1.3   The manager's role in the decision to make changes could be:
(a)   receiving instructions from his boss to implement the change;
(b)   recommending changes to his boss, who then makes the decision;
(c)   making changes without consulting his boss.

1.4   The 'tree' shown below illustrates the different ways in which a manager might become involved in decisions to change.

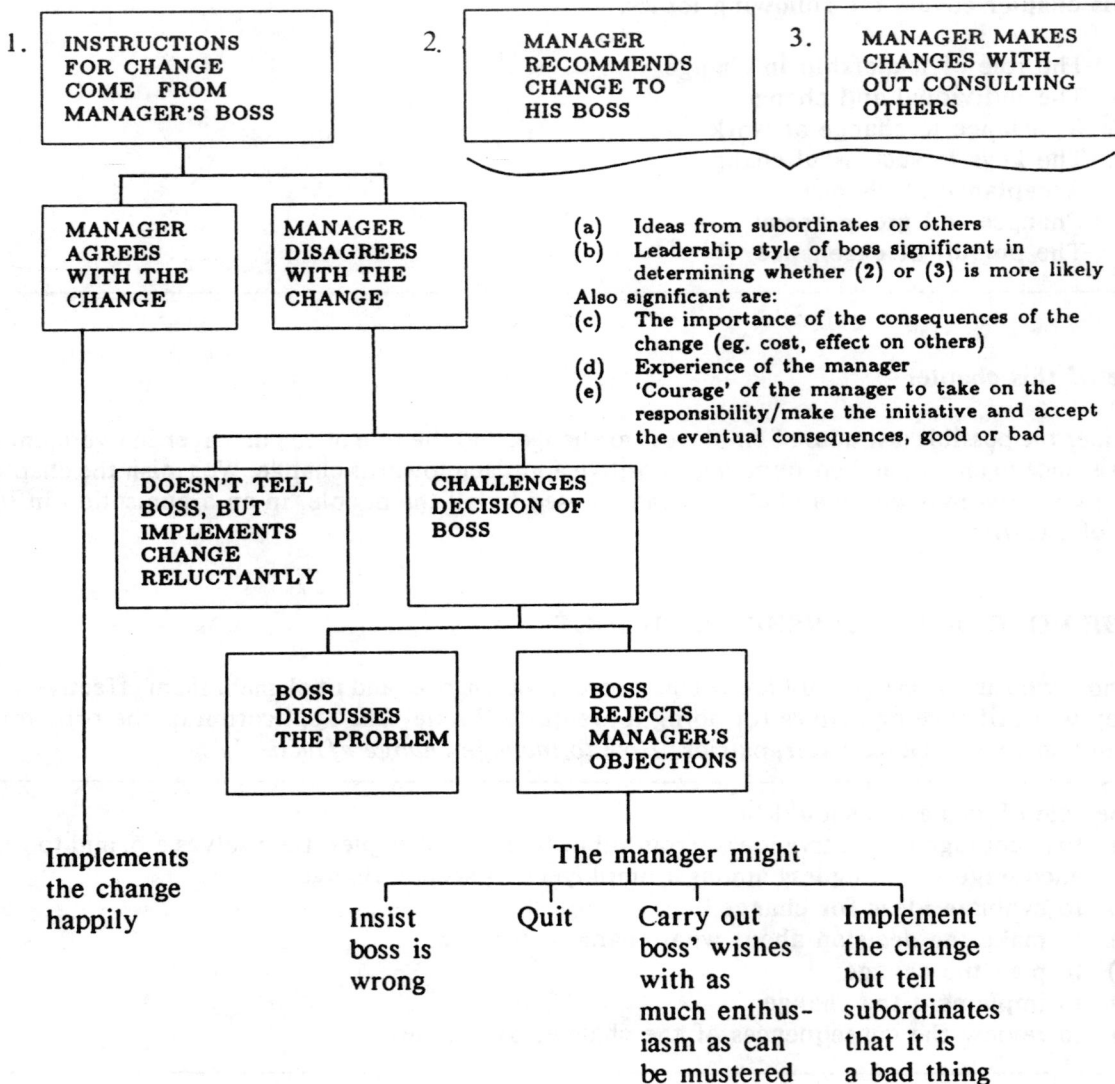

1.   **INSTRUCTIONS FOR CHANGE COME FROM MANAGER'S BOSS**

2.   **MANAGER RECOMMENDS CHANGE TO HIS BOSS**

3.   **MANAGER MAKES CHANGES WITHOUT CONSULTING OTHERS**

MANAGER AGREES WITH THE CHANGE

MANAGER DISAGREES WITH THE CHANGE

(a)   Ideas from subordinates or others
(b)   Leadership style of boss significant in determining whether (2) or (3) is more likely

Also significant are:
(c)   The importance of the consequences of the change (eg. cost, effect on others)
(d)   Experience of the manager
(e)   'Courage' of the manager to take on the responsibility/make the initiative and accept the eventual consequences, good or bad

DOESN'T TELL BOSS, BUT IMPLEMENTS CHANGE RELUCTANTLY

CHALLENGES DECISION OF BOSS

BOSS DISCUSSES THE PROBLEM

BOSS REJECTS MANAGER'S OBJECTIONS

Implements the change happily

The manager might

Insist boss is wrong

Quit

Carry out boss' wishes with as much enthus- iasm as can be mustered

Implement the change but tell subordinates that it is a bad thing

2.   THE INDIVIDUAL AND CHANGE

2.1   Change may affect individuals in several areas.

(a)   There may be *physiological* changes in a person's life, both as the natural product of development, maturation and ageing, and as the result of external factors: a change in the pattern of shift-working, for example, may temporarily throw the individual's eating, waking and sleeping routine out of sync. with the body's 'clock', or sense of time. A change of location may have physical side effects, related to different drinking water, levels of pollution in the air, altitude etc.

(b)   *Circumstantial* changes - living in a new house, establishing new relationships, working to new routines etc. - will involve letting go of things, perhaps 'unlearning' old knowledge, and learning new ways of doing things.

(c)   Above all, changes affect individuals *psychologically.*

   (i)   It may create feelings of disorientation before new circumstances have been assimilated: you may have felt this on waking up in an unfamiliar room, or performing familiar tasks in an unfamiliar setting at work.

   (ii)   Uncertainty may lead to insecurity - which is especially acute in changes involving work. ('What if I can't pick up the technology?' 'What if the new supervisor doesn't like me?'). Individuals who are not averse to risk, who have handled uncertainty before, are more likely to adapt than risk-averse people. Similarly, people whose goals are more 'open' (usually younger ones, and those without parental or peer pressure to perform in a particular way) are more flexible.

   (iii)   The secure basis of warm, accepting relationships may be up-rooted and the business of forging new inter-relations can be fraught with personal insecurity, risk of rejection and the feeling of being an outsider.

3.   RESISTANCE TO CHANGE AT WORK

3.1   Resisting change means attempting to preserve the existing state of affairs - the status quo - against pressure to alter it. Despite the possibly traumatic effects of change per se, as discussed above, most people do *not* in fact resist it on these grounds alone. Many people - think of your own study or work situation - long for change, and have a wealth of ideas about how it should be achieved.

3.2   Sources of resistance to particular proposed changes - e.g. in location, methods of working, pay structure - may include:

(a)   attitudes or beliefs, perhaps arising from cultural, religious or class influences (eg. resistance to change in the law on Sunday trading);

(b)   loyalty to a group and its norms, perhaps with an accompanying rejection of other groups, or 'outsiders' (e.g. in the case of a relocation so that two departments share office space). Groups tend to close ranks if their independent identity is threatened;

(c)   habit, or past norms. This can be a strong source of clinging to old ways, whether out of security needs, respect for tradition, or the belief that 'you can't teach an old dog new tricks' (e.g. resistance to the introduction of new technology);

(d) politics - in the sense of resisting changes that might weaken the power base of the individual or group, strengthen a rival's position etc. Changes involving increased delegation may be strongly resisted by senior management, for example. In the same way, the introduction of automation, or new methods, may be seen by the workforce as an attempt to devalue their skills and experience in the job market: they will be superfluous, or will be 'starting at the bottom again', and will have lost their position of strength as suppliers of labour in demand;

(e) the *way* in which any change is put forward and implemented.

3.3 Arthur Bedeian cites four common *causes* of resistance:

(a) *self-interest:* if the status quo is perceived to be comfortable, or advantageous to the individual, or the group with which he identifies himself;

(b) *misunderstanding and distrust:* if the reasons for, or the nature and consequences of, the change have not been made clear: this aggravates uncertainty and suspicion, ie the perceived threat;

(c) *contradictory assessments:* different individuals' evaluations of the likely costs and benefits of some change. Resistance arises from individuals' perceptions of the undesirability of change;

(d) *low tolerance of change itself:* differences in tolerance of ambiguity, uncertainty, challenge to self-concept etc.

3.4 Reactions to proposed change may range from:

(a) *acceptance* - whether enthusiastic espousal, co-operation, grudging co-operation or resignation; to

(b) *indifference* - usually where the change does not directly affect the individual: apathy, lack of interest, inaction etc.; to

(c) *passive resistance* - refusal to learn, working to rule etc; to

(d) *active resistance* - deliberate 'spoiling', go-slows, deliberate errors, sabotage, absenteeism or strikes.

3.5 The reasons for resisting change or welcoming change might be listed as follows:

Reasons for resisting change

(a) Fear of personal loss
  - security
  - money (eg. travelling costs to work, when a change of office location is proposed)
  - pride and job satisfaction
  - friends and contacts
  - freedom
  - responsibility
  - authority/discretion
  - good working conditions
  - status

(b) Can't see the need for change

(c) Believes change will do more harm than good

(d) Lack of respect for the person initiating the change

(e) Objection to the manner in which the planned change was communicated

(f) No participation "We weren't asked"

Probably the most important factor

(g) Negative attitude to the job

(h) Belief that the change is a personal criticism of what the individual has been doing

(i) Change requires effort

(j) The change comes at a bad time "We have enough on our plate already"

(k) Challenge to authority in the act of resisting change

Reasons for welcoming change

(a) Expectations of personal gain

(b) Change provides a new and welcome challenge

(c) Change will reduce the boredom of work

(d) Likes/respects the source of the change

(e) Likes the manner in which the change was suggested

(f) Participation in the decision

Probably the most important factor

(g) Wants the change

(h) The change improves the employee's future prospects

(i) The change comes at a good time

16: CHANGE: THE LEADER'S ROLE AND EMPLOYEE ATTITUDES

Example of resistance

3.6 John Hunt highlights a number of responses that may not *look* like resistance on the face of things, but are behaviours aimed at reinforcing the status quo. Apart from the 'behind the scenes' political manoeuvres - withholding or distorting information, gossip, undermining the authority of management, blaming the agents of change for small failures etc. There are a number of responses that the manager should learn to recognise, e.g.:

(a) pleas of ignorance ('I need more information');

(b) delayed judgement ('let's wait and see...'), perhaps stalling for time with comparisons ('there are other ways...');

(c) defensive stances - ('This isn't going to work', 'It'd be too expensive', 'It's the wrong time to...');

(d) the display of various personal insecurities: ('I won't be able to cope', 'I won't see my team anymore', 'We won't have control over our planning any more', 'Why can't we just go on as we are?'); fear, anxiety, resentment at the manner of change, frustration at perceived losses etc.;

(e) withdrawal, or disowning of the change: ('Oh, well. On their heads be it', 'I'm not interested in flexitime anyway').

> 'Most of us are all in favour of progress so long as it doesn't involve change'.
>
> Ray Proctor.

Overcoming resistance to change

3.7 Three factors which should be considered by managers in overcoming resistance to change are:

(a) the pace of change;
(b) the manner of change; and
(c) the scope of change.

3.8 Changes ought generally to be introduced slowly. Apart from 'people problems', there may be a long planning and administrative process and/or financial risks to be considered, e.g. in a re-location of offices or a factory: a range of alternatives will have to be considered, information gathered etc. Change is, however, above all a 'political' process: relationships are changed, and must be reformed, old ways have to be unlearned and new ways learned.

3.9 The more gradual the change, the more time is available for questions to be asked, reassurances to be given and retraining (where necessary) embarked upon. People can get used to the idea of new methods - can get acclimatised at each stage, with a consequent confidence in the likely success of the change programme, and in the individual's own ability to cope.

Presenting the individuals concerned with a *fait accompli* ('Let's get it over with - they'll just have to get used to it!') may short-circuit resistance at the planning and immediate implementation stages. But it may cause a withdrawal reaction (akin to 'shock'), if the change is radical and perceived as threatening, and resistance is likely to surface later, as the change is consolidated, in any case - probably strengthened by resentment.

3.10 *Timing* will also be crucial: those responsible for change should be sensitive to incidents and attitudes that might indicate that 'now is not the time'.

3.11 The *manner* in which a change is put across is very important: the climate must be prepared, the need made clear, fears soothed, and if possible the individuals concerned positively motivated to embrace the changes as their own.

(a) Resistance should be welcomed and confronted - not swept under the carpet. Talking through areas of conflict may lead to useful insights and the adapting of the programme of change to advantage. Repressing resistance will only send it underground, into the realm of rumour and covert hostility.

(b) There should be free circulation of information about the reasons for the change, its expected results and likely consequences. That information should appear sensible, clear, consistent and realistic: there is no point issuing information which will be seen as an attempt to 'pull the wool over the eyes' of the people concerned, or to 'blind them with science' - or which is a blatant misrepresentation of the situation. Competent experts should be used. Expectations should not be inflated - otherwise disappointment will be inevitable if the plan doesn't succeed as far or as fast as expected.

(c) The change must be 'sold' to the people: ie people must be convinced that their attitudes and behaviours *need* changing. Objections must be overcome - but it is also possible to get people *behind* the change in a positive way.

(d) Individuals must be helped to learn - ie to change their attitudes and behaviours. Learning programmes for any new skills or systems necessary will have to be designed according to the abilities, previous learning experience etc. of the individuals concerned.

(e) The effects of insecurity, perceived helplessness and therefore resentment, may be lessened if the people can be involved in the planning and implementation of the change, ie if it is not perceived to have been imposed from above. The degree to which *consultation* or *participation* will be possible (or genuine) will depend on management's attitude towards the competence and trustworthiness of its workforce.

3.12 The *scope* of change should also be carefully reviewed. Total transformation will create greater insecurity - but also greater excitement, if the organisation has the kind of innovative culture that can stand it - than moderate innovation. There may be 'hidden' changes to take into account: a change in technology may necessitate changes in work methods, which may in turn result in the breaking up of work groups. Management should be aware of how many various aspects of their employees' lives they are proposing to alter - and therefore on how many 'fronts' they are likely to encounter resistance.

4.   THE KEYS TO SUCCESSFUL CHANGE

4.1   Donald Kirkpatrick ('*How to Manage Change Effectively*') identified three keys to successful change:

> (a)   empathy
> (b)   communication; and
> (c)   participation.

4.2   *Empathy* means 'putting yourself in the shoes of the other person' and getting to know the people involved in and affected by changes. The manager should consider each person's (or group's) reaction to change accordingly. In other words: 'If I were in his shoes, what would I be thinking about this, and how would I be reacting?'

4.3   To show empathy, a manager has to get to know various matters about each individual. Kirkpatrick calls these 'must know' factors, which include name and nickname, where the individual lives, whether he or she is married or single, the individual's work experience, formal education, outside hobbies, health, children, religion, politics, attitudes, problems, friends, financial situation, intelligence, personality, ambitions, date of employment, social background and continuing education (eg. still studying for the ICSA examinations).

4.4   *Communication* is not just telling subordinates what to do, but it is the process of creating an understanding. The importance of communication and the barriers to proper communication were discussed in an earlier chapter of this text. However, the aspects of communication which might be particularly relevant to change are as follows.

   (a)   Who *needs* to know and who else will *want* to know? These people should be told.

   (b)   When should the information be given about planned changes?
      (i)   Bosses ought to be told before subordinates;
      (ii)   Trade union officials ought to be told before workers.

   (c)   How should the information be given? Should it be given verbally, face-to-face? Or in writing? Or a mixture of both?

      (i)   If emotions are likely to run high, the communication ought to be verbal, and face-to-face. If individuals need persuading, the manager must give himself the opportunity to talk to them, and to try to persuade them.

      (ii)   If the changes are complex, and individuals need time to study them or to refer to them later (eg. proposed changes to the company pension scheme) they should be set out in writing.

      (iii) The information should be communicated directly, not via a go-between or middleman.

   (d)   Feedback from the people affected should be obtained. The feelings of employees should be allowed to come out, by encouraging them to ask questions and voice any doubts or worries they might have.

4.5 *Participation* by subordinates in decisions to make changes is Kirkpatrick's third key element for successful change. He argues that a participative approach is needed for innovation; otherwise new ideas will get stifled and discouraged. Examples of a participative approach to change include:

(a) quality circles;
(b) task forces; and
(c) problem-solving groups.

4.6 Two important aspects to participation determine the nature and extent of the participation. These are:

(a) *when* should the manager start to involve his staff; and
(b) *how* should participation be made to work?

When to start participation – 3 approaches	*How participation is achieved in practice*
(a) From the beginning, discuss ideas. Gradually, acceptable ideas will emerge. (b) Make tentative plans for change, and then start to discuss them with subordinates. (c) Decide to make a change and then try to sell the idea to subordinates. Approaches (a) or (b) are preferred for 'real' participation.	The desire of the manager for participation must be genuine. It won't work if 'participation is something the top orders the middle to do from the bottom'. (*Kanter 1983*) 1. Ask for input of ideas. 2. Seriously consider input and evaluate it objectively. 3. Use good ideas. 4. Reject bad ideas. 5. Give credit/rewards to providers of good ideas. 6. Convince the providers of bad ideas that their ideas were bad.

4.7 The practical difficulties with achieving participation for change are that:

(a) managers might pay lip service to participation, but don't believe in it;
(b) employees have suspicions about the consequences of their ideas – eg. that their good ideas will result in lost jobs;
(c) if there is no 'culture' of participation at the moment, it would be difficult to introduce suddenly. Participation would have to be introduced gradually, perhaps starting with one or two pilot groups.

Exercise

You might like to try, as an exercise in empathy, to put yourself in the shoes of a 28-year old accountant, Sam Francisco, who works for a growing manufacturing company in its accounting department, as a junior manager. He has just qualified, but has so far had relatively little experience with computerised accounting systems. He is quite ambitious.

The chief executive of the company now announces that owing to the continuing growth of the company, new product divisions will be created, and the company will switch from a functional to a divisionalised organisation structure, each with its own production, marketing, personnel and accounting functions. Each division might be re-located in a different part of the country. The authority for most decision-making will be delegated to each division (although head office will exercise control) and, to improve the company's control system, there will be a new networked database system, which the accounting and marketing departments of the new divisions will set up. The changes will be explained in more detail by the new divisional managers, and will start to take effect immediately.

Discussion

If you were in Sam Francisco's shoes, how would you react to these changes? Sam will probably be worried by quite a few things. First of all, where does he fit into the new structure? Which division will he be working for? Will he be separated from his colleagues, who might go to work in different divisions? Where might he be working, and is the threat of relocation to a different area a serious one? Does he like the idea of living somewhere else? He hasn't had much experience with computer systems, and so is he worried about the prospect of having to work with a new database system? Will he get any training? He is ambitious, and so how does the reorganisation affect his career prospects? Does the divisional management structure make it more difficult for a specialised functional manager (eg. an accountant) to reach a general management position, or easier?

The company's management should have thought about the fears and doubts of its employees *before* it announced any changes, and done something pro-active to overcome them.

---

5. ACCEPTANCE OF CHANGE

5.1 It takes time for changes to get accepted. Conner and Patterson (1981) identified three phases and eight stages in the process of accepting change by the people affected.

Phase 1: Preparation phase

Stage 1	Contact	First knowledge that a change is 'in the air'
Stage 2	Awareness	Knowledge that change will happen

Phase 2: Acceptance phase

Stage 3	Understanding	Gaining an understanding of the nature and purpose of the change
Stage 4	Positive perception	Developing a positive view towards the change, and accepting the need for it

Phase 3: Commitment phase

Stage 5	Installation	The change becomes operational
Stage 6	Adoption	The change has been in force for long enough and its value has become apparent
Stage 7	Institutionalisation	The change has been in for long enough to become 'routine' and the 'norm'
Stage 8	Internalisation	Individuals are highly committed to the change because it is now congruent with their personal interests, goals and value systems.

5.2 Conner and Patterson argued that *commitment* to change is necessary for its successful implementation.

(a) Getting commitment is expensive, and calls for an investment of time, effort and money - eg. providing information, involving subordinates in the planning and implementation process, rewarding them for their participation etc.

(b) Strategies for commitment ought to be developed. For any change, management needs to decide how far through the eight stages the acceptance process needs to go. Some changes can stop at Stage 5; other must go to Stage 7 or Stage 8, otherwise the benefits of the change will be lost.

(c) Management must plan to win the commitment of employees, or prepare for the adverse consequences.

(d) Human reactions to change are a function of both intellect and emotion. Reactions can be either positive or negative, on both an intellectual and an emotional level.

6. CHANGES AND GROUP NORMS

6.1 Participation in decisions for making changes should recognise the strength of group attitudes and group norms. A norm, you should remember, is 'any uniformity of attitude, opinion, feeling or action shared by two or more people. Groups are characterised by the norms their members share.' *(Blake and Mouton 1982)* A group couldn't be a group if it lacked norms to co-ordinate and regulate the interactions between group members.

6.2 A boss can try to use his power and authority to break up prevailing norms, ie. to make changes. This might work successfully, but it is more likely to fail due to the passive resistance from the group members. Blake and Mouton suggested that the most effective way of changing group norms is to involve the people affected in studying what the existing norms are and what would be better. 'Only after prevailing norms are understood can specific steps necessary for shifting from the old to the new be considered and implemented. The key factor is to involve those who are controlled by a norm to change the norm itself.'

(a) The group should be led by the manager who is responsible for the ultimate decisions.

(b) However, all 'norm carriers' should actively participate, and be involved in the problem of deciding how to change.

(i)   The group should be allowed to study their situation objectively, and be given the information they need to carry out a full analysis. The reasons for the current problems should be identified after discussions and by common agreement.

(ii)   Agreements for change should be reached, made explicit and introduced.

(iii)   Changes in norms should be followed up (monitored and enforced), to prevent backsliding. New group norms are always weaker than old ones, until they become well-established.

6.3   It is worth adding the point that although Blake and Mouton favoured group participation in decisions to make changes, imposed or 'coerced' changes will sometimes work better. Hersey and Blanchard (1972) suggested that coerced change is better for 'immature' groups and can be introduced comparatively quickly whereas participative change is better for 'mature' groups, to overcome the problem of resistance.

6.4   In an article in the Financial Times (June 25, 1986), Christopher Lorenz reviews *The Change Masters* by Rosabeth Moss Kanter, quoting the following list of personal 'do's' and 'don'ts' for the would-be 'change master':

"(1)   Tune into the company's external environment much more effectively. Only then will you be able to identify new needs.

(2)   Use 'kaleidoscope thinking' to create new approaches, by combining known facts and fragments to form different patterns. (This is one of the various definitions of creativity). This way of thinking can be stimulated throughout an organisation by encouraging playfulness and irreverence.

(3)   Develop the ability to create and communicate a clear vision. The importance of this is underlined by the fact that venture capitalists place more weight on the person behind a project than on the project itself.

(4)   Build coalitions, and don't spring new things on people. Moss Kanter uses colourful jargon to describe four phases of coalition-building: planting seeds; 'tin-cupping' around the organisation (getting other people to contribute to the new idea); horse-trading; and 'sanity checking' (final checking of possible problems).

(5)   Work through highly-motivated teams. 'Successful change efforts are associated with heightened teamwork.'

(6)   Persevere and persist. 'Everything looks like a failure halfway through, which is when the political problems arise.'

(7)   Share credit and recognition - 'make everyone a hero.' "

CASE STUDY 1: INTRODUCING FLEXIBLE WORKING HOURS

It might be useful now to look at a couple of simple case studies in the management of change. Before reading the discussion of each case, try to develop your own ideas of how you would handle each situation yourself.

You are the manager in charge of a department, which is located in a separate office building. Your divisional manager has suggested that the company should offer a system of flexible working hours to all its staff, including those in your department. In response, you have said that you are in favour of the idea, because you can see benefits for both the organisation and your staff. However, you can see problems too.

The divisional manager asks you to look further into the possibility of introducing flexible working hours in your department.

How would you tackle this job? What problems would you foresee, and how would you propose to resolve them?

Discussion

The most significant problem with introducing any change in personnel policy, such as offering flexible working hours, is how to win the support of employees. The three key factors in making a successful change, as Kirkpatrick argues, are empathy, communication and participation.

(a) It would be inadvisable to introduce flexible working hours unless employees wanted the change, and might benefit from it.

(b) The proposals for change, the reasons for suggesting a change and details of how the new system might operate, should be communicated to staff, who should be asked to express their doubts or worries about the change.

(c) The idea has come from the divisional manager, but staff can participate in the decision by voicing their objections, or making suggestions for improvements in the scheme and how it would work. The proposed change might be modified - or abandoned - accordingly.

The process of communication should include explaining the potential benefits of a flexible working hours system to both the organisation and the staff.

(a) *For the staff*

   (i) There is the convenience of choosing when to start and finish work each day. This could help to improve the individual's use of each day - leading to a better social life.

   (ii) Supervisors can't be there all the time that other staff are on duty, and so there will be more delegation of authority.

   (iii) The change is likely to make the organisation more receptive to any future suggestions that employees might have for part-time jobs or job sharing.

(b) *For the organisation*

    (i)   Telephones in the office will be manned for more hours each day.

    (ii)   Work will start earlier in the day and end later.

    (iii) There will probably be a drop in late arrivals at work, absenteeism and employee turnover.

Some problems of detail will inevitably arise, and in discussing the proposed changes with the staff, these problems must be recognised and brought out. For example:

(a)   there will be a shortage of supervision at some times of the day when staff are working, especially early in the morning and late in the evening;

(b)   there might be no one in an office at times to answer the telephone;

(c)   there could be some difficulty in scheduling meetings for a time that everyone can attend.

This problem could be resolved mainly by getting the staff to accept that flexible working hours are being offered as a privilege, but not as a right, and that the hours they work must be compatible with maintaining an efficient work flow.

This acceptance should come through recognising the problem and involving the staff in a discussion of how to resolve it - eg. how can steps be taken to ensure that the telephones are manned at all times between the hours of, say, 8.30 am and 5.30 pm?

CASE STUDY 2: INTRODUCING NEW TECHNOLOGY INTO THE OFFICE

The accounting department at A Ltd uses a typing pool which comprises six female staff, who have all been at the company for years. They deal with all correspondence except invoices and statements, and the more senior do some secretarial work for specific managers. Their work has always been satisfactory. The amount of both secretarial and routine work is expected to increase in the course of the next few years, and the manager feels that a switch to word processing is indicated. One of the typists is pregnant and another has expressed an interest in early retirement.

(a)   What effects could the introduction of word processors be expected to have on the staff?

(b)   What steps should be taken to avoid any problems?

Discussion

Effects on the staff on introducing WPs. This is this process of trying to show empathy – ie recognising how staff might be affected by a change.

(a) There might be general fear and resistance to the idea. The typists have worked in their present way 'for years', and feel insecure, threatened and unable to cope with new methods. They may lack confidence in their ability to learn 'new technology'. They may fear that the resulting increased productivity will lead to redundancies.

(b) There might be some loss of interest in the work. *If* the work were organised in a way which no longer allowed the typists to liaise with specific managers, and to perform other duties, this could seriously affect their job satisfaction and morale.

(c) New working arrangements, office layout, and greater demands on the concentration of the typists, might also mean that valued work group relationships and opportunities for social interaction suffer.

(d) Although the keyboard action itself is easier with a WP, the lack of task variety and increased speed of operating create physical and mental demands on the typists. They are spending more continuous time at the keyboard which taxes the muscles, eyes etc, and also having to pay attention to matters such as file maintenance and data security. The pregnancy of one of the typists might also raise fears associated with the supposed health hazard of VDUs.

(e) On the positive side, there is opportunity for new skill development and the satisfaction that it affords. For example, the typists would learn how to use the operating system, codes of editing and formatting text etc and would also be given new responsibilities for file maintenance, security (eg backing up disks) etc.

(f) The demands made by technology in the office frequently lead to the creation of a better-designed environment with a 'hi-tech' appearance. This may also be a source of pride and satisfaction to staff.

Steps to avoid problems.
These should encompass a full communication of the proposed changes to the staff, and their participation in the process of deciding when and how the changes should be made.

Taking the adverse effects envisaged above one by one, ways can be found to combat them.

(a) The introduction should be carefully planned, to minimise disruption and insecurity. *Consultation* with staff on areas in which they are able to participate (eg requirements of the new system, design of furniture etc) may help to involve staff and decrease resistance. At the very least, there should be early, open and full *communication* of the manager's plans, purposes, proposals etc, to minimise fear of the unknown.

(b) A programme of training will help to minimise insecurity, and will ease the transition period.

(c) If increased productivity creates the possibility of staff reductions, this should be accomplished by non-aversive means as far as possible. A Ltd are facing an increased workload, and they also have the opportunity to take advantage of natural wastage (with at least one voluntary leaver), so should not face too many problems here.

(d) To counter the loss of interest in the job, the new skills element of word processing should be stressed; the operators should be given the opportunity to discover and utilise the advanced capabilities of their machines. If possible, work should be organised to allow the typists to retain their secretarial duties for specific managers.

(e) If work group relationships must be stifled by working arrangements, the department might be able to compensate for this by allowing or positively encouraging social interaction during rest-pauses, or non-work hours eg by providing rest areas, canteen or social facilities.

(f) Working conditions and the office environment will have to be carefully designed to minimise physical discomfort and fatigue.

(g) The whole 'culture' of the department should be geared to appreciation of the skills and effort involved. Management should try to make it clear that the WP operators are valued employees, and will not become 'drones', or irrelevant additions to precious new technology.

7. THE PURSUIT OF EXCELLENCE

7.1 In 1982 Tom Peters and Robert Waterman published what became a seminal book in management theory, *"In Search of Excellence"*. By an anecdotal technique they set about describing and analysing what it was that made successful companies successful.

7.2 By 'excellent' companies Peters and Waterman mean companies which have achieved a certain kind of innovative performance:

(a) they are usually good at producing commercially viable new products; *and*

(b) they are especially adroit at continually responding to changes of any sort in their environment.

> An excellent company is a continuously innovative big company.

7.3 By observing and analysing in depth about thirty highly successful American companies (in terms of growth, market value, return on capital etc), Peters and Waterman noted that excellent companies share certain common characteristics:

(a) *thinking*, *wisdom* and *action* by managers were considered more important than tools, intellect and analysis;

(b) they worked hard to keep things *simple* in a complex world;

(c) they insisted on *top quality*;

(d) they paid huge attention to *customer care*;

(e) they listened to *employees* and treated them like adults;

(f) they gave rein to *innovators;* and

(g) they were prepared to put up with some *chaos* in return for quick action and experimentation.

7.4 These observed characteristics were analysed into eight key attributes of an excellent company and its culture.

1.	A bias for action.
2.	Closeness to the customer - quality, service and reliability.
3.	Autonomy and entrepreneurship.
4.	Productivity through people.
5.	Hands-on management, driven by value.
6.	'Stick to the knitting' - stick with what you know and can run.
7.	Simple structures, small numbers of top-level staff.
8.	Simultaneous loose-tight properties - they are at once centralised and decentralised. Autonomy is allowed on the shop-floor and in project teams but *all* parts of the organisation must adhere to core values.

Excellence and leadership

7.5 It is interesting to note that many of the 'excellent' companies showing these attributes were associated with very strong leaders who seemed to have a lot to do with making the company excellent in the first place. Provided this happened at an early stage in the company's life, the excellent values remained after the leader departed. The role of managers was to manage the *values* of the company.

7.6 A later work by Tom Peters with Nancy Austin, *A Passion for Excellence,* focusses on the importance of leadership and values. In particular, it advocates 'management by wandering about' (MBWA), by which it means that managers should keep in touch with what customers want, how products are produced and how employees are carrying out their work.

Excellence and the rational model of management

7.7 For many years the central theme of Western thinking on management was that managers make decisions in a rational way. Complex logical and mathematical methods were developed for the process: decision trees, critical path analysis etc.

7.8 However, behaviour in organisations is also about creativity, emotion, hunches, gut reactions, politics, enthusiasm and other unquantifiable human qualities that do not fit well into the rational model.

> "'Rational' has come to have a very narrow definition in business analysis. It is the 'right' answer, but it's missing all of that messy human stuff, such as good strategies that do not allow for persistent old habits, implementation barriers and simple human inconsistencies." *(Peters and Waterman)*

7.9 Peters and Waterman enumerate several shortcomings of the rational model of organisation, including the fact that:

- the numerative analytical component has in-built conservative bias and stifles innovation;
- it does not celebrate informality, internal competition and experimentation;
- it denigrates the importance of values: culture is essentially irrational;
- 'the rationalist approach takes the living element out of situations that should, above all, be alive'.

7.10 They suggest that the 'technology of reason' should be supplemented with a 'technology of foolishness': that sometimes, individuals should be free to act before they think. The right side of the brain - artistic and irrational - has its place in human behaviour. The decision making process should be like a 'garbage can': lots of ideas swirling around, mixing etc.

(Note that to a large extent these comments reflect the researchers' own attitudes as to what is desirable in an organisation.)

7.11 Above all, Peters and Waterman find that the central problem with the rationalist view of organising people is that people are not very rational.

> "Logic, reason and analysis are necessary, but not sufficient for success. To ignore this is to confuse a part of the process with the whole. And such a confusion can lead to a state of corporate constipation known as 'analysis paralysis'." *Ray Proctor*

Excellence and motivation

7.12 Peters and Waterman also discuss the central importance of positive reinforcement in any method of motivation. "Researchers studying motivation find that the prime factor is simply the self-perception among motivated subjects that they are in fact doing well ... Mere association with past personal success apparently leads to more persistence, higher motivation, or something that makes us do better."

7.13 For instance at Mars Inc in America, Peters and Waterman observed that every employee - including the president - received a 10% pay bonus for each week in which he got to work on time every day. "That's an ... example of creating a setting in which virtually everybody wins regularly ... When the number of awards is high, it makes the perceived possibility of winning something high as well. And then the average man will stretch to achieve. *[cf expectancy theory]* Many companies do believe in special awards, but use them exclusively to honour the top few (who already are so highly motivated that they would probably have done their thing anyway)."

7.14 The observations of Peters and Waterman on the 'culture' and motivational environment of 'excellent' companies in the USA may seem slightly eccentric to British managers, but part of the writers' profile of an excellent company is that 'excellent companies require and demand extraordinary performance from the average man'.

7.15 Positive reinforcement – whether in the form of bonuses, prizes, 'reaffirming the heroic dimension' of the job itself, identifying workers with the company's success, or enhancing self-image in the workforce – is the method Peters and Waterman observed *succeeding*, although some research has shown that 'tough' managers, applying sanctions on undesirable behaviour, can also get improved performance out of their subordinates.

7.16 Peters and Waterman argue that employees can be 'switched on' to extraordinary loyalty and effort if:

(a) the cause is perceived to be in some sense great – 'reaffirming the heroic dimension' of the work. Commitment comes from believing that a task is inherently worthwhile. Devotion to the *customer*, and his needs and wants, is an important motivator in this way.

> "Owing to good luck, or maybe even good sense, those companies that emphasise quality, reliability, and service have chosen the *only* area where it is readily possible to generate excitement in the average down-the-line employee. They give people pride in what they do. They make it possible to love the product."

Shared values and 'good news swapping' – a kind of folklore of past success and 'heroic' endeavour – create a climate where intrinsic motivation is a real driving force;

(b) they are treated as winners. "Label a man a loser and he'll start acting like one." Repressive control systems and negative reinforcement break down the employee's self-image. Positive reinforcement, 'good news swapping', attention from management etc enhance the employee's self-image and create positive attitudes to work and to the organisation;

(c) they can satisfy their dual needs:

(i) to be a conforming, secure part of a successful team; and
(ii) to be a 'star' in their own right.

7.17 This means applying control (through firm central direction, and shared values and beliefs) but also allowing maximum individual autonomy (at least, the *illusion* of control) and even competition between individuals or groups within the organisation. Peters and Waterman call this 'loose-tight' management. Culture, peer pressure, a focus on action, customer-orientation etc are 'non-aversive' ways of exercising control over employees.

7.18 The implication of this for work behaviour affects the way in which individuals can be motivated and managed. As Peters and Waterman argue, a strong 'central faith', which binds the organisation together as a whole, should be combined with a strong emphasis on individual self-expression, contribution and success: individuals should be given at least the 'illusion of control' over their destinies, while still being given a sense of belonging and a secure, perceived meaningful framework in which to act.

Excellence and group behaviour

7.19 Peters and Waterman *(In Search of Excellence)* outline the cultural attributes of successful *task force* teams. They should:

- be small - requiring the trust of those who are not involved;
- be of limited duration and working under the 'busy member theorem' - "get off the damned task force and back to work";
- be voluntary - which ensures that the business is 'real';
- have an informal structure and documentation - no bulky paperwork, and open communication;
- have swift follow-up - be *action* oriented.

Excellence and people

7.20 One of the prime attributes of 'excellent' companies identified by Peters and Waterman is what they call 'Productivity through People'.

> "We are not talking about mollycoddling. We are talking about tough-minded respect for the individual and the willingness to train him, to set reasonable and clear expectations for him, and to grant him practical autonomy to step out and contribute directly to his job." *In Search of Excellence.*

7.21 The emphasis is on *enabling contribution*. They quote IBM: "Our early emphasis on human relations was not motivated by altruism but by the simple belief that if we respected our people and helped them to respect themselves, the company would make the most profit."

7.22 'Happy workers' are unlikely to be an end in themselves. A business organisation tries to get the best *out* of its people, not necessarily *for* them - unless the one cannot be achieved without the other.

7.23 We should also note that there are a great many other work and non-work variables in the equation. A 'happy' workforce will not *necessarily* make the organisation profitable (eg if the market is unfavourable): they will not necessarily be more productive (eg if the task itself is badly designed, or resources scarce) nor even more highly motivated. Nor is there a magic formula for making them happy by offering them opportunities suitable to their personality development (increased responsibility etc): their priorities may lie elsewhere, or they may be suffering frustration and failure in other areas of their lives that work cannot influence.

```
┌─────────────────────────────────────────────────────────────────────────┐
│                          TEST YOUR KNOWLEDGE                              │
│                                                                           │
│       (the numbers in brackets refer to the paragraphs in this chapter)   │
│                                                                           │
│    1.  What is the role of a leader in change?  (1.1-1.3)                 │
│                                                                           │
│    2.  List reasons why employees might (a) resist or (b) welcome change. │
│        (3.2-3.4, 3.5)                                                     │
│                                                                           │
│    3.  What is the value of introducing changes slowly?  (3.9, 4.6)       │
│                                                                           │
│    4.  What, according to Kirkpatrick, are the three keys to successful   │
│        change?  (4.1)                                                     │
│                                                                           │
│    5.  When might you start the process of involving subordinates in      │
│        decisions to make changes? How might participation be achieved in  │
│        practice?  (4.6, 4.7)                                              │
│                                                                           │
│    6.  What is the relevance of group norms to change?  (6.1)             │
│                                                                           │
│    7.  What common characteristics are shared by excellent companies?     │
│        (7.3, 7.4)                                                         │
│                                                                           │
│    8.  Account for the importance of the leadership role of general       │
│        management for the effective implementation of major               │
│        organisational change.                                             │
│                                                                           │
│    9.  The goals of an organisation are usually altered on a gradual      │
│        basis. Why?                                                        │
│                                                                           │
│   10.  What is the role of staff participation in the effective           │
│        implementation of organisational changes?                          │
│                                                                           │
│   11.  What can managers do to ensure that organisations are flexible and │
│        adaptable? To what extent can a policy of decentralisation achieve │
│        that end?                                                          │
└─────────────────────────────────────────────────────────────────────────┘
```

Discussion points

Question 8
The role of leadership change is discussed in paragraphs 1.1-1.3. This question asks about the role of *general* management, and so you should consider the functions of general managers - planning, organising, controlling, communicating, co-ordinating, motivating - and relate them to the management of change.

Question 9
The need for gradual change is partly because overcoming resistance among employees takes time, and participation is a slow process. However, major innovation must be planned carefully. The planning horizon might be quite long (eg. a new product development might take several years). Innovation can be expensive and it might take time to build up the resources to make the change.

Question 10
This problem is well covered in the chapter. Don't ignore the importance of group norms.

Question 11

The responsibility for creating an organisation in which innovation and creativity are encouraged were discussed in the previous chapter. As an example, the setting up of quality circles is discussed in this chapter.

One of the advantages of decentralisation is to give the authority for making decisions to someone closer to the 'scene of the action'. This encourages flexibility and adaptability in short term decisions. You might argue, however, that longer-term innovations are probably made better at a central headquarters - eg. decisions about product research might be entrusted to a central R & D unit in preference to smaller divisional R & D sections.

SECTION E
SOCIAL RESPONSIBILITIES
OF MANAGEMENT

Chapter 17

SOCIAL RESPONSIBILITY OF MANAGEMENT

This chapter covers the following topics:

1. Social and ethical obligations of organisations
2. Political and legal constraints on management
3. The social and ethical environment
4. The social responsibility of organisations and managers
5. Management as a profession
6. Stakeholder analysis
7. Management responsibilities
8. Public relations and corporate image
9. Accountability of management

Purpose of this chapter

To consider the environmental, legal and other contraints on the exercise of managerial responsibility. We also look at the responsibilities of management to consumers, suppliers, employees, the environment and the general public, and at the way in which the organisation is perceived by the public.

1. SOCIAL AND ETHICAL OBLIGATIONS OF ORGANISATIONS

1.1 A business supplies goods and services to customers, and employs people; it is therefore an integral part of society and is subject to the pressures of that society. Most companies:

   (a) seek a good public image;

   (b) are increasingly conscious of the need to conserve energy, and to protect the environment from the pollution of industrial wastage and spillages;

   (c) attempt to be good employers;

(d) attempt to provide facilities or welfare to the local community or the country as a whole (eg. the sponsorship of sports, which is not always associated with a blaze of advertising and publicity, donations to charity etc.).

1.2 There are differing views about the extent to which external environmental constraints modify business objectives.

(a) The *stakeholder view* of company objectives is that many groups of people have a stake in what the company does. Shareholders own the business, but there are also suppliers, managers, workers and customers. Each of these groups has its own objectives, so that a compromise or balance is required. Management must balance the profit objective with the pressures from the non-shareholder groups in deciding the strategic targets of the business.

(b) The *consensus theory* of company objectives was developed by Cyert and March. They argued that managers run a business but do not own it and that 'organisations do not have objectives, only people have objectives'. Managers do not necessarily set objectives for the company, but they rather look for objectives which suit their own inclinations. However, objectives emerge as a consensus of the differing views of shareholders, managers, employees, suppliers, customers and society at large, but (in contrast to the stakeholder view) they are not all selected or controlled by management.

1.3 Ansoff suggested that a company has:

(a) a primary objective, which is financial or economic, aimed at optimising the efficiency and effectiveness of the firm's 'total resource-conversion process';

(b) social or non-economic objectives, which are secondary and modify management behaviour. These social objectives are the result of inter-action among the individual objectives of the differing groups of 'stakeholders';

(c) in addition to economic and non-economic objectives, there are two other factors exerting influence on management behaviour:

(i) *responsibilities*: these are obligations which a company undertakes, but which do not form a part of its 'internal guidance or control mechanism'. Responsibilities would include charitable donations, contributions to the life of local communities etc;

(ii) *boundaries*: these are rules which restrict management's freedom of action, and include government legislation (on pollution levels, health and safety at work, employment protection, redundancy, monopolies, illegal business practices etc) and agreements with trade unions.

2. POLITICAL AND LEGAL CONSTRAINTS ON MANAGEMENT

2.1 The government acts as a constraining influence on managers of other organisations, in both the public and private sectors.

    (a)   In the public sector, senior management is accountable to a government department, and decisions taken by the management might be dictated by government policy.

    (b)   For both the public and private sectors, the government enacts and enforces the law. Managers are sometimes compelled to take certain actions, because of the law. Examples are company law (filing of accounts etc), consumer law (pollution controls, dangerous goods legislation), employment law (minimum wage, health and safety) and contract law (limitations on exclusion of liability).

    (c)   The government is also able to exert considerable influence on organisations without the need for legal backing.

        (i)   Fiscal policy and economic policy have implications for corporate taxes, interest rates, foreign exchange rates, inflation, and so on, which influence the corporate planning decisions by organisations.

        (ii)   The government might provide financial incentives (eg grants) to encourage organis- ations to make certain investments, employ more people, or provide more training.

2.2 There is a two-way relationship between government and management, and management can influence the policy decisions of a government, perhaps by means of organised lobbying - eg lobbying by the book trade in the mid 1980s to persuade the government not to impose VAT on newspapers and books.

2.3 The legal constraints or controls affecting the management of an organisation come from the Companies Acts and a wide range of legislation and case law. The controls can be categorised under six broad headings:

    (a)   *personnel*: employment law might extend to minimum wages, sex and racial discrimination, dismissal, hours of work, redundancy payments, formal worker participation in Board decisions;

    (b)   *operations*: laws might place restrictions on the operations of the organisation; for example, health and safety at work and product safety standards, the banning of dangerous materials or substances in products. In the case of the transport of goods, legislation might extend to permitted routes for lorries or maximum hours/distances per driver per day;

    (c)   *marketing*: the selling of goods might be restricted by laws on the description of goods, sending unsolicited goods to customers, dangerous packaging, misleading advertising, weights and measures;

    (d)   *environmental*: certain products or production operations might be banned because they are damaging to mind and health, or pollute the environment. Major construction works (eg new power plants and oil pipelines) might be required to cater for protection of the environment. Organisations might be forbidden to pollute rivers, the air or land with dangerous effluent materials. There are likely to be continuing pressures from environ- mental and scientific groups for further legislation to protect the environment (eg to take steps to prevent acid rain or nuclear radiation and to restrict damage to the ozone layer);

(e) *finance*: legislation on financial matters involves, for instance, consumer credit. Taxation affects organisations in two ways:
(i)   they act as tax collectors for the government (PAYE income tax, VAT);
(ii) they pay tax to the government (corporation tax).

There are also legal requirements to produce financial information (eg annual returns, annual report and accounts);

(f) *organisation*: legislation might affect the organisation structure of an organisation, eg by establishing the duties of directors of a company.

2.4   An organisation may also act to prevent changes in the law from taking place. A well-publicised example is the success of the firearms manufacturers in the USA in preventing anti-gun legislation from being enacted. Other organisations have attempted to delay legislation which would affect their operations (eg cigarette manufacturers have successfully postponed anti-smoking legislation in the UK).

2.5   On a larger scale, national governments may be frustrated in their attempts to regulate the activities of multi-national companies by the fact that companies can switch their activities to other countries where similar legislation and controls do not exist.

3. THE SOCIAL AND ETHICAL ENVIRONMENT

3.1   Whereas the political environment in which an organisation operates consists of laws, regulations and government agencies

> - the social environment consists of the customs, attitudes, beliefs and education of society as a whole, or of different groups in society; and
>
> - the ethical environment consists of a set (or sets) of well-established rules of personal and organisational behaviour.

3.2   *Social* attitudes, such as a belief in the merits of education, progress through science and technology, and fair competition, are significant for the management of a business organisation. Other beliefs which have either gained strength or been eroded in recent years include the following.

(a) There is a growing belief in preserving and improving the quality of life by reducing working hours, reversing the spread of pollution, developing leisure activities etc. Pressures on organisations to consider the environment are particularly strong because most environmental damage is irreversible and some is fatal to humans and wildlife.

(b) Many pressure groups have been organised in recent years to protect social minorities and under-privileged groups. Legislation has been passed in an attempt to prevent racial discrimination and discrimination against women and disabled people.

(c) The conflict between 'them and us' - management and workers - has bedevilled British industry for many years and shows signs of abating only in restricted areas. To some extent, this view is the product of social attitudes which exist outside a particular work situation.

(d) There has possibly been some erosion in respect for authority.

(e) A growth in materialism and consumerism has meant that money is once again a very strong motivator.

(f) It is government policy to involve the private sector in areas that would previously have been the responsibility of the state. Business sponsorship of the arts is one such example.

(g) Health and fitness issues are on the social agenda as never before. At one level, *stress* is increasingly recognised as a cause of illness: as stress is often work-generated organisations may find they have to address this issue as a management problem. A more simple issue is that some organisations are introducing restrictions on smoking on company premises.

3.3 The *ethical* environment refers to justice, respect for the law and a moral code. The conduct of an organisation, its management and employees will be measured against ethical standards by the customers, suppliers and other members of the public with whom they deal.

3.4 Managers have a duty (in most enterprises) to aim for profit. At the same time, modern ethical standards impose a duty to guard, preserve and enhance the value of the enterprise for the good of all touched by it, including the general public. Large organisations tend to be more often held to account over this than small ones.

3.5 The types of ethical problem a manager may meet with in practice are very numerous. A few of them are suggested in the following paragraphs.

3.6 In the area of products and production, managers have responsibility to ensure that the public and their own employees are protected from danger. Attempts to increase profitability by cutting costs may lead to dangerous working conditions or to inadequate safety standards in products. In the United States, product liability litigation is so common that this legal threat may be a more effective deterrent than general ethical standards. The Consumer Protection Act 1987 is beginning to ensure that ethical standards are similarly 'enforced' in the UK.

3.7 The pharmaceutical industry is one where this problem is particularly acute. On the one hand managers may be influenced by a genuine desire to benefit the community by developing new drugs which at the same time will lead to profits; on the other hand, they must not skimp their research on possible side-effects in rushing to launch the new product. In the UK, the Consumer Protection Act 1987 attempts to recognise this dilemma. Drugs companies are not held liable for side-effects which could not have been foreseen by scientific knowledge as it existed at the time the drug was developed - the 'development risk' defence.

3.8 Another ethical problem concerns payments by companies to officials (particularly officials in foreign countries) who have power to help or hinder the payers' operations. In *The ethics of corporate conduct* Clarence Walton refers to the fine distinctions which exist in this area:

(a) *Extortion*. Foreign officials have been known to threaten companies with the complete closure of their local operations unless suitable payments are made.

(b) *Bribery*. This refers to payments for services to which a company is not legally entitled. There are some fine distinctions to be drawn; for example, some managers regard political contributions as bribery.

(c) *Grease money*. Multinational companies are sometimes unable to obtain services to which they are legally entitled because of deliberate stalling by local officials. Cash payments to the right people may then be enough to oil the machinery of bureaucracy.

(d) *Gifts*. In some cultures (such as Japan) gifts are regarded as an essential part of civilised negotiation, even in circumstances where to Western eyes they might appear ethically dubious. Managers operating in such a culture may feel at liberty to adopt the local customs.

3.9 Another difficult area for managers concerns the extent to which an organisation's activities may appear to give support to undesirable political policies. In modern times, the conspicuous example of this has been the apparent support given to apartheid by companies with South African trading links. Supermarkets find themselves under pressure not to stock South African fruit, and increasingly companies are quietly withdrawing from their South African links.

Social and ethical objectives

3.10 However, companies are not passive in the social and ethical environment. Many organisations pursue a variety of social and ethical objectives. The following list is not comprehensive.

(a) For employees:
   (i)   a minimum wage, perhaps with adequate differentials for skilled labour;
   (ii)   job security (over and above the protection afforded to employees by government legislation);
   (iii) good conditions of work (above the legal minima);
   (iv)   job satisfaction.

(b) For customers:
   (i)   to provide a product of a certain quality at a reasonable price;
   (ii)   to make products that should last a certain number of years (eg. for consumer durable goods).

(c) For suppliers, to offer regular orders in return for reliable delivery and good service.

(d) For shareholders, to remain independent and resist takeover offers.

(e) For society as a whole:
   (i)   to control pollution, noise and smell;
   (ii)   to provide financial assistance to charities, sports and community activities;
   (iii) to co-operate with government authorities in identifying and preventing health hazards in the products sold.

3.11 As far as it is possible, social and ethical objectives should be expressed quantitatively, so that actual results can be monitored to ensure that the targets are achieved. This is often easier said than done - more often, they are expressed in the organisation's mission statement which is rarely a quanitfied amount.

4. THE SOCIAL RESPONSIBILITY OF ORGANISATIONS AND MANAGERS

4.1 It will be apparent from the preceding paragraphs that not only does the environment have a significant influence on the structure and behaviour of organisations, but also the organisation will have some influence on its environment.

4.2 Since organisations have an effect on their environment, it is arguable that they should act in a way which shows social awareness and responsibility.

> 'A society, awakened and vocal with respect to the urgency of social problems, is asking the managers of all kinds of organisations, particularly those at the top, what they are doing to discharge their social responsibilities and why they are not doing more.' (Koontz, O'Donnell and Weihrich)

4.3 Social responsibility is expected from all types of organisation, be they businesses, governments, universities and colleges, the church, charities etc.

(a) Local government is expected to provide services to the local community, and to preserve or improve the character of that community, but at an acceptable cost to the ratepayers.

(b) Businesses are expected to provide goods and services which reflect the needs of users and society as a whole. These needs may not be in harmony - arguably, the development of the Concorde aeroplane and supersonic passenger travel did not contribute to the public interest, and caused considerable inconvenience to residents near airports who suffer from excessive aircraft noise. A business should also be expected to anticipate the future needs of society; an example of socially useful products might be energy-saving devices and alternative sources of power.

Pollution control is a particularly important example of social responsibility by industrial organisations, and some progress has been made in the development of commercial processes for re-cycling waste material. British Coal attempts to restore the environment by planting on old slag heaps.

(c) Universities and schools are expected to produce students whose abilities and qualifications will prove beneficial to society. One view of education, by no means universally shared, is that greater emphasis should be placed on vocational training for students.

(d) In some cases, legislation may be required to enforce social need, for example to regulate the materials used to make crash helmets for motor cyclists, or to regulate safety standards in motor cars and furniture. Ideally, however, organisations should avoid the need for legislation by taking earlier self-regulating action.

5. MANAGEMENT AS A PROFESSION

5.1 If it is accepted that the managers of organisations should have certain social and ethical responsibilities, the next question is 'should there by a formal code of behaviour for managers, and if so, who should issue such a code?'

5.2 A code of social and ethical behaviour might be issued:
   (a) by a professional or management institution; or
   (b) by an organisation, as a guide for its own managers and employees.

5.3 Professional bodies such as those for accountants, lawyers and doctors issue and enforce a code of ethical conduct for their members. Breaches of the code are punishable, *in extremis*, by expulsion from the profession.

5.4 There is a view that, in a broader sense, management is a profession too, and managers of all organisations ought to share a common code of professional ethics. One such code in the UK has been issued by the British Institute of Management (BIM).

The BIM's Code of Conduct

5.5 A *Code of conduct* (and supporting *Guides to good management practice*) is published by the British Institute of Management and gives guidance on the ethical and professional standards required of BIM members.

5.6 According to the *Code* managers should:
   (a) comply with the law;
   (b) respect the customs and practices of any country in which they work as managers;
   (c) not misuse their authority or office for personal or other gains.

5.7 The supporting *Guides* lay down a number of professional ethics.

(a) In pursuing their personal ambitions, managers shall take account of the interests of others.

(b) Managers should never maliciously injure the professional reputation or career prospects of others, nor the business of others.

(c) Managers should make immediate and full declaration of any personal interests which may conflict with the interests of the organisation.

(d) Managers should be concerned in the working environment for the health, safety and well-being of all, especially those for whom they are responsible.

(e) Managers should respect the confidentiality of any information if so requested by customers and suppliers.

(f) Managers should neither offer nor accept any gift, favour or hospitality intended as, or having the effect of, bribery and corruption.

(g) Managers should ensure that all public communications are true and not misleading.

5.8 The need for this kind of ethical guidance may not be immediately obvious. You might think that adequate legislation exists to prevent any abuse of their position by managers. But professional standards go beyond compliance with the law to ensure that not even an appearance of unethical conduct is given. 'The law is a floor. Ethical business conduct should normally exist at a level well above the minimum required by law.'

5.9 It is not clear to what extent moral ethics will determine the decisions of management. An international survey reported in 1983 found that even with a published code of ethics, the business executive is still more likely to make the expedient rather than the moral decision. The problem, it appears, is 'group think' - a result of companies, especially multi-nationals, creating their own morality. A group of managers, especially when working closely together on an important project, tends to come to a consensus view of the world which may not always be the same as the views held by outsiders or be in accordance with society's normal codes of morality.

Codes of conduct issued by organisations themselves

5.10 If this is so, it would seem to follow that the imposition of social and ethical responsibilities on its management should come from within the organisation itself, and the organisation should issue its own code of conduct for its employees.

5.11 One such set of guidelines has been issued by United Biscuits plc as follows.

> "These 'guiding principles', taken in conjunction with our budget and strategic objectives, are important as a description of the way in which we operate.
>
> United Biscuits' business ethics are not negotiable - a well-founded reputation for scrupulous dealing is itself a priceless company asset and the most important single factor in our success is faithful adherence to our beliefs. While our tactical plans and many other elements constantly change, our basic philosophy does not. To meet the challenges of a changing world, we are prepared to change everything about ourselves except our values.
>
> Some employees might have the mistaken idea that we do not care how results are obtained, as long as we get results. This would be wrong: we do care how we get results. We expect compliance with our standard of integrity throughout the company, and we will support an employee who passes up an opportunity or advantage that can only be secured at the sacrifice of a principle.
>
> While it is the responsibility of top management to keep a company honest and honourable, perpetuating ethical values is not a function only of the chief executive or a handful of senior managers. Every employee is expected to take on the responsibility of always behaving ethically whatever the circumstances. Beliefs and values must always come before policies, practices and goals; the latter must be altered if they violate fundamental beliefs."

5.12 It is easier for a single 'family' organisation than it is for a large organisation to hold firmly to ethical beliefs, because there are fewer employees to give direction to. A published code of conduct, which has the backing of top management, is arguably needed for large organisations, in order to foster a proper sense of ethical and social behaviour.

6. Stakeholder analysis

6.1 The 'stakeholder view' is a way of looking at an organisation's social responsibility which states that many different groups of people have a 'stake' in what the organisation does. From their various perspectives they have different objectives which they would like to see the organisation fulfil.

6.2 There are three broad types of stakeholder in an organisation, such as a company, as follows:

(1) internal stakeholders - employees, management
(2) connected stakeholders - shareholders, customers, suppliers, financiers
(3) external stakeholders - the community, government, pressure groups.

These types are indicated in the diagram below.

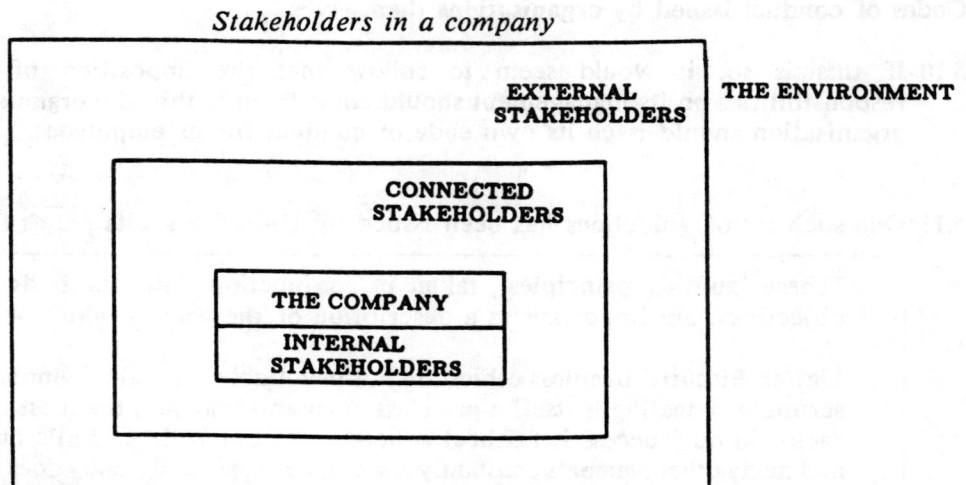

Stakeholders in a company

```
                                          THE ENVIRONMENT
  ┌─────────────────────────────────────────┐
  │                        EXTERNAL          │
  │                        STAKEHOLDERS      │
  │   ┌───────────────────────────────────┐ │
  │   │            CONNECTED              │ │
  │   │            STAKEHOLDERS           │ │
  │   │   ┌───────────────────────────┐   │ │
  │   │   │      THE COMPANY          │   │ │
  │   │   ├───────────────────────────┤   │ │
  │   │   │      INTERNAL             │   │ │
  │   │   │      STAKEHOLDERS         │   │ │
  │   │   └───────────────────────────┘   │ │
  │   └───────────────────────────────────┘ │
  └─────────────────────────────────────────┘
```

We shall consider each of them in turn.

6.3 *Internal stakeholders*
Because employees and management (which includes the Chairman and the Board of Directors) are so intimately connected with the company, their objectives are likely to have a strong and immediate influence on how it is run.

6.4 *Connected stakeholders*
The objective of shareholders - which is generally that of making a profit - is often taken as the prime objective which the company's management seeks to fulfil. But clearly financiers such as banks have similar objectives which must be met (usually the payment of loan interest is a contractual obligation whilst the payment of dividends is not), whilst the customer's objectives, in a market-led company, must also be fulfilled if the company is to be successful. Other stakeholders directly 'connected' with the company are suppliers, trade unions and distributors.

6.5 *External stakeholders*
These groups - the government, local authorities, pressure groups, the community at large, professional bodies - are likely to have quite diverse objectives and have a varying ability to ensure that the company meets them.

6.6 How stakeholders relate to the management of the company depends very much on what type of stakeholder they are – internal, connected or external – and on the level in the management hierarchy at which they are able to apply pressure. Clearly a company's management will respond differently to the demands of, say, its shareholders and the community at large. This is because both the character of the relationship and the means by which the relationship is conducted depend on the relative bargaining power and philosophy of the stakeholder on the one hand and the company on the other.

6.7 The relationship may be characterised by a number of stances. Each party (stakeholder and company) may actively seek dominance or they may each adopt defensive roles. Ideally they should seek a balance of objectives but in turn this can mean that they may actively seek agreement or may merely react to circumstances as they arise. Hence the company and its employees/trade unions may have a relationship characterised by each party seeking dominance over the other, whilst with its customers the company may find itself reacting to the demands made of it by them. This shows that the ability to influence management does not necessarily arise from mere closeness to the company (employees are internal to the company but often the shareholders' and customers' objectives are more important).

6.8 The way in which the relationship between company and stakeholders is conducted again is a function of the relationship's character, the parties' relative bargaining strength and the philosophy underlying each party's objectives. This can be shown by means of a spectrum as follows.

	Weak				Stakeholders' bargaining strength		Strong
Company's conduct of relationship	Command dictat by company	Consultation and consideration of stakeholders' views	Negotiation	Participation and acceptance of stakeholders' views	Democratic voting by stakeholders	Command/ dictat by stakeholders

Influence of stakeholders

6.9 Stakeholders can influence and constrain the management of the company at a number of different levels, which can be defined at the *strategic level* (the main mission and objectives of the company), the *planning level* (how those objectives are going to be met) and the *operations level* (how plans are put in practice day-to-day). But in addition management is constrained at every level by the legal environment in which it exists and the regulations with which it must comply. These can be said to arise from the objectives of the community at large and of the government, and can affect things such as employment rights, financial control and reporting, safety and environmental protection and the way in which competition is handled.

Strategic level

6.10 When deciding on the company's mission and objectives, and the strategies to be adopted in meeting them, the company's board will almost certainly be constrained primarily by the interests of the shareholders (profit) but also by those of the customers (price, variety, reliability) and of other financiers (interest and capital repayments, value of security, value of shares). But the extent to which management has discretion to make profits for shareholders is itself constrained by the demands of customers for value and of financiers for reducing risk to their investment. A balance must clearly be reached.

6.11 The company must comply with identifiable constraints such as its statutory duty to exercise 'stewardship' over its shareholders' assets, its contractual duty to pay interest on loans and its legal duties regarding employment and environment protection. These may come into conflict with other stakeholders' interests and even with the company's preferred strategy such as to be 'market-led'.

6.12 Finally the company's strategy may be influenced by intangible constraints from the external stakeholders and the environment as a whole such as 'green' culture and concern for Third World development and good employment practices.

Planning level

6.13 In order to achieve objectives and ultimately fulfil the company's mission, the management must make tactical plans. These will be influenced to a greater or lesser extent by stakeholders.

(a) *Customers'* demands will dictate decisions for investment in new products, development of existing ones and setting-up of new outlets. They will also affect the standards adopted for quality control, and the extent to which they can be enticed away by competitors' products will affect the planned advertising spend.

(b) *Suppliers'* and *distributors'* demands will affect the timing and amount of production, the amount of raw material and finished goods stock held and hence the financial planning which allows production to take place.

(c) *Employees'* attitudes and objectives will greatly affect the organisation and co-ordination required to put production plans into effect. Construction of departments and work groups, job design, workflow and the amount of training undertaken will all be matters in which management will have to take the employees' stake into account.

(d) *Specialised or professional employees* have two sets of priorities - their jobs, and the requirements of their professional bodies. The management must be careful not to bring these two into conflict, say by asking a qualified construction engineer to operate with untrained staff.

(e) *Trade unions* represent employees *en masse* and seek to ensure that pay, terms and conditions of employment, disciplinary and grievance procedures and employment protection policies are formulated with the employees in mind. Management will have to consider these and will have to involve unions in the planning process in order to preserve good industrial relations.

(f) *Legislation, regulations and the community at large*. At the planning level management discretion can be contrained by a great number of restrictions which are put in place to protect the community as a whole. Examples are planning restrictions on a construction company, pollution controls on a chemical works and disclosure requirements for a financial services group.

Operations level

6.14 Clearly many of the constraints affecting management at the strategic and planning levels will also filter down to the running of day-to-day operations. Certainly consumers will affect production aims (size, quality, colour) and procedures (planning, stockholding, computerisation etc) when demand is variable (as in the fashion and high-tech industries). Health and safety legislation for employees and consumer protection legislation also mean that day-to-day operations must be constantly reviewed for compliance.

7. Management responsibilities

7.1 Management is be responsible not only to the organisation's owners (shareholders) but also to:

(a) employees;
(b) customers;
(c) suppliers;
(d) competitors;
(e) the local community; and
(f) the general public (and government).

7.2 *Employees*

An organisation's broad responsibilities to its *employees* are well set out by United Biscuits plc as follows:

> To achieve the dynamic morale and team spirit based on mutual confidence without which a business cannot be successful, people have to be cared for during their working lives and in retirement. In return we expect from all our staff loyalty and commitment to the company. We respect the rights and innate worth of the individual. In addition to being financially rewarding, working life should provide as much job satisfaction as possible. The company encourages all employees to be trained and developed to achieve their full potential.
>
> United Biscuits takes a responsible attitude towards employment legislation requirements and codes of practice, union activities and communications with staff.
>
> We place the highest priority on promoting and preserving the health and safety of employees. Employees, for their part, have a clear duty to take every reasonable precaution to avoid injury to themselves, their colleagues and members of the public.

7.3 General principles have to be converted into practice, and should take the form of good pay and working conditions, and good training and development schemes. They should also extend into:

(a) recruitment policy;
(b) redundancy and retirement policies.

7.4 *Recruitment* of new staff should be done as carefully as possible, because if an organisation recruits an individual who turns out to be bad at his job the company has to sack him. Dismissals will be inevitable in any large organisation, but careful recruitment methods should manage to keep such demoralising incidents down to a small number.

7.5 Staff who are about to retire, after years of service with the organisation, should be provided for in their *retirement*.

    (a) The organisation might have a good pension scheme.

    (b) One of the problems for retired people is learning what to do with their leisure time. Some organisations provide training courses and discussion groups for employees who are coming up for retirement, to help them to plan their future time constructively.

7.6 Dealing with *redundancies* is a more difficult problem. Even for organisations which show an ethical sense of responsibility towards their employees, there may be occasions when parts of the business have to be closed down, and jobs lost. In such a situation, the organisation:

    (a) should try to redeploy as many staff as possible, without making them redundant; and
    (b) where necessary, should provide retraining to give staff the skills to do their new job.

7.7 For those staff who *are* made redundant, the organisation should take steps to help them to get a job elsewhere. Measures could include:

    (a) counselling individuals to give them suggestions about what they might try to do;

    (b) providing retraining, or funds for training, in other skills which the employees could use in other organisations and industries;

    (c) arranging 'job fairs', by inviting other employers to come and display the jobs that they have on offer, and to discuss job opportunities with redundant employees;

    (d) providing good redundancy payments, which employees might be able to use to set up in business themselves or which at least should tide them over until they find employment again.

7.8 *Customers*

Ethical responsibilities towards customers are mainly those of providing a product or service of a quality that customers expect, and to deal honestly and fairly with customers.

7.9 The guidelines of United Biscuits plc again provide a good example of how these responsibilities might be expressed.

UB's reputation for integrity is the foundation on which the mutual trust between the company and its customers is based. That relationship is the key to our trading success.

Both employees and customers need to know that products sold by any of our operating companies will always meet their highest expectations. The integrity of our products is sacrosanct and implicit in the commitment is an absolute and uncompromising dedication to quality. We will never compromise on recipes or specification of products in order to save costs. Quality improvement must always be our goal.

No employee may give money or any gift of significant value to a customer if it could reasonably be viewed as being done to gain a business advantage. Winning an order by violating this policy or by providing free or extra services, or unauthorised contract terms, is contrary to our trading policy.

7.10 *Suppliers*

The responsibilities of an organisation towards its suppliers are expressed mainly in terms of trading relationships.

(a) The organisation's size could give it considerable power as a buyer. One ethical guideline might be that the organisation shouldn't use its power unscrupulously (say to force the supplier to lower his prices under threat of withdrawing business).

(b) Suppliers might rely on getting prompt payment in accordance with the terms of trade negotiated with its customers. Another ethical guideline is that an organisation should not delay payments to suppliers beyond the agreed credit period.

(c) All information obtained from suppliers and potential suppliers should be kept confidential.

(d) All suppliers should be treated fairly, and this means:

  (i) giving potential new suppliers a chance to win some business; and also

  (ii) maintaining long-standing relationships that have been built up over the years with some suppliers. Long-established suppliers should not be replaced unless there is a significant commercial advantage for the organisation from such a move.

7.11 *Competitors*

Some ethical responsibilities should exist towards competitors.

> "We compete vigorously, energetically, untiringly but we also compete ethically and honestly. Our competitive success is founded on excellence - of product and service. We have no need to disparage our competitors either directly or by implication or innuendo....
>
> No-one may attempt improperly to acquire a competitor's trade secrets or other proprietary or confidential information. 'Improper' means are activities such as industrial espionage, hiring competitors' employees to get confidential information, urging competitive personnel or customers to disclose confidential information, or any other approach which is not completely open and above board."
>
> (United Biscuits plc)

7.12 *The community*

An organisation is a part of the community that it serves, and it should be responsible for:

(a) upholding the social and ethical values of the community;

(b) contributing towards the well-being of the community, eg by sponsoring local events and charities, or providing facilities for the community to use (eg sports fields);

(c) responding constructively to complaints from local residents or politicians (eg about problems for local traffic caused by the organisation's delivery vehicles).

8. PUBLIC RELATIONS AND CORPORATE IMAGE

8.1 The Institute of Public Relations defines the role of public relations (PR) as 'a planned and sustained effort to establish and maintain mutual understanding between an organisation and its public.'

A large organisation is likely to have a PR department, and smaller companies might hire the services of a PR agency to perform the same function for them. PR is a form of boundary within which management must act because it is always better to have good relations with the public than bad. This can involve doing something which is good for PR and/or not doing something which is bad.

8.2 An important element of public relations is publicity. Publicity can be a useful selling aid, depending on:

(a) the newsworthiness of any item;
(b) relations between the public relations department and the news media; and
(c) the item's credibility.

8.3 Publicity is often relatively inexpensive in comparison with the cost of advertising. The need for publicity probably varies significantly from industry to industry. The tourist trade, for example, relies heavily on publicity to attract customers, whereas a small industrial firm might restrict its interest in PR and publicity to the locality of its factories and offices (as a local employer, a firm ought to be conscious of its relationship with the local community).

8.4 The role and purpose of a PR department are:

(a) to obtain favourable publicity for the organisation, usually through the national and local press or television, and to prevent adverse publicity. The publicity sought is through an 'independent' channel, and is not paid for – advertising and sales promotions are paid for by an organisation, and would not normally be handled by PR staff;

(b) in some cases, to obtain a high profile for the organisation in the public mind;

(c) to arrange for the announcement of events to the news media. For example, if one company decided to take over another company, its PR department would call a press conference to announce the event, and hope to obtain widespread coverage;

(d) to provide information about new products – eg by inviting the press to a 'product launch';

(e) to establish a good working relationship with journalists and other news reporters, so that 'official leaks' to the press can be made through favoured contacts;

(f) to deal with all other relations with the press (except for advertising matters) – eg most public companies will arrange to pay for the inclusion of their shares in the price lists in the *Financial Times*;

(g) to liaise with the customer relations department about the response of customers to the organisation's products and services;

(h) to produce the in-house journal and be responsible for all internal communications of this type – eg distributing to employees statements made by the MD or chairman;

(i) if appropriate, to organise exhibitions and visits by the general public to the organisation's premises;

(j) to be involved, perhaps, in sponsored events paid for by the company (eg sports events, many of which are now sponsored);

(k) to lobby the government and other authorities for decisions which would be of benefit to the organisation; and

(l) to identify and perhaps to establish a relationship with stakeholder groups (eg environmental groups, local interest groups etc) with a view to establishing a communications link for liaising with them.

Corporate image

8.5 Corporate image describes the public attitude towards a company, or the image of the company in the mind of the general public, and perhaps more specifically in the minds of potential customers. It is possible to promote a desired corporate image through a combination of PR, advertising and the experience and attitudes built up by customers over the years (for example, the favourable corporate image of Marks and Spencer grew up over the years, without the need for excessive PR or advertising).

8.6 There are various reasons why an organisation might attempt to build up a corporate image.

(a) The organisation may want to strengthen customer loyalty, and so a corporate image of good quality products and services, and concern for the customer's interests, could be fostered. British Home Stores, for instance, have successfully built up such an image in recent years, partly through advertising.

(b) Rather than strengthen customer loyalty, a corporate image might be developed to create customer awareness. Some companies have faced the problem that customers do not know what they are, and have never heard of them. A corporate image is then needed to give the company a public identity (eg fairly recently, Racal plc spent large sums advertising itself as one of the largest companies no one had ever heard of).

(c) Corporate image can strengthen an employee's attachment to the company he or she works for, because of corporate identity. People may want to work for a company because of its image in the mind of the public ('prestige' jobs) or because the company has a 'get-ahead' image.

(d) Some companies may wish to develop a corporate image of social responsibility, in order to avoid unfavourable legislation, to prevent adverse publicity or to prevent pressure from stakeholder groups. Examples of this motive are:

(i) the attempt by oil companies to establish an image of care for the environment and for the future needs of society;
(ii) the attempt by British Nuclear Fuels to promote an image of deepest concern for the safety of nuclear waste;
(iii) the attempt by fur traders to counter the adverse publicity built up against them by the efforts of animal rights activists; and
(iv) the efforts of independent TV companies to promote an image of 'quality' programme-makers, to strengthen their chances of winning a bid for franchises.

(e) Some companies may wish to have a favourable corporate image which they can subsequently use to win public and political support. For example, the corporate image of Land Rover as a successful and very British manufacturer of a quality product was used in 1986 to stir up public and political support against a takeover by the US company General Motors.

(f) A good corporate image has a variety of benefits for management, in addition to strengthening customer loyalty. An image of a sound, well-established company might encourage investors to put more money into the business, and suppliers to grant longer credit.

8.7 As mentioned above, the most commonly used methods of communicating information about a company and company image are:

(a) public relations (PR); and
(b) advertising, especially TV advertising, although this is expensive.

Market research by MORI has shown that:

(a) two out of every three people in the UK believe that a company which has a good reputation would not sell poor quality products (this suggests that customers would be more willing to try a new product if it is promoted by a well-known corporate name than if it is made by an unknown company); and

(b) nine times out of ten, the better known a company is, the more highly it is regarded.

8.8 In an article on the subject, the *Financial Times* made the following interesting comments about corporate advertising:

> 'Anyone who doubts the efficacy of corporate messages might consider the famous McGraw-Hill advertisement which features a daunting company executive who asks: "I don't know who you are. I don't know your company. I don't know your company's product. I don't know what your company stands for. I don't know your company's customers. I don't know your company's reputation. Now – what was it you wanted to sell me?"
>
> Some industries have learnt the corporate lesson. Banks and building societies have shown consistent commitment to pushing the corporate 'brand' ... remember 'the listening bank', 'the action bank' and 'a thoroughbred among banks'?
>
> Before them, the oil companies knew well the dividends reaped by keeping the public informed. They handled a messy product which carried a pollution risk, involved an unsightly production process and had a premium price tag (as customers saw it). Which is why Shell, BP, Esso, Mobil and the rest have kept up a constant public information programme.'

8.9 A popular way for UK companies to project a corporate image is to identify itself with an animal – on the basis that British people love animals more than anything else. Hence we have the Esso tiger, the Peugeot lion and the black horse of Lloyds Bank. In 1989, Woolworth plc adopted the name 'Kingfisher', the qualities of this bird being deemed appropriate in some way to represent the organisation's corporate objectives. Moreover, it was felt necessary to get away from the much-loved but essentially downmarket image associated with the threepenny store's name.

9. ACCOUNTABILITY OF MANAGEMENT

9.1 Social responsibility, which is desirable in theory, is not easily achieved in practice, because managers are commonly judged by a different set of results - profits, sales growth, market share, earnings per share etc - and not in terms of achievements for society. After all, why should company A incur high costs on improving the safety standards of its product when a competitor, company B, does not spend any money on such improvements, and would therefore be able to undercut company A's prices on the market?

9.2 Managers are unlikely to act with proper responsibility unless they are made accountable for what they do. Social and ethical responsibilities are unlikely to be anything more than fine words and phrases unless managers are judged according to their achievements.

9.3 If an organisation sets its own social and ethical guidelines, managers should be given objectives to achieve, and actual performance should be measured against those objectives in a formal system of control reporting. For example, any manager found guilty of a breach of the code of conduct should be reprimanded, or other disciplinary measures should be taken against him.

9.4 Social responsibility is to some extent forced on managers by the wishes of consumers.

> *Consumerism* has been defined (by Mann and Thornton) as a 'social movement seeking to augment the rights and powers of buyers in relation to sellers up to the point where the consumer is able to defend his interests'.

9.5 Aspects of business activity on which consumer organisations have focused include:

- dangerous products (such as cigarettes and the content of car exhaust emissions);
- dishonest marketing or promotion. In the UK there is legislation designed to deal with this kind of abuse;
- the abuse of power by organisations which are large enough to disregard external constraints and even government pressure;
- the availability of information. Consumers are anxious, for example, to be informed of any artificial additives in foodstuffs.

The accountability of managers in the public sector

9.6 Social responsibility ought to be particularly important for the management of public sector organisations, such as local authorities, and it could be argued that management in central or local government ought to be accountable, not just to their political 'bosses' but also to the general public.

9.7 However, the concept of checks and balances in the British Constitution results in a system of government in which no single department or agency is entirely responsible for anything. Several different departments will always be involved, none of them entirely responsible for the tasks in hand and so none of them fully accountable. It is all too easy to 'pass the buck' and blame another department when members of the general public complain.

9.8 Some examples of shared responsibilities, and so the lack of management accountability to the public, were described in an article by Richard C Carr in the *Administrator* (January 1988).

(a) *Education*. Local authorities build schools and employ teachers. Central government sets rules about how education should be provided and even what should be taught. Because central government provides much of the finance for schools, it can also put indirect pressure (the threat of refusing to give payments of grants) on local authorities. And what 'powers' do school governors have to direct the running of their school?

(b) *Police*. Similarly, the police are employed by local authorities to enforce laws made mainly by central government. Police activity is constrained by decisions of the courts and the local chief constable of police is also answerable to a police authority.

(c) *Gypsy encampments*. The article described a problem in Cambridgeshire with unauthorised gypsy encampments, and public complaints about them. County councils have a duty to provide official encampments, but local residents near such proposed sites complain. The costs of developing official sites are paid for by central government. District councils have to manage the sites, and are also involved as planning authorities. The police, county highway authority and district council environment health officers and planning officers are all involved in dealing with or acting against unauthorised encampments. Central government might issue instructions that dwellers on unauthorised encampments should not be harrassed. So who should members of the general public complain to, with a demand for action?

9.9

The points being made here are that:

(a) management might only feel socially responsible, in the long run, if they are held accountable;

(b) how can managers be made accountable to the public? For private companies, we have seen that accountability can be achieved through the exercise of law, or adverse public reaction and the threat of lost customer demand. For public sector organisations, however, where social responsibility *ought* to be strong, management might choose to escape their responsibility by passing the blame on to someone else. Responsibility does not lie with just one department, nor even just one organisation.

TEST YOUR KNOWLEDGE

(The numbers in brackets refer to paragraph numbers in this text)

1. List some of the social and ethical objectives that an organisation might pursue. (1.3)

2. What are the legal constraints affecting management? (2.3, 2.4)

3. What ethical problems face management? (3.4-3.9)

4. To whom does management arguably have responsibilities, and what are some of those responsibilities? (4.1-4.3)

5. What are the professional ethics of the British Institute of Management? (5.7)

6. What is stakeholder analysis? (6.1-6.5)

7. At what levels do stakeholders influence an organisation? (6.9-6.14)

8. What responsibilities have managers to persons outside their organisation? (7.8-7.12)

9. What is the role of the PR department? (8.4)

10. How might a company justify expenditure on its corporate image? (8.6)

INDEX

INDEX

INDEX

FURTHER READING

For further question practice on Management, BPP publish a companion Practice and Revision Kit. This contains a bank of 70 questions, mostly drawn from past examinations, and each one is accompanied by a fully worked suggested solution. The current (1989) edition is priced at £6.95; a new edition will be published in July 1991.

You may also wish to test your grasp of the subject by tackling short questions in multiple choice format. BPP publish the Password series of books, each of which incorporates a large collection of multiple choice questions with solutions, comments and marking guides. The Password title relevant to Management is Organisation and Management. This is priced at £6.95 and contains 307 questions.

To order your practice and Revision Kit and Password books, ring our credit card hotline on 081-740 6808 or tear out this page and send it to our Freepost address.

To: BPP Publishing Ltd, FREEPOST, London W12 8BR   Tel: 081-740 6808

Forenames (Mr / Ms) _____

Surname: _____

Address: _____

_____

Post code: _____

Please send me the following books:	*Quantity*	*Price*	*Total*
ICSA Management: Principles and Policy Kit		£6.95	
Password Organisation and Management		£6.95	

Please include postage:

UK: Single book £1; two or more books £1.50 ....

Overseas: £3 for first plus £1.50 for each extra book ....

I enclose a cheque for £_____ or charge to Access/Visa

Card number ☐☐☐☐☐☐☐☐☐☐☐☐☐☐☐☐☐☐

Expiry date _____ Signature _____

> If you are placing an order, you might like to look at the reverse of this page. It's a Review Form, which you can send in to us with comments and suggestions on the text you've just finished. Your feedback really does make a difference: it helps us to make the next edition that bit better. So if you're posting the coupon, do fill in the Review Form as well.

ICSA – MANAGEMENT: PRINCIPLES AND POLICY

Name: _____

How have you used this text?

Home study (book only) ☐ With 'correspondence' package ☐

On a course: college_____ Other _____

How did you obtain this text?

From us by mail order ☐ From us by phone ☐

From a bookshop ☐ From your college ☐

Where did you hear about BPP texts?

At bookshop ☐ Recommended by lecturer ☐

Recommended by friend ☐ Mailshot from BPP ☐

Advertisement in _____ Other _____

Have you used the companion kit for this subject? Yes/No

Your comments and suggestions would be appreciated on the following areas.

Syllabus coverage

Illustrative questions

Errors (please specify, and refer to a page number, if you've spotted anything!)

Presentation

Other (index, cross-referencing, price – whatever!)